American Foreign Policy and the Politics of Fear

This edited volume addresses the issue of threat inflation in American foreign policy and domestic politics. The Bush administration's aggressive campaign to build public support for an invasion of Iraq reheated fears about the president's ability to manipulate the public, and many charged the administration with "threat inflation," duping the news media and misleading the public into supporting the war under false pretences.

Presenting the latest research, these essays seek to answer the question of why threat inflation occurs and when it will be successful. Simply defined, it is the effort by elites to create concern for a threat that goes beyond the scope and urgency that disinterested analysis would justify. More broadly, the process concerns how elites view threats, the political uses of threat inflation, the politics of threat framing among competing elites, and how the public interprets and perceives threats via the news media.

The war with Iraq gets special attention in this volume, along with the "War on Terror." Although many believe that the Bush administration successfully inflated the Iraq threat, there is not a neat consensus about why this was successful. Through both theoretical contributions and case studies, this book showcases the four major explanations of threat inflation – realism, domestic politics, psychology, and constructivism – and makes them confront one another directly. The result is a richer appreciation of this important dynamic in US politics and foreign policy, present and future.

This book will be of much interest to students of US foreign and national security policy, international security, strategic studies and IR in general.

Trevor Thrall is Assistant Professor of Political Science and directs the Master of Public Policy program at the University of Michigan-Dearborn. **Jane Kellett Cramer** is an Assistant Professor of Political Science at the University of Oregon.

Routledge Global Security Studies
Series editors: Aaron Karp, Regina Karp and Terry Teriff

American Foreign Policy and the Politics of Fear

Threat inflation since 9/11

Edited by
A. Trevor Thrall and
Jane K. Cramer

LONDON AND NEW YORK

First published 2009
by Routledge
2 Park Square, Milton Park, Abingdon, Oxon OX14 4RN

Simultaneously published in the USA and Canada
by Routledge
270 Madison Avenue, New York, NY 10016

*Routledge is an imprint of the Taylor & Francis Group,
an informa business*

© 2009 Selection and editorial matter, A. Trevor Thrall and Jane K. Cramer;
individual chapters, the contributors

Typeset in Times New Roman by Swales & Willis Ltd, Exeter, Devon
Printed and bound in Great Britain by
CPI Antony Rowe, Chippenham, Wiltshire

British Library Cataloguing in Publication Data
A catalogue record for this book is available from the British Library

Library of Congress Cataloging in Publication Data
American foreign policy and the politics of fear : threat inflation since 9/11/
edited by A. Trevor Thrall and Jane K. Cramer.
p. cm.
1.United States—Foreign relations—2001—Psychological aspects.
2. Threats—United States. I. Thrall, A. Trevor. II. Cramer, Jane K.
JZ1480.A959 2009
327.73—dc22
2008046236

ISBN 10: 0–415–77768–2 (hbk)
ISBN 10: 0–415–77769–0 (pbk)
ISBN 10: 0–203–87909–0 (ebk)

ISBN 13: 978–0–415–77768–1 (hbk)
ISBN 13: 978–0–415–77769–8 (pbk)
ISBN 13: 978–0–203–87909–2 (ebk)

Contents

List of tables

List of figures

Notes on contributors

Jane K. Cramer is Assistant Professor of Political Science at the University of Oregon. She focuses on the study of international relations, specializing in international security. Her research examines the multiple causes of national security panics in the United States. She also researches the domestic politics behind U.S. foreign policy, and the diversionary theory of war.

Benjamin H. Friedman is a PhD candidate in Political Science at M.I.T and Research Fellow in Defense and Homeland Security Studies at the Cato Institute. His writing deals with counter-terrorism, homeland security and defense politics. His work has appeared in *Foreign Policy*, *Regulation* and other newspapers and journals.

Rocio Garcia-Retamero is an associate professor in the Department of Experimental Psychology, University of Granada (Spain). Her current research interests involve risk perceptions, leadership and gender, decision-making in groups, causal learning, and learning and emotions.

Robert Jervis is the Adlai E. Stevenson Professor of International Affairs at Columbia University. Specializing in international politics in general and security policy, decision-making, and theories of conflict and cooperation in particular, his most recent book is *System Effects: Complexity in Political and Social Life* (Princeton University Press).

Daniel Kahneman is a Senior Scholar at the Woodrow Wilson School of Public and International Affairs and a fellow of the Center for Rationality at the Hebrew University in Jerusalem. Daniel Kahneman won the Nobel Prize in Economic Sciences in 2002 for his work on prospect theory and decision-making under uncertainty.

Chaim Kaufmann is Associate Professor of International Relations at Lehigh University. His research interests include international relations theory, international security, nationalism and ethnic conflict, political psychology, social science research methods, and epistemology. His recent work has appeared in *International Studies Perspectives*, *Harvard International Review*, and *Peace Review*.

Ronald R. Krebs is Associate Professor of Political Science at the University of Minnesota. His research interests focus on the origins and consequences of international conflict and military service as well as on rhetoric and politics. His most recent book is *Fighting for Rights: Military Service and the Politics of Citizenship* (Cornell University Press).

Jennifer K. Lobasz is a PhD candidate in the Department of Political Science at the University of Minnesota. Her research interests include international human trafficking, feminist security studies, and the construction of meaning in world politics.

John Mueller is Woody Hayes Chair of National Security Studies, Mershon Center, and professor of political science at Ohio State University. His most recent book is *Overblown: How Politicians and the Terrorism Industry Inflate National Security Threats, and Why We Believe Them* (Free Press). He is currently finishing a book on nuclear proliferation and nuclear terrorism, *Atomic Obsession*.

Jonathan Renshon is a PhD candidate in the Department of Government at Harvard University. Renshon studies national security decision-making, foreign policy analysis and political psychology. He is the author of *Why Leaders Choose War: The Psychology of Prevention* (Greenwood) and several journal articles.

David Rousseau is Associate Professor of Political Science at the University at Albany (SUNY). His research interests focus on military conflict, shared identity, political development, and foreign policy. His most recent book, entitled *Identifying Threats and threatening Identities: The Social Construction of Realism and Liberalism* (Stanford University Press), explores the impact of shared identity on threat perception.

Jack Snyder is the Robert and Renée Belfer Professor of International Relations in the Political Science department and the Saltzman Institute of War and Peace Studies at Columbia University. His most recent book is *Electing to Fight: Why Emerging Democracies Go to War* (MIT Press), co-authored with Edward D. Mansfield.

A. Trevor Thrall is Assistant Professor of Political Science at the University of Michigan – Dearborn. His research focuses on the intersection of war, the news media, and public opinion. He is the author of *War in the Media Age* (Hampton Press), which traces the evolution of the U.S. government's strategy for dealing with the press during war.

Stephen Van Evera is Professor of Political Science at the Massachusetts Institute of Technology. His research interests include the causes and prevention of war, U.S. foreign policy, U.S. national security policy, and social science methods. He is author of *Causes of War: Power and the Roots of Conflict* (Cornell University Press).

Jon Western is Five College Associate Professor of International Relations at Mt. Holyoke College. His teaching and research interests focus on U.S. foreign policy, military intervention, human rights and humanitarian affairs. He is the author of *Selling Intervention and War: The Presidency, the Media, and the American Public* (Johns Hopkins University Press).

Foreword

Stephen Van Evera

Threat inflation is a pervasive feature of international politics and an important cause of international conflict. States have a chronic tendency to exaggerate the aggressiveness and offensive capabilities of other states. As a result states often believe they are less secure than in fact they are. They then take unneeded or counterproductive steps to gain security that they already enjoy. A self-fulfilling prophecy develops: by their belligerent efforts to address imaginary threats, states provoke others to pose real threats to their safety.

States sometimes underestimate the threats they face. For example, at times Britain and France underestimated German power and aggressiveness during the 1930s. The George W. Bush administration underestimated the threat of an al-Qaeda terrorist attack in the U.S. before 9/11 (Van Evera 2006).

But threat inflation is far more common than threat underestimation.

Britain was provoked to war against France in 1756 by false reports that French forces had invaded east of the Alleghenies and were preparing a general invasion of British North America. The resulting Seven Years' War (1756–63) was a vast conflict that saw fighting from North America and the Caribbean to West Africa and South Asia. Its origins lay largely in inflated British fears of aggressive French intentions (Higgonet 1968; Smoke 1977).

A later generation of British leaders were led by similar mistakes to adopt hardline policies toward Russia, sparking the Crimean War (1854–56). Specifically, the British badly overestimated Russian aggressiveness and Russian capabilities. Frightened by these illusions, Britain used force to contain the expansion of a Russia that was not pursuing expansion, and was too feeble to expand successfully in any case. In the Crimean conflict Britain spent 45,000 British lives to avert a Russian threat that existed largely in the imagination of the British government. (Greenville 1976; Smoke 1977).

Before 1914, Germans widely believed they were surrounded by hostile states that were plotting aggressive war against them, and that Germany could well be destroyed in such a war. This was untrue on both counts. Germany's neighbors did not seek war against Germany; and even if war somehow erupted between Germany and its neighbors, Germany would have easily survived had it played its hand wisely. In the test of World War I, Germany was defeated only because it foolishly provoked Britain to enter the war against it in 1914 by invading Belgium and

France, and then even more foolishly provoked the United States to enter against it in 1917 by attacking American shipping. A Germany under more prudent leadership would have emerged from the war unbeaten or even victorious. And a Germany that sought to avoid war in 1914 would have enjoyed a safe, peaceful and prosperous existence. Over time a peaceful Germany's relative power would have only grown, because Germany's economy was growing faster than other European economies. The threats that fueled German pre-1914 belligerence were illusions (Geiss 1976; Fischer 1975; Mombauer 2002; Moses 1975).

During the interwar years Germans continued to inflate the threats that Germany faced. Germans wrongly believed they were innocent of causing World War I, thinking instead that Britain, France and Russia had conspired to organize the war (Herwig 1991). This misreading of history fueled arguments that Germany lived in a vicious neighborhood and might soon be attacked again. Hitler rode this paranoid climate to power and used it to persuade Germans to follow him into self-ruinous wars of aggression during 1939–1945, launched in the name of gaining security for Germany.

In the 1930s Japan's leaders wrongly believed that Japan faced what they called "ABCD encirclement," an imagined conspiracy by America, Britain, China and the Dutch to subjugate and colonize Japan. This illusion fueled arguments in Japan that Japan had to grow or die, and kindled their decision to launch the Pacific war in 1941.

During 1955–61 Americans vastly exaggerated Soviet military capabilities, first during the "bomber gap" period (1955–57), and then during the "missile gap" (1957–61) Bottome (1971; Cramer 2002). These overestimates sometimes reached remarkable proportions. For example, in late 1959 U.S. intelligence agencies forecast that by 1961–62 the Soviet Union would have 1000–1500 intercontinental ballistic missiles (ICBMs), compared to less than 100 ICBMs for the U.S (Bottome 1971: 39–40, 55–56). In fact by September 1961 the Soviets had deployed only four ICBMs – less than one half of one percent of the missiles expected by U.S. intelligence (Kaplan 1983). There was a missile gap, but it lay vastly in favor of the United States.

These overestimates of Soviet bomber and missile building fed Cold War tensions by fueling American military over-building and American fear that Soviet intentions were aggressive. Americans wondered why the Soviets would seek military superiority, if not to bully the west into concessions or to launch aggressive war? Such fears stoked outsized U.S. military programs. This U.S. military over-building in turn provoked the USSR to desperate measures to strengthen its nuclear capability by covertly moving intermediate range missiles to Cuba in 1962. This reckless move triggered the Cuban Missile Crisis, our closest brush with World War III.

The U.S. again exaggerated Soviet military capabilities in the late 1970s and early 1980s. U.S. press commentators widely warned of Soviet nuclear and conventional superiority. But Soviet military superiority was an illusion. Both the Soviets and the U.S. maintained vast secure nuclear deterrents during this period – neither came anywhere near superiority over the other – and NATO conventional forces could have defeated a Soviet conventional attack in Europe (Salman, Sullivan, and Van Evera 1989; Mearsheimer 1982, 1988; Posen 1984–85, 1988).

The George W. Bush administration famously overestimated the threat posed by Saddam Hussein's Iraqi regime during the run-up to the 2003 American attack on Iraq. The administration wrongly claimed that Saddam possessed chemical and biological weapons, and maintained an active nuclear program. The administration also wrongly suggested that Saddam was allied with al-Qaeda and shared responsibility for al-Qaeda's 9/11 attack. The American people supported the war largely because it believed these false arguments.

Professional militaries are especially prone to inflate foreign threats. For example, the pre-1914 German military warned that Germany was surrounded by rapacious enemies ready to pounce. In the late 1880s and early 1890s General Alfred von Waldersee's military attaché in Paris "filled his reports with hair raising accounts of the imminence of a French attack." He told Berlin that "the present peaceful exterior is only a thin covering over France, a slight puff of wind and the bayonets are through," although French leaders actually had no belligerent plans (Kitchen 1968: 73). In 1904, the German naval attaché in London so alarmed Berlin with his reports that the Kaiser became persuaded that Britain might attack the next spring – a groundless fear (Steinber 1966). In 1909, former Chief of the General Staff Alfred von Schlieffen wrongly imagined that Germany and Austria–Hungary faced sudden attack by Britain, France, Russia and even Italy, which was then Germany's ally (Ritter 1958 [1978]). In 1911, General Friedrich von Bernhardi, the German army's top publicist, echoed Schlieffen, writing that "France aims solely at crushing Germany by an aggressive war," and that Germany's eastern territories were "menaced" by "Slavonic waves." "Our German nation is beset on all sides" (Bernhardi 1914). And in 1912 Admiral Alfred von Tirpitz wrongly claimed that the Anglo-French Entente "has the character of an offensive alliance" (Fischer 1975).

During the cold war U.S. military commanders often drew alarming pictures of Soviet and Chinese intentions. General Thomas Power, a former commander of the Strategic Air Command (SAC), wrongly forecast in 1964 that Soviet leaders would resort to "all-out military action" if they could not subdue the United States by other means. "They have long prepared for such a contingency" (Power and Arnhym 1965). Former SAC commander General Nathan Twining dubiously divined in 1966 that "the ultimate objectives of China's leaders are certainly the subjugation and communization of all Southeast Asia, the Indonesian area, the Philippines, and Australia" and described a "Hitler-like mentality which now dominates Red China" (Twining 1966). Cold War-era polls showed that U.S. military officers had darker views of Soviet intentions than their civilian counterparts (Holsti 1998/99).

Special interest groups that stand to gain from aggressive foreign policies are another source of threat inflation. The false reports of French aggression that provoked Britain to war against France in 1756 (described earlier) were concocted largely by Governor Robert Dinwiddie of Virginia. Dinwiddie was a principle shareholder in the Ohio Land Company, which stood to profit greatly from British expansion in North America. This private motive likely explains Dinwiddie's deceit (Higonnet 1968). Likewise, during 1953–54 the United Fruit Company (UFCo) organized a publicity campaign to warn the American public that Guatemala was coming under Soviet influence (Kinzer and Schlesinger 1999). But UFCo's claims were false. The Soviets actually had no significant presence in Guatemala. UFCo's motive doubtless lay in its wish to persuade the U.S. government to oust a leftist Guatemalan government that was threatening UFCo's privileged economic position in Guatemala.

Foreign lobbies will inflate threats if they can mobilize help for their cause by doing so. During the 1940s and 1950s the China Lobby relentlessly exaggerated the threat posed to the U.S. by communism in Asia (Koen 1974). This propaganda nurtured a public climate of fear about Asian communism in the U.S., which in turn helped to foster America's unfortunate decision to prosecute the Vietnam War.

Threat inflation often takes the form of monolith thinking, in which the closeness of ties among unfriendly states, or between neutral and unfriendly states, is exaggerated. Monolith thinking has a double threat-inflating effect. It causes the monolith-thinker to impute the hostility of the more hostile state to the less hostile state; and to assume that the leader-state of the assumed monolith commands the capabilities of its alleged vassals, and so to believe that the leader-state is stronger than in fact it is. Hence, monolith thinking leads states to exaggerate the hostility and capabilities of others.

During the Cold War Americans often fell sway to monolith thinking, wrongly assuming that nationalist/communist Third World movements were Soviet puppets, when in fact they were independent of Soviet control. At various times the U.S. wrongly saw China, Iran, Guatemala, North Vietnam, the Viet Cong of South Vietnam, Nicaragua, and leftists in El Salvador as obedient to Soviet command. In the 1960s U.S. leaders also believed Vietnam's communists were vassals of China, a mistaken notion that crucially supported arguments for American involvement in Vietnam. Soviet cold war-era leaders held similar notions about the capitalist world, wrongly seeing neutral non-communist states as obedient American proxies.

More recently, the George W. Bush administration wrongly argued that Saddam Hussein and Osama Bin Laden's al-Qaeda were partners, when in fact they were hostile adversaries.

Threat inflation can sometimes prevent war by deterring states that would act more aggressively if they accurately gauged others capabilities or intentions. In the early 1950s Stalin and his successors may have moderated their foreign policies because they wrongly thought the U.S. was gearing up to attack the USSR, and they sought to avoid offering a provocation (Khrushchev 1990).

More often, however, threat inflation raises the risk of war. It leaves states feeling less secure than they would feel if they estimated others intentions and capabilities accurately. As a result states take belligerent measures to secure themselves. Specifically, they may seek bigger borders to gain assets they believe will enhance their power. They may launch aggressive wars to cut neighbors down to size, or to destroy what they believe to be hostile regimes in neighboring states. They may launch preemptive or preventive war to forestall attack by others.

States that feel insecure may also adopt belligerent policies short of war that raise the risk of war. Such policies include the use of *fait accompli* tactics in diplomacy, the enshrouding of foreign and military policy in dark secrecy, and the pursuit of more intense arms-racing. The first of these policies, *faits accomplis*, can cause war if the state taking the *fait accompli* unwittingly oversteps another state's red line, creating a *casus belli*. The second policy, dark secrecy, can foster war-causing false optimism in others. The third, arms racing, can open windows of opportunity or vulnerability. These windows in turn can tempt states in relative decline to launch preventive war before their situation deteriorates further.

When states are conquered and destroyed, their own threat inflation is often a large part of the cause. Since 1815 great powers have been conquered on eight occasions. On two of these eight occasions the great power was conquered by unprovoked aggressors (France was overrun by Prussia in 1870 and by Nazi Germany in 1940), while on six occasions it was overrun by provoked aggressors. On five of these six occasions the aggressors were provoked by the victim's fantasy-driven defensive bellicosity. Napoleonic France, Wilhelmine and Nazi Germany, Austria-Hungary and Imperial Japan were all destroyed by dangers that they created through their efforts to escape from exaggerated or imaginary threats to their safety. Mussolini's Italy, which provoked its own destruction for non-security reasons, forms the sole exception.

If so, threat inflation is a prime danger to the safety of modern great powers. Their nemesis lies in their own tendency to exaggerate the threats they face, and to respond with counterproductive belligerence. The causes of this syndrome pose a large question for students of international relations, and form the subject of this volume.

References

Bernhardi, F. (1914) *Germany and the Next War*, trans. Allen H. Powles, London: Edward Arnold.

Bottome, E. M. (1971) *The Balance of Terror: A Guide to the Arms Race*, Boston: Beacon Press.

Cramer, J. K. (2002) "National Security Panics: Overestimating Threats to National Security," Ph.D. dissertation, Massachusetts Institute of Technology.

Fischer, F. (1975) *War of Illusions: German Policies from 1911 to 1914*, trans. Marian Jackson, New York: W. W. Norton.

Geiss, I. (1976) *Germany Foreign Policy 1871-1914*, Boston: Routledge and Kegan Paul.

Grenville, J. A. S. (1976) *Europe Reshaped*, London: Fontana.

Herwig, H. (1991) "Clio deceived: Patriotic self-censorship in Germany after the great war," in Steven E. Miller, Sean M. Lynn-Jones and Stephen Van Evera (eds) *Military Strategy and the Origins of the First World War*, rev. edn., Princeton: Princeton University Press.

Higonnet, P. L. (1968) "The origins of the seven years' war," *Journal of Modern History*, 40: 57–90.

Holsti, O. R. (1998/99) "A widening gap between the U.S. military and civilian society? Some evidence, 1976–96," *International Security*, 23: 5–42.

Kaplan, F. (1983) *The Wizards of Armageddon*, New York: Simon and Schuster.

Kinzer, S. and Schlesinger, S. (1999) *Bitter Fruit: The Story of the American Coup in Guatemala* (exp. ed.), Cambridge MA: Harvard University Press.

Kitchen, M. (1968) *The German Officer Corps, 1890–1914*, Oxford: Oxford University Press.

Koen, R. Y. (1974) *The China Lobby in American Politics*, NY: Harper & Row.

Khrushchev, N. (1990) *Khrushchev Remembers: The Glasnost Tapes* (trans. and ed.) J. L. Schecter with V. V. Luchow, Boston: Little, Brown.

Mearsheimer, J. J. (1982) "Why the Soviets can't win quickly in central Europe," *International Security*, 7: 3–39.

—— (1988) "Numbers, strategy, and the European balance," *International Security*, 12: 174–185.

Mombauer, A. (2002) *The Origins of the First World War: Controversies and Consensus*, New York and London: Longman.

Moses, J. A. (1975) *The Politics of Illusion: The Fischer Controversy In German Historiography*, London: George Prior.

Posen, Barry R. "Measuring the European conventional balance: Coping with complexity in threat assessment," *International Security*, 9: 47–88.

—— (1988) "Is NATO decisively outnumbered?" *International Security*, 12: 186–202.

Power, T. S. with Arnhym, A. A. (1964) *Design For Survival*, New York: Coward-McCann.

Ritter, G. (1979) *The Schlieffen Plan: Critique of a Myth*, London: Oswald Wolff, 1958; reprint edn, Westport, Conn.: Greenwood Press.

Salman, M., Sullivan, K. J. and Van Evera, S. (1989) "Analysis or propaganda? Measuring American strategic nuclear capability, 1969–1988," in L. Eden and S. E. Miller (eds) *Nuclear Arguments: Understanding the Strategic Nuclear Arms and Arms Control Debates*, Ithaca: Cornell University Press.

Smoke, R. War (1997) *Controlling Escalation*, Cambridge: Harvard University Press.

Steinberg, J. (1966) "The Copenhagen complex," in W. Laqueur and G. L. Mosse, (eds) *1914: The Coming of the First World War*, New York: Harper & Row.

Twining, N. F. (1966) *Neither Liberty Nor Safety*, New York: Holt, Rinehart and Winston.

Van Evera, S. (2006) "Bush administration, weak on terror," *Middle East Policy*, 13: 28–38.

Acknowledgements

Every book represents the efforts and support of a great many people beyond the authors and editors. In addition to the great support from our families and friends, we need to thank the Social Sciences department at the University of Michigan – Dearborn and the Political Science Department at the University of Oregon for providing necessary funding and every form of logistical support. We would also like to thank Sue Peterson for first suggesting the idea for this edited volume and Robert Art for connecting us with Sue Peterson. We would also like to thank the contributors to this volume, all of whom have been extremely pleasant under short deadlines and without whom there would be no book. Finally, we thank Sage Publications, the MIT Press, the National Interest, and John Wiley and Sons for permission to reprint portions of material previously published in their journals.

A. Trevor Thrall
Jane K. Cramer

1 Introduction

Understanding threat inflation

Jane K. Cramer and A. Trevor Thrall

The Bush administration's launching of a global war on terrorism in the wake of 9/11, coupled with its aggressive campaign to build public support for war against Iraq, have brought the term "threat inflation" into popular use. President Bush's ability to stoke public fear about Iraq's connections to Al Qaeda and about its weapons of mass destruction despite the lack of any hard evidence has fueled both public outcry as well as a vigorous debate among academics about why the administration argued with such certainty about Iraq and how its arguments came to dominate debate. The implications of the debate are profound. To the extent that the president can dominate debate about foreign threats, it becomes difficult for the United States to rely on the marketplace of ideas (i.e., the news media and public vetting of foreign policy) to assess accurately the pros and cons of competing arguments about foreign policy and the use of force. In extreme cases, as several scholars have labeled the invasion of Iraq, a president may convince the public to support a war that it would otherwise strenuously oppose.

This volume focuses on the whys and hows of the threat inflation process. Threat inflation, most simply understood, is the attempt by elites to create concern for a threat that goes beyond the scope and urgency that a disinterested analysis would justify. Many scholars, including several in this volume, do not find this definition a perfect one to describe the process. Nonetheless, this view sits at the heart of both public and academic debate over Iraq, and for many it describes the handling of threats since 9/11, thus providing an important baseline definition with which to compare and contrast competing explanations for the same historical cases.

To date scholars have offered a wide range of arguments about why the Bush administration has sought to inflate threats since 9/11 and Iraq in particular. Many observers insist that much of the threat exaggeration since 9/11 has been intentional, politically opportunistic and even self-serving. Others see the administration as sincere, led by long-held ideology to see the post 9/11 world as extremely threatening. Some scholars point the finger at neoconservatives in key positions; arguing that they pressed their worldview on the administration and hijacked the decision-making process regarding Iraq. Others have argued that common psychological short cuts in reasoning biased the threat perception process and most likely significantly account for the widespread misperceptions among administration leaders and their followers. Still others find the threat inflation process likely to be at root politically motivated, but nonetheless primarily institutionally determined and perhaps even necessary to exaggerate threats to enable bold foreign policy initiatives. Finally, a few scholars have assessed the post 9/11 era and found simply a series of heightened fears, unavoidable intelligence failures, and mistakes in judgment.

With regard to how the threat inflation process actually impacts public opinion change and the policy-making process, scholars are likewise in conflict. Why does threat inflation sometimes succeed when clearly, at many other moments in history, elite attempts to inflate the threat do not succeed? Even in cases where scholars agree threat inflation was successful, as with Iraq, observers disagree about what factors moved the needle. Was Bush's ability to manage the news the critical ingredient, his information dominance as president with respect to Congress, or simply the fact that Congress was unwilling or unable to challenge him so soon after 9/11?

Given the rising interest in the question of threat inflation and the tremendous diversity of competing explanations for recent events, the time is ripe to bring together the different theoretical approaches and make them speak to one another. Too often scholars studying different aspects of threat inflation have not confronted each other's work. Scholars who have studied intelligence failures, psychological misperceptions, intentional elite manipulation of threats, the formation of public opinion and the power of identity have often been analyzing the same historical cases and evidence without explicitly recognizing either the challenges or the synergies from other perspectives. Thus, in these pages, we asked our contributors to do two things. First, we asked them to address specifically the concept of threat inflation as we have defined it here. Second, we asked them to consider the extent to which their understanding of threat inflation is complementary or competitive with other explanations. In short, these essays on threat inflation have been brought together here to begin a more comprehensive discussion of the causes of threat inflation and the factors that contribute to its success or failure in the United States. Our hope is that a robust debate on this topic will shed light on an important period in U.S. foreign policy and prove fruitful for scholars trying to build theories that offer enduring lessons about threat inflation.

Theories of threat inflation

There are four broad theoretical approaches explaining threat inflation: realist, psychological, domestic political and constructivist. Part of what makes it difficult to reconcile these approaches is that they often operate on different levels of analysis and highlight different elements as most crucial to the process. At times, scholars appear to be in near-agreement as to the causes of threat inflation, but slight differences in emphasis or characterization of what the most important causes of threat inflation are lead to major differences in policy prescriptions as to what the cure for threat inflation might be, if a cure is indeed possible. Nonetheless, a complete theory must explain the causal chain outlined in Figure 1.1. The figure provides the simplest possible model of the threat inflation process, in which elites perceive threats, create communication strategies to inflate threats, implement those

Figure 1.1 A simple model of threat inflation

strategies within the news media, or marketplace of ideas, in an attempt to shape opinions and influence policy, and either succeed or fail to do so.

Looking at the model, a useful way to understand the major differences between the four theoretical approaches is simply to ask in case of each approach: Where does threat inflation begin? Realists begin at the far left of the model, highlighting the uncertainty that elites face in trying to assess threats. Unable to be certain of other's intentions, elites often feel they have little or no choice but to focus on the worst case, and they may even spin threats to the public in order to prepare for the same. Psychological theorists generally start a step further to the right from realists, arguing most often that the key problems arise in the information-processing step as elites fall prey to various cognitive and emotional biases in perception. Some psychological theorists emphasize the fifth step in that they emphasize ways in which the very same cognitive biases lead the public to overreact to certain threats and to be most receptive to elites who emphasize worst case scenarios.

Constructivist perspectives on threat inflation similarly suggest that threat inflation begins with elite threat perception, but argue that elite threat perceptions are not discrete events but are historically and culturally determined, rooted in national identity, norms and values, which in turn reflect collective discursive processes within the society. As with psychological theories, many constructivist theories are also used to explain how public perceptions are determined. Instead of looking at cognitive processes, constructivists aim to understand how and why certain arguments become hegemonic among the public from a social perspective.

Domestic politics explanations of threat inflation primarily focus on the middle two steps of the process, arguing that many elites have institutional, electoral, bureaucratic, personal or material incentives to promote threats and that threat inflation's success or failure rides on the political maneuvering, competition between President and Congress, the influence of interest groups and lobbies, public opinion, and the behavior of the mass media.

Most scholars, regardless of general theoretical approach, acknowledge that threat inflation has multiple and interacting causes. To date, however, there have been few attempts to bring these different perspectives together in a complete explanation of the entire threat inflation process. In this chapter we provide a brief overview of these four types of explanations and how the phenomenon of "threat inflation" has been explored previously.

Realist explanations of threat inflation

Realist scholars emphasize that what appears to be "threat inflation" is really the result of leaders attempting to cope with uncertainty. For realists, overestimations of threats are the inevitable, regular consequence of insufficient intelligence and the opacity of other states' intentions. (Knorr 1976; Waltz 1979; Walt 1987; Mearsheimer 2001; Tang 2008). Large overestimations of threats are most likely to happen at times of increased uncertainty and perceived high risk such as after a surprise attack because leaders need to constantly analyse ambiguous and incomplete intelligence in real time and pay close attention to worst case analyzes as they decide how to respond to possible threats within the international system (e.g. how could a leader ever know for sure that Iraq really did not have weapons of mass destruction somewhere, even with inspections?) (Freedman 2004; Jervis 2006a). Realist analysis emphasizes the primary importance of uncertainty as the root cause of what appears to be "threat inflation."

Realist arguments stress that analyses of threats at all times vary greatly, and what appears to be "threat inflation" is most often a disagreement over the probability or significance of worst case analyses. Realists argue that people can sometimes know with the benefit of hindsight that threats were inflated at a particular time, but for many analysts that does not mean that seemingly extreme estimates were insincere, unreasonable or implausible. Many interpretations of a threat are always possible, so deciding what threat analysis is beyond the range of plausible at a particular time is most often unknowable (Krebs 2005).

Realists who stress disagreements over intelligence as the root cause of what appears to be "threat inflation" often acknowledge other contributing factors such as understandable and excusable "spinning" of threats for political mobilization purposes (Mearsheimer 2004). This does not mean that leaders are lying or pursuing self-serving domestic political interests. Instead, leaders are primarily rationally coping with international threats that are unknowable and largely unpredictable. Leaders are acting responsibly in an uncertain and anarchic system where states must constantly search for security. It is a tragic reality that leaders' actions and frequent over-reactions often leave them worse off, but this is the result of the usually unavoidable security dilemma (Jervis 1978). Future capabilities and intentions of adversaries can never be known with certainty, and thus "threat inflation" is to be expected as leaders attempt to "play it safe" by anticipating unknowable threats. For many realists, "threat inflation" cannot be "cured." Vigilance by states against possible threats is necessary and hyper-vigilance that can be counterproductive can only be somewhat guarded against through better intelligence collection and analysis.

Psychological explanations of threat inflation

Many scholars believe that there is a significant amount of "threat inflation" that cannot be explained by uncertainty, intelligence failure and rational worst case analysis alone. One approach turns to theories of social and cognitive psychology to explain the central misperceptions of national security threats (Jervis 1976). Based on years of laboratory experiments, psychological theories suggest that people may misperceive national security threats due to common cognitive biases that limit the ability to assess threats rationally (Janis and Mann 1977; Nisbett and

Ross 1980; Janis 1982; Larson 1989; Lebow 1981; Khong 1992; Johnson 1994; Kaufmann 1994; Jervis 2006b).

A common argument with respect to Iraq in line with the psychological perspective generally begins with the observation that people often interpret facts in ways that support their expectations and in ways that support plausible arguments about potential threats even when the facts do not warrant such conclusions. In the case of Iraq, this tendency may have led the Bush administration to assume (and possibly the American public to accept) that Saddam Hussein's uncooperative behavior was hiding his pursuit of nuclear weapons. Since the United States knew he had sought such weapons in the past and expected him to continue doing so, the Bush administration and the U.S. intelligence community may have been unable to read the true underlying situation, leading them to inflate the threat (Jervis 2006b).

Relatedly, psychologists have argued that people do not update their beliefs in response to new information in the manner assumed by rational actor theories. Instead, once people form beliefs they tend to stick with them and use them as guidance for interpreting and understanding the world (Jervis 2006a). Having decided and argued that Iraq was the central front in the war on terror and that terrorism was an existential threat that had to be confronted aggressively, for example, it would be psychologically difficult and even painful for President Bush and his supporters to acknowledge at a later point that Al Qaeda did not represent an existential threat and that the war in Iraq was unnecessary and costly, even if a great deal of factual evidence pointed in that direction. Thus, psychological theories also suggest the potential for threat inflation to persist once it has begun.

The psychological biases that underlie these misperceptions come in two main types: unmotivated biases and motivated biases. Unmotivated biases are thought of as "short cuts in reasoning" and are unconscious, systematic errors, operating at all times or at least often, leading to theoretically predictable and observable divergences from rationality within individuals. In contrast, motivated biases reflect people's attempts to protect their egos, rationalize prior decisions, or prevent cognitive dissonance, and involve affect and emotion, not just cognition. Harder to predict, these biases help to explain how leaders who appear self-serving actually sincerely believe they are not self-serving and are instead acting in the best interest of the nation or cause. Taken together, scholars argue, these two types of biases can lead to a range of misperceptions and beliefs that make threat inflation more likely (Jervis 2006a; Renshon 2006; Gilovich *et al.* 2002).

One of the most famous unmotivated biases with threat inflationary capability is what psychologists call the fundamental attribution error (Kelley and Michela 1980). When one person observes another, the observer tends to attribute the other's actions to their character, nature or deeply held motives. At the same time, the observer tends to reason that her own actions are in response to her situation and to the other's actions, and not due to her own character, motives or nature since these aspects of herself are less "salient" or apparent to her. Thus, an observer is likely to reason that the other is buying arms or behaving threateningly because she is innately hostile and aggressive, while she is buying arms and behaving aggressively because she was provoked by the other and needs to defend herself. This type of cognitive bias could cause leaders and members of the public to see themselves as significantly less hostile than their adversaries, while blinding them to the ways in which their adversary was provoked by them or by the situation. Such patterns in reasoning could be an important root cause of threat inflation.

Numerous other cognitive shortcuts in reasoning have been identified by scholars and are possibly important to national misperceptions of threats. Studies have shown, for example, that once people become anxious about a threat, they attend more carefully to threat-related information, identify threatening information as more salient than other information, and develop more negative attitudes toward out groups, often leading to an increased willingness to use force (Huddy *et al.* 2005; Gordon and Arian 2001; Eysenck 1992; Hermann *et al.* 1999). With particular relevance to the threat of terrorism, scholars have also long noted that people tend to overestimate the probability of extremely unlikely, yet dreadful, risks such as major terrorist attacks. In an uncertain world, scholars argue, these tendencies make it likely that hawkish arguments will win the day in policy debates and that nations will tend to inflate threats beyond their reasonable proportions (Sunstein 2003; Kahneman and Renshon 2007).

Psychological arguments may complement other lines of inquiry, but should also be considered potential competitors with other explanations of threat inflation. Domestic political arguments, for example, typically suggest that leaders intentionally mislead the public because of their political and material interests. Such an explanation clearly does not rule out the possibility that psychological factors also play a role in threat perception, perhaps compounding the misperception of threat. On the other hand, a contrary psychology based argument might suggest either that unmotivated bias is enough to explain the case without regard to domestic politics or that elites' political and material interests led to motivated biases. In the latter case, the psychological argument would suggest that leaders were acting sincerely rather than in a manipulative way.

Domestic political explanations of threat inflation

Domestic politics arguments begin with two central observations. First, that the electoral, institutional, bureaucratic and even material interests of elites help determine which threats elites will find it useful to inflate. Second, that the process of threat inflation is determined by the array of domestic political institutions and the advantages conferred by these institutions on the elites who occupy certain positions within them, as well as the obstacles those institutions present to anyone seeking to influence the policy process or public opinion.

The domestic politics viewpoint acknowledges that the causes of threat inflation might take the form either of sincere efforts to act in the public interest or manipulative strategies to gain political advantage, increase institutional budgets, or to advance other goals kept hidden from the public and political opposition. For example, many scholars have argued that overselling threats may in fact be a necessary evil. The inertia caused by the separation of powers and the difficulty of working with Congress routinely delays decisions and neutralizes bold policy initiatives. To generate the political capital needed to mobilize the government, the president must first mobilize an apathetic public that typically pays little attention to foreign affairs. Thus this view finds that the president is essentially forced to make dramatic, even outlandish, arguments about potential threats to accomplish what he or she deems best for the country (Friedman this volume; Lowi 1979; Nye 1984; Kaufmann 2004; Kernell 2007).

Most scholars making domestic political arguments to explain threat inflation, however, identify a range of interests and motivations that point to less seemly reasons for presidents and other elites to hype threats. One set of likely threat inflators would be powerful narrow ideological and military special interests who find overseas expansion or intervention beneficial to their cause or goals in one way or another (Snyder 2003; Mearsheimer and Walt 2007). In looking at the Iraq case, for example, some scholars have pointed to neoconservatives as the root of threat inflation. Neoconservatives in and out of the Bush administration, they argue, had long sought an invasion of Iraq in particular, and more U.S. military engagement in the Middle East in many ways. These leaders likely were primarily interested in better securing Israel, while also presumably believing that these actions would better secure U.S. interests, just at a cost the U.S. public would not accept without threat inflation. These analysts argue that 9/11 merely provided the window of opportunity to take actions these narrow interests desired for other reasons long before 9/11. In this view, the war on terror has merely been mostly a convenient device to sell the Iraq war (and a more aggressive foreign policy overall) to an otherwise recalcitrant public (Lustick 2006; Cramer and Thrall 2005).

Once a threat has been established, wrongly or rightly, there is an incentive for interest groups, corporations, government agencies, and politicians to continue to inflate the threat in order to achieve material, policy, and electoral goals. In the wake of 9/11, scholars argue, interest groups and companies sought to sell themselves as critical to the war on terror, giving them an organizational incentive to make sure that the American public stayed focused on and afraid of the terrorist threat. Federal agencies used 9/11 as a window to advance policy priorities that had been stalled or denied in the past. Likewise, members of Congress, seeking to build favor back in their districts, had incentive to try to funnel abundant terrorism-related monies home to pet projects. In order to reap dividends at home, politicians had an incentive to argue that the government was not doing enough to protect ports, cities, transportation nodes, etc. Aspiring politicians as well could use threat inflation to challenge incumbents as being soft on terrorism, promising to do more and bring home more bacon. This competition leads incumbents and bureaucrats to work hard to attend to the terrorist threat in order to be sure that they could not be criticized by opponents or blamed should something actually happen. Scholars have suggested that such dynamics are unlikely to disappear quickly. While incentives to inflate the threat are numerous and the dividends gained by narrow interests are tangible, no one has such strong incentives to work to deflate threats (Lustick 2006; Mueller 2006; Snyder 2003).

Another theme from the domestic politics literature on threat inflation is the role and contribution of the mass media to public fears. This argument takes several forms. First, many scholars argue that the news media tend to accept presidential claims and framing of threats uncritically and only occasionally give much space to the opposition, helping presidents inflate threats as in the case of terrorism and Iraq (Entman 2004; Kaufmann 2004; Chomsky 1997; Rampton and Stauber 2003; Massing 2004, 2005a, 2005b). Second, given its sensationalist bias, short attention span, and superficiality, the news media tend to focus on the most vivid and frightening aspects of threats, providing little balance or sense of perspective and stoking public fears essentially to sell papers or gain viewers and ratings (Kushner 2005; Mueller 2006; Lustick 2006). Additionally, it has recently been argued that the superficiality and sensationalism of the media may be greater than it has been historically in the U.S. marketplace of ideas since media consolidation and increased corporate ownership has taken place. Finally, as Lustick notes, popular movies, books, and television shows have amped the threat of terrorism by generating an endless stream of catastrophic plots and end-of-the-world scenarios with little relation to reality (2006).

Other domestic political approaches partially set aside arguments about motives or incentives, and instead focus upon why threat inflation succeeds in the U.S. marketplace of ideas. A major theme here focuses on the role of the president in threat inflation. Scholars focused on the president have offered three main arguments about why the president is especially capable of threat inflation. First, the executive branch has some enhanced control of information, especially intelligence, however the significance of this control is disputed. It appears that because of this control of information, in dealings with Congress, the press, and the public, presidents have a very strong position from which to debate the scope and urgency of threats. In the case of Iraq, for example, many of the administration's key claims about WMD and Iraq's connections to terrorism and 9/11 seemed to be unverifiable by outsiders at the time. Secretary of State Colin Powell's dramatic testimony to the United Nations in which he summarized the U.S. intelligence system's case on Iraqi WMD made a sizeable impact on short term public support for the invasion, despite the fact that its most important elements were fully revealed later to be false (Kaufmann 2004; Western 2005a).

By contrast, while some analysts argue the president's control of information was one of the main reasons the executive branch's threat inflation succeeded, other scholars dispute the importance of the president's alleged informational advantage, and instead argue that the political opposition to the president understood the lack of evidence against Iraq and the full folly of the administration's invasion plans, yet this opposition failed to oppose the executive branch for other reasons, such as a lack of rhetorical space or because of dominant norms of patriotism based in militarism (Krebs and Lobasz; Cramer, both in this volume).

The second advantage the president enjoys is the power to set the political agenda. Given the president's role as the prime mover in foreign-policy making, the president can mobilize the armed forces and confront foreign leaders at any time, thus shaping the terms of debate in ways opponents cannot match (e.g. moving troops into ready positions in the Persian Gulf and making conflict with Iraq seem inevitable). In doing this the president also has the power to time events to shape the ensuing debate to maximize political advantage over important issues and over upcoming electoral contests (Snyder, Shapiro and Bloch-Elkon 2009). In the case of Iraq, for example, President Bush made sure to time his introduction of the debate over war in Iraq so that the Congressional vote to authorize the use of force would come right before the mid-term elections, making it difficult for Democrats in Congress to mount a vigorous opposition lest they be viewed as unpatriotic by voters (Western 2005a; Cramer 2007).

The third major advantage the president enjoys is the power of the bully pulpit and the cohesion of the executive branch, which makes it possible to exercise that power effectively. Thanks to the routines of modern journalism the president is guaranteed the opening salvo in debates about foreign threats as well as far more coverage than his opponents (Kaufmann 2004; Bennett *et al.* 2007). Some scholars argue that this tendency reflects a compliant press seeking to enable its government handlers; others view it as an unhappy result of financial pressures on an increasingly profit-focused media system (Hutcheson *et al.* 2004; Chomsky 1997). Regardless of which view is correct, this advantage allows the president great latitude to frame debate in ways that maximize his persuasive impact while minimizing the potential for opponents to challenge his arguments (Entman 2004; Gershkoff and Kushner 2005). This advantage is bolstered by the fact that the president benefits from having a dedicated communications staff and a coordinated message while his opponents are more scattered and less organized (Western 2005a). Many scholars identify the news media as the last and most important failure of the marketplace of ideas in the case of Iraq. Scholars like Chaim Kaufmann (this volume), for example, believe that the war would never have taken place had the press offered greater resistance to Bush administration claims about Iraq and provided more space and time to political opponents seeking to debate the administration's case for war.

A final consideration on the domestic political process of threat inflation is the role of public attitudes and partisanship. As both Western and Thrall argue in this volume, the resonance of elite arguments about threats will depend on the distribution of general public attitudes toward the international arena as well as their support for the president in particular. Thus, in the case of Iraq, Bush had more success generating support among conservatives who shared his worldview than he did among liberals who supported working multilaterally and through the United Nations. This suggests that the potential for threat inflation will vary depending on what kind of president occupies the White House, on the president's current popularity, as well as on public predispositions toward certain types of threats.

Constructivist explanations of threat inflation

The constructivist approach to considering threat inflation might best be summarized by the argument that threats are what we make of them. From this perspective, threats are not objective material facts, waiting to be perceived correctly or incorrectly, waiting to be inflated, deflated, or communicated honestly to the public. Constructivists do not argue, of course, that threats do not exist. The central contribution of the constructivist perspective, however, is that national and cultural identities, norms, and myths will heavily color threat perceptions and the success of elite threat inflation efforts (Johnston 1995; Wendt 1999; Payne 2001; Rousseau 2006).

Constructivist scholars have challenged the realist assumption that relative power is the sole determinant of threat perception. Instead, constructivists have focused on the role of identity and the process of categorizing other nations as other, lesser, or evil. To the extent that two nations differ with respect to national identity (government structure, religion, cultural values), constructivists argue, the more each is likely to feel threatened by the other and, by extension, the more likely threat inflation will become. A constructivist perspective also predicts that the public will be most responsive to threat inflation efforts when leaders use rhetoric that high-lights cultural and national differences (Rousseau 2006; Rousseau and Garcia-Retamero this volume; Kaufman 2001). In this way, constructivism offers a way to predict when the uncertainty identified by realism will be most likely to result in threat inflation efforts and successful threat inflation.

Constructivist theories are a form of social-psychological argument and as such have much in common with psychological theories. Constructivists argue that people's unconscious categorization of self and other plays a critical role in threat perception, much like a cognitive bias. Likewise, constructivists also acknowledge the power of ideas to influence perception even in the face of contrary facts. They move beyond individual level psychological theories, however, in their emphasis of the way in which ideas and beliefs are constructed over time. For constructivists, the political, social, and economic structures in society, along with the processes of mass communication, must be accounted for in any explanation of national identity and, in turn, national threat perceptions. In the constructivist view, ideas that sup-port a society's power structure are likely to be those with the greatest influence on national identity. In turn, elites with access to the mass media will have the greatest influence on how people think about their national identity and what aspects of it are most salient. In the case of Iraq, for example, both Presidents Bush spoke of the "Iraqi regime," highlighting the distinction between the democratic (and thus "good") United States and the totalitarian (and thus "bad") Iraq and encouraging U.S. citizens to view the conflict in such terms rather than encouraging them to cal-culate what sort of threat Iraq represented to the U.S. in more material terms (Krebs and Lobasz in this volume).

Finally, constructivist arguments also provide a different take on the standard domestic political understanding of the role of the marketplace of ideas in the threat inflation process. While many scholars have focused on the importance of factual reporting and the quality of information available to the public as a bulwark against threat inflation (Kaufmann 2003; Van Evera 1990; Snyder and Ballantine 1996; Cramer 2007), the constructivist perspective suggests that symbolic politics and framing efforts based on worldviews and values will be more important to public opinion formation (Sears 1993; Kaufman 2001; Western 2005; Thrall 2007). With respect to Iraq, for example, Thrall in this volume argues that elite misrepresentation of Iraqi WMD in the news was far less important than many scholars have assumed in building and maintaining public support for war.

Threat inflation: the search for enduring lessons

Though the immediate impetus for this volume is the effort to understand the events since 9/11, we believe that the search for enduring lessons about threat inflation provides its real justification. A more complete understanding of how elites and the public perceive and respond to threats may help provide counsel to future leaders attempting to cope with an uncertain world. A fuller assessment of the strengths and limits of the marketplace of ideas should give us earlier warning about when unhealthy threat inflation may occur. We believe that the contributions in this volume represent a step in the right direction and urge our colleagues to join the debate.

Roadmap of the book

In Chapter 2 Robert Jervis provides an overview of his current take on some of the most important arguments from the psychological approach to understanding threat perceptions, and threat inflation. Jervis focuses on understanding beliefs and their influence on both elite perceptions and elite behavior. He emphasizes that to find that beliefs were important determinants of action it is not enough to simply find records of private elite conversations demonstrating the elites were sincere in their beliefs. Instead, he proposes that beliefs must be shown to be "powerful and autonomous" and not simply the direct product of the objective situation (determined by interests and incentives).

Alternatively, from a more domestic political angle, Jack Snyder takes a different approach to explaining why great powers tend to frequently display a remarkable pattern of exaggerating threats. In Chapter 3 Snyder argues that the United States has fallen prey to several common "myths of empire." He argues that the emergence of these myths of empire occurred thanks to the confluence of the shocking attacks of 9/11, the Bush administration's ideological worldview, and the domestic politics of the time period, particularly the utility of "wedge issues" in the currently polarized American party system.

In Chapter 4 David Rousseau and Rocio Garcia-Retamero offer a constructivist explanation for individual threat perception. Using experimental data to test what they call the construction of threat model, they show that both the realist focus on relative balance of power and the constructivist focus on shared national identity help explain people's willingness to use force to settle international disputes. Their conclusions call for us to question our ability to measure threats objectively.

In Chapter 5 Kahneman and Renshon argue that hawkish and threat inflationary arguments tend to be more persuasive than they should be, thanks to an array of cognitive biases that shape how we process information, make decisions, and ultimately judge the scope and urgency of foreign threats.

In Chapter 6, the first of several chapters that focus on explaining the Iraq case, Chaim Kaufmann argues that the marketplace of ideas failed to counter the Bush administration's misuse of intelligence information. Citing executive advantages in information, a privileged role in shaping the news agenda, and successful framing of the issue by the White House, Kaufmann argues that the U.S. marketplace of ideas is highly susceptible to threat inflation thanks to the structure and processes of domestic politics.

Ronald Krebs and Jennifer Lobasz agree in Chapter 7 that the Bush administration was successful in its threat inflation efforts, but identify its use of powerful rhetoric as the most critical component of success. Krebs and Lobasz argue that because the Bush administration was able to fix the meaning of the September 11 attacks in terms of the broad and urgent "War on Terror," this discourse about Iraq became hegemonic, rhetorically forcing the Democrats to accede to this interpretation of the events instead of contesting it.

In Chapter 8, Jane K. Cramer suggests that to understand why Bush's arguments were so powerful, one has to go back to the Cold War and trace the development of what she calls "militarized patriotism." Cramer argues that this form of patriotism, forged during the long confrontation with the Soviet Union, generally silences opponents of military force by making dissent unpatriotic. This argument about patriotism rests on the evidence that the executive branch did not trick or mislead the majority of Democrats or the many Republicans who strongly opposed the invasion just days before they turned around and passed the Iraq War Resolution.

In Chapter 9, Jon Western provides another take on the Iraq case, arguing that latent public support for the administration's arguments about Iraq and the need for an invasion played a larger role in Bush's ability to take the nation to war than some have acknowledged. Despite this, Western also argues that Bush administration used its information and communication advantages to mislead the public and stymie the opposition until it was too late to stop the invasion.

A. Trevor Thrall offers a critique of the standard conception of the marketplace of ideas and threat inflation in Chapter 10. Thrall argues that the realist focus on facts and debate misses the true process by which the public forms opinions. Thrall also challenges the notion that Bush was in fact successful in inflating public concerns about Iraq, noting that though Bush had support from republicans and some independents before the war, he never managed to persuade a majority of democrats to support the war until it was essentially underway.

John Mueller offers a historically informed argument about threat inflation in Chapter 11. Observing that the U.S. government has tended to inflate foreign threats since the dawn of the Cold War, Mueller argues that the military and the "terrorism industry" have strong incentives to keep people afraid of terrorist threats.

In Chapter 12 Benjamin Friedman looks at the flip side of threat inflation and argues that the U.S. perceptions of the threat of terrorism in the 1990s were in fact accurate, contrary to what most people have argued in the wake of 9/11. Friedman argues that elite threat perception flows not from perceptual biases but primarily from institutional interests. Unless military and government institutions have an incentive to adopt a new threat, he argues, they will be unlikely to seek its inflation in the public mind.

References

Bennett, W. L., Lawrence, R. G. and Livingston, S. (2007) *When the Press Fails: Political Power and the News Media from Iraq to Katrina*, Chicago, IL: Chicago University Press.

Chomsky, N. (1997) *Media Control: The Spectacular Successes of Propaganda*, New York: Seven Stories.

Cramer, J. K. (2007) "Militarized patriotism: why the marketplace of ideas failed before the Iraq war," *Security Studies*, 16: 489–524.

Cramer, J. K. and Thrall, A. T. (2005) "Why did the United States invade Iraq?" Paper presented at the 2005 meeting of the International Studies Association, Chicago, IL.

Entman, R. M. (2004) *Projections of Power: Framing News, Public Opinion, and U.S. Foreign Policy*, Chicago: University of Chicago Press.

Eysenck, M. W. (1992) *Anxiety: The Cognitive Perspective*, London: Lawrence Erlbaum Associates Ltd.

Freedman, L. (2004) "War in Iraq: selling the threat," *Survival*, 46: 7–50.

Gershkoff, A. and Kushner, S. (2005) "Shaping public opinion: The 9/11-Iraq connection in the Bush administration's rhetoric," *Perspectives on Politics*, 3: 525–37.

Gilovich, T., Griffin D. W. and Kahneman, D. (2002) *Heuristics and Biases: The Psychology of Intuitive Judgment*, Cambridge: Cambridge University Press.

Gordon, C. and Arian, A. (2001) "Threat and decision making," *Journal of Conflict Resolution*, 45: 196–215.

Herrmann, R. K., Tetlock, P. E. and Visser, P. S. (1999) "Mass public decisions to go to war: A cognitive-interactionist framework," *American Political Science Review*, 93: 553–573

Huddy, L., Feldman, S., Taber, C. and Lahav, G. (2003) "Fear and terrorism: Psychological reactions to 9/11," in Norris, P., Kern, M. and Just, M. R. (eds) *Framing Terrorism: The News Media, the Government, and the Public*, New York: Routledge.

Hutcheson, J., Domke, D., Billeaudeaux, A. and Garland, P. (2004) "U.S. national identity, political elites, and a patriotic press following September 11," *Political Communication*, 21: 27–50.

Janis, I. and Mann, L. (1977) *Decision Making: A Psychological Analysis of Conflict, Choice and Commitment*, New York: Free Press.

Janis, I. (1982) *Groupthink: Psychological Studies of Policy Decisions and Fiascoes*, 2nd edn, Boston: Houghton Mifflin.

Jervis, R. (1976) *Perception and Misperception in International Politics*, Princeton, NJ: Princeton University Press.

—— (1978) "Cooperation under the security dilemma," *World Politics*, 30: 167–214.

—— (2003) "Understanding the Bush doctrine," *Political Science Quarterly*, 118: 365–88.

—— (2006a) "Reports, politics, and intelligence failures: The case of Iraq," *Journal of Strategic Studies*, 29: 3–52.

—— (2006b) "Understanding beliefs," *Political Psychology*, 27: 641–663

Johnson, R. H. (1994) *Improbable Dangers: U.S. Conceptions of Threat in the Cold War and After*, New York: St. Martin's Press.

Johnston, A. I. (1995) *Cultural Realism: Strategic Culture and Grand Strategy in Chinese History*, Princeton, NJ: Princeton University Press.

Kahneman, D. and Renshon, J. (2007) "Why hawks win," *Foreign Policy*, January/February: 34–38.

Kaufman, S. J. (2001) *Modern Hatreds: The Symbolic Politics of Ethnic War*, Ithaca, NY: Cornell University Press.

Kaufmann, C. (1994) "Out of the lab and into the archives: A method for testing psychological explanations of political decision making," *International Studies Quarterly*, 38: 557–586.

—— (2004) "Threat inflation and the failure of the marketplace of ideas: The selling of the Iraq war," *International Security*, 29: 5–48.

Kelley, H. H. and Michela, J. M. (1980) "Attribution theory and research," *Annual Review of Psychology*, 31: 457–501.

Kernell, S. (2007) *Going Public: New Strategies of Presidential Leadership*, 4th edn, Washington, DC: CQ Press.

Khong, Y. F. (1992) *Analogies at War: Korea, Munich, Dien Bien Phu, and the Vietnam Decisions of 1965*, Princeton, NJ: Princeton University Press.

Knorr, K. (1976) "Threat perception," in K. Knorr (ed.) *Historical Dimensions of national Security Problems*, Lawrence, Kansas: Allen Press, Inc.

Krebs, R. R. (2005) "Selling the market short? The marketplace of ideas and the Iraq war," *International Security*, 29: 196–202.

Kushner-Gadarian, S. (2005) "Threat, media, and foreign policy opinion," Paper presented at the 2005 meeting of the American Political Science Association, Washington, DC.

Larson, D. W. (1989) *Origins of Containment: A Psychological Explanation*, Princeton: Princeton University Press.

Lebow, R. N. (1981) *Between Peace and War: The Nature of International Crisis*, Baltimore, MD: Johns Hopkins University Press.

Lowi, T. J. (1979) *The End of Liberalism: The Second Republic of the United States*, New York: W.W. Norton & Company.

Lustick, I. (2006) *Trapped in the War on Terror*, Philadelphia: University of Pennsylvania Press.

Massing, M. (2004) "Now they tell us: The American press and Iraq," *New York Review of Books*, February 26.

—— (2005a) "The end of news?" *New York Review of Books*, December 1.

—— (2005b) "The press: The enemy within," *New York Review of Books*, December 15.

Mearsheimer, J. J. (2001) *The Tragedy of Great Power Politics*, New York: Norton.

—— (2004) "Lying in international politics." Paper presented at the 2004 Annual Meeting of the American Political Science Association, Chicago, IL.

Mearsheimer, J. J. and Walt, S. (2007) *The Israel Lobby and U.S. Foreign Policy*, New York: Farrar, Straus and Giroux.

Miller, D. (ed.) (2004) *Tell Me Lies: Propaganda and Media Distortion in the Attack on Iraq*, London: Pluto Press.

Mueller, J. E. (1973) *War, Presidents, and Public Opinion*, New York: Wiley.

—— (2005a) "The Iraq syndrome," *Foreign Affairs*, 84: 44–54.

—— (2005b) "Simplicity and spook: Terrorism and the dynamics of threat exaggeration," *International Studies Perspectives,* 6: 208–34.

—— (2006) *Overblown*, New York: Free Press.

Nisbett, R. and Ross, L. (1980) *Human Inference: Strategies and Shortcomings of Social Judgement*, Englewood Cliffs, NJ: Prentice-Hall, Inc.

Nye, J. S. (ed.) (1984) *The Making of America's Soviet Policy*, New Haven: Yale University Press.

Payne, R. A. (2001) "Persuasion, frames and norm construction," *European Journal of International Relations*, 7: 37–61.

Renshon, J. (2005) *Why Leaders Choose War: The Psychology of Prevention*, New York: Praeger.

Rousseau, D. L. (2006) *Identifying Threats and Threatening Identities: The Social Construction of Realism and Liberalism*, Stanford, CA: Stanford University Press.

Sears, D. O. (1993) "Symbolic politics: A socio-psychological theory," in S. Iyengar and W. J. McGuire (eds) *Explorations in political psychology*, Durham, NC: Duke University Press.

Snyder, J. (2003) "Imperial temptations," *The National Interest*, Spring: 29–40.

Snyder, J. and Ballantine, K. (1996) "Nationalism and the marketplace of ideas," *International Security*, 21: 5–40.

Snyder, J., Shapiro, R. Y. and Bloch-Elkon, Y. (2009) "Free hand abroad, divide and rule at home," *World Politics*, 61.

Sunstein, C. R. (2003) "Terrorism and probability neglect," *Journal of Risk and Uncertainty*, 26: 121–36.

Tang, S. (2008) "Fear in the international politics," *International Studies Review*, 10: 451–471.

Thrall, A. T. (2007) "A bear in the woods? Threat framing in the marketplace of values," *Security Studies*, 16: 452–488.

Van Evera, S. (1990) "Primed for peace: Europe after the Cold War," *International Security*, 15: 7–57.

Walt, S. M. (1987) *The Origins of Alliances*, Ithaca, New York: Cornell University Press.

Waltz, Kenneth N. (1979). *Theory of International Politics*, New York: McGraw-Hill.

Wendt, Alexander. (1999). *Social Theory of International Politics*, Cambridge: Cambridge University Press.

Western, J. (2005a) *Selling Intervention and War: The Presidency, the Media, and the American Public*, Baltimore, MD: The Johns Hopkins University Press.

—— (2005b) "The war over Iraq: Selling war to the American public," *Security Studies*, 14: 106–39.

2 Understanding beliefs and threat inflation

Robert Jervis

The question with which Smith, Bruner and White (1956) began their classic *Opinions and Personality* over 50 years ago is still appropriate today, albeit with a change in the pronoun: "Of what use to man are his opinions?" (for further discussion on Smith, Bruner and White see: 1; Eagly and Chaiken 1998: 303–309; George 1958; Hammond 1996: Ch. 11; Herek 1987; Katz 1960; Sarnoff and Katz 1954; Tetlock 2002). I think their answer was essentially correct as well: People adopt opinions not only to understand the world, but also to meet the psychological and social needs to live with themselves and others. In this chapter I use this basic insight to examine some of the puzzles in what people believe generally, drawing most of my examples from the realm of international politics. I believe these insights cast light on what many people assume to be intentional "threat inflation." I recognize that proving that actors actually believed in what they were doing at the time is a monumental challenge, one that even access to private conversations and records of the time cannot reliably solve. Attempting to sort out sincere beliefs from intentional threat inflation is a necessary knot to disentangle as best we can, however, because it is a fundamental question for foreign-policy making – are grievous foreign policy errors primarily unavoidable outcomes of sincere beliefs and misperceptions or the result of intentional deception on the part of political leaders? I propose here ideas about how to determine if beliefs caused behavior – i.e., if beliefs are powerful and autonomous as opposed to *ex post* rationalizations for behavior. If beliefs cause behavior, as my study of history suggests they often do, then the problem of steering clear of beliefs such as the domino theory, the acceptability of slavery or belief in Saddam Hussein's hiding of weapons of mass destruction in Iraq – beliefs known to be wholly wrong-headed with the benefit of hindsight – will be much more difficult than is suggested by those who argue that politicians are intentionally deceiving the public with self-serving policies such as threat inflation and need to be kept politically and bureaucratically in check.

Beliefs and related concepts

There are terminological and conceptual thickets surrounding the words we use here. I will focus on beliefs partly about facts but more about cause-and-effect relationships. How do things work? Why do others act as they do? What will be the consequences of my own behavior? Definitions of related terms differ and the notions of beliefs, opinions, attitudes, ideas, and even policy preferences overlap and interweave. Attitudes and opinions involve a strong evaluative component. Indeed, this dimension often dominates, as when people say they have a negative attitude toward radical Islam even if they know little about it. But when an attitude is different from a purely subjective taste, it also involves causal claims. For example, I abhor radical Islam because I think it produces oppression and violence toward other religions.

Overtones of beliefs

Although my focus is on beliefs in the sense of what people think about causes and effects, it is noteworthy that the term is used in other senses as well, and I think this tells us that equating beliefs with scientific or social scientific knowledge would be limiting. Although political psychologists rarely deal with statements like the following, they are important to people's lives: "I believe in God." "I believe I am falling in love." "I believe that it is vital to win the war in Iraq." Even this abbreviated list illustrates three things. First, beliefs can refer to inner states as well as outer realities. We often interpret our feelings and seek to understand exactly what it is that we believe. Second, beliefs and statements about beliefs can be exhortatory. To say "I believe we must do this" is to urge others – and ourselves – on. Statements like "I believe my views will prevail" combine these two elements.

The third and perhaps most important point is that many beliefs have a strong element of commitment and faith, even when religion is not involved. Scientists say that they believe in their theories or findings, and this often means not only that they have confidence in their validity, but that they are important to them and it is important that others accept them as well. When people talk about "beliefs to live by," moral and empirical considerations are fused. When people say that they believe that democracy can be brought to the Middle East and that doing so will make this a better world, they are combining how they see the evidence and what their values and desires lead them to think should and must be true. The other side of this coin is revealed by a doctor's response to his critics' rejection of his findings that a controversial treatment helped many victims of a heart attack: he said they suffered from "emotional disbelief" (quoted in Wade 2005).

One can argue that this only shows that the word "belief" has multiple meanings and that we would be better off separating them and attaching different labels to each. I suspect, however, that the common term may be pointing to something deeper, which is the inextricable role of emotion in sensible thought. Over the past decade or so, psychologists and political psychologists have come to see (to "believe"?) that a sharp separation between cognition and affect is impossible and that a person who embodied pure rationality, undisturbed by emotion, would be a monster if she were not an impossibility (for summaries on belief, see McDermott 2004; Marcus 2000, 2003; Zajonc 1998).

Investigating beliefs

We want to understand why people believe what they do, whether these beliefs are warranted by the available evidence, and whether they are correct. Although these tasks are different, we often fuse them. Thus we often think that correct beliefs require no explanation, implicitly assuming that they are self-evident and follow directly from commonly available evidence. But we often believe as much in the face of evidence as because of it, and in some of these cases we turn out to be correct. In other cases, correct beliefs may be adopted to smooth our relations with others or to increase our psychological comfort.

Wrong beliefs may be sensible and sincere

It is then tempting, but a mistake, to seek to explain correct beliefs in a way fundamentally different from the way we explain incorrect ones (Laudan 1977). Nevertheless, people are prone to associate faulty reasoning processes with incorrect beliefs even when more careful analysis would indicate that this comforting association does not hold. Given the complexity and ambiguity of our world, it is unfortunately true that beliefs for which a good deal of evidence can be mustered often turn out to be mistaken (for an application to intelligence, see Jervis 2006).

In parallel, we often have difficulty taking seriously beliefs with which we disagree. This is not only a mistake; it is also disrespectful of the people we are trying to understand. When someone believes something that we cannot, we often ask whether she is a fool or a knave. This is obviously most likely to be the case with beliefs that are now unpopular. Thus because most academics believe that it was a mistake for the United States to have fought in Vietnam, they cannot believe that a sensible person could have accepted the domino theory. Rather than explore what evidence the people who held these beliefs pointed to, what theories of politics were implicitly evoked, and why a more complacent view did not seem compelling, they seek hidden motives and psychological pressures. These may indeed have been present, but the fact that most of us now find the domino theory disastrously incorrect should not lead us to conclude it was not central to decision makers. Similarly, if the reconstruction of Iraq and other events in the Middle East continue to go badly, future generations are likely to reject the idea that Bush and his colleagues actually believed that Saddam had weapons of mass destruction (WMD) or expected his overthrow to produce democracy, concluding instead that they must have been motivated by concern for oil and Israel.

Grasping others' incorrect beliefs also poses severe difficulties for contemporary observers. Thus it was very hard for American leaders to believe that Japan would attack Pearl Harbor, even though they (partly) expected an attack against the Philippines. Knowing that Japan could not win this war made the Japanese beliefs inaccessible. During the run-up to the war in Iraq it was similarly impossible for outsiders to see that Saddam was more afraid of his generals, his people, and Iran than he was of the United States, with the result that everyone – even opponents of the war – concluded that his refusal to fully cooperate with the UN showed that he was developing WMD.

It is especially hard to appreciate the empirical beliefs that underpin views that are now morally unacceptable, for example those supporting slavery. It is then very tempting to attribute the beliefs to economic interests, which spares us the difficulty and the pain of reconstructing a worldview in which slavery appeared appropriate, effective, and beneficial for all. The line between understanding and approving is too thin to make this a comfortable task.

Ambivalence and unawareness

It may be hard to tell what a person believes because she is ambivalent, confused, or contradictory. We sometimes say that a person does not know her own mind, and we often half believe something, or simultaneously believe it and do not. I think this was the case with whether Kissinger and Nixon believed that the peace agreement with North Vietnam could be sustained. They were under no illusions that the North had given up its commitment to take over the South. With its troops already in the South and a large army on its own territory, the North could be restrained only by the fear that blatantly breaking the agreement would call forth an American military response, most obviously a resumption of bombing. Nixon and Kissinger told themselves, each other, and the South Vietnamese that this threat was credible enough to prevent major North Vietnamese violations and that they would carry it out if it were not. While it is impossible to be certain whether they believed what they were saying, my guess is that what they were expressing was something between a hope and an expectation. They partly believed it, or believed it on some days but not others, or believed it with some probability but less than certainty. A related way of thinking was revealed by the diary entry of a top Foreign Office official after Hitler seized the non-German parts of Czechoslovakia: "I always said that, as long as Hitler *could pretend* he was incorporating Germans in the Reich, we *could pretend* that he had a case" (Dilks 1972: 161, emphasis added).

Further problems are created by the fact that the driving beliefs may be so widely shared they need never be expressed, at least not in a way that is connected with specific actions. Because they are rarely analyzed by the person, we often call them "assumptions," and we need to excavate them, as Joll (1972) did in "1914: The Unspoken Assumptions" in which he argues that the specific beliefs discussed later say less about the origins of World War I than does the prevailing intellectual climate that was built on Social Darwinism and the outlook that the leaders absorbed when they were in school. In other cases, the driving beliefs may not be voiced because they are disreputable or illegitimate. Thus a search of even confidential or private documents will rarely reveal an American decision maker saying that he favored overthrowing a Third World regime in order to benefit American corporations or further his own domestic political interests. Although the person will not express these views, here he or she perhaps is aware of them.

In a third category of cases even this is not true (and one might therefore question whether they should be called beliefs at all). It is not only those schooled in psychoanalysis who argue that we do not understand how we reach many of our conclusions because much cognitive processing is beyond the reach of conscious thought (Nisbett and Wilson 1977; Wilson 2002). The reasons we give for many of our beliefs are sincere in that we do believe them, but these are stories we tell ourselves as well as others because we understand as little about what is driving our beliefs as we do about what is driving others. To extend the previous example, someone who was in fact moved to favor military intervention because of economic or political interests might not be aware of this because of the strong societal norms of putting national security interests first. All we can do is infer operative beliefs from behavior, often by arguing that the explicit reasons given are implausible. As I noted earlier, this is how many scholars explain the U.S. policy in Vietnam. It is not surprising that arguments in this vein will be particularly contentious. Those who use ego-dynamic may look for Freudian slips and Marxists will look for benefits accruing to large corporations, but it is hard to get evidence that will carry weight with people who approach these questions from different perspectives. Skepticism here, like that called up by the concept of false consciousness, is warranted but does not do away with the problem that people's self-knowledge is sharply limited.

Understanding beliefs

Understanding beliefs means trying to fathom what caused them and what consequences they had. We are interested in whether beliefs are powerful in the sense of producing behavior and autonomous in the sense of not directly following from other factors. To return to the Smith, Bruner, and White formulation, this means trying to determine the relative weights of reality appraisal, personal needs, and social adjustment. The latter two are similar in that they serve purposes other than seeking an accurate view of the world, and we can refer to them together as a functional explanation because they explain the person's beliefs by the social and psychological functions that they serve.

This is not to say that the line between appraisal and functionality is always clear or to deny that many of the ways in which we try to make sense of our world combine them. Susan Clancy's (2005) fascinating and empathetic but not credulous study of why people come to believe that they had been abducted by space aliens shows how this belief not only renders coherent what was previously confused, but also provides an explanation that, while disturbing on one level, gives a meaning that restores a form of integrity to the person's life. The book has a chapter titled "Why Would I Want to Believe It?" which indicates both that people ward off attacks on their beliefs by claiming there could be no ulterior (or interior) motive and that there can be quite different but reinforcing reasons for holding beliefs.

Consistency and excess reasons

It is often hard to tell what beliefs were causal, not only in separating statements the person knows are false from what she "really" believes, but in the sense of determining which of a plethora of justifications played the largest role. In examining the beliefs that precede action, we often find claims that either contradict or are in some tension with one another and see people generating more arguments for the conclusions than would be necessary to produce them. While these two phenomena are in one sense opposites, the first revealing inconsistencies and the second displaying excess reasons or belief overkill, they have common psychological roots in the conflicting needs of reality appraisal and serving psychological, social, and political functions. In the end, definitive conclusions are often beyond reach, but the exploration of why this is so is itself illuminating, as we can see in the beliefs leading to World War I.

The story, especially on the German side, at first seems straightforward. The war was essentially a preventive one. German leaders felt that an eventual war was inevitable, that Germany could win it at a relatively low price if it were fought in 1914, and that growing Russian military strength meant that Germany would lose or at least greatly suffer if the war was postponed. At bottom there remains much to this argument; indeed, I do not think there is a better one-sentence explanation of the war. But there are problems (a good summary is given in Herwig 2003).

We find forms of troubling inconsistency. One is temporal: these beliefs were quite long-lasting yet did not produce war prior to 1914. Part of the reason for the different effect is that events in the preceding years deepened the beliefs and created a sense of urgency, compounded by the fact that the assassination of Archduke Franz Ferdinand allowed Germany to mobilize both its Austro-Hungarian ally and its domestic opinion. But I do not think this entirely disposes of the problem since the basic German geostrategic problem was not new.

There are other forms of inconsistency as well. German policy in July 1914 had as its preferred outcome not war with Russia, but the Russian abandonment of its Serbian client, perhaps because Russia itself feared being deserted by Britain and France if it fought. The problem is not so much that such a Russian retreat was unlikely (German leaders recognized this) as it is this "solution" would not have dealt with the fundamental threat of growing Russian strength. Indeed, if Russia had been forced to back down it probably would have stepped up its rearmament, and even if the bonds between Russia, Britain, and France were severed, there was no reason to believe that this would be permanent. At best, Germany's nightmare would be postponed, not eliminated. This means that it is hard to square German hopes for peace with the beliefs that are posited to be central for the decision to go to war.

Another inconsistency appears in the beliefs themselves. Although many statements support the position that the decision makers thought that the war would be short, there were discordant notes. The Russian defense minister realized that signing the mobilization orders might be sentencing his country to death, the British Foreign Secretary famously said at dawn of the day Britain went to war: "The lamps are going out all over Europe; we shall not see them lit again in our life-time," and the Chief of the German General Staff declared that war "would destroy the culture of almost the whole of Europe for decades to come" (quoted in Mombauer 2001: 202, also see 206). Furthermore, Germany respected Holland's neutrality in order to permit the entry of supplies from neutrals and most German leaders were deeply disturbed when Great Britain joined the war. These responses would not make sense if the war was expected to end quickly.

In casting doubt on what the decision makers believed, these inconsistencies open up four lines of inquiry. First, it can be extremely difficult to determine what people really believe. We might want to rule this a metaphysical question that we should not ask. But then we would have to abandon much of the notion of beliefs.

The second point shows why this would be a mistake: knowing whether German leaders thought the war would be long or short points us toward very different explanations of their behavior. If they thought a war would be short (and that they would win it), it would be seen as relatively cheap, which means that any number of impulses could have produced war. But if the war was expected to be long (and therefore very costly), only the strongest motivation would have been sufficient to overcome the obvious reasons not to fight. In the same way, the initial scholarship on the Vietnam War assumed that American decision makers believed that they could win quite quickly. This focused people on why the officials were so wrong (the "quagmire theory"), with less attention paid to the motives to fight because the decision seemed relatively easy if the price tag was believed to be low. But when the publication of the *Pentagon Papers* revealed that the leaders had fairly accurate perceptions of the costs and risks, the question to be answered was not why they so misperceived the likely course of the war, but what goals and beliefs were so pressing as to make them fight in the face of such daunting prospects.

A third line of inquiry is whether we can explain the contradiction in the beliefs in 1914 by reality appraisal or whether they were strongly functional. I will discuss this general topic in more detail later, but the obvious point is that holding to discrepant beliefs allowed decision makers to keep in touch with the possibility that turned out to be the case without having to abandon the belligerent policy that they felt was necessary. They *had* to believe that the war would be short. To have seen that it would not be would have put them in an intolerable position because if they could not fight, they would have had to alter many of their policies, beliefs, and values. The historian Elie Halevy argues that the diplomatic and strategic interconnections linking the European states were so tight and obvious that "every one knew, *who chose to know*" that an Austrian attack on Serbia would bring in all the other Continental powers (1966: 232–233). But the phrase I have italicized is a telling one – people can indeed choose not to know things when knowing them would generate terrible pressures.

A final question in this series is about the consistency of people's beliefs. Scholars greatly value consistency. Consistency to them means rigor, logic, and rationality; its lack implies error if not moral weakness. Although as I will discuss later, decision makers do feel pressures for consistency on some occasions, they do not appear to put it among their highest values. Perhaps because they are not trained to seek great rigor, perhaps because they see life as full of contradictions, and perhaps because they appreciate the extent to which seeming inconsistencies can bring political success, they do contradictory things and hold contradictory beliefs. When Franklin D. Roosevelt famously said, "I am a juggler, and I never let my right hand know what my left hand does" (quoted in Kimball 1991: 7), he was only being more explicit than most. So when we look at his policy toward Japan before Pearl Harbor it may not be surprising that in November 1941 he seemed to believe: the United States should enter the war as soon as possible; Germany not Japan was the main enemy; the United States was so much stronger than Japan that the latter would not dare attack; economic sanctions against Japan might not force that country to comply with American demands; Japan was likely to attack the Philippines (an American possession) in the belief that the United States would otherwise use it as a base to interdict Japanese attacks on British Malaya and the Dutch East Indies; but Japan would not attack Pearl Harbor.

At times, inconsistencies can be used to uncover the beliefs that are driving a person's stance. This is especially true when people claim to be following a principled belief but change their conclusions depending on the principle's substantive implications. For example, at first glance it would seem that American conservatives uphold the principles of decentralization, Federalism, and states' rights and that liberals want to give more power to the central government. But each group has no difficulty endorsing the "wrong" position when it leads to the "right" outcome. Thus conservatives favor taking class-action suits out of the hands of state courts, pass legislation that removes much of the state and local control over education, and prevent states from permitting assisted suicide or the medicinal use of marijuana. Liberals, being no more consistent, shamelessly call for states' rights here. Conservatives generally see genes as playing a large role in human behavior, but make an exception for sexual orientation, which liberals, who usually stress the role of the environment, see as fixed. In the foreign policy area, beliefs about whether a policy of "engagement" will be efficacious are almost always driven not by general beliefs about cause-and-effect relationships, but rather by how deeply the person abhors the regime in question. During the Cold War liberals urged engagement with Eastern Europe but isolation for South Africa, while conservatives took the opposite position.

If it is sometimes difficult to analyze the causal role of beliefs because they are inconsistent, in other cases people adduce more beliefs than are necessary to produce the behavior. The war in Iraq provides a nice example. Bush and his colleagues apparently believed that: Saddam had a large and growing WMD program; there were close links between his regime and Al Qaeda; the war would be quick; political reconstruction would be relatively easy; and liberation would light the path for the rest of the Middle East. This is odd. If a nuclear-armed Iraq could not have been deterred from coercing its neighbors, then this menace to American interests was sufficient to have triggered war. If Saddam was harboring Al Qaeda, this by itself could have led to an invasion, as it did in Afghanistan. Had the prospects for establishing democracy in Iraq been great and likely to trigger positive domino effects throughout the region, then overthrowing Saddam would have been a great opportunity even if there were no pressing danger. It is the excess rather than the paucity of reasons that confuses us. This is probably why Richard Haass, who was head of the State Department Policy Planning Staff during the run-up to the war and personally heard all of these beliefs expressed, replied to the question of why the administration went to war by declaring: "I will go to my grave not knowing that. I can't answer it" (quoted in Lemann 2004: 157).

In order to disentangle excess beliefs and determine which of them were primarily responsible for the policy, we can try to see which was most compatible with what the person believed over a prolonged period as well as fitting with other actions she had taken (see May 1975). Although this assumes a degree of consistency that, as I have noted, may be problematic, it is noteworthy that Bush and his colleagues consistently held a healthy – or unhealthy – respect for the utility of American force in world politics. Although this still leaves us with the question of the sources of these beliefs (and there is no logical stopping place once we start down that road, important as it is to explore – see Roberts 1996), this at least tells us that the claim that force would work was not developed in order to justify the war.

A second long-standing belief was that while force is efficacious, deterrence is flawed. This position was taken by leaders of the Bush administration during the Cold War when they (except for Bush, who was not deeply involved in these questions) strongly favored nuclear counterforce and missile defense. Their belief that an Iraq armed with nuclear weapons could not be deterred from coercing its neighbors fit with this outlook, even if it was badly flawed (Jervis 2005: Ch. 3).

It is harder to find roots for the belief that there were serious links between Al Qaeda and Saddam, even putting aside the lack of evidence and plausibility for the claim. No one reached this conclusion before they contemplated invading Iraq, and the speed and avidity with which Bush and his colleagues searched for Saddam's connections to terrorism suggest a conclusion in need of justification. So I think it would be reasonable to doubt that this belief was an independent pillar of the behavior.

The final set of beliefs supporting the war concerned democracy: democracies are peaceful and share interests with each other; democracy could readily be established in Iraq once Saddam was overthrown; the example of Iraq would encourage democratic movements throughout the region. Were these beliefs a foundation of the policy? Bush and the advisors he most relied on did not have a history of propounding these beliefs and had not hesitated to cooperate with tyrannical regimes in the past. Furthermore, although September 11, 2001, changed a great deal, there is no reason why it should have led anyone to have greater faith in democracy as the antidote to world problems. Indeed the value of democracy and the possibility of spreading it was not stressed during the run-up to the war but only became salient in the wake of the failure to find WMD. So here too the causal role of the beliefs is questionable.

Reality appraisal

The difficulty of determining whether and how particular beliefs affect behavior stems in part from the fact that they can form for quite different reasons. Further exploration then requires us to return to the categories used by Smith, Bruner and White.

Many of our beliefs are dominated by the need to understand our environments, and almost all of them embody an element of this objective. It is impossible here to summarize how reality appraisal operates, but central is the fact that the world is so complex and our information processing capabilities so limited that in significant measure people must be theory driven. Beliefs are hard won from our world, and so it is not only ego that leads us to be quite attached to them. Although this model of people as "cognitive misers" (see, e.g., Fiske and Taylor 1991) needs to be modified by the findings that people will deploy more cognitive resources in areas that are most important to them, that people vary in the extent to which they are theory driven, and that people who are more open to discrepant evidence tend to make more accurate predictions (see, e.g., Chaiken 1980; Tetlock 2005), there remains much to the basic argument.

Four implications follow for how beliefs operate. First, people are strongly influenced by their expectations: people tend to see what they expect to see. In international politics perhaps the most striking examples come from cases of surprise attack (the literature is very large: key works include Betts 1982; Whaley 1973; Wohlstetter 1962; Bar-Joseph and Kruglanski 2003; also see Jervis 1976: Ch. 4). The Israelis were certain that Egypt lacked the military strength to attack in 1973 and so misinterpreted what in hindsight were obvious tip-offs that an attack was coming; in April 1940 the British and Norwegians were so sure that Germany would not expose its forces to British naval superiority that they were unmoved by their sinking a transport containing German soldiers who told them that they were on their way to invade Norway; when Secretary of War Stimson was told of the Japanese attack on Pearl Harbor, he said "My God, this can't be true. This [message] must mean the Philippines," where he had expected the attack; when a Soviet front-line unit reported coming under German artillery fire as the latter country attacked, it received the reply, "You must be insane. And why is your signal not in code?" (quoted in Ransom 1958: 54; quoted in Erickson 1962: 587).

Of course these cases are selected on the dependent variable, to use a phrase common in political science, because we are looking only at instances of surprise. This makes it impossible for us to say that this cognitive bias is a central cause of error. Indeed most correct inferences are also strongly influenced by expectations, leading to the second implication of the role of theory-driven beliefs, which is that a proposition is most likely to be accepted when it is seen as plausible – i.e., when it fits with more general beliefs. This is why almost everyone interpreted the scattered and ambiguous evidence as showing that Saddam Hussein had vigorous WMD programs (Jervis 2006). This inference made a great deal of sense, as the regime had used gas against Iran and its own Kurds, pursued nuclear weapons before the Gulf War, initially tried to maintain these programs despite UN sanctions, and engaged in a great deal of denial and deception. Without this background, the intelligence reports would have been read very differently.

The third general proposition is that judgments of plausibility can be self-reinforcing as ambiguous evidence is taken not only to be consistent with preexisting beliefs, but to confirm them. Logically, the latter is the case only when the evidence both fits with the belief and does not fit with competing ones. But people rarely probe the latter possibility as carefully as they should, assuming it instead.

The fourth implication of theory-driven processing is that the model of Bayesian up-dating not only does not but cannot fully apply (for a good review, see Gerber and Green 1999). The basic point of Bayesianism is that people should and do modify their beliefs according to the likelihood that observed new events or information should occur if the prior beliefs are correct. The difficulty is that people who hold different beliefs will see the new event or information in different ways, and there is no objective arbiter to which we can appeal. This is not a problem when we are trying to adjust our estimate of whether a jar has more blue balls than red ones as they are drawn out at random. The evidence of a ball's color is clear enough so that people can agree on it irrespective of their priors. This is sometimes true in politics, but often is not. For example, supporters of the Bush administration would argue that the events in countries like Lebanon and Egypt in the months following the Iraqi elections in January 2005 show how the American policy is reshaping the Middle East. Those who disagree not only argue that their beliefs need not be fundamentally changed because they are underpinned by so much other evidence, but dispute the interpretation of these events themselves, seeing them as either superficial or as products of internal politics. In other words, the inevitable impact of priors on new "facts" undercuts the thrust of a significant part of the Bayesian model.

Although – and because – we need theories, strong beliefs, and expectations in order to make any sense of our complex and contradictory world, reality appraisal can lead us astray. But, more importantly, this is not the only impulse shaping our beliefs, as Smith, Bruner, and White so clearly showed.

Functions of beliefs

Functional explanations of beliefs cast doubt on their causal role. A full understanding of how beliefs operate requires backward as well as forward linkages; we need to look for the causes as well as the consequences of the beliefs in order to see whether the connection between beliefs and behavior is spurious with both being driven by a common third factor. Beliefs may be rationalizations for policies as well as rationales for them. When social, political, and personal needs are strong, the results can be summarized by the saying, "If you want something really bad, you will get it really bad." The explanation for why a policy is adopted and why it was carried out so incompetently often are linked as the need to see that it can succeed will diminish reality appraisal and draw the actor into a conceptual and perceptual world that, while comfortable, cannot provide good guidance for behavior.

If the discussion of reality appraisal and how it goes wrong is linked to cognitive biases, the functions of beliefs are linked to motivated ones (Spencer *et al.* 2003; Pears 1984; On the difficulties and possibilities of separating kinds of biases see Kaufmann 1994; Tetlock and Levi 1982). People's needs to work with others, further their political goals, and live with themselves tap into their emotions and drive them to certain beliefs. A classic demonstration is the study by Hastorf and Cantril (1954), "They Saw a Game." Purely cognitive biases cannot explain why students at Dartmouth and Princeton who viewed films of a penalty-filled game between their two football teams saw the other side as at fault. When we look at elite beliefs and decision making, we see four overlapping areas in which motivated biases are at work and beliefs are highly functional. These are the hesitancy to recognize painful value trade-offs, the psychological and political need for people to see that their policies will work, the impact on beliefs of goals and feelings of which people are unaware, and the propensity of people to infer their own beliefs from how they behave.

One can reply that these sorts of functional pressures are unlikely because they imply knowledge of the very cognitions that people are trying to ward off, if not the conclusions to which they are being steered. At times, the line between awareness and lack of it is very thin. People often say things like "I don't think that this is something I want to hear about," or "That is a subject we are better off not analyzing." But beyond this borderline a great deal of cognitive processing is preconscious, and the understanding that a certain position *must* be affirmed can affect the person's thinking without her being aware of it. One does not have to accept Freudian notions of the unconscious and repression to conclude that we can be strongly influenced by impulses of which we are unaware (see Gladwell 2005; Larson 2003). The requirement for bolstering beliefs can be triggered by the implicit realization that the decision is a hard one and that more thorough analysis could lead to high conflict. When people lack good choices, they are likely to imagine that the one they select is better than it is.

Varied forms of self-deception are then common in politics, but they are not unique to this realm, as novels make clear. Scientists also feel the same social and psychological pressures, and Richard Feynman famously said to his fellow scientists: "The first principle is that you must not fool yourself – and you are the easiest person to fool." This is one reason why errors in science are often detected by people not involved in the original discoveries and why the scientific community cannot be trusted to make unbiased judgments about the danger of experiments and technologies in which it has a large stake.

Avoiding painful trade-offs

In difficult political and psychological situations, reality appraisal, far from pointing the way out, can be a menace to the person if the reality it points to is too painful to contemplate. My first discussion of the tendency to avoid value tradeoffs (Jervis 1976: 128–142) treated it as cognitive, but this was a mistake because its roots are primarily motivated or functional. Although people often have to make trade-offs – budgets, for example, force them on us – avoidance is often possible and necessary (On the possibility of leaders avoiding trade-offs, however, see Farnham 1997; Neustadt 1986). People are especially prone to shy away from trade-offs when dealing with incommensurable realms and moral choices (Fiske and Tetlock 1997), which explains why those who oppose the use of torture on moral grounds resist the argument that its use might save lives. I would similarly predict that if Bush and his colleagues decide that the prospect of Iranian nuclear weapons is truly intolerable, they will come to see the negative consequences of an air strike as quite small.

The desire to avoid trade-offs is clear in the discussion of Iraq. As a soldier's mother put it: "I know my son's there for a reason. And whatever might happen, that's the way it's supposed to be. And if I took it any other way, I'd be in a funny farm" (Abramsky 2004: 11). Elites do not put it this revealingly, but their beliefs often serve the same functions. As I discussed above, proponents of the war had more reasons than they needed, and opponents differed on all these points. If reality testing were shaping the beliefs, then one should have found quite a few people who believed that while the war was necessary, it would be very costly, or who thought that while threat was present, opportunity was not (or vice versa), or that the war would be cheap, but was not necessary. But these positions are uncomfortable, and so it is not surprising that we do not find people taking them. For political leaders as well as the mother quoted earlier, if they took it any other way, they'd be in a funny farm.

Policies call up supporting beliefs

The second and related functional source of foreign policy beliefs is the pressure generated by policies. One reason why political leaders are slow to see that their policies are failing is that good reality appraisal would force them to acknowledge the high costs and risks they are facing. Thus building on the psychological work on defensive avoidance (Janis and Mann 1977), Richard Ned Lebow and others (Jervis *et al.* 1985; Lebow 1981) have shown that if the actor is committed to proceeding, even highly credible threats by the adversary are likely to be missed, misinterpreted, or ignored. This is one reason why attempts to explain wars as the product of rational choices on both sides will often fail, just as the policies themselves fail.

One of the hallmarks of the functional source of beliefs is that planning on the surface looks meticulous, but in fact is terribly deficient because it is built on unrealistic and unexamined assumptions. As Hull (2005) notes in regard to Germany thinking about colonial warfare in the early twentieth century, "realistic planning would have revealed the impossibility of the grand goals; rather than giving these up, planning itself was truncated" (143; see also Herwig 2003: 155 for a similar discussion of German planning for World War I). Indeed, when a part of the organization does engage in effective reality appraisal, it may be neutered, as was the case with a planning division in the Japanese army in the 1930s (Barnhart 1987: 200–202, 240, 258). It is tempting to dismiss this as the product of military culture, but the U.S. Forest Service, committed to stamping out all forest fires, disbanded its research arm when it showed that healthy forests required periodic burning (Schiff 1962: 169–173).

British planning for the bombardment of Germany throughout the 1930s illustrates the ways in which beliefs supporting the efficacy of a policy can be shielded from reality appraisal. The incredible costs of fighting World War I not only contributed to the subsequent appeasement policy, but also convinced the British that if war were to come, they could not fight it as they had done before. A way out was strategic bombardment that could deter devastating German air attack on Britain and win the war without having to suffer the horrendous losses of ground warfare. It then *had* to be true that an effective bomber force could be developed, and supporting beliefs were called up to meet this demand. So it is not surprising that British planners convinced themselves that the bomb loads their planes could carry would be sufficient to do grave damage to German industries and cities that British bombers could fly without protection from fighter escorts, that the aircraft could readily find their targets and that bombing would be accurate. Although many plans were cranked out, these central assumptions were never scrutinized. In fact, even rudimentary questioning and military exercises would have revealed that German cities were obscured by clouds much of the year, that navigation systems were not adequate to direct planes to them, that bombs would miss their targets, and that even direct hits would rarely put factories out of action for long (Carter 1998; Jervis 1982/83). A history of Bomber Command notes that "seldom in the history of warfare has a force been so sure of the end it sought – fulfillment of the Trenchard doctrine [of strategic bombardment] – and yet so ignorant of how this might be achieved as the RAF between the wars" (Hastings 1979: 44). In fact, the certainty with which the ends were held and the ignorance about means were closely linked. Reality appraisal was unacceptable because it would have called the highly valued goals into question.

The same pressures for beliefs to support policy explain many of the deficiencies in American planning for the aftermath of the overthrow of Saddam. Reality appraisal would have been politically and psychologically painful; to have recognized that reconstruction was likely to be long, costly, and uncertain would have been to give ammunition to the war's critics. When confronted with the Army Chief of Staff's estimate that it would take several hundred thousand troops to garrison Iraq, Deputy Secretary of Defense Paul Wolfowitz told Congress "it's hard to conceive that it would take more forces to provide stability in post-Saddam Iraq than it would take to conduct the war itself. . . . Hard to imagine" (quoted in Slevin and Priest 2003). This was indeed a failure of imagination, but under these circumstances imagination could not be allowed free rein. It is hard to ask important questions and conduct unbiased analysis when the answers may be unacceptable.

Beliefs supporting the established order

The third function of beliefs is much broader, consisting of people's conceptions of the political and social structures that gratify them. In his pioneering study, Lippmann argued that stereotypes form not only because they permit "economy of effort," but because they "may be the core of our personal tradition, the defenses of our position in society" (1922: 95). Marxists – and cynics – analyze the beliefs of the ruling classes in this way. During the Cold War, members of the political and economic elite who incorrectly said that the establishment of revolutionary regimes anywhere in the world would menace American security interests were not lying. Rather, the knowledge that such regimes would adversely affect their economic interests led them to believe that American national security was at stake as well. People in the upper income brackets can cite many reasons why cutting their taxes would benefit the entire economy and pull others out of poverty. These beliefs, which can involve somewhat complicated economics, are not insincere, but they nevertheless derive from personal interest.

Beliefs about what is right and just may have similar roots. Carr (1946) famously showed how the morality espoused by status quo states nicely justified the prevailing arrangements that suited them so well; most Americans join president Bush in believing that the vigorous exercise of American power abroad is in the world's interest. Looking within U.S. society, trial lawyers believe that unimpeded access to the courts for liability and class action suits is the best way to control rapacious companies; police officers believe that the establishment of civilian oversight boards will encourage criminals to produce false claims and defy the police; professors believe that government support for universities in general and their specializations in particular will produce a stronger and better society (but that government direction of research harms these goals). Some or all of these beliefs may be correct, but they are remarkably convenient.

Beliefs produced by actions

In contrast to the usual method of explaining actions by the beliefs that we think generated them, the previous pages have discussed how beliefs form to provide rationalizations for actions. In the final category of cases, actions not only produce beliefs, but, once formed, these new beliefs influence later actions. The theory was developed over 30 years ago by Daryl Bem, and the basic point is related to the one noted earlier that people often do not know why they act as they do. They then implicitly analyze their own behavior in the same way they analyze that of others and ask what beliefs and motives could have been responsible for it (Bem 1972; also see Shafir *et al.* 1993). Answers like inadvertence, fleeting impulses, the desire to do something and get on with it, all seem inappropriate if not frivolous and, although often correct, are rejected. Instead, the person looks for more serious and lasting beliefs and motives, and then attributes her behavior to them. This would be no more than a psychological curiosity if the effects stopped there. But, once formed, these explanations guide future behavior. If I think that I gave money on one occasion because I am a generous person, I will give more in the future; if as a national leader I ordered the use of force to free hostages, I must believe that this instrument is efficacious and therefore should respond similarly in other situations; if as president I gave a stiff response to another country, it must be because that state is deeply hostile and that deterrence if not force is required to meet it.

The last example is not hypothetical but is the foundation for Larson's (1985) fascinating analysis of the psychological origins of American Cold War policy. Most scholars have seen Truman's containment policy as growing out of his steady response to increasing Soviet provocations. Revisionist scholars disagree, seeing the impulse as being generated by the need to keep the world open to capitalist penetration, but they too explain Truman's actions as following from his beliefs, albeit ones that were formed by the functional process noted previously. Larson argues that both these views fail to see that Truman was at first unsure of himself and inconsistent and that his position hardened only after he came to interpret his hesitant steps as implying that the Soviet Union was aggressive and could only be countered by firmness. Having attributed these beliefs to himself, Truman then acted on them more consistently.

Beliefs: powerful and autonomous

An intriguing article on learning and reality testing begins: "The Aztecs apparently believed that the corn on which their civilization depended would not grow unless there were human sacrifices. What seems to us an absurd belief caused thousands of people to be sacrificed each year" (Boulding 1967: 1). This brings us back to the question of whether beliefs are powerful and autonomous. Boulding claims that here they were. They were powerful in that they drove human sacrifices and the wars that were necessary to procure them, and they were autonomous in the sense of not being a direct product of the Aztecs' objective situation. It is easier to demonstrate the former than the latter. The Aztecs did indeed act on their belief in the potency of human sacrifices. Such a correspondence is not automatic. A classic study in the 1930s showed that many people who said that they would discriminate against nonwhites in fact did not do so (LaPiere 1934; for a review of the literature see Schuman and Johnson 1976). Overall, the relationship between expressed attitudes and behavior is mediated and complex, but we often do find beliefs to be linked to behavior. One important example is that Ronald Reagan's readiness to deal with Mikhail Gorbachev (on American terms, to be sure) can in part be explained by his image of the Soviet Union, which despite being highly skeptical and critical, involved more openness to change than was true of the beliefs of his hard-line advisors (Shimko 1991).

But beliefs are not unmoved movers. Although an explanation of behavior in terms of beliefs does not have to trace all their roots, it does have to rule out spurious correlation by meeting the objection that they were formed to meet social, political, or psychological needs and that, relatedly, they merely reflect self-interest. Upton Sinclair put it crudely but correctly: "It is difficult to get a man to understand something when his salary depends on his not understanding it" (quoted in Krugman 2005). In cases like these, we can explain both the beliefs and the behavior by some underlying factor, and we need to scrutinize statements like Boulding's in this light. Without claiming any expertise on this case, I doubt that the Aztec practices of human sacrifices are best explained by their beliefs, or, at the very least, we cannot leave it at that but need to ask how and why those beliefs formed. This would not be a problem if there were reasonable grounds for the conviction that corn would not grow without human blood, but it probably developed because it was highly functional for the maintenance of Aztec society, justifying as it did constant warfare, the prominence of warriors and warrior values, and hierarchical control.

While ideas can indeed have consequences, in this case I doubt if we should make them the center of our attention. It is similarly doubtful that we can explain

President Clinton's initial refusal to intervene in the former Yugoslavia by his reading Kaplan's *Balkan Ghosts* and being convinced that the conflict was generated by "ancient hatreds." Instead, it is likely that he was attracted to the book and its claim because of his need for reasons not to intervene. In much the same way, when in a private note vice president Cheney characterized as "a junket" ambassador Joseph Wilson's trip to Niger to investigate the reports that Saddam had sought uranium from that barren country (quoted in Johnston 2006), it is hard to avoid the conclusion that he saw it in this way in order to discredit Wilson's motives in his own mind. By contrast, Reagan's image of the Soviet Union, flawed as it may have been, was relatively autonomous. The perception that change was possible pre-dated Gorbachev's rise to power and does not seem to be a rationalization for anything else.

The relationship between interests and ideas (and of course neither concept is unproblematic) is one of the oldest in social science and if Marx, Mannheim, and Weber could not settle it, I certainly cannot. The extremes are easy enough to rule out. Even if we believe in the existence of objective interests, they do not dictate all beliefs. Not only do some wealthy people think that tax cuts for the rich are ethically wrong, they believe that such policies are bad for the economy (but note that those who think that such cuts violate our obligations to fellow citizens also think they will reduce overall economic growth).

Reality appraisal and the functional role of beliefs conflict and combine in complex ways. While few of us can accept Richard Nixon's claims that national security required harassing Vietnam dissenters, punishing his political adversaries, and covering up the Watergate break-in, this was not a conscious rationalization. Nixon made these claims in private (Haldeman 1994; Kutler 1997), and I am sure that he could have passed a lie-detector test. Furthermore, one can defend his conclusions. The North Vietnamese were looking for signs about what the American public would support, and Soviet leaders may have looked to Nixon's handling of domestic opponents for clues as to whether he would back down in a crisis. Nevertheless, the coincidence between these beliefs and Nixon's strong impulses to quash his opponents in order to gratify his psychological needs and maintain his domestic power invites suspicion and no leader likes to recognize that he is more concerned about his own future than with the good of the country.

Others displayed similar patterns. One of Reagan's associates reported that he had the capacity to "convince himself that the truth is what he wants it to be. Most politicians are unable to do this, but they would give their eye teeth if they could" (Nofziger 1992: 45, 285). Thus Reagan was able to make himself believe that he was not trading arms for hostages in Iran, although later he had enough self-insight to realize that this is what he had done. But he was not unique and perhaps not unusual in this regard. Nixon not only thought his version of Watergate was accurate, but earlier told his top assistant that "PR [public relations] is right if it emphasizes the truth. It's wrong, at least for us, if it isn't true" (Haldeman 1994: 287, 521). An associate of Slobodan Milosevic similarly reports: "He decides first what is expedient for him to believe, then he believes it" (Burns 1992). Bill Clinton convinced himself that the donors he invited for overnight stays at the White House were his friends (Kurtz 1998: 138–139), and Harry Truman noted in his diary that "I have told Sec. of War, Mr. Stimson, to use [the atomic bomb] so that military objectives and soldiers and sailors are the target and not women and children" (Ferrell 1980: 55).

The capacity for self-deception bordering on delusion enables people to work their way through difficult situations (on more limited and often healthy forms of self-deception, see Taylor 1989; Gilbert 2006). Before World War I British leaders were able to pursue a policy of containing Germany without building a large army by convincing themselves that the intervention of its small army would be decisive. When the war started, Woodrow Wilson was able to reconcile his preference for a British victory with his desire that the U.S. should remain neutral by believing in the face of clear facts that Britain was abiding by international law and respecting the rights of neutral trade (Coogan 1981).

But as these and other cases show, self-deception often eventually brings political and personal grief. It was very convenient for Nixon to believe that his actions were required by the imperatives of national security, but in the end they served neither the country nor his own interests. What he did was extremely risky, and he was unable to make an accurate cost-benefit calculation in terms of his own political stakes in part because he had convinced himself that the national interest required these unacceptable tactics. He and the country would have been better off if he had been more of a hypocrite. Had he realized that while his own and the national interest were both legitimate, they were not identical he might have seen the world more clearly and sought a better way to deal with the conflicts between them. Wilson might have been able to develop an effective strategy to preserve neutral rights, restrain both Britain and Germany, and put the U.S. in a position to end the war sooner had he not quickly avoided the trade-offs but instead carefully thought about them (Coogan 1981: 217–219). A fuller if more painful search might similarly have revealed better ways for Germany to deal with its dilemmas before 1914 (Snyder 1984).

Beliefs are filled with puzzles and ironies like this, and I think they deserve more attention. A scientist starts his book on the brain by declaring that "Believing is what we humans do best" (Gazzaniga 1985: 3). We certainly are quick to form beliefs, but how and how well we do so is another question. According to Bob Woodward, on his deathbed CIA Director William Casey gave a deceptively simple answer to the question of why he had engaged in a series of arguably illegal covert actions: "I believed" (Woodward 1987: 507).

Beliefs and the perception of threat

This implies that in a significant number of cases in which threat was exaggerated, the causes were rooted in the beliefs that people held rather than in the communication strategies they pursued, although the latter can at times produce the former. We need to take beliefs seriously even – or especially – when we find them flawed. This analysis leads to some informal hypotheses about when threat will be over-perceived and when it will be under-perceived. Both cognitive and motivated biases play a role, and some processes blend them.

To begin with, the conscious belief held by most decision-makers that "it is better to be safe than sorry" predisposes to over-perception of threat. This may be a slightly misleading way to put it, because when people follow this principle they consciously err in a certain direction, or act as though they are doing this. That is, they say to themselves (and often to their colleagues): "I cannot be sure of the other state's capabilities and intentions, but for this very reason I and our country should act as though the other is strong and hostile." The underlying idea is that under-perception of threat is much more dangerous than is over-perception. In the former case, the state will be vulnerable to the other's threats and use of force and the state's security and other vital interests will be put at risk. To perceive greater hostility than is present and to follow policies such as building up one's arms will be "only" to waste money. Unfortunately, this belief is incorrect (Jervis 1976: Ch. 3), but it is common. Threat is inflated in a way that may not serve the state well, but the reason is not the need to generate public support but a mistaken sense of prudence.

This could be termed a substantive cognitive error in that the substance of an incorrect belief leads to over-perception. Other biases, largely if not completely cognitive, also push in this direction, as Kahneman and Renshon (this volume) have shown. Let me just add a bit to their discussion of attribution. They are clearly right that the "fundamental attribution error" is particularly troublesome in distorting perceptions of other's hostility. Perhaps even more than individuals, states are rarely willing to recognize the extent to which their actions may have triggered the apparently malign behavior of others. In part, this is because actors know their own motives, or think they do, and they forget that others play it safe in the way I described in the previous paragraph. If leaders do not wish to harm the other state, they will expect others to understand that any inappropriate or rough behavior on their part was well-intentioned and aimed only at inducing a more cooperative relationship in the long run. Since leaders want to think well of themselves and their countries, they have trouble recognizing the degree to which their behavior threatens others and the extent to which they have acted contrary to their promises. Thus, in a great many cases each side sincerely believes that it has acted in accord with an agreement but that the other has not. The latter perception is more often accurate than the former, and US–North Korean relations provide a textbook case.

Furthermore – and this is a point missed by the fundamental attribution error – the problem is compounded because when the other acts as the state wants it to, the state is likely to attribute this not to the other's dispositions, but to the state's own actions (Jervis 1976: Ch. 9). Thus, if the state has used threats and the other has acted as desired, the state is likely to conclude that it is this tactic that has brought the adversary into line rather than entertaining the possibility that the other was not hostile in the first place.

As I argued earlier, expectations strongly guide perceptions and beliefs, producing a strong but not unidirectional impact on the level of hostility that is seen. Individuals and states that expect hostility will perceive it; those that do not will treat equivocal evidence as indicating a more benign environment. I suspect that there are significant personality differences here, although this is a difficult and contentious area. It is more obvious that there is a correlation between how American officials perceived the Soviet Union during the Cold War and the level of threat they perceive today from a variety of countries, not only Russia but also China and "rogue" states like Iran and North Korea. Expectations are also influenced by previous events and the lessons people draw from them (Jervis 1976: Ch. 6; Khong 1992; May 1973). Wars can then breed wars, not only between the same participants, but more generally because the experience of other's hostility can lead decision-makers to be (over) sensitive to later threats. Prolonged periods of peace may lead to the tendency to be more relaxed and to under-perceive threats. Of course it is not easy to find all the sources of expectations, and there may be endogeneity here as perceptions of threat influence expectations. Nevertheless, an appreciation of the causes and effects of beliefs does lead to the conclusion that expectations are sometimes separate from the immediate case under consideration and that however they are caused, they will exert a powerful influence.

Personal and political needs and the resulting motivated biases are also a major influence on threat perception, and these too can lead to errors in both directions. The crucial question is what perceptions will meet the person's pressing needs for self-justification, minimizing painful value trade-offs, and reduce the possibility that he or she will end up "in a funny farm" as discussed earlier. Here the need to oversell (or undersell) the menace can influence beliefs that, once established, take on a life of their own. If it is true that Bush's main impulse for overthrowing Saddam derived from the belief that this would establish democracy in Iraq and the wider region (McClellan 2008: 128–129; Tenet 2007: 321), then in order to provide additional justification for his policy he would have been prone to overestimate the threat posed by Saddam. As a generalization, whenever political or personal needs mean that perceiving threat will ease leaders' problems, they are likely to do so even in the face of a fairly benign environment. On the other hand, if they become psychologically or political committed to a policy of conciliation, they will under-perceive threat, as Neville Chamberlain and his colleagues did in the 1930s. Ironically, the last year of the Bush administration may reveal this phenomenon in its policy toward North Korea. After the policy of intransigence led North Korea to resume its nuclear program, Bush finally authorized serious negotiations. At first these met with success, but ran into major problems in 2008. One might have expected Bush to have reinstated his older view of North Korea as dangerous and deceptive, but this would have required him to abandon his new policy. He could not afford to do this, however, because Korea was his only potential foreign policy success, and so he had to continue his belief that the agreement could be consummated on reasonable terms. Here the need to undersell the threat in order to maintain the policy has perhaps been responsible for changing Bush's beliefs.

In summary, understanding beliefs help us see when people are likely to exaggerate the threats they face and when they are likely to minimize them. But the task of understanding beliefs is itself as difficult as it is important.

References

Abramsky, S. (2004) "Supporting the troops, doubting the war," *The Nation,* October 4: 11–15.

Bem, D. (1972) "Self-perception theory," in L. Berkowitz (ed.) *Advances in Experimental Social Psychology*, New York: Academic Press.

Bar-Joseph, U. and Kruglanski, A. W. (2003) "Intelligence failures and need for cognitive closure: On the psychology of the Yom Kippur surprise," *Political Psychology,* 24: 75–99.

Barnhart, M. (1987) *Japan prepares for total war*, Ithaca, NY: Cornell University Press.

Betts, R. K. (1982) *Surprise attack*, Washington, DC: The Brookings Institution.

Boulding, K. E. (1967) "The learning and reality-testing process in the international system," *Journal of International Affairs*, 21: 1–15.

Burns, J. F. (1992) "Serbia's enigma: An aloof leader who stoked fires of nationalist passion," *New York Times*, December 22.

Carr, E. H. (1946) *The twenty years' crisis: 1919–1939*, New York: Harper Torchbooks.

Carter, J. R. (1998) *Airpower and the cult of the offensive*, Maxwell Air Force Base, AL: Air University Press.

Chaiken, S. (1980) "Heuristic versus systematic information processing and the use of source versus message cues in persuasion," *Journal of Personality and Social Psychology*, 39: 752–766.

Clancy, S. A. (2005) *Abducted: How People Come to Believe They Were Kidnapped by Aliens*, Cambridge, MA: Harvard University Press.

Coogan, J. W. (1981). *The End of Neutrality: The United States, Britain, and Maritime Rights, 1899–1915*, Ithaca, NY: Cornell University Press.

Dilks, D. (1972) *The Diaries of Sir Alexander Cadogan*, New York: G. P. Putnam's.

Eagly, A. H. and Chaiken, S. (1998) "Attitude structure and function," in D. T. Gilbert, S. T. Fiske and G. Lindzey (eds) *The Handbook of Social Psychology*, NewYork: Oxford University Press.

Erickson, J. (1962) *The Soviet High Command*, London: Macmillan.

Farnham, B. F. (1997) *Roosevelt and the Munich Crisis: A study of Political Decision-Making*, Princeton, NJ: Princeton University Press.

Ferrell, R. H. (1980) *Off the Record: The Private Papers of Harry S. Truman*, New York: Harper & Row.

Fiske, S. T. and Taylor, S. E. (1991) *Social Cognition*, New York: McGraw-Hill.

Fiske, A. P. and Tetlock, P. E. (1997) "Taboo trade-offs: Reactions to transactions that transgress the spheres of justice," *Political Psychology*, 18: 255–297.

Gazzaniga, M. S. (1985) *The Social Brain: Discovering the Networks of the Mind*, New York: Basic Books.

George, A. L. (1958) "Comment on 'Opinions, personality, and political behavior,'" *American Political Science Review*, 52: 18–26.

Gerber, A. and Green, D. (1999) "Bias," *Annual Review of Political Science*, 2: 189–210.

Gilbert, D. (2006) *Stumbling on Happiness*, New York: Knopf.

Gladwell, M. (2005) *Blink: The Power of Thinking Without Thinking*, New York: Little Brown.

Haldeman, H. R. (1994) *The Haldeman Diaries: Inside the Nixon White House*, New York: G. P. Putnam's.

Halevy, E. (1966) *The Era of Tyrannies*, New York: New York University Press.

Hammond, K. R. (1996) *Human Judgment and Social Policy*, New York: Oxford University Press.

Harris, M. (1979) *Cultural Materialism: The Struggle for a Science of Culture*, New York: Random House.

Hastings, M. (1979) *Bomber command*, New York: Dial Press.

Hastorf, A. and Cantril, H. (1954) "They saw a game," *Journal of Abnormal and Social Psychology*, 49: 129–134.

Herek, Gregory M. (1987) "Can functions be measured? A new perspective on the functional approach to attitudes," *Social Psychology Quarterly*, 50: 285–303.

Herwig, H. H. (2003) "Germany," in R. F. Hamilton and H. H. Herwig (eds) *The Origins of World War I,* Cambridge: Cambridge University Press.

Hull, I. V. (2005) *Absolute Destruction: Military Culture and the Practices of War in Imperial Germany*, Ithaca, NY: Cornell University Press.

Janis, I. L. and Mann, L. (1977) *Decision Making: A Psychological Analysis of Conflict, Choice, and Commitment*, New York: Free Press.

Jervis, R. (1976) *Perception and Misperception in International Politics*, Princeton, NJ: Princeton University Press.

—— (1982/83) "Deterrence and perception," *International Security*, 7: 3–30.

—— (2005) *American Foreign Policy in a New Era*, New York: Routledge.

—— (2006) "Reports, politics, and intelligence failures: The case of Iraq," *Journal of Strategic Studies*, 29: 3–52.

Jervis, R., Lebow, R. N. and Stein, J. G. (1985) *Psychology and Deterrence*, Baltimore, MD: Johns Hopkins University Press.

Johnston, D. (2006) "Notes are said to reveal close Cheney interest in a critic of Iraq policy," *New York Times*, May 14.

Joll, J. (1972) "1914: The unspoken assumptions," in H. W. Koch (ed.) *The Origins of the First World War*, London: Macmillan.

Kaplan, R. D. (1993) *Balkan Ghosts: A Journey through History*, New York: St. Martin's Press.

Katz, D. (1960) "The functional approach to the study of attitudes," *Public Opinion Quarterly*, 24: 163–204.

Kaufmann, C. (1994) "Out of the lab and into the archives: A method for testing psychological explanations of political decision making," *International Studies Quarterly*, 38: 557–586.

Khong, Y. F. (1992) *Analogies at War: Korea, Munich, Dien Bien Phu, and the Vietnam Decisions of 1965*, Princeton, NJ: Princeton University Press.

Kimball, W. F. (1991) *The Juggler: Franklin Roosevelt As Wartime Statesman*, Princeton, NJ: Princeton University Press.

Krugman, P. (2005) "The free lunch bunch," *New York Times*, January 21 Section A, 23.

Kurtz, H. (1998) *Spin cycle: How the White House and the Media Manipulate the News*, New York: Simon and Schuster.

Kutler, S. I. (1997) *Abuse of Power: The New Nixon tapes*, New York: Free Press.

LaPiere, R. T. (1934) "Attitudes versus actions," *Social Forces*, 13: 230–237.

Larson, D. W. (1985) *Origins of Containment*, Princeton, NJ: Princeton University Press.

—— (2003) "Truman and the Berlin blockade: The role of intuition and experience in good foreign policy judgment," in D. W. Larson and S. A. Renshon (eds) *Good Judgment in Foreign Policy: Theory and Application*, Lanham, MD: Rowman & Littlefield.

Laudan, L. (1977) *Progress and Its Problems: Toward a Theory of Scientific Growth*, Berkeley: University of California Press.

Lebow, R. N. (1981) *Between Peace and War: The Nature of International Crisis*, Baltimore: Johns Hopkins University Press.

Lemann, N. (2004) "Remember the Alamo," *New Yorker*, October 18: 148–163.

Lippmann, W. (1922) *Public opinion*, New York: Macmillan.

McClellan, S. (2008) *What Happened: Inside The Bush White House and the Culture of Deception*, New York: Public Affairs.

Marcus, G. E. (2000) "Emotions in politics," *Annual Review of Political Science*, 3: 221–250.

—— (2003) "The psychology of emotion and politics," in D. O. Sears, L. Huddy, and R. Jervis (eds) *Oxford Handbook of Political Psychology*, New York: Oxford University Press.

May, E. R. (1973) *"Lessons" of the past: The use of and misuse of history in American foreign policy*, New York: Oxford University Press.

—— (1975) *The Making of the Monroe Doctrine*, Cambridge: Harvard University Press.

McDermott, R. (2004) "The feeling of rationality: The meaning of neuroscientific advances for political science," *Perspectives on Politics*, 2: 691–706.

Mombauer, A. (2001) *Helmuth von Moltke and the Origins of the First World War*, New York: Cambridge University Press.

Neustadt, R. E. (1986) "Presidents, politics and analysis," Paper presented at Graduate School of Public Affairs, University of Washington, Seattle, WA.

Nisbett, R. E. and Wilson, T. D. (1977) "Telling more than we can know: Verbal reports on mental processes," *Psychological Review*, 84: 231–259.

Nofziger, L. (1992) *Nofziger*, Washington, DC: Regnery Publishing, Inc.

Pears, D. (1984) *Motivated Irrationality*, New York: Oxford University Press.

Ransom, H. H. (1958) *Central Intelligence and National Security*, Cambridge: Harvard University Press.

Roberts, C. (1996) *The Logic of Historical Explanation*, University Park: Pennsylvania State University Press.

Sarnoff, I. and Katz, D. (1954) "The motivational bases of attitude change," *Journal of Abnormal and Social Psychology*, 49: 115–124.

Schiff, A. (1962) *Fire and Water: Scientific Heresy in the Forest Service*, Cambridge, MA: Harvard University Press.

Schuman, H. and Johnson, M. P. (1976) "Attitudes and behavior," *Annual Review of Sociology*, 2: 167–207.

Shafir, E., Simonson, I. and Tversky, A. (1993) "Reason-based choice," *Cognition*, 49: 11–36.

Shimko, K. L. (1991) *Images and Arms Control*, Ann Arbor: University of Michigan Press.

Slevin, P. and Priest, D. (2003) "Wolfowitz concedes Iraq errors," *Washington Post*, July 24 Section A: 1.

Smith, M. B., Bruner, J. S. and White, R. W. (1956) *Opinions and Personality*, New York: Wiley.

Snyder, J. (1984) *The Ideology of the Offensive: Military Decision Making and the Disasters of 1914*, Ithaca, NY: Cornell University Press.

Spencer, S., Fein, S., Zanna, M. and Olson, J. (eds) (2003) *Motivated Social Perception: The Ontario Symposium Volume 9*, Mahwah, NJ: Erlbaum.

Taylor, S. E. (1989) *Positive Illusions: Creative Self-Deception and the Healthy Mind*, New York: Basic Books.

Tenet, G., with Harlow, B. (2007) *At the Center of the Storm: My Years at the CIA*, New York: HarperCollins.

Tetlock, P. E. (2002) "Social-functionalist metaphors for judgment and choice: The politician, theologian and prosecutor," *Psychological Review*, 109: 451–472.

—— (2005) *Expert Political Judgment: How Good Is It? How Can We Know?* Princeton, NJ: Princeton University Press.

Tetlock, P. E. and Levi, A. (1982) "Attribution bias: On the inconclusiveness of the cognition-motivation debate," *Journal of Experimental Social Psychology*, 18: 68–88.

Trivers, R. (2002) *Natural Selection and Social Theory*, New York: Oxford University Press.

Wade, N. (2005) "The uncertain science of growing heart cells," *New York Times*, March 14 Section A: 1.

Whaley, B. (1973) *Codeword Barbarossa*, Cambridge, MA: MIT Press.

Wilson, T. D. (2002) *Strangers to Ourselves*, Cambridge, MA: Harvard University Press.

Woodward, B. (1987) *Veil: The Secret Wars of the CIA 1981–1987*, New York: Simon and Schuster.

Wohlstetter, R. (1962) *Pearl Harbor: Warning and Decision*, Stanford, CA: Stanford University Press.

Zajonc, R. B. (1998) "Emotions," in D. T. Gilbert, S. T. Fiske and G. Lindzey (eds) *The handbook of Social Psychology*, Boston, MA: McGraw-Hill.

3 Imperial myths and threat inflation

Jack Snyder

Historically, modern great powers have often engaged in preventive wars premised on ideas that military expansion would enhance security. Typically these preventive strategies have proved counter-productive, lessening security at great expense and even leading in some cases to imperial collapse. The arguments by advocates of these preventive wars have been eerily similar across time and place: they claimed that offense was cheaper and easier than remaining on the defense or deterring threats, and that offense was immediately necessary because waiting would only make the threats grow larger. Moreover, the modern imperial powers repeatedly adopted a paradoxical paper tiger image of the adversary: undeterrably threatening, yet at the same time easy to destroy with a timely attack. These notions of offensive bias and paradoxical threat perception lie at the core of what I have termed the myths of empire.

Since the end of the Cold War, America has enjoyed unprecedented and unrivaled disproportionate power. The U.S. military budget is greater than those of the next 14 countries combined and the American economy is larger than the next three combined. Yet, after 9/11, Americans going about their daily lives perceived greater risk of sudden death from terrorist attack than ever before. This situation of a real increased threat fostered a psychology of vulnerability that made Americans hyperalert to foreign dangers and predisposed many Americans to be willing to use military power to forestall possible threats. However, with the benefit of hindsight, a majority of Americans came after a few years to view the U.S. attack on Iraq as unnecessary and counterproductive for national security.

The Iraq war was justified largely in terms of the myths of empire. In the fall of 2002, as the Bush Administration began to press for war against Iraq, the administration introduced a new national security doctrine (Office of the President 2002a – National Security Strategy, hereafter NSS) which provided a superficially attractive rationale for preventive war, reflecting the uneasy state of mind of many Americans after 9/11. This "Bush Doctrine" argued that in an open society, no strictly defensive strategy against terrorism could be foolproof. Moreover, deterring terrorist attack by the threat of retaliation seemed impossible when the potential attackers seemed to welcome suicide. Additionally, it was argued that bizarre or diabolical leaders of potentially nuclear-armed rogue states would likewise be undeterrable. If so, attacking the sources of potential threats before they could mount their own attacks seemed the only safe option. Such a strategy presented a great temptation to a country as strong as the United States, which could project overwhelming military power to any spot on the globe.

In adopting this strategy, however, America began marching in the well-trod footsteps of virtually every imperial power of the modern age. Unlike past imperial powers, America had virtually no formal colonial empire and sought none, but like other great powers over the past two centuries, it had often sought to influence the tortured politics of weaker societies. Consequently, it faced many of the same strategic dilemmas as did the great powers that had gone before it. The Bush Administration's rhetoric of preventive war did not reflect a sober appreciation of the American predicament, but instead echoed point by point the disastrous strategic ideas of those earlier keepers of imperial order.

This chapter first briefly reviews the modern history of imperial overstretch and delineates the imperial myths that have been the repeated pattern of faulty and illogical strategic arguments that have undergirded multiple cases of overexpansion. Threat inflation played a key role in this pattern historically and in the United States after 9/11. The chapter concludes by discussing the multiple sources of these imperial myths.

Imperial overstretch

Like America, the great empires of the nineteenth and twentieth centuries enjoyed huge asymmetries of power relative to the societies at their periphery, yet they rightly feared disruptive attack from unruly peoples along the turbulent frontier of empire. Suspecting that their empires were houses of cards, imperial rulers feared that unchecked defiance on the periphery might cascade toward the imperial core. Repeatedly they tried the strategy of preventive attack to nip challenges in the bud and prevent their spread.

Typically, the preventive use of force proved counterproductive for imperial security because it often sparked endless brushfire wars at the edges of the empire, internal rebellions, and opposition from powers not yet conquered or otherwise subdued. Historically, the preventive pacification of one turbulent frontier of empire has usually led to the creation of another one, adjacent to the first. When the British conquered what is now Pakistan, for example, the turbulent frontier simply moved to neighboring Afghanistan. It was impossible to conquer everyone, so there was always another frontier.

Even inside well-established areas of imperial control, the use of repressive force against opponents often created a backlash among subjects who came to reassess the relative dangers and benefits of submission. The Amritsar massacre of 1919, for example, was the death knell for British India because it radicalized a formerly circumspect opposition. Moreover, the preventive use of force inside the empire and along its frontiers often intensified resistance from independent powers outside the empire who feared that unchecked, ruthless imperial force would soon encroach upon them. In other words, the balance of power kicked in. Through all of these mechanisms, empires have typically found that the preventive use of force expanded their security problems instead of ameliorating them.

As the dynamic of imperial overstretch became clearer, many of the great powers decided to solve their security dilemmas through even bolder preventive offensives. None of these efforts worked. To secure their European holdings, Napoleon and Hitler marched to Moscow, only to be engulfed in the Russian winter. Kaiser Wilhelm's Germany tried to break the allies' encirclement through unrestricted submarine warfare, which brought America's industrial might into the war against it. Imperial Japan, facing a quagmire in China and a U.S. oil embargo, tried to break what it saw as impending encirclement by seizing the Indonesian oil fields and preventively attacking Pearl Harbor. All sought security through expansion, and all ended in imperial collapse.

Some great powers, however, have pulled back from overstretch and husbanded their power for another day. Democratic great powers, notably Britain and the United States, are prominent among empires that learned how to retrench. At the turn of the twentieth century, British leaders saw that the strategy of "splendid isolation" – what we would now call unilateralism – was getting the empire into trouble. The independence struggle of Boer farmers in South Africa drained the imperial coffers while, at the same time, the European great powers were challenging Britain's naval mastery and its hold on other colonial positions. Quickly doing the math, the British patched up relations with their secondary rivals, France and Russia, to form an alliance directed at the main danger, Germany. Likewise, when the United States blundered into war in Vietnam, it retrenched and adopted a more patient strategy for waiting out its less capable communist opponents.

Contemporary America, too, has begun to retrench after recognizing the counterproductive effects of offensive policies and has begun moderating its preventive war strategy before irreversible damage has been done. The democratic marketplace of ideas, however imperfect, has worked to curb overexpansion. Even in 2002, guided by wary public opinion, the Bush team was pushed to make an extensive effort to work through existing UN resolutions to increase multilateral support for its threats of preventive war against Iraq. Most significantly, important administration leaders and respected critics repeatedly stressed the likely counterproductive effects of a unilateral offensive strategy, and their warnings have proved prophetic and have been recognized as such.

Moreover, the Bush administration itself declined to apply mechanically its preventive war principles against North Korea in the same 2002–2003 time period when the United States invaded Iraq even though North Korea renounced international controls on its nuclear materials and later pursued nuclear weapons capability. Strikingly, too, a December 2002 codicil to the famous "Bush Doctrine" NSS, dealing specifically with the proliferation of weapons of mass destruction, never mentioned the option of preventive attack (Office of the President 2002b). Thus, it appears that while the Bush administration espoused the virtues of preventive attack in its primary strategy document and rhetorically to the public, it simultaneously did not take its own policy to heart as it seemed to recognize that the costs of a general preventive war policy against weapons of mass destruction could well outweigh the benefits. A brief tour through the misguided strategic ideas of previous empires underscores the wisdom of such self-restraint.

Myths of security through expansion

Every major historical instance of imperial overstretch has been propelled by arguments that security could best be achieved through further expansion – the myths of empire (Snyder 1991). Since many of these myths were revived full force by the Bush Administration's strategic rhetoric in 2002, it is worthwhile recalling how earlier advocates of imperial overstretch similarly made their dubious cases. Eight themes deserve mention.

Offensive advantage

The most general of the myths of empire is that the attacker has an inherent advantage. Sometimes this is explained in terms of the advantages of surprise. More often, it relies on the broader notion that seizing the initiative allows the attacker to impose a plan on a passive enemy and to choose a propitious time and circumstance for the fight. Even if the political objective is self-defense, in this view, attacking is still the best strategy. As the Bush NSS said, "our best defense is a good offense" (2002a).

Throughout history, strategists who have blundered into imperial overstretch have shared this view. For example, General Alfred von Schlieffen, the author of Germany's misbegotten plan for a quick, decisive offensive in France in 1914, used to say that "if one is too weak to attack the whole" of the other side's army, "one should attack a section" (quoted in Snyder 1984: 113). This idea defies elementary military common sense. In war, the weaker side normally remains on the defensive precisely because defending its home ground is typically easier than attacking the other side's strongholds.

The idea of offensive advantage also runs counter to the most typical patterns of deterrence and coercion. Sometimes the purpose of a military operation is not to take or hold territory but to influence an adversary by inflicting pain. This is especially true when weapons of mass destruction are involved. In that case, war may resemble a competition in the willingness to endure pain. Here too, however, the defender normally has the advantage, because the side defending its own homeland and the survival of its regime typically cares more about the stakes of the conflict than does a would-be attacker. For example, even as North Korea acquired nuclear weapons capability, it was difficult to imagine North Korea using nuclear weapons or mounting a conventional artillery barrage on the South Korean capital of Seoul for purposes of conquest, but it was much easier to envision such desperate measures in response to "preventive" U.S. attacks on the core power resources of the regime. Because the Bush Administration saw such retaliation as feasible and credible, it was deterred from undertaking preventive strikes against North Koreans even as North Korea defied the Bush Administration's insistence to cease its nuclear pursuits. Indeed, deterring any country from attacking is almost always easier than compelling it to disarm, surrender territory or change its regime. Once stated, this point seems obvious, but the logic of the Bush Doctrine strategy implied the opposite. This most prevalent myth, that a good offensive strategy provides the best defense, does not directly require or include threat inflation as a number of the following myths do, but this myth is typically accompanied by arguments claiming threats are large, imminent or inevitable as part of the argument that it is necessary to urgently employ the required offensive strategy to gain the advantage.

Power shifts

One reason that blundering empires have been keen on offensive strategies is that they have relied on preventive attacks to forestall unfavorable shifts in the balance of power. Seeing unfavorable shifts of power as existentially threatening appears with hindsight to have included extensive marked threat inflation. For example, in both World War I and II, Germany's leaders sought war with Russia in the short run because they expected the Russian army to gain relative strength over time and this shift was seen as too great a threat to endure (Copeland 2000). But the tactic of heading off this potential threat backfired badly. Preventive aggression not only turned a possible enemy into a certain one, but in the long run it helped bring other powers into the fight to prevent Germany from gaining hegemony over all of them. This reflects a fundamental realist principle of the balance of power: in the international system, states and other powerful actors tend to form alliances against the expansionist state that most threatens them. Attackers provoke fears that drive their potential victims to cooperate with each other.

Astute strategists learn to anticipate such cooperation and try to use it to their advantage. For example, one of the most successful diplomats in European history, Otto von Bismarck, achieved the unification of Germany by always putting the other side in the wrong and, whenever possible, maneuvering the opponent into attacking first. As a result, Prussia expanded its control over the German lands without provoking excessive fears or resistance. Pressed by his generals on several occasions to authorize preventive attacks, Bismarck said that preventive war is like committing suicide from fear of death; it would "put the full weight of the imponderables . . . on the side of the enemies we have attacked" (Ritter 1969: 245; Craig 1978: 24–25). Instead, he demanded patience: "I have often had to stand for long periods of time in the hunting blind and let myself be covered and stung by insects before the moment came to shoot" (Pflanze 1963: 90). Germany fared poorly under Bismarck's less-able successors, who shared his ruthlessness but lacked his understanding of the balance of power.

Because Saddam Hussein attacked Kuwait, the elder Bush enjoyed a diplomatic advantage in the 1991 war. That's why the coalition against Iraq was so large and willing. This advantage is vastly and inherently more difficult to achieve in a strategy of preventive attack, as the younger Bush learned after the 2003 attack on Iraq. Especially when an adverse power shift is merely hypothetical and not imminent, it hardly seems worthwhile to incur the substantial diplomatic disadvantages of a preventive attack.

Paper tiger enemies

Empires also become overstretched when they view their enemies as paper tigers, capable of becoming fiercely threatening if appeased, but easily crumpled by a resolute attack. These images are often not only wrong as they are generally based on a large amount of threat inflation, but they are also self-contradictory. For example, Japanese militarists saw the United States as so strong and insatiably aggressive that Japan would have to conquer a huge, self-sufficient empire to get the resources to defend itself; yet at the same time, the Japanese regime saw the United States as so vulnerable and irresolute that a sharp rap against Pearl Harbor would discourage it from fighting back.

Similarly, the Bush Administration's arguments for preventive war against Iraq portrayed Saddam Hussein as being completely undeterrable from using the weapons of mass destruction it claimed he possessed, yet Secretary of Defense Donald Rumsfeld said he expected that Iraq would not use them even if attacked because "wise Iraqis will not obey his orders to use WMD" (Testimony before the House Armed Services Committee, September 18–19, 2002). In other words, administration strategists thought that deterrence was impossible even in the situation in which Saddam lacked a motive to use weapons of mass destruction, but they simultaneously thought deterrence would succeed during a U.S. attack which would provide Iraq the strongest imaginable motive to use its weapons. The NSS said "the greater the threat, the greater is the risk of inaction" (2002a); but this was a rationale for preventive attack only if a paper tiger image of the enemy was accepted.

Bandwagons

Another recurrent myth of empire is the argument that states tend to jump on the bandwagon with threatening or forceful powers. During the Cold War, for example, the Soviet Union thought that forceful action in Berlin, Cuba and the developing world would demonstrate its political and military strength, encourage so-called progressive forces to ally actively with Moscow, and thereby shift the balance of forces still further in the favor of the communist bloc. The Soviets called this the "correlation of forces" theory. In fact, the balance of power effect far outweighed and erased the bandwagon effect. The Soviet Union was left far weaker in relative terms as a result of its pressing for unilateral advantage. As Churchill said of the Soviets in the wake of the first Berlin Crisis, "Why have they deliberately acted for three long years so as to unite the free world against them?" (Churchill 1949).

During the 1991 Gulf War, the earlier Bush Administration argued that rolling back Saddam Hussein's conquest of Kuwait was essential to discourage Arabs throughout the Middle East from jumping on the Iraqi bandwagon. The second Bush Administration hoped in 2002 that bandwagon dynamics could be made to work in its own favor. Despite the difficulties that the United States had in lining up support for the invasion of Iraq, the administration nonetheless asserted that its strategy of preventive war would lead others to jump on the U.S. bandwagon. Secretary Rumsfeld said that "if our leaders do the right thing, others will follow and support our just cause – just as they have in the global war against terror" (Testimony before the House Armed Services Committee September 18–19, 2002).

At the same time, some self-styled realists in the administration argued that this NSS preventive war policy was consistent with the concept of the balance of power, but the rhetoric of the NSS pulled this concept inside out: "Through our willingness to use force in our own defense and in the defense of others, the United States demonstrates its resolve to maintain a balance of power that favors freedom" (2002a). What this Orwellian statement really seems to mean is that preventive war will attract a bandwagon of support that creates an imbalance of power in America's favor, a conception that is logically the same as the wrongheaded Soviet theory of the "correlation of forces." Administration strategists liked to use the terminology of the balance of power, but they understood that concept exactly backwards. A common essential ingredient of making bandwagon arguments is frequently to inflate the threat from the other side, and argue that others will join you to *maintain* a balance of power through preventive war, while others typically view preventive war as aggression, disrupting the balance of power.

Big stick diplomacy

A closely related myth is the big stick theory of making friends by threatening them. Before World War I, Germany's leaders found that its rising power and belligerent diplomacy had pushed France, Russia and Britain into a loose alliance against it. In the backwards reasoning of German diplomacy, they decided to try to break apart this encirclement by trumping up a crisis over claims to Morocco, threatening France with an attack and hoping to prove to French leaders that its allies would not come to its rescue. In fact, Britain did support France, and the noose around Germany grew tighter.

How did the Bush administration seek to win friends abroad? The NSS offered some reassuring language about the need to work with allies, but this was not sincerely pursued. President Bush did at first seem to work hard for a UN resolution to authorize an attack on Iraq, a move President Clinton did not even attempt in the Kosovo war. Nonetheless, on the Iraq issue and a series of others, the Bush administration attempted to extort cooperation primarily by threats to act unilaterally, and it did not work to gain cooperation by persuasion or concessions. For example, Russia was forced to accept a new strategic arms control regime on take-it-or-leave-it American terms in lieu of a SALT III Treaty. EU member states were similarly compelled to accept an exemption for U.S. officials from prosecution by the International Criminal Court (ICC). Germany was snubbed for resisting the war against Iraq. Multilateral initiatives on the environment were summarily rejected. Secretary Rumsfeld, in his personal jottings on strategy, raised to the level of principle the dictum that the United States should "avoid trying so hard to persuade others to join a coalition that we compromise on our goals" (Quoted in *New York*

Times, October 4, 2002). Either the administration believed allies were dispensable, or a powerful faction within that administration adhered to the Kaiser Wilhelm Big Stick theory of diplomacy.

Falling dominoes

Another common myth of empire is the famous domino theory. According to this conception, small setbacks at the periphery of the empire will tend to snowball into an unstoppable chain of defeats that will ultimately threaten the imperial core. Consequently, empires must fight hard to prevent even the most trivial setbacks. Various causal mechanisms are imagined that might trigger such cascades: The opponent will seize ever more strategic resources from these victories, tipping the balance of forces and making further conquests easier. Vulnerable defenders will lose heart. Allies and enemies alike will come to doubt the empire's resolve to fight for its commitments. An empire's domestic political support will be undermined. Above all, lost credibility is the ultimate domino. This myth incorporates threat inflation in spades as small threats are predicted to have devastating consequences.

Such reasoning has been nearly universal among overstretched empires (Kupchan 1994). For example, in 1898 the British and the French both believed that if a French scouting party could claim a tributary of the Upper Nile – at a place called Fashoda – France could build a dam there, block the flow of the Nile, trigger chaos in Egypt that would force Britain out of the Suez Canal, cut Britain's strategic lifeline to India, and thus topple the empire that depended on India's wealth and manpower. Britain and France, both democracies, nearly went to war because of this chimera. Similarly, Cold War America believed that if Vietnam fell to communism, then the credibility of its commitment to defend Taiwan, Japan and Berlin would be debased. Arguably, the peripheral setback in Vietnam tarnished American deterrent credibility only because the United States so often and so insistently said it would.

Similar arguments about small losses leading to larger and larger losses, especially ones that hinged on lost credibility, informed Secretary Rumsfeld's brief for preventive war against Iraq. In a nice rhetorical move, Rumsfeld quoted former President Clinton in September 2002 to the effect that if "we fail to act" against Saddam's non-compliance with inspections,

> he will conclude that the international community has lost its will. He will conclude that he can go right on and do more to rebuild an arsenal of devastating destruction. . . . Some day, some way, I guarantee you he will use that arsenal.
> (Rumsfeld Testimony, September 18–19 2002)

Rumsfeld could have added (but didn't) that the Clinton Administration made the same argument even more strongly about the dire precedent that would be set by permitting the further expansion of North Korea's nuclear weapons capability. Ironically, the credibility of the United States is on the line in such cases mainly because of its own rhetoric. Beyond any problem of rhetoric, it appears the threat of an American attack was all too credible. The main motivation for North Korea to break out of the 1994 agreement constraining its nuclear program was apparently its perceived need, in light of the Bush Administration's preventive war doctrine and reluctance to negotiate, for more powerful weapons to deter the United States from attacking.

A ubiquitous corollary of the domino theory holds that it is cheap and easy to stop aggressors if it is done early on. Secretary Rumsfeld repeatedly made this kind of argument to justify a preventive attack on Iraq. Between 35 and 60 million people died needlessly, he claimed, because the world didn't attack Hitler preventively: "He might have been stopped early – at minimal cost in lives – had the vast majority of the world's leaders not decided at the time that the risks of acting were greater than the risks of not acting." Apart from its questionable relevance to the case of Iraq, the historical point is itself debatable: Britain and France were militarily ill-prepared to launch a preventive attack at the time of the Munich crisis, and if they had, they probably would have had to fight Germany without the Soviet Union and the United States as allies. As Bismarck had understood, preventive war is bad strategy in part because it often leads to diplomatic isolation.

El Dorado and manifest destiny

Most of the central myths of empire focus on a comparison of the alleged costs of offensive versus defensive strategies. In addition, myths that exaggerate the benefits of imperial expansion sometimes play an important role in strategic debates. For example, German imperialism before World War I was fueled in part by the false idea that Central Africa would be an El Dorado of resources that would strengthen Germany's strategic position in the same way that India had supposedly strengthened Britain's. In debates about preventive war in Iraq, some commentators portrayed an anticipated oil windfall as a comparable El Dorado. Astutely, the Bush Administration refrained from rhetoric about this potential boon, realizing that it would be counterproductive and unnecessary to dwell on it.

Sometimes the promised benefits of imperial expansion are also ideological – for example, France's civilizing mission or America's mission to make the world safe for democracy. In a surprising moment of candor, John Foster Dulles, a decade before he became Dwight Eisenhower's Secretary of State, wrote that all empires had been "imbued with and radiated great faiths [like] Manifest Destiny [and] The White Man's Burden." We Americans "need a faith", said Dulles, "that will make us strong, a faith so pronounced that we, too, will feel that we have a mission to spread throughout the world" (quoted in Pruessen 1982: 200). An idealistic goal is patently invoked here for its instrumental value in mobilizing support for the imperial enterprise.

The idealistic notes that graced the Bush Administration's NSS had the same hollow ring. The document was chock full of high-sounding prose about the goal of spreading democracy to Iraq and other countries living under the yoke of repression. President Bush's preface to the strategy document asserted that "the United States enjoys a position of unparalleled military strength" (2002a), which creates "a moment of opportunity to extend the benefits of freedom across the globe. We will actively work to bring the hope of democracy, development, free markets, and free trade to every corner of the world" (2002a). This sounded like insincere public relations in light of the fact it came less than two years after candidate Bush's warnings against the temptations of nation-building abroad. The theme of promoting democracy is rare in Secretary Rumsfeld's statements, which appears to have been a better index of the administration's underlying views.

No tradeoffs

A final myth of empire is that in strategy there are no tradeoffs. Proponents of imperial expansion tend to pile on every argument from the whole list of myths of empire. It is not enough to argue that the opponent is a paper tiger, or that dominoes tend to fall, or that big stick diplomacy will make friends, or that a preventive attack will help to civilize the natives. Rather, proponents of offensive self-defense inhabit a rhetorical world in which all of these things are simultaneously true, and thus all considerations point in the same direction. Undergirding these multiple myths are threat inflated arguments making it urgent for the state to act.

The Bush Administration's strategic rhetoric about Iraq in late 2002 did not disappoint in this regard. Saddam was portrayed as undeterrable, as getting nuclear weapons unless deposed and giving them to terrorists, the war against him would be cheap and easy, grumbling allies would jump on the U.S. bandwagon, Iraq would become a democracy, and the Arab street would thank the United States for liberating it. In real life, as opposed to the world of imperial rhetoric, it is surprising when every conceivable consideration supports the preferred strategy. As is so often the case with the myths of empire, this piling on of reinforcing claims smacks of ex post facto justification rather than serious strategic assessment.

During the 2000 presidential campaign, Condoleezza Rice wrote of Iraq that "the first line of defense should be a clear and classical statement of deterrence—if they do acquire WMD, their weapons will be unusable because any attempt to use them will bring national obliteration" (Rice 2000). Two years later, however, the possibility of deterrence became unthinkable as administration rhetoric regarding Iraq was piled higher and higher. "Given the goals of rogue states [and] the inability to deter a potential attacker" of this kind, said the NSS, "we cannot let our enemies strike first" (2002a). Administration dogma left no room for any assessment of Iraq that did not reinforce the logic of the prevailing preventive strategy.

Why are myths of empire so prevalent?

It is striking that in America in the fall of 2002, in the wake of 9/11, many strategic experts, including many self-styled realists – people who pride themselves on accepting the hard reality that the use of force is often necessary in the defense of national interests – considered the Bush Administration's strategic justifications for preventive war against Iraq to be unconvincing. Indeed, 32 prominent international relations scholars, most of them realists, bought an ad in the *New York Times* to make their case against the Bush strategy. Included among them was the leading proponent of the "offensive realism" school of thought, John Mearsheimer, a professor at the University of Chicago (*New York Times*, September 26 2002; Mearsheimer 2002).

Proponents of Bush's preventive strategy at the time charged that these realists were out of touch with a world in which forming alliances to balance against overwhelming U.S. power had simply become impossible. These proponents argued both that threats were grave and needed to be addressed immediately, while at the same time small rogue states and their ilk could not on their own offset American power in response to American initiatives. It was clearly true that potential great-power backers, Russia and China, had so far been wary of overtly opposing U.S. military interventions, and thus would likely stand aside from balancing American power in any traditional sense. But even if America's unprecedented power reduced the likelihood of traditional balancing alliances arising against it, realists argued the United States could find that its own offensive actions would likely create the functional equivalents of traditional balancing in some form. Some earlier expansionist empires found themselves overstretched and surrounded by enemies even though balancing alliances were slow to oppose them. For example, although the prospective victims of Napoleon and Hitler found it difficult to form effective balancing coalitions, these empires attacked so many opponents simultaneously that substantial de facto alliances eventually did form against them. In the twenty-first century, an analogous form of self-imposed overstretch – political as well as military – could happen if the need for military operations to prevent nuclear proliferation risks were deemed urgent on several fronts at the same time, or if an attempt to impose democracy by force of arms on a handful of Muslim countries were seriously undertaken.

It was argued by realists that even in the absence of highly coordinated balancing alliances, simultaneous resistance by several troublemaking states and terrorist groups would be a daunting challenge for a strategy of universal preventive action. Highly motivated small powers or rebel movements defending their home ground had often prevailed against vastly superior states that lacked the sustained motivation to dominate them at extremely high cost, as in Vietnam and Algeria. Even when the challengers did not prevail, as on the West Bank, they often fought on, imposing high costs over long periods.

Realists noted that precisely because America was so strong, weak states on America's target list would likely increasingly conclude that weapons of mass destruction joined to terror tactics were the only feasible equalizer to its power. Despite America's aggregate power advantages, weaker opponents could eventually get access to outside resources to sustain this kind of cost-imposing resistance. Even a state as weak and isolated as North Korea had been able to mount a credible deterrent, in part by engaging in mutually valuable strategic trade with Pakistan. Iran bought a nuclear reactor from Russia that the United States viewed as posing risks of nuclear proliferation. Palestinian suicide bombers had repeatedly successfully imposed severe costs with minimal resources. In the September 11 attack, Al-Qaeda famously had meager resources and had used its enemy's own resources against it.

In short, both historically and after 9/11, it seems hard to explain the prevalence of the myths of empire in terms of objective strategic analysis. So what, then, explains it?

In some historical cases, narrow interest groups that profited from imperial expansion or military preparations hijacked strategic debates by controlling the media or bankrolling imperial pressure groups. In imperial Japan, for example, when a civilian strategic planning board pointed out the implausibilities and contradictions in the militarists' worldview, its experts were thanked for their trenchant analysis and then summarily fired. In pre-World War I Germany, internal documents showing the gaping holes in the offensive strategic plans of the army and navy were kept secret, and civilians lacked the information or expertise to criticize the military's public reasoning. The directors of Krupp Steelworks subsidized the belligerent German Navy League before 1914, and then in the 1920s monopolized the wire services that brought nationalist-slanted news to Germany's smaller cities and towns. These were precisely the constituencies that later voted most heavily for Hitler.

In other cases, myths of empire were propounded by hard-pressed leaders seeking to rally support by pointing a finger at real or highly inflated enemies. For example, in the aftermath of the French Revolution, a series of unstable regimes found that they could increase their short-run popularity by inflating the threat from monarchical neighboring states and from aristocratic traitors to the Revolution. Napoleon perfected this strategy of rule, transforming the republic of the Rights of Man into an ever-expanding empire of popular nationalism.

Once the myths of empire gain widespread currency in a society their origins in political expediency are often forgotten. Members of the second generation become true believers in the domino theory, big stick diplomacy and the civilizing mission. Kaiser Wilhelm's ministers were self-aware manipulators, but their audiences, including the generation that formed the Nazi movement, believed in German nationalist ideology with utmost conviction. In a process that Stephen Van Evera has called "blowback," the myths of empire may become ingrained in the psyche of the people and the institutions of their state.

Thus, one deep reason for the prevalence of the myths of empire in American debates in the recent past is the legacy of Cold War rhetoric in the tropes of American strategic discourse. The Rumsfeld generation grew to political maturity inculcated with the Munich analogy and the domino theory. It was also true that an opposite metaphor, the quagmire, was readily available for skeptics to invoke as a result of the Vietnam experience. But after the September 11 attack and the easy victory over the Taliban, the American political audience seemed primed for Munich analogies and preventive war, not for quagmire theories. Indeed, it was striking how many Senate speeches on the resolution authorizing the use of force in Iraq began with references to the effect of September 11 on the American psyche. Senators did not necessarily argue that the Iraqi government was in fact a terrorist organization like Al-Qaeda. They simply noted the emotional reality that the attacks on the World Trade Center and the Pentagon seemed to have left Americans fearful and ready to fight back forcefully against threats of many sorts. In this sense,

Senators expressed that they thought America was psychologically primed to accept the myths of empire. These myths seemed to "feel right"; but this was no way to run a grand strategy.

Another major reason why America was primed to accept the myths of empire was simply the temptation of great power. As the German realist historian Ludwig Dehio wrote about Germany's bid for a hegemonic position in Europe, "since the supreme power stands in the solitude of its supremacy, it must face daemonic temptations of a special kind" (Dehio 1967 [1959]: 15). More recently, Christopher Layne chronicled the tendency of unipolar hegemonic states since the Spain of Philip II to succumb to the temptations of overstretch and thereby to provoke the enmity of an opposing coalition (Layne 1993). In 2002, the United States was so strong compared to everyone else that almost any imaginable military objective seemed achievable. This circumstance, supercharged by the rhetoric of the myths of empire, made the temptation of preventive war almost irresistible.

In addition to the opportunity presented by the confluence of the World Trade Center attacks and America's unprecedented international power, skeptics about attacking Iraq suspected that domestic political dynamics played a major role in spawning the Bush doctrine of preventive war. Indeed it appears that while some members of Bush's inner circle had been spoiling for a rematch with Iraq for years, the reason this policy prevailed in the fall of 2002 had to do in large part with the increased polarization of the American party system and the subsequent value of this policy as a "wedge issue." This national security issue appeared to be capable of mobilizing the Republican conservative base and at the same time raiding voters from the Democrats' traditional middle and working class constituencies. Republicans under Ronald Reagan had previously successfully staked out divisive stances on non-economic social issues such as abortion, affirmative action for minorities, homosexuality, and religion as well as trying to consolidate ownership of the national security issue. Even though Republicans' electoral payoff from domestic wedge issues had been fading by the late 1990s, September 11 created an opportunity for empire to become the new wedge issue (Snyder *et al.* 2009). This argument does not claim the Bush Administration invaded Iraq in order to reap domestic political benefits, but rather that party polarization interacted with America's unipolar dominance and the shock of September 11 to create a situation in which preventive war seemed an attractive option to the Bush Administration, both internationally and domestically.

The historical record warrants a skeptical attitude toward arguments that security can be achieved through imperial expansion and preventive war. President Bush's National Security Advisor, former Stanford political science professor and provost Condoleezza Rice, advanced a view in the fall of 2002 of the interplay of power-political realism and democratic idealism where she argued that realism and idealism should not be seen as alternatives: a realistic sense of power politics should be used in the service of ideals. Who could possibly disagree? But contrary to what she and Bush had once argued on the campaign trail about humility and a judicious sense of limits, Rice just two years later believed that America's vast military power should be used preventively to spread democratic ideals. She also said that the aim of the Bush strategy was "to dissuade any potential adversary from pursuing a military build-up in the hope of surpassing, or equaling, the power of the United States and our allies." Even though no combination of adversaries could hope to equal America's traditional military power under any circumstances, if others fear the unbridled use of America's power, they would likely perceive overwhelming incentives to wield weapons of terror and mass destruction to deter America's offensive tactics of self-defense. Indeed, the history of the myths of empire suggests that a strategy of preventive war to ward off inflated threats is likely to undermine the security goals that preventive war was intended to achieve.

References

Churchill, W. (1949) *Speech at the Massachusetts Institute of Technology*, 31 March.

Copeland, D. C. (2000) *The Origins of Major War*, Ithaca, NY: Cornell University Press.

Craig, G. (1978) *Germany: 1866–1945*, New York: Oxford University Press.

Dehio, L. (1967 [1959]) *Germany and World Politics in the Twentieth Century*, New York: W. W. Norton.

Pruessen, R. (1982) *John Foster Dulles: The Road to Power*, New York: Free Press.

Kupchan, C. (1994) *The Vulnerability of Empire*, Ithaca, NY: Cornell University Press.

Layne, C. (1993) "The unipolar illusion: Why new powers will rise," *International Security*, 17: 5–51.

Mearsheimer, J. J. (2002) "Hearts and minds," *The National Interest*. Fall.

New York Times (2002) "In Rumsfeld's words," *New York Times*, October 14, section A; 9

Office of the President (2002a). *National Security Strategy of the United States*, September 2002.

Office of the President (2002b) *National Strategy to Combat Weapons of Mass Destruction*, December 2002.

Pflanze, O. (1963) *Bismarck and the Development of Germany: The Period of Unification, 1815–1871*, Princeton, NJ: Princeton University Press.

Rice, C. (2000) "Promoting the national interest," *Foreign Affairs*, January/February.

Ritter, G. (1969) *The Sword and the Scepter: The Problem of Militarism in Germany, Vol. 1*, Coral Gables, FL: University of Miami Press.

Rumsfeld, D. (2002) *Testimony before the House Armed Services Committee*, 18–19 September.

Snyder, J. (1984) *Ideology of the Offensive: Military Decision Making and the Disasters of 1914*, Ithaca, NY: Cornell University Press.

—— (1991) *Myths of Empire: Domestic Politics and International Ambition*, Ithaca, NY: Cornell University Press.

Snyder, J., Shapiro, R. Y. and Bloch-Elkon, Y. (2009) "Free hand abroad, divide and rule at home," *World Politics*, 61.

4 Estimating threats

The impact and interaction of identity and power

David L. Rousseau and Rocio Garcia-Retamero

The Bush Administration's selling of the Iraq War to the American people has highlighted the issue of threat inflation. In their introduction to this volume, the editors define threat inflation as the depiction of a threat "that goes beyond the scope and urgency that a disinterested analysis would justify" (page 1). This definition of threat inflation immediately raises a number of interesting questions:

1 can we measure threats "objectively"?
2 how much of an error is necessary for us to label an assessment as "inflated" or "deflated"? and
3 why do some people see particular countries as more threatening than other people?

Realists in international relations have traditionally argued that threats are an objective function of the material balance of power (e.g., Waltz 1979: 131). Although some realists emphasize the importance of a common culture for measuring threats (e.g., Gulick 1955: 19), many realists argue that competition within the international system will weed out states that ignore this objective function (e.g., Waltz 1979: 127). However, the existence of an objective material-based threat function does not eliminate uncertainty and error. State leaders have private information about their capability that they often attempt to conceal through bluffs and deception. In addition, it is inherently difficult to assess the impact of new battlefield technologies and tactics. Thus, even if threats can be measured objectively, individual threat assessments tend to fall in a distribution around a modal estimate.

But how are threat assessments actually made? Threat assessments are persuasive arguments made to convince ourselves or those around us. An argument is a series of claims coupled with evidence supporting or refuting these claims. Thus, the central claim (e.g., Saddam Hussein's Iraq is a threat to the United States) is built up from a series of sub-claims (e.g., Saddam supports terrorists, Iraq is developing weapons of mass destruction, Saddam cannot be deterred, toppling the Iraqi regime will spread democracy). In a "strong" argument, evidence is brought to bear on each claim and counter-arguments (e.g., Saddam is deterrable) are rigorously explored. Although we expect intelligence analysts to build strong arguments (Heuer 1999), the same cannot be expected of politicians. Politicians attempt to persuade an audience by building an argument in favor of a proposition; only rarely will a politician carefully layout the pros and cons of a position in public. (In private, we would expect politicians to build strong arguments as they grapple with issues.) This situation creates two important but distinct dangers:

1 politicians will pressure intelligence analysts to make political rather than strong arguments, and
2 the mass public will only be exposed to one-sided political arguments unless the political opposition has access to evidence and an incentive to step up to the bully pulpit.

Given this view of threat assessment, it should come as no surprise that we suspect that threat assessments are both rhetorically and socially constructed. The assessments are rhetorically constructed in that individuals (politicians and intelligence analysts) must choose which arguments to include, the types of evidence to present, and the rationale for weighting the individual sub-claims. These choices imply that all arguments are framed and that the persuasive power of an argument depends on how the frame resonates with the audience (see Krebs and Lobasz, this volume). The assessments are socially constructed in that as members of a community we are socialized to find some claims more salient, some evidence more available, and some inferences more believable.

In this chapter, we focus on this last issue: the social construction of threats. Specifically, we compare the importance of "objective" material factors such as the balance of military power with "subjective" ideational factors such as a common social identity. We develop a general "construction of threat model" at the individual level and test its predictions using three laboratory experiments (one conducted in the United States and two conducted in Spain). Four key findings emerge from the experiments:

1 a weak position in terms of military power increases threat perception, as realists predict;
2 shared identity decreases threat perception, as constructivists predict;
3 an interactive relationship between power and identity appears in two of the three studies; and
4 shared identity increases cooperation in economic policy areas.

In sum, the results strongly support the construction of a threat model and demonstrate how both power and identity play a role in threat perception.

The remainder of this chapter is divided into eight sections. The next section examines the theoretical relationship between power asymmetries and threat perception. The second section explores the theoretical relationship between shared identity and threat perception. The third section introduces the causal logic of our construction of a threat model. The results of the three laboratory experiments are presented in sections four, five, and six. The seventh section discusses the contribution of the experimental findings to our understanding of realism and liberalism. The final section provides a brief conclusion to the study.

Power and threat perception

In the international relations literature, a threat is defined as a situation in which one agent or group has either the capability or intention to inflict a negative consequence on another agent or group (Davis 2000: 10). Threats are probabilistic because they may or may not be carried out. From the broadest perspective, we can divide threats into two categories: threats against us as individuals and threats against collections of individuals (MacKuen *et al.* 1992). International relations focuses mostly, but not exclusively on the second category of threats. Threats against collectives can be in the form of

1   military threats,
2   economic threats, or
3   cultural threats.

In contrast, threats against an individual can be in the form of negative consequences for his or her

1   physical security,
2   personal wealth and income, or
3   personal values and beliefs.

In some cases, a threat against a collective can also represent a personal threat against an individual. For example, an American worker in the textile industry may view the rise of China as a collective economic threat against the United States and a personal income threat against himself or herself.

Power can be used to threaten (or reward). Dahl (1957) defines power as the ability of actor A to get actor B to do what actor A wants (and that which actor B was not going to do anyway). Dahl's definition focuses on observable conflict between two actors. Bachrach and Baratz (1962, 1963) supplement this vision of power with behind the scenes power, such as agenda setting, that may lessen the observable conflict between actors. Finally, Lukes (1974) argues that power should be extended to include preference shaping activities. If an individual or group can alter another actor's preferences to conform with its own through socialization or persuasion, then there will be no observable conflict and no need for the manipulation of agendas.

Power by definition is a relative concept; the power of actor A can only be assessed relative to the remaining actors in the environment (Grieco 1990: 40; Fiske 1993; Jones 1972). This relational aspect of power separates it from other variables central to the study of international relations. For example, the level of democracy is not a relational variable in that the rise in one state's level of democracy does not by definition correspond to the loss by another state. The relative nature of power leads many realists in international relations to view power in particular and international relations in general in zero-sum terms (Waltz 1979: 70, 105).

In international relations, the balance of power among states is typically measured using some combination of "size of population and territory, resource endowment, economic capability, military strength, political stability, and competence" (Waltz 1979: 131). For realists in international relations, the immediate military balance provides the best measure of the ability of one actor (or alliance) to influence another actor (or alliance). The remaining elements of power are important because power is fungible; the other elements of power can be transformed into military power in the long run. Therefore, in the short run, realists worry about the immediate balance of military forces, and in the long run, realists worry about any economic or territorial gains by potential competitors.

Both classical (e.g., Gulick 1955) and structural realists (e.g., Waltz 1979) argue that threats are a function of power asymmetries (Doyle 1997: 168). If a neighboring state has more power than you, your state should feel at risk because nothing in the anarchical international system prevents that state from using force against you to resolve a conflict. In this "self-help" world, states are forced to rely on domestic military spending and temporary international alliances to balance against the power of other states. Even allies are suspect in this Hobbesian world because "today's friend may be tomorrow's enemy in war, and fear that achievements of joint gains that advantage a friend in the present might produce a more dangerous potential foe in the future" (Grieco 1988: 487).

Realistic conflict theory (Levine and Campbell 1972; Sherif 1966) is similar to realism in that power (or resource) asymmetries are the root cause of conflict among groups. The theory is realistic in that there is a "real" conflict over material resources. In a series of field studies at a boys' summer camp, Sherif and Sherif (1953) demonstrated how intense competition could quickly spiral into open conflict. Twenty-two 11-year-old boys were divided into two groups that were isolated from each other during phase 1 of the study and competed in sports and other activities in phase 2. The rapid emergence of prejudice and open conflict (e.g., taunting, burning of flags, ransacking cabins) forced the researchers to separate the boys. While attempts to lessen conflict by bringing the two groups into contact failed, the researchers were able to reduce prejudice and discrimination by getting both groups to solve a collective problem. In related work at the national level, Simpson and Yinger (1985) illustrated how political and economic competition among nationalities can lead to the perception of threat (e.g., competition among immigrants and non-immigrants). When power among the groups is unevenly distributed, both parties in the asymmetric relationship may have cause for alarm. The weaker side may fear exploitation and/or resent their position of inferiority. Conversely, the stronger side may fear an inevitable shift in the balance of power in the long run and a challenge to the status quo.

Identity and threat perception

Social identity theory (SIT; Tajfel 1978; Tajfel and Turner 1979) and its offshoot self-categorization theory (SCT; Turner 1985; Turner *et al.* 1987) provide two non-material explanations for identity construction and threat perception. Both theories were developed to explain prejudicial attitudes and discriminatory behavior toward members of the out-group. Given that prejudice is often (but not always) associated with a fear that the out-group has the capability or intention to inflict a negative consequence on the in-group, these theories can provide a competing explanation for the rise and fall of the perception of threat.

SIT (Tajfel 1978; Tajfel and Turner 1979) begins with the assumption that individuals automatically sort themselves into categories. This is a natural cognitive process that occurs in any social setting. Although the speed of the sorting and salience of the categorization can vary (e.g., high salience when you are a very distinct minority on a sorting dimension), the placement of objects into categories always occurs and the placement of the "self" in one category immediately creates an "other" (Brewer and Brown 1998). Given that groups naturally differ in power and prestige, Tajfel argues that the categorization automatically triggers a motivational need to view one's own group positively. This motivation leads to behaviors in which the members of the in-group are favored over members of the out-group. Thus, SIT postulates a multistep process that encompasses both cognitive and motivational elements.

SCT (Turner *et al.* 1987) emphasizes the cognitive aspect of identity construction rather than the motivational aspect. The first step in the process is identical to SIT: individuals automatically sort themselves into categories and thus automatically create an "us" and a "them." The second step involves the adoption of norms, beliefs, values, attitudes, and behaviors associated with the in-group. If the individual desires to adopt these traits to fit with the in-group, SCT remains similar to SIT in that it combines cognitive and motivational aspects. However, Turner *et al.* emphasize a purely cognitive process in the second step: individuals adopt the norms, beliefs, values, attitudes, and behaviors associated with the in-group because they are part of a readily accessible schema (e.g., an individual categorizes himself or herself as "Catholic," and this makes elements of the "Catholic schema" readily available). In this case, motivation or desire does not play a role. But regardless of the underlying causal mechanisms, SCT (just like SIT) predicts that the categorization process will lead to the emergence of prejudicial attitudes toward the out-group and discrimination against them. International relations scholars have adopted the logic of SIT to predict that "outsiders" in international affairs will be viewed as more threatening than "insiders" (Wendt 1999).

Construction of threat theory

We conceptualize collective identities as "bundles" of shared values, beliefs, attitudes, norms, and roles that are used to draw a boundary between the "in-group" and the "out-group" (Rousseau 2006: 12). Although proponents of SIT and SCT routinely discuss movement between identities based on the social context (e.g., shifting a personal identity from "father" to "professor" or shifting a collective identity from "Scottish" to "British"), there has been insufficient discussion of the process through which individuals construct identities for the collective in-group and the collective out-group. What building blocks are utilized? How are they aggregated? How can they be manipulated to alter a sense of identity? The construction of threat theory has been developed to answer these questions within the context of international relations (Rousseau 2006).

How do individuals in a country such as the United States construct a collective American identity, and how stable is this construction across time and space? Consider the process through which individuals construct opinions in response to survey questions. Sudman, Bradburn, and Schwarz (1996) present a four-step model of opinion formation. First, the respondent must interpret the question. Second, the respondent must generate an opinion. In some cases, the individual simply retrieves the opinion from memory. However, in many if not most instances, individuals do not hold readily accessible responses for survey questions (Sudman, Bradburn, and Schwarz 1996: 70). When faced with this situation, individuals compute a response using accessible information. How this is done is still a matter of great controversy. The traditional explanation proposes that individuals simply balance salient considerations for and against the proposition retrieved from memory (Dawes 1979; Keeney and Raiffa 1976; Zaller 1992). Third, the respondent must format the response for closed-ended questions. Finally, the respondent must decide whether to edit the response. For instance, individuals may feel reluctant to report to the interviewer that they watch 27 hours of television a week.

We believe that a similar process takes place when constructing collective identities of the self and other. For example, when a survey research organization telephones an American citizen and asks, "Should Japan become a permanent member of the United Nations Security Council?" this individual must immediately construct some image of Japan. This image will be based on the categorization of Japan and the United States along a set of dimensions (e.g., beliefs, values, norms, attitudes). If the individual were asked this question repeatedly across time, we would find that he or she tended to rely on a handful of dimensions to categorize the other state. That is, while the individual would probably not construct the same image of Japan on every occasion, there would be a discernible pattern to his or her responses across time.

In Figure 4.1, we present the hypothetical case of "Jane Doe." Jane tends to use eight different dimensions to evaluate Japan, ranging from wealth to great power status. However, these dimensions are "latent" in that they are in memory but not necessarily immediately available. On any given day, only a subset of the latent

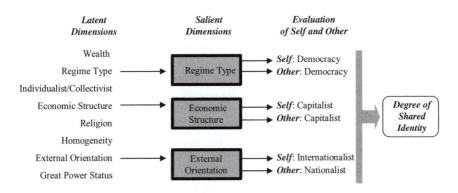

Figure 4.1 The aggregation of latent and salient identity dimensions

dimensions will be "salient" or readily accessible. Only dimensions that are salient influence the construction of the opinion (e.g., influence the aggregation process). In Figure 4.1, we see that on this particular day, three dimensions are salient: regime type, economic structure, and external orientation. Jane Doe evaluates both her own country and the other country using these salient dimensions. She concludes that both countries are democratic and capitalist but that the United States is more internationalist than Japan. Her net assessment is that the two states are pretty similar (but not identical).

The process is iterative in that the individual's assessment of the self may make certain dimensions more salient for the construction of the other and vice versa (Hopf 2002). So when Jane Doe thinks of the United States, certain dimensions come to mind, and when she thinks of Japan, other dimensions come to mind. Ultimately, a comparison will be made on each dimension because both countries are salient. For example, if Jane Doe believes Japan is different because it is Buddhist, she is implicitly categorizing the United States as non-Buddhist. More important, the process is a subjective assessment. Although surveys indicate that more Japanese citizens profess adherence to the Shinto religion than to Buddhism, this "objective" fact is irrelevant to the subjective assessment of Jane Doe. If she believes Japan is a Buddhist country, her categorization scheme will reflect this belief. Moreover, the categorization will ultimately influence the degree of perceived shared identity and her perception of threat (Gries 2005: 237).

How does this conceptualization of identity creation relate to threat perception? The construction of threat model claims that the perception of threat is a function of the line drawn between the in-group and the out-group. The model predicts that power influences people's threat perceptions only after identity between the self and the other has been established. If the other is completely unlike the self (i.e., if no shared identity exists), the material balance of power between the self and the other will be a good predictor of threat perception. However, the higher the level of shared identity between the self and the other, the less threatening the other will appear. In the extreme case in which the other and the self are members of the same in-group, the other will not be seen as a threat regardless of the particular balance of power. In sum, the construction of threat model predicts that both a shared sense of identity and power interact with each other when influencing people's threat perceptions.

The perception of a highly similar or shared identity will also have important consequences in terms of affect, beliefs, and behaviors (Crisp and Hewstone 2006). The greater the sense of shared identity, the stronger the affective attachment the individual will have toward the other (see Figure 4.2). In addition, a shared sense of identity will lead individuals to categorize themselves as closer to the other. Thus, shared identity will manifest itself in both "hot" emotional and "cold" cognitive terms. More important, a shared sense of identity will decrease the belief that the other has the intention to inflict negative consequences on the individual. Therefore, a shared sense of identity will alter behavior by increasing the willingness of the individual to cooperate with the other. Returning to our example of Jane Doe, if she believes that the United States and Japan share a common identity, she

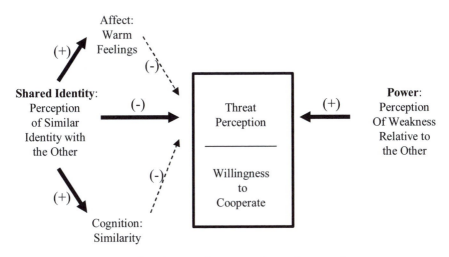

Figure 4.2 Competing explanations for threat perception and cooperation

should believe that Japan is less threatening than other states, and she should be more willing to take a chance on cooperating with Japan because the risks of exploitation are lower. Therefore, by making specific attitudes and beliefs salient, shared identity increases the probability of cooperation.

Experiment #1: abstract scenario in the United States

Experiment #1 tests whether a perception of threat posed by another country is influenced by the material balance of power and/or a shared sense of identity. The experiment employed an abstract scenario involving two unnamed countries engaged in a territorial dispute (Geva and Hanson 1999). Specifically, participants were asked to play the role of a foreign policy advisor in an unnamed country. They were informed that a simmering international dispute had erupted into conflict, and they were asked to advise their boss on the best possible course of action. The scenario was intentionally vague with respect to the party responsible for the outbreak of fighting. After completing the short scenario, participants answered a series of questions about the source of conflict and the utility of using military force.

The experimental survey varied along two dichotomous dimensions: the balance of military forces between the countries (strong vs. weak power) and the degree of shared identity between the countries (shared vs. non-shared identity). Our main experimental hypotheses then focused on the relationship between power, identity, and threat perception. The causal process linking these elements is illustrated in Figure 4.2. Specifically, we hypothesized the following:

Hypothesis 1: Power If the foreign country is framed as a strong military power, then the participant's perception of threat will increase. This hypothesis is derived from the realist school of thought in international relations (Mearsheimer 2001;

Waltz 1979) and the realistic conflict theory of social psychology (Levine and Campbell 1972; Sherif 1966).

Hypothesis 2: Identity   If the foreign country is framed as similar to the home country (e.g., similar language, religions, and culture), then the perception of threat will decrease. This hypothesis is derived from the social constructivism school of thought in international relations (Wendt 1999) and the SIT in psychology (Tafjel 1978).

Hypothesis 3: Interaction between power and identity   While most explanations treat power and identity as completely independent dimensions, the construction of threat model predicts an interactive effect. At one theoretical extreme, in which identity is completely shared, power asymmetries should have no impact on threat perception. At the other theoretical extreme, in which no shared identity exists at all, power will determine threat perception. Between these theoretical extremes (in which most real-world cases will fall), we should observe that the degree of shared identity modulates the impact of power asymmetries on threat perception. Therefore, if a foreign country is framed as both a strong military power and diverging from democratic institutions and a market economy, then the perception of threat should increase beyond what one should expect from a simple linear additive model.

Hypothesis 4: Similarity   If the foreign country is framed as having an identity similar to the home country, then the perceived similarity between the countries will increase. This manipulation check probes the cold cognitive causal mechanism behind the shared identity claim. If the identity manipulation does not produce a recategorization of the other with respect to the self, we cannot claim to have a strong understanding of the causal mechanisms supporting the theoretical predictions.

Hypothesis 5: Affect   If the foreign country is framed as having an identity similar to the home country, then the positive affect toward the foreign country will increase (Furia and Lucas 2006). In addition to providing a robustness check for the identity manipulation, this hypothesis explores whether the shared sense of identity is, in part, the function of a hot affective process. While it is possible for the identity manipulation to only increase the perceived similarity between countries, it could also trigger positive affect toward the other.

To probe the robustness of the analysis, the survey included several questions that allow us to control for competing explanations that fall outside the central focus of our study. Although the results reported below are statistically significant with or without these controls, the controls have been reported to reassure the reader that competing arguments have been explored systematically. Hypothesis 6 predicts that individuals with realist belief systems are more likely to view the other as threatening than individuals with liberal belief systems. Rousseau (2002) has shown that participants scoring high on a realist–liberal index are more likely to view other states as threatening and more likely to support the use of military force to resolve conflicts. The realist–liberal variable has a theoretic range of –20 (extreme liberal views) to +20 (extreme realist views). The exact wording of the questions used to create the realist–liberal variable appears in Rousseau and Garcia-Retamero 2007. Hypothesis 7 predicts that male participants are more likely to view the other as threatening (Heskin and Power 1994). Hypothesis 8 predicts that American participants are more likely to take a militarist view of international politics and therefore perceive the other as threatening (Hurwitz *et al.* 1993). Finally, Hypothesis 9 predicts that self-described "conservative" participants are more likely to view outsiders as threatening than non-conservative participants (i.e., self-described middle of the road or liberal; Heskin and Power 1994). Conservatism was self-reported using a question virtually identical to that used in the American National Election Study.

Participants and procedure

The experiment was conducted in the United States during the fall semester of 2004 at the University of Pennsylvania with a sample of 169 undergraduates enrolled in introductory political science classes. The sample included 102 men and 67 women. All participants were between the ages of 18 and 25. The ethnicity survey question indicated that the sample was 65 percent white, 20 percent Asian, 3 percent black, 3 percent Hispanic, and 9 percent "other" (or refused to answer). The participants were offered extra credit for participating in a one-hour experiment exploring the role of news coverage in international affairs. After completing an initial survey and "distracting" sorting exercise, the participants were randomly assigned to one of four scenarios based on the balance of military power and the degree of shared identity between the countries. The wording of all versions of the scenarios appears in Rousseau and Garcia-Retamero 2007.

The power and identity hypotheses were tested using a 2 × 2 between-subjects experimental research design. The scenarios varied along two dichotomous dimensions:

1 the balance of military forces (strong vs. weak); and
2 the degree of shared identity in terms of ancestry, language, and religion (shared identity vs. no shared identity).

In the "strong opponent" scenario, the army and navy of the southern neighbor were described as double the size of the "home" state. In the "weak opponent" scenario, the situation was reversed. In the shared identity scenario, the southern neighbor was described as sharing a common language, culture, and religion. In the "different identity" scenario, the two hypothetical states did not share any similar dimensions. After reading the scenario, participants answered a short twelve-question survey. The manipulation checks in this survey indicated that only 2 of the 169 participants could not correctly identify either the balance of power between the two states or the degree of cultural similarity. While the findings reported here include these 2 participants, the results are virtually identical if the 2 participants are deleted from the sample.

Dependent variables

The experiment explores three dependent variables: threat perceptions, feelings of warmth, and perceptions of similarity.

1   Threat perceptions. On a 10-point scale, participants evaluated how much of a military threat the neighboring country in the scenario represents. A score of 0 meant no threat at all, and a score of 10 meant extremely threatening.
2   Perceptions of similarity. On a 5-point Likert scale, participants estimated the extent to which they view the neighboring country as similar or dissimilar to the home country, ranging from very similar to very dissimilar.
3   Feelings of warmth. On a scale ranging from 0 to 100, participants estimated their feelings toward the neighboring country. Ratings between 50 and 100 meant that they felt favorable and warm toward the neighbor. Ratings between 0 and 50 meant that they did not feel favorable toward the neighbor. A rating of exactly 50 meant that they did not feel particularly warm or cold. For many years, the American National Election Study has used this type of "feeling thermometer" to measure how much respondents like particular candidates and political parties.

Results from experiment #1

The hypotheses are tested using regression analysis with robust standard errors. Table 4.1, which displays models 1, 2, and 3, presents results using the "threat perception" dependent variable, which ranges from 0 (no threat) to 10 (extremely threatening) and has a mean of 6.6 in our sample. Model 1 presents the results with the two variables manipulated in the experiment; model 2 adds an interactive variable to the equation. Finally, model 3 includes all the control variables controlling for competing explanations. Given that the coefficients and standard errors are stable across the three models, we will restrict our discussion to model 3.

Hypothesis 1 predicts that if the other state is powerful, then the perception of threat should increase. The results in model 3 strongly support this realist claim; the coefficient is positive ($b = 2.15$; $SE = 0.34$) and statistically significant at the better than the 0.001 level of significance. Hypothesis 2, which predicts that a shared identity will decrease threat perception, is also supported by the data. The coefficient is negative as expected ($b = -0.59$; $SE = 0.28$) and statistically significant at the better than the 0.05 level of significance. The much larger size of the power coefficient indicates that the marginal impact of the power manipulation was about four times the marginal impact of the identity manipulation. But despite this asymmetry, the analysis clearly demonstrates that both power and identity matter; realists focusing only on the material balance of power and constructivists focusing

Table 4.1 Experiment #1: regression with threat dependent variable

Independent variables	Model 1 Dependent variable: Threat perception (range 0–10) OLS	Model 2 Dependent variable: Threat perception (range 0–10) OLS	Model 3 Dependent variable: Threat perception (range 0–10) OLS
Unfavorable Balance of Power	2.14*** 0.24	2.07*** 0.33	2.15*** 0.34
Shared Identity	−0.61** 0.25	−0.54* 0.27	−0.59* 0.28
Interaction: Strong* Different Power Identity	—	−0.13 0.49	−0.06 0.49
Realist–Liberal Index	—	—	0.005 0.02
Male	—	—	−0.31 0.25
American	—	—	0.41 0.43
Self-described Conservative	—	—	0.20 0.28
Constant	8.03 0.17	7.99 0.16	7.81 0.48
Number of Observations	169	169	169
Probability > F (6, 162)	0.000	0.000	0.000
R-squared	0.33	.033	0.34

Notes: Model estimated with Stata 8.0 using robust standard errors. Standard errors appear below the estimated coefficients. All significance tests are one-tailed. *$p<.05$, **$p<.01$, ***$p<.001$.

only on ideational factors miss half the story. Finally, model 3 indicates that there is no interactive impact of these variables; the interactive term is not statistically different from zero in Table 4.1.

None of the remaining control variables in model 3 are statistically significant. Realists are no more likely to view the "southern neighbor" as more threatening than liberals. Threat assessments by males and Americans are no different from their female and non-American counterparts. Nor are conservatives more likely to view the other as threatening compared with liberals.

Models 4 and 5, which are displayed in Table 4.2, probe the causal mechanisms behind the identity argument. In model 4, the dependent variable is the perception of similarity. After the scenario, participants were asked, "Do you view your southern neighbor as similar or dissimilar to your country?" For coding purposes, the response categories were collapsed into similar (very or somewhat) and dissimilar (very or somewhat). The probit analysis using this dichotomous variable indicates that the shared identity scenario significantly increases the categorization

Table 4.2 Experiment #1: regression with warmth and similarity dependent variables

Independent variables	Model 4 Dependent variable: Similarity perception (range 0/1) Probit	Model 5 Dependent variable: Warmth perception (range: 0–100) OLS
Unfavorable Balance of Power	−0.48 0.42	0.78 3.42
Shared Identity	2.33*** 0.37	12.35*** 3.54
Interaction: Strong* Different Power Identity	0.87 0.56	3.93 4.78
Realist–Liberal Index	−0.01 0.02	−0.15 0.27
Male	0.04 0.28	−1.41 2.36
American	−0.2 0.55	−5.28 4.29
Self-described Conservative	−0.74 0.32	−0.4 3.1
Constant	0.97 0.57	34.75 4.49
Number of Observations	169	169
Probability > F (6, 162)	—	0
R-squared	0.57 (pseudo)	0.019
Log Likelihood	−50.8	—

Notes: Model estimated with Stata 8.0 using robust standard errors. Standard errors appear below the estimated coefficients. All significance tests are one-tailed. *$p<.05$, **$p<.01$, ***$p<.001$.

of states as similar (b = 2.33; SE = 0.37). The marginal impact of the variable is quite large. Using Clarify software to calculate the marginal impacts, we find that a shift from no shared identity to shared identity increases the predicted probability of perceiving the states as similar by approximately 74 percentage points when holding all other variables at their means or modes (Tomz *et al.* 2003). In contrast, neither the favorable balance of power nor any of the control variables have a statistically significant impact on the categorization of the other.

In model 5, the dependent variable is the level of positive affect felt toward the other. The warmth variable has a mean of 36 degrees, a standard deviation of 17 degrees, and a range of 5 to 100 degrees in our sample. The results in model 5 strongly support hypothesis 5: the shared identity scenario produces much warmer feelings toward the other. The estimated coefficient (b = 12.35; SE = 3.54) is statistically significant at the better than the 0.001 level of significance. A shift from a dissimilar to similar identity increases the warmth felt toward the other by over 12 degrees. Thus, the identity manipulation influenced both the participant's cold cognitive categorization process and a hot affective process. As with the previous model, neither the prevailing balance of power nor the control variables had an impact on the assessment of warmth.

Experiment #2: abstract scenario in Spain

In experiment #2, we replicate the central findings of the prior experiment with one important difference: to demonstrate the cross-national applicability of the construction of threat model, we test the hypotheses using Spanish participants rather than American participants. Although countries may differ with respect to the most common dimensions used to separate the self from the other, we expect the process of identity construction at the individual level to be similar across countries. The hypothetical territorial dispute scenario was translated into Spanish, and the experiment was administered at a Spanish university. As in the last experiment, the scenarios varied along two dimensions: the balance of military forces between the countries (strong vs. weak power) and the degree of shared identity between them (shared vs. non-shared identity). Given the absence of significant results for the control variables in the prior study, this experiment focused solely on the five hypotheses tested in the first study: the power hypothesis, the identity hypothesis, the interaction hypothesis, the similarity hypothesis, and the affect hypothesis.

Participants and procedure

The participants in experiment #2 were 112 undergraduates enrolled in a psychology course from the University of Granada (Spain) in the spring of 2005. The participants included 46 men and 66 women. They had a median age of 20 years (range 17 to 55), and all were Caucasian. They were randomly assigned to one of four groups based on the power and identity of the framed country. The participants received course credit for their participation in the experiment. The hypothetical scenario, survey questions, and dependent variables were virtually identical to experiment #1 (see Rousseau and Garcia-Retamero (2007: 767) for minor changes made to frame identity in the Spanish context).

Results from experiment #2

The results of experiment #2 appear in Table 4.3. As predicted by realist theories, an unfavorable balance of power increased the perception of threat (see model 1 Table 4.3). The coefficient is positive ($b = 2.71$; $SE = 0.52$) and statistically significant at the better than the 0.001 level of significance. Similarly, the data strongly support the identity hypothesis proposed by constructivists. Describing the two states as having a similar culture, religion, and language significantly decreased the perception of a military threat. The estimated coefficient is negative ($b = -1.07$; $SE = 0.44$) and statistically significant at the better than the 0.01 level of

Table 4.3 Experiment #2: regression with threat, warmth, and similarity dependent variables

Independent variables	Model 1 Dependent variable: Threat perception (range 0–10) OLS	Model 2 Dependent variable: Similarity perception (range 0/1) OLS	Model 3 Dependent variable: Warmth perception (range: 0–100) Probit
Unfavorable Balance of Power	2.71*** 0.52	−0.34 0.57	3.32 5.16
Shared Identity	−1.07** 0.44	2.37*** 0.51	11.29** 4.31
Interaction: Strong* Different Power Identity	1.73** 0.65	−0.16 0.69	−0.15 0.27
Constant	4.25*** 0.29	0.57** 0.25	33.98 4.42
Number of Observations	112	112	112
Probability > F (6, 162)	0.000	—	0.000
R-squared	0.60	0.47 (pseudo)	0.019
Log Likelihood	—	−39.8	—

Notes: Model estimated with Stata 8.0 using robust standard errors. Standard errors appear below the estimated coefficients. All significance tests are one-tailed. *$p<.05$, **$p<.01$, ***$p<.001$.

significance. As was the case in the first experiment, the balance of power has a more powerful impact than the shared identity variable. Unlike the first experiment, the interaction term, which isolates the situation in which the opposing state is strong and culturally different, produces a positive ($b = 1.73$; $SE = 0.65$) and statistically significant coefficient. Although the addition of this interactive term slightly weakens the power and identity coefficients, it does not alter the conclusions we draw from the results of the regression. Thus, both power and identity influence threat perception, and the most feared states of all have both the power to injure and a different identity.

As predicted by the similarity hypothesis, the identity manipulation increased the closeness of the categorization of the self and the other (see model 2 Table 4.3). The shared identity coefficient was positive, as predicted ($b = 2.37$; $SE = 0.51$), and statistically significant at the better than the 0.001 level of significance. The marginal analysis indicates that a shift from no shared identity to shared identity increases the predicted probability of perceiving the states as similar by approximately 60 percentage points when holding all other variables at their means or modes (Tomz *et al.* 2003). Neither the power manipulation nor the interaction term produced significant changes in the assessment of similarity.

Finally, Table 4.3 also shows that as predicted by the affect hypothesis, the identity manipulation increased a sense of warmth toward the southern neighbor (see model 3). The warmth dependent variable has a mean of 50 degrees, a standard deviation of 17 degrees, and a range from 10 to 99 degrees. Describing the other state as religiously, linguistically, and culturally similar led to a statistically significant increase in warmth (b = 11.29; SE = 4.31; p<0.05). A shift from different identity to similar identity increases the sense of warmth by just over 11 degrees. In contrast, neither the power manipulation nor the interaction term had an impact on the perception of warmth.

Experiment #3: concrete situation in Spain

The purpose of experiment #3 was threefold. First, we wanted to alter the power and identity manipulations to demonstrate that a very minor difference in a framing could produce the types of dependent variable changes seen in the previous two studies. Therefore, the manipulation in experiment #3 begins with a very short introduction (approximately 85 words) in which shared identity and power are framed for the participants (Hiscox 2006). This new manipulation is suitable for both a paper and pencil study (employed in the current study) and a telephone survey with a nationally representative sample (which we hope to employ in future research to demonstrate the generalizability of our findings). Moreover, we employed a real world situation rather than a hypothetical scenario to probe the robustness of previous findings. Critics of laboratory experiments often claim the studies lack external validity because the manipulations are abstract and devoid of real-world content (e.g., studying responses to alpha or beta state). Thus, in this experiment, we tackle the much more difficult task of manipulating perceptions of power and perceptions of identity of a real-world great power: Russia.

Second, we investigate the interaction between identity and power in the decision process. Although most versions of realism and constructivism predict that only power or only identity matters, the empirical findings in the previous studies

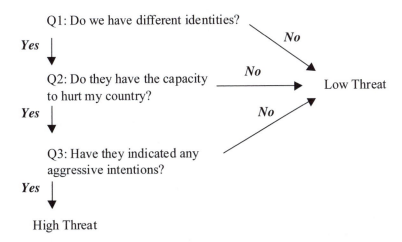

Figure 4.3 Simple heuristic for threat assessment privileging identity

indicate both factors play a central role in threat perception. But how do these two variables interact in the decision process? Participants could simply average over two independent variables (Meyer 1981). However, the significance of the interactive term in the second experiment hints at a more interesting relationship. For example, participants might use a simple heuristic that privileges one dimension over the other. This type of decision-making heuristic is referred to as a "fast and frugal decision tree" (see Martignon *et al.* 2003). Figure 4.3, which is adapted from the work of Gigerenzer, Todd, and the ABC Research Group (1999: 4), displays a fast and frugal decision tree heuristic that privileges identity (Rousseau 2006: 217). In this heuristic, power and identity are treated as dichotomous variables. The individual begins the decision process by asking: is the other state a member of the outgroup? If the answer is yes, the individual asks a second question: does the other state have more power than my state? If the answer to this second question is also a yes, then the other state is classified as a threat. While the simple fast and frugal decision tree is valuable because it does not involve any computationally difficult averaging for individuals, it does privilege one variable by placing it first in the series of questions. More important, the heuristic implies that power asymmetries and dissimilar identities are necessary conditions for the perception of threat: only if a foreign country is framed as both a strong military power and diverging from democratic institutions and a market economy will the perception of threat increase.

Finally, the third experiment examines the public policy implications of the manipulations of power and identity. Although the prior two laboratory studies established the fact that shared identity decreases threat perception and military weakness increases threat perception, the experiments did not demonstrate that public policy positions (e.g., trade and investment with the other) would be impacted by the assessment. Therefore, we hypothesize that if the foreign country is framed as becoming more like the home country, then individuals will be more willing to support cooperation (e.g., a trade treaty, an arms control agreement, and trade in general) with the foreign country.

Thus, we test four hypotheses in this third experiment: the power hypothesis, the identity hypothesis, the revised interaction hypothesis, and the new public policy hypothesis.

Participants and procedure

The participants were 112 undergraduates enrolled in psychology from the University of Granada (Spain) in the spring of 2005. The participants included 50 men and 62 women; all participants were Caucasian. Participants had a median age of twenty years (range 18 to 51). The participants, who received course credit for participating in the experiment, were randomly assigned to one of four groups based on the balance of military power and the degree of shared identity between the countries.

Participants completed a 20 minute questionnaire that began with a very short paragraph (approximately 85 words) framing the power and collective identity of

Russia relative to Spain and the European Union. The four introductory descriptions delivered at the start of the experiment are reproduced in Rousseau and Garcia-Retamero 2007. For illustrative purposes, the condition "strong power" and "similar identity" is presented here:

> We would like to ask you a few questions about relations with Russia. Many people focus on the fact that the Russians have increased defense spending by over 10 percent a year for the last several years. Many others believe that Russia is becoming more like the countries of the European Union due to the expanding role of markets in the economy and recent increases in freedom of expression and assembly for many groups in society. We are interested in your opinions.

The assignment of the order of the statements about the balance of military power and identity in the scenario was counterbalanced across participants. Given that we did not find significant differences between assignments, the results reported below are based on an analysis across assignments. Following the introductory scenario, participants were asked a series of questions that directly tested our hypotheses. The resulting factorial design of experiment #3 was a 2 (balance of military power: strong vs. weak power) × 2 (degree of shared identity: shared vs. non-shared identity) between-subjects design.

Dependent variables

In the third experiment, we employ two dependent variables: threat perception and willingness to cooperate.

1   Threat perceptions. On a 10-point scale, participants evaluated how much of a military threat Russia is to the countries of the European Union. A score of 0 in both questions meant no threat at all and a score of 10 meant extremely threatening.
2   Policy cooperation assessments. On a 5-point scale, participants evaluated whether they would favor or oppose:

   a   an international trade agreement that results in small economic gains by the countries of the European Union but major economic gains by Russia,
   b   cutting troop totals by 50,000 for both Spain and Russia, and
   c   increasing trade with Russia. For the statistical analysis presented below, we created a dichotomous "favors cooperation" by combining the "strongly favors" and the "somewhat favors" categories.

Results from experiment #3

The results from the regression analysis with the threat dependent variable are presented in Table 4.4. Given that the central findings are similar with or without the interaction term, we will restrict our discussion to model 2 in Table 4.4. As with the

Table 4.4 Experiment #3: regression with threat and dependent variable

Independent variables	Model 1 Dependent variable: Threat perception (range 0–10) OLS	Model 2 Dependent variable: Threat perception (range 0–10) OLS
Unfavorable Balance of Power	2.29*** 0.40	1.46** 0.56
Shared Identity	−2.64*** 0.40	−1.82*** 0.55
Interaction: Strong* Different Power Identity	—	1.64* 0.79
Constant	3.23*** 0.91	3.54*** 0.40
Number of Observations	112	112
Probability > F (3, 108)	0.000	0.000
R-squared	0.41	0.43

Notes: Model estimated with Stata 8.0 using robust standard errors. Standard errors appear below the estimated coefficients. All significance tests are one-tailed. *$p<.05$, **$p<.01$, ***$p<.001$.

first two experiments, we once again find that an unfavorable military balance increases the perception of threat. The estimated coefficient is positive (b = 1.46; SE = 0.56) and statistically significant at the better than the 0.01 level of significance. Conversely, emphasizing a shared identity between Spain and Russia decreased threat perception. The shared identity coefficient is negative (b =−1.82; SE = 0.55) and statistically significant at the better than the 0.001 level of significance. Unlike the prior two experiments, the identity variable has a larger marginal impact than the power variable in the real-world situation. Finally, model 2 indicates that the interaction between identity and power is positive (b = 1.64; SE = 0.79) and statistically significant at the 0.05 level. When the other state is described as both more powerful and possessing a different identity, the perception of threat grows above and beyond simply summing the impact of the two independent variables.

But how are participants using the interaction? The Interaction Hypothesis predicted a simple necessary condition heuristic: states would only be viewed as threatening if they possessed both a different identity and greater military power. The results in Table 4.5 do not support this type of heuristic. The interaction hypothesis correctly predicts that the highest level of military threat perception occurs when Russia was described a strong power with a non-shared identity (mean threat equals 6.64). However, the necessary condition hypothesis also predicts that the values in all the remaining cells should be low and indistinguishable from each other. This is not the case. Moreover, a purely realist explanation has trouble

Table 4.5 Military threat assessments by treatment in experiment #3

	Shared identity		Non-shared identity	
	Weak power	Strong power	Weak power	Strong power
Military threat	1.71_a (1.98)	3.18_b (2.21)	3.54_b (2.15)	6.64_c (2.04)

Notes: The means and deviations (in parentheses) about identity and power. Military threat was measuring using a scale ranging from 1 to 10. The means that do not share a common subscript differ at the 0.05 level or lower by Tukey's HSD test.

explaining the results because it would predict both strong power conditions would trigger a similar level in threat regardless of identity (i.e., realists expect the 3.18 mean would be expected to be closer to the 6.64 mean). Similarly, a purely constructivist explanation has trouble explaining the results because it would predict both shared identity conditions would trigger a similar level of threat (i.e., constructivists expect the 1.71 mean would be expected to be close to the 3.18 mean). Thus, while the necessary condition hypothesis (or fast and frugal decision tree hypothesis) failed with respect to military threat, the findings strongly support a positive interaction between the power variable and the identity variable.

The final set of analyses, which is displayed in Table 4.6, explores the policy implications of the framing experiment. The survey question examined in model 1 asked, "Would you support or oppose an international trade agreement that results in small economic gains by Spain, but major economic gains by Russia?" Fifty-two percent of the participants supported such an agreement either somewhat or strongly. The survey question is important because wording explicitly states that

Table 4.6 Experiment #3: impact of identity and power on policy positions

	Model 1 Dependent variable:	Model 2 Dependent variable:	Model 3 Dependent variable:
	Support for trade agreement	Support for cutting military personnel	Support for increasing trade
Independent variables	Probit	Probit	Probit
Unfavorable Balance of Power	0.27 0.24	−0.51* 0.25	0.35 0.29
Shared Identity	0.45* 0.24	0.31 0.25	0.79** 0.30
Constant	−0.32 0.21	0.38* 0.21	0.40* 0.23
Number of Observations	112	112	112
Wald chi2(2)	4.79	5.54	−7.80
prob > chi2	0.09	0.06	0.02
Log Likelihood	−75.1	−67.5	−49.6

Notes: Model estimated with Stata 8.0 using robust standard errors. Standard errors appear below the estimated coefficients. All significance tests are one-tailed. *$p<.05$, **$p<.01$, ***$p<.001$.

Russia will achieve relative gains from the agreement. Realists such as Waltz (1979) and Grieco (1988) expect leaders to be wary of relative gains by other states. The results in model 1 of Table 4.6 indicate that framing Russia as a member of the in-group increases support for the trade agreement despite the disproportionate gains by Russia (b = 0.45; SE = 0.24, p<0.05). In contrast, the framing of power had no impact. A second survey question probed support for defense cuts that were equal in absolute terms but relatively larger for Spain because of its smaller military. Model 2 in Table 4.6 indicates that when the issue area is military affairs, participants are less willing to support such an agreement when in a position of military weakness (b = –0.51; SE = 0.25, p<0.05). In this case, shared identity did not influence the policy preference. Finally, a third survey question explored support for increasing trade with Russia in general. Overall, 81 percent of the participants supported increasing trade either somewhat or strongly. However, while the military balance did not influence support for increasing trade, when Russia was described as becoming more like Spain, support for increasing trade grew significantly (b = 0.79; SE = 0.30, p<0.01). In sum, the framing of the other in terms of power and identity had a powerful impact on public policies regulating interaction between the two societies.

General discussion

Realists tend to emphasize material factors because power is viewed as the best predictor of threat (Waltz 1986: 329), and it is relatively easy to measure (Waltz 1979: 98, 131). In contrast, many constructivists tend to focus exclusively on ideational factors. The three experiments discussed here suggest both these exclusive viewpoints are misguided; both power and identity influence threat perception. In all three experiments, a position of military weakness increased the perception of threat, and a different identity increased the perception of threat. This was true for both American participants and Spanish participants. This was also true in both hypothetical and real-world situations. Furthermore, this was true even after controlling for several alternative explanations for threat perception in experiment #1.

In addition, there is a strong interaction between power and identity. In experiments #2 and #3, the interactive term was positive and statistically significant. In other words, specific combinations of power and identity (e.g., both military strength and a different identity) produced an increase in threat perception more than the simply additive impact of each independent variable. This raises a very interesting question: how are power and identity combined in the calculation of threat? Unfortunately, constructivist theories of international relations developed to date provide little guidance on this issue. Solving this empirical puzzle will require us to turn to the decision analysis literature. Although the "necessary condition" interaction hypothesis (or fast and frugal decision tree hypothesis) drawn from this literature was not confirmed in experiment #3, scratching this explanation off the long list of plausible explanations is an important first step toward solving this critical question.

It is important to note that not all constructivist scholars neglect material factors. Wendt (1999), for example, is one of the few authors that explicitly links identity and power in a model of systemic conflict and cooperation. While power tends to dominate considerations in a Hobbesian world and identity dominates calculations in a Kantian world, Wendt claims that both power and identity influence state assessments and international patterns in the intermediate Lockean world. Unfortunately, Wendt's desire to create a systemic social theory of international politics (to directly challenge Waltz's systemic realist theory of international politics) leads him to explicitly "black box" the state and implicitly drop individuals from the analysis. In his review of Wendt's book, Smith (2000: 161) asks, "Where in Wendt's model are the only moving forces in the social world: human beings?" The answer is nowhere. As with Smith, we contend that it is impossible to develop a complete social theory of international politics without explaining the role of people in the process.

The construction of threat model proposed in this article provides an individual level mechanism that explains the interaction of power and identity. It articulates the causal mechanisms at the individual level that can explain how humans can create the Hobbesian, Lockean, and Kantian worlds that Wendt discusses at the systemic level. Although the purpose of this article has been to provide empirical support for the model at the individual level, it provides a foundation for discussion diffusion at the state and international levels (Rousseau and van der Veen 2005; Rousseau 2006).

Finally, the construction of threat model provides a precise and fully specified way to synthesize realism and liberalism into a single framework. International relations scholars have long sought to integrate the two models in a systemic fashion. For example, in *Power and Interdependence*, Keohane and Nye (1977) proposed a continuum from "pure realism" to "complex interdependence." As one moved toward the realist pole, the authors expected realist theories to have greater explanatory power. Similarly, Grieco (1988) proposed a "k" factor that measured the salience of relative gains. As k became closer to 1.0, we moved toward a zero-sum realist world of pure competition. The construction of threat model contends that identity is an important explanation for placement on Keohane and Nye's (1977) continuum and for the level of Grieco's k. The experimental evidence demonstrates that identity moderates the subject's interpretation of the material balance of power. When shared identity is high, threat perception and the salience of relative gains are lower. This increases the probability of unilateral, bilateral, and multilateral cooperation. Conversely, when shared identity is low, threat perception and the salience of relative gains are higher. In this Hobbesian world, cooperation is more difficult. Thus, shared identity is a crucial variable that determines whether individuals behave according to the predictions of realism or liberalism.

Conclusion

Threat inflation is a hot topic today in both the popular press and academic research. The American foreign policy disaster in Iraq has fueled this interest and has led to calls from both liberals and conservatives for more accurate threat assessments. Unfortunately, the central findings of this chapter highlight how difficult this task will be because the evidence demonstrates that threats are social constructs that include both material and ideational factors. Threats cannot simply be measured using objective material factors such as the number of missiles or infantry divisions possessed by another state; ideational factors such as the degree of shared identity are an important part of the threat formula. This finding makes determining whether a threat is inflated – whether it "goes beyond the scope and urgency that disinterested analysis would justify" – extremely difficult. If ideational factors add variance to the threat assessment distribution, we should expect a broad range of threat assessments even if there is agreement on the level and consequences of material factors. Just how far from the modal point would an assessment have to be in order to be labeled as biased?

This chapter has demonstrated that both power and ideas are central to threat assessments. In the process, we have shown that the particular frame chosen for describing the "other" has an important impact on the threat assessment. We should expect politicians to carefully select from among alternative frames as they attempt to maximize the persuasive power of their argument. However, it would be misleading to assume that politicians are the only ones selecting frames. We suspect that everyone (i.e., politicians, intelligence analysts, and average citizens) selects particular claims and evidence because they are salient or readily available in that society. Intelligence analysts and average citizens interested in making a "strong" argument have to be cognizant of framing and willing to probe competing claims even more rigorously. Recognizing that threats are a social construct naturally heightens ones awareness of this perennial problem.

Note

This chapter is adapted from Rousseau and Garcia-Retamero 2007. We would like to thank Sage Publications for permission to reproduce portions of that article.

References

Bachrach, P. and Baratz, M. S. (1962) "Two faces of power," *American Political Science Review*, 56: 947–52.
—— (1963) "Decisions and nondecisions: An analytical framework," *American Political Science Review*, 57: 632–42.
Brewer, M. B. and Brown, R. J. (1998) "Intergroup relations," in D. T. Gilbert, S. T. Fiske and G. Lindzey (eds) *The Handbook of Social Psychology*, 4th edn, Boston, MA: McGraw-Hill.
Crisp, R. J. and Hewstone, M. (2006) *Multiple Social Categorization: Processes, Models, and Applications*, New York: Psychology Press.
Dahl, R. A. (1957) "The concept of power," *Behavioral Science*, 2: 201–5.
Davis, J. W. (2000) *Threats and Promises: The Pursuit of International Influence*, Baltimore, MD: Johns Hopkins University Press.
Dawes, R. M. (1979) "The robust beauty of improper linear models in decision making," *American Psychologist*, 34: 571–82.

Doyle, M. W. (1997) *Ways of War and Peace: Realism, Liberalism, and Socialism*, New York: Norton.

Fiske, S. T. (1993) "Controlling other people: The impact of power on stereotyping," *American Psychologist*, 48: 621–8.

Furia, P. A. and Lucas, R. E. (2006) "Determinants of Arab public opinion on foreign relations," *International Studies Quarterly,* 50: 585–605.

Geva, N. and Hanson, D. C. (1999) "Cultural similarity, foreign policy actions, and regime perception: An experimental study of international cues and democratic peace," *Political Psychology*, 20: 803–27.

Gigerenzer, G., Todd, P. M. and the ABC Research Group (1999) *Simple Heuristics That Make Us Smart*, Oxford, UK: Oxford University Press.

Grieco, J. M. (1988) "Anarchy and the limits of cooperation: A realist critique of the newest liberal institutionalism," *International Organization*, 42: 485–507.

—— (1990) *Cooperation among Nations: Europe, America, and Non-Tariff Barriers to Trade*, Ithaca, NY: Cornell University Press.

Gries, P. H. (2005) ["Social psychology and the identity-conflict debate: Is a 'China threat' inevitable?"] *European Journal of International Relations*, 11: 235–65.

Gulick, E. V. (1955) *Europe's Classical Balance of Power*, New York: Norton.

Heskin, K. and Power, V. (1994) "The determinants of Australians' attitudes toward the Gulf War," *The Journal of Social Psychology*, 134: 317–31.

Heuer, R. J. (1999) *Psychology of Intelligence Analysis*, Center for the Study of Intelligence, Central Intelligence Agency, Langley, VA.

Hiscox, M. (2006) "Through a glass and darkly: Attitudes toward international trade and the curious effects of issue framing," *International Organization*, 60: 755–80.

Hopf, Ted. (2002) *Constructing Allies at Home: Identities and Interests in Soviet and Russian Foreign Policy, 1955–99*, Ithaca, NY: Cornell University Press.

Hurwitz, J., Peffley, M. and Seligson, M. A. (1993) "Foreign policy belief systems in comparative perspective: The United States and Costa Rica," *International Studies Quarterly*, 37: 245–70.

Jones, J. M. (1972) *Prejudice and Racism*, Philadelphia: Addison-Wesley.

Keeney, R. L. and Raiffa, H. (1976) *Decisions with Multiple Objectives: Preferences and Value Tradeoffs*, New York: John Wiley.

Keohane, R. O. and Nye, J. S. (1977) *Power and Interdependence: World Politics in Transition*, Boston, MA: Little, Brown.

Levine, R. A. and Campbell, D. T. (1972) *Ethnocentrism: Theories of Conflict, Ethnic Attitudes, and Group Behavior*, New York: John Wiley.

Lukes, S. (1974) *Power: A Radical View*, London: Macmillan.

MacKuen, M. B., Erikson, R. S. and Stimson, J A. (1992) "Peasants or bankers? The American electorate and the U.S. economy," *American Journal of Political Science*, 86: 597–611.

Martignon, L., Vitouch, O., Takezawa, M. and Forster, M. R. (2003) "Naive and yet enlightened: From natural frequencies to fast and frugal decision trees," in D. Hardman and L. Macchi (eds) *Thinking: Psychological Perspectives on Reasoning, Judgment and Decision Making*, West Sussex, UK: John Wiley.

Mearsheimer, J. J. (2001) *The Tragedy of Great Power Politics*, New York: Norton.

Meyer, R. J. (1981) "A model of multiattribute judgments under attribute uncertainty and information constraint," *Journal of Marketing Research*, 18: 428–41.

Rousseau, D. L. (2002) "Motivations for choice: The salience of relative gains in international relations," *Journal of Conflict Resolution*, 46: 394–426.

—— (2006) *Identifying Threats and Threatening Identities: The Social Construction of Realism and Liberalism*, Stanford, CA: Stanford University Press.

Rousseau, D. L. and Garcia-Retamero, R. (2007) "Identity, power and threat perception: A cross-national experimental study," *Journal of Conflict Resolution*, 51: 744–71.

Rousseau, D. L. and Maurits van der Veen, A. (2005) "The emergence of a shared identity: A simulation," *Journal of Conflict Resolution*, 49: 686–712.

Sherif, M. (1966) *Group Conflict and Co-operation: Their Social Psychology*, London: Routledge & Kegan Paul.

Sherif, M. and Sherif, C. (1953) *Groups in Harmony and Tension*, New York: Harper.

Simpson, G. and Yinger, J. M. (1985) *Racial and Cultural Minorities: An Analysis of Prejudice and Discrimination*, 5th edn, New York: Plenum.

Smith, S. (2000) "Wendt's world," *Review of International Studies*, 26: 151–63.

Sudman, S., Bradburn, N. M. and Schwarz, N. (1996) *Thinking about Answers: The Application of Cognitive Processes to Survey Methodology*, San Francisco: Jossey-Bass.

Tajfel, H. (1978) "Social categorization, social identity, and social comparison," in H. Tajfel (ed.) *Studies in the Social Psychology of Intergroup Relations*, London: Academic Press.

Tajfel, H. and Turner, J. C. (1979) "An integrative theory of intergroup conflict," in W. Austin and S. Worchel (eds) *The Social Psychology of Intergroup Relations*, Monterey, CA: Brooks/Cole.

Tomz, M., Wittenberg, J. and King, G. (2003) "Clarify: Software for interpreting and presenting statistical results," Unpublished paper, Harvard University, Cambridge, MA.

Turner, J. C. (1985) "Social categorization and the self-concept: A social cognitive theory of group behaviour," in E. J. Lawler (ed.) *Advances in Group Processes: Theory and Research*, vol. 2, Greenwich, CT: Jai, 77–122.

Turner, J. C., Hogg, M. A., Oaks, P. J., Reicher, S. D. and Wetherell, S. M. (1987) *Rediscovering the Social Group: A Self-Categorization Theory*, Oxford: Blackwell.

Waltz, K. N. (1979) *Theory of international politics*, New York: Random House.

—— (1986) "A response to my critics," in R. O. Keohane (ed.) *Neorealism and its Critics*, New York: Columbia University Press.

Wendt, A. (1999) *Social Theory of International Politics*, Cambridge: Cambridge University Press.

Zaller, J. R. (1992) *The Nature and Origins of Mass Opinion*, Cambridge: Cambridge University Press.

5　Hawkish biases

Daniel Kahneman and Jonathan Renshon

In a short article in *Foreign Policy* in 2007, we put forward a hypothesis of "directionality" in cognitive biases that generated a fair amount of debate and some controversy (Kahneman and Renshon 2007). This chapter is an attempt to expand upon and clarify our original argument.

In the last few decades, cognitive and social psychologists have described many cognitive biases – predictable errors in the ways that individuals interpret information and make decisions. More specifically, a bias exists when an error in estimating or assessing a value is more likely in one direction than another. For example, in estimating our own skills as drivers, a bias exists because we are far more likely to *over*-estimate our abilities relative to others than to *under*-estimate them. In the absence of an objective criterion, we take the opinions of knowledgeable but uninvolved observer as a definition of an unbiased judgment. The perspective of history provides another "unbiased" view of the situation that decision makers faced. An unexpected and significant pattern emerges when theses biases are viewed as a set: we find, almost without exception, that the biases recently uncovered by psychological research favor hawkish decisions in conflict situations. We use the term "hawkish" to describe a propensity for suspicion, hostility and aggression in the conduct of conflict, and for less cooperation and trust when the resolution of a conflict is on the agenda. Actors who are susceptible to hawkish biases are not only more likely to see threats as more dire than an objective observer would perceive, but are also likely to act in a way that will produce unnecessary conflict. We do not contend, of course, that all decisions in the international political context will be hostile or aggressive as a result of biases of cognition and preference, only that more decisions will be so more often than they would be in the absence of bias. Nor do we contend that all suspicions are produced by biased thinking, and therefore unjustified. Our point is only that the collective effect of the biases that psychology has identified is to increase the probability that agents will act more hawkishly than an objective observer would deem appropriate. For a more concrete image, suppose that a national leader is exposed to conflicting advice from a hawk and a dove. Our contention is that cognitive biases will tend to make the hawk's arguments more persuasive than they deserve to be.

The biases discussed in this chapter pose a difficult methodological problem for political scientists, since we cannot "prove" the bias to have been at fault in any given decision. Instead, we define the bias and invite readers to consider its consequences in conflict situations by invoking a hypothetical objective observer. We can only hope that this perspective allows dispassionate analysts to take that role. And we can only hope that the retrospective judgments are not overly tainted by the familiar hindsight bias, which makes it all too easy to explain past disasters by finding flaws in the decisions of actors who cannot defend themselves. The test of our approach is whether it offers historians and political scientists a useful heuristic. The biases that we list are to be viewed as hypotheses, to be confirmed by examining evidence of what the decision makers believed, desired or feared at the critical time. For example, students of conflict should expect to find evidence of unreasonably negative interpretations of the opponent's intentions, and overly optimistic assessments of the situation by both sides, because these biases have been established by prior research.

In our original analysis, we compiled a list of known biases, and proceeded to trace the implications of those biases for international conflict. This chapter proceeds in much the same way. For each bias, we first present empirical evidence illustrating how and when it is likely to affect judgment and decision-making. Note that the evidence on which we rely was documented in experimental situations that did *not* involve conflict – the biases are considered to be general features of cognition and preference. We then proceed to examine the potential behavioral implications of each bias in situations in international conflict. The biases and their main effects are listed in Table 5.1.

Table 5.1 Biases examined in this chapter

Bias	Primary Effect in Conflict Situations
Positive Illusions	Biased overconfidence raises the probability of violent conflict occurring and of deadlock in negotiations (when the parties overestimate their bargaining position or ability).
FAE	Perceive hostile actions of adversaries as due to unchanging, dispositional factors and discount the role of contextual factors; neglect the effects of one's own hostility on the behavior of adversaries.
Illusion of Transparency	Ignore how one's actions are likely to be perceived by others, resulting in behavior that is likely to provoke aggression or hostility.
Endowment Effect/Loss Aversion	Induces an aversion to making concessions and a reluctance to accept objectively "fair" exchanges.
Risk Seeking in Losses	Reluctance to settle, prolongation of conflict.
Pseudo-Certainty	Lowers probability of concessions if there is a potential that those concessions might advantage an opponent in a possible future conflict and concurrently *raises* the probability of conflict occurring by adopting a worst-case scenario of the other's intentions.
Reactive Devaluation	Unconscious devaluation of offers, concessions or plans suggested by rivals or adversaries makes it difficult to reach agreement.

Positive illusions

One of the most robust findings in cognitive and social psychology is that individuals often fall victim to "positive illusions."[1] Among these positive illusions are: unrealistically positive views of one's abilities and character, the illusion of control, and unrealistic optimism (Taylor and Brown 1988: 195–196; Heine and Lehman 1995).

Unrealistically positive views of the self have been documented in many domains. Among other things, most people believe themselves to be better than average drivers, decision-makers and negotiators (Svenson 1981: 143; Bazerman 1998: 69). A survey of university professors found that 94 percent believed themselves to be better teachers than the average at their institution, which of course is a statistical impossibility (Cross 1977). Because individuals resist information that conflicts with positive self-assessments, these unrealistically positive views of oneself are generally robust over time (Crary 1966: 246; Marks 1984: 203).

The "illusion of control" is an exaggerated perception of the extent to which outcomes depend on one's actions. When people were given a button and instructed to cause a particular color to appear on the screen, they erroneously believed that they had substantial control over events, even when the outcomes were actually determined by a computer (Martin *et al.* 1984). Experiments have shown that people act as if they can control the outcome of rolling a die, and are more willing to bet when they do the rolling (Silverman 1964: 114; Langer 1975: 312, 324; Campbell 1986: 290). It has also been demonstrated that stress (common in conflict or crisis decision-making) increases the preference for strategies that engender a feeling of control, even if it is illusory, and even if it leads to worse outcomes (Friedland *et al.* 1992: 923). In a competitive situation, the illusion of control causes each side to believe that the outcome of the competition depends mostly on its own actions and abilities, even when it depends equally on the achievements of competitors.

The third positive illusion is "unrealistic optimism." The evidence for "illusory," or biased, optimism comes from the comparisons of individuals' judgments of themselves and of others. People generally believe that the probability of positive outcomes (such as having a gifted child, or enjoying their first job) is higher for themselves than for their peers, and judge the probability of negative events (such as being the victim of a crime or being in a car accident) as less likely for themselves than for others (Robertson 1977: 136; Weinstein 1980: 806; Perloff and Fetzer 1986: 502). In addition, experimental evidence suggests that people's predictions of what *will* occur correspond closely to what they would *like* to happen, rather than what is objectively likely to occur (Sherman 1980: 211). A study of entrepreneurs who had started small businesses revealed a striking discrepancy between their expectations of success (typically .80 or more) and the actual probability of success for a small business, which is about 1/3 (Cooper *et al.* 1988). One important cause of this bias seems to be "reference group neglect," in which individuals discount the abilities or skills of the peer group against which they are competing (Camerer and Lovallo 1999: 307). Experts are not immune to these positive illusions. One recent experiment, for example, found that professional financial analysts, making judgments and predictions about their areas of expertise, were just as overconfident as the base group of students (Glaser *et al.* 2005).

Within political science, many scholars have found evidence supportive of the notion that leaders' positive illusions have led to more wars than would have occurred in the absence of that bias. Stephen Van Evera argued, for instance, that leaders often have unrealistically positive views of the balance of military power, overestimate their "will" relative to their adversary, overestimate the loyalty and abilities of key allies, and underestimate the cost of potential wars (Van Evera 1999).

A group of researchers has recently documented the link between overconfidence and war in a simulated conflict situation (Johnson *et al.* 2006). Johnson *et al.* conducted an experiment in which participants (drawn from the Cambridge, MA area, but not exclusively composed of students) played an experimental wargame. Subjects gave ranked assessments of themselves relative to the other players prior to the game, and in each of the six rounds of the game chose between negotiation, surrender, fight, threaten or do nothing; they also allocated the fictional wealth of their "country" to either military, infrastructure or cash reserves. Players were paid to participate and told to expect bonuses if they "won the game" (there was no dominant strategy and players could "win" using a variety of strategies). Players were generally overly optimistic, and those who made unprovoked attacks were especially likely to be overconfident (Johnson *et al.* 2006: 2516).

The consequences of positive illusions in conflict and international politics are overwhelmingly harmful. Except for relatively rare instances of armed conflicts in which one side knows that it will lose but fights anyway for the sake of honor or ideology, wars generally occur when each side believes it is likely to win – or at least when rivals' estimates of their respective chances of winning a war sum to more than 100 percent (Johnson 2004: 4). Fewer wars would occur if leaders and their advisors held realistic assessments of their probability of success; that is, if they were less optimistically overconfident.

Positive illusions also have damaging implications for negotiations. Neale and Bazerman found that overconfident negotiators (those with biased expectations of their likelihood of success) exhibited less concessionary behavior, and experienced more impasses, than realistically confident individuals (Neale and Bazerman 1985: 34; Bazerman 2001: 222).

Positive illusions generally favor hawkish, aggressive behavior when conflict exists or when a side already contemplates hostile actions. The implications of optimistic biases are less clear for tense situations that may lead either to conflict or to negotiated settlement. Actors can be overly optimistic about the prospects of negotiating a peaceful settlement. Of course, optimism in negotiations does not necessarily yield good outcomes.

Fundamental attribution error (FAE)

The Fundamental Attribution Error (FAE) is a systematic bias in the explanation of the behavior of others, and is perhaps the most studied bias in social cognition.

Because the mental states of others are not directly observable, people inevitably rely on inferences to explain the behaviors they observe as due to personal dispositions or to situational pressures. The robust finding is that these causal attributions are biased, exaggerating the role of the other's dispositions and intentions and discounting the role of the situation as the other perceives it (Heider 1958; Tversky and Kahneman 1974: 1128; Quattrone 1982: 596).[2]

There is a vast literature on the FAE, but one of the earliest examples is still among the most evocative. In a famous early experiment, Jones and Harris asked participants to read short essays about Cuba that were either pro- or anti-Castro in content. In the "choice" condition participants were told that the writers had freely chosen the position for which they argued in their essay. In the "no choice" condition participants were told that the writers had been assigned the position for which they were to argue.

The participants then estimated the writers' actual attitude toward Castro. The surprising result of the experiment was that these estimates were strongly influenced by the position of the essay, *even when the position was not chosen by the writer.* Indeed, there was only a minor difference between the judgments made of the same essays in the "Choice" and "No choice" condition (Jones and Harris 1967: 6). The authors of this classic experiment concluded that people are prone to attribute behaviors they observe to personal dispositions, and prone to neglect the influence of situational pressures – even the overwhelming pressure of a specific instruction to adopt a particular position in an essay (Jones and Harris 1967: 22). Some years later, the tendency to underestimate the role of the situation in explaining the behaviors of others was called the Fundamental Attribution Error (Ross 1977).

This attribution error is remarkably robust, and people who are informed about the bias are not immune to it. Students who had learned about the attribution error continued to over-emphasize dispositional factors and to neglect the importance of situational context or constraints (Darley and Batson 1973: 100; Pietromonaco and Nisbett 1982: 1). More recent research suggests that "rumination" (i.e., spending more time thinking about something) actually increases attribution errors. Subjects who were asked to take several minutes to imagine the motives, intentions and strategies of the other players were more likely to be suspicious of their partners in a computer game (Kramer 1994: 218–219). In line with previous research on the subject (Wilson and Kraft 1993: 409), rumination also increased the subjects' confidence in the accuracy of their erroneous judgments.

Explanations of another person's behavior reflect prior beliefs and attitudes toward that person: actions that are consistent with expectations are attributed to internal, or dispositional factors, while actions that appear inconsistent with prior beliefs are attributed to situational factors (Regan *et al.* 1974). Thus, subjects attributed to stable dispositions the good actions of people they liked and the bad actions of people they did not like, and attributed behaviors that violated expectations to fleeting, situational variables. Thus, the FAE – the tendency to over-attribute behavior to disposition – effectively reverses when disliked or distrusted actors commit positive actions.

Field evidence from the Middle East supports the same conclusion. Heradstveit conducted interviews with political activists in Egypt, Israel, Jordan, Lebanon and Syria and found strong support for the predictions of the FAE: actors tended to over-attribute the hostile behavior of adversaries to dispositions and correspondingly disregarded contextual factors. However, this effect was reversed for positive behaviors (Heradstveit 1981: 4). Beliefs in the hostile intentions of adversaries tend to be self-perpetuating – and of course they also tend to be self-fulfilling.

When another country acts in an aggressive, belligerent or deceptive manner, the explanation of its behavior is of paramount importance. Were its actions driven by domestic political necessity – or perhaps provoked by our own actions? Or do their hostile actions reflect the true goals and character of the other side? The alternative attributions lead to different policy choices. If, for instance, the behavior is a response to one's own aggressive behavior, then attempts to restore trust may be appropriate. If, however, the same behavior reflects a deeper hostility, friendly gestures are likely to be futile.

The FAE strongly favors hawkish arguments in conflict situations. When hostility and suspicion already exist, actors will tend to attribute moderate behavior of antagonists to situational constraints ("they *had* to do that") while attributing more hostile actions to dispositions. Bad behavior by adversaries will reinforce prior beliefs, while good behavior will be disregarded as "forced." The hawkish position is justified both when the opponents yield and when they do not. Of course, antagonists do often have hostile dispositions, but that does not disprove our argument, which is that leaders will make these inferences to an excessive degree – beyond the level of suspicion that an objective observer would consider appropriate. Furthermore, the same bias will hinder efforts toward conciliation by causing leaders and their advisors to disregard the positive actions taken by adversaries.

Of course, the FAE will not cause hawkish arguments to prevail every time. And in some cases, history might judge an argument that was biased to have been correct in retrospect. One need only think of Europe in the 1930s to wish that perhaps more politicians had adopted a dispositional attribution of Hitler's actions, instead of excusing them as a reaction to the position of Germany following the Treaty of Versailles.

Illusion of transparency

We have thus far made the case for hawkish arguments being advantaged by cognitive biases in how actors explain behavior. But how do people believe *their own* behavior will be explained? Individuals realize, of course, that they are not as transparent to others as they are to themselves. However, they typically do not make sufficient allowances for this difference in perspective. As a result, people tend to overestimate the extent to which their own feelings, thoughts or motivations "leak out" and are apparent to observers (Gilovich and Savitsky 1999: 167).

In recent demonstrations of this bias, participants in a "truth-telling game" overestimated the extent to which their lies were readily apparent to others, witnesses to a staged emergency believed their concern was obvious even when it was not, and negotiators overestimated the degree to which the other side understood their preferences (even in the condition in which there were incentives to maintain secrecy) (Gilovich *et al.* 1998; Van Boven *et al.* 2003: 117). The common theme is that people generally exaggerate the degree to which their internal states are apparent to observers.

The transparency bias has pernicious implications for international politics. When the actor's intentions are hostile, the bias favors redoubled efforts at deception. When the actor's intentions are *not* hostile, the bias increases the risk of dangerous misunderstandings. Because they believe their benign intentions are readily apparent to others, actors underestimate the need to reassure the other side. Their opponents – even if their own intentions are equally benign – are correspondingly more likely to perceive more hostility than exists and to react in kind, in a cycle of escalation. The transparency bias thus favors hawkish outcomes through the mediating variable of misperception.

The memoirs of U.S. Secretary of State Dean Acheson provide an illustration. Commenting on the American decision to drive to the Yalu River during the Korean War, he wrote that "no possible shred of evidence could have existed in the minds of the Chinese Communists about the non-threatening intentions of the forces of the United Nations" (Jervis 1980: 583). Though the U.S./U.N. forces did not have any intention of attempting to directly invade China, it should have been clear to Acheson and other U.S. decision-makers that their march toward the Yalu River would be perceived as threatening by Chinese leaders. Indeed, the People's Republic of China had already issued warnings that they would intervene militarily if any non-South Korean forces crossed the 38th parallel separating North and South Korea. Ignoring those warnings and being unable to see their actions as China would perceive them cost the U.S. dearly: China intervened with almost 800,000 troops and at one point pushed U.S./South Korean forces to a line well south of Seoul.

Loss aversion

The assertion that "losses loom larger than gains" was the most important claim of Prospect Theory (Kahneman and Tversky 1979: 279). It implied an abrupt change in the slope of the value function at the point that separates gains from losses, as seen in Figure 5.1. The difference in the slopes of the value function in the positive and negative domains is labeled loss aversion.

The main evidence for loss aversion in Prospect Theory was the extreme reluctance of people to accept gambles with equal probabilities to win and lose. A majority of respondents will typically refuse to play a gamble in which they face equal probabilities to lose x or to win $2x$ (for example, 50 percent chance to lose $100 and 50 percent chance to win $200). Soon after the publication of Prospect Theory, Richard Thaler (1980) noted that loss aversion could explain the observation that he labeled the endowment effect: the fact that the monetary value that people assign to a good depends on whether or not it is already part of their endowment. This conceptual advance extended Prospect Theory from a theory of choice between gambles to

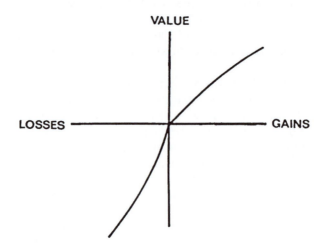

Figure 5.1 Hypothetical value function

a more general model of decision-making, and provided the foundation of behavioral economics.

Some years later, Kahneman, Knetsch, and Thaler (1991: 195) reported a demonstration of the endowment effect that has become standard. The critical experiment was conducted in a classroom. Half of the participants were given an attractive coffee mug. They were told the mug was theirs to keep, but were given an opportunity to sell it and were asked to record their cash equivalent (minimal selling price) for the mug. The other participants were told that they could choose between receiving a mug and receiving an amount of money, and were asked to indicate their cash equivalent for the mug. The options that faced the two groups were effectively identical: they could go home with a mug or with a sum of money. But the cash equivalents were quite different: the participants who owned a mug valued it at $7.12 while the participants who did not own a mug valued it at $3.50 (for more recent demonstrations of this effect see Sen and Johnson 1997: 105; Carmon and Ariely 2000: 360).

The point of this demonstration – and by extension, of the endowment effect – is that people do not put value on the states of "having a mug" or "not having a mug." Depending on their endowment, they value the *changes* of "getting a mug" and "giving up a mug." Furthermore, the psychological aversion to giving up a mug is more intense than the attraction of receiving one, by loss aversion. Recent work has suggested that one determinant of the endowment effect is emotional attachment; and that loss aversion occurs in proportion to the emotion experienced when an individual considers giving up a good (Ariely *et al.* 2005: 134; Novemsky and Kahneman 2005: 139–140).

Loss aversion also contributes to the explanation of an important phenomenon of choice known as the *status-quo bias*. Samuelson and Zeckhauser (1988), who coined that term, illustrated the bias by the choices that Harvard University employees made when new options were added to health-care coverage. New employees chose a plan from the set of options, and continuing employees were free to switch to the new plan. Because new and continuing employees faced the same options, the distribution of their choices should have been the same, but it was not. The continuing employees were very likely to retain their current plan, regardless of the advantages of the new options.

It is easy to see that loss aversion contributes to the status-quo bias. An individual who considers switching from her current plan A to an alternative plan B will naturally evaluate the features of the alternative plan from the reference point of her current plan. Plan B is viewed as a bundle of advantages and disadvantages relative to Plan A – and the disadvantages are given more weight than the advantages, a manifestation of loss aversion. If the individual owned Plan B, of course, she would think of the same choice in terms of the advantages and disadvantages of Plan A – and the disadvantages of that plan would loom larger than its advantages.

There are important exceptions to the endowment effect. In particular, the effect does not apply to "exchange goods" – goods that are specifically held to be traded, not to be used (Kahneman *et al.* 1990: 1344). Furthermore, highly experienced traders exhibit little loss aversion even for goods they have purchased as personal possessions (List 2003). Individuals with much experience trading sports memorabilia were less likely to exhibit an endowment effect for assorted sports collectibles.

Loss aversion has an unfortunate effect on negotiations, because actors treat their own concessions as "losses," but evaluate the concessions they receive as gains. This "concession aversion" can be illustrated by negotiations over mutual disarmament (Kahneman and Tversky 1995: 56). Because our own losses carry more psychological weight, offers that are objectively fair or equal will not seem so to either side: a country will feel the *loss* of a 10 percent reduction of its arsenal more than it will experience the *gain* of an equal reduction in the arsenal of its adversary. The asymmetric evaluation of gains and losses poses a serious obstacle to agreement (Levy 1997: 105).

Concession aversion is exacerbated by two additional factors: anticipated regret and the "sucker's payoff." Individuals faced with choice problems anticipate the regret they may experience if they do not achieve the best outcome. And the outcome of being betrayed by an opponent one has trusted – known as the "sucker's payoff" – constitutes an especially severe form of regret. Actors are reluctant to expose themselves to this outcome by making concessions that could be exploited by their opponents. Anticipated regret favors both an aversion to concessions and the avoidance of risky cooperation.

The second implication of loss aversion for world politics concerns the relative speed at which people adapt to (or "integrate") gains and losses. The endowment effect appears to be largely instantaneous. The mug that was received a minute ago is immediately absorbed as part of one's endowment. In contrast, it appears that people are slower to adjust their reference point following losses (Kahneman *et al.* 1990: 1342).

Consider a scenario in which Country A has lost a valuable strategic territory to

Country B during the course of a war. Because of the quick adjustment to its new endowment, B is likely to adopt the new territory into its "status quo portfolio", with a corresponding increase in its willingness to expend blood and treasure to defend it.[3] However, if actors do not adapt to losses as quickly as gains, Country A is likely to view the new situation as a loss relative to the 'normal' reference situation in which it held the territory. In this scenario, both countries will be operating in the domain of losses: B because of the instant endowment effect and Country A because of the slow adaptation to losses. As we see in the next section, actors are likely to take substantial risks in order to avoid accepting a loss – when both sides face losses, the likelihood of conflict increases.

Risk seeking in losses

Formal models of rational choice do not prescribe a particular risk attitude. Rational decision makers can be as risk-averse or risk-seeking as they wish – the only requirement is that they must be internally consistent. Furthermore, models of rational choice do not explicitly specify the nature of the outcomes to which utilities are attached. However, the relevant outcomes and the appropriate risk attitude are both specified when the rational choice model (aka utility theory) is applied to a particular situation. In most applications, the outcomes are assumed to be final states – e.g., a complete description of the state of affairs when uncertainty is resolved. In the context of financial decisions, for example, rational agents are said to evaluate the outcomes of decisions as states of wealth, not as gains and losses. Furthermore, a moderately risk averse attitude is widely assumed to be characteristic of reasonable (rational) agents.

Prospect Theory questioned both these aspects of rational choice models. The idea that the carriers of value are gains and losses – not final states – helps explain robust observations that are difficult to reconcile with rationality, including the endowment effect, the status-quo bias and the susceptibility to many framing manipulations. A further departure from the rational model is the observation that risk-seeking preferences are prevalent when people face difficult choices, especially when one of the options involves accepting a sure loss.

For an example, consider the following problem:

Problem 1   Choose between:
 A. a sure loss of $900
 B. a 90 percent chance to lose $1000 and 10 percent chance to lose nothing

A large majority of people who have been asked this question choose the gamble over the sure loss – a risk-seeking preference. According to Prospect Theory, this preference is explained by two separate factors. The first is the shape of the value function (see Figure 5.1). Because of diminishing marginal disutility, the difference between a loss of $900 and a loss of $1,000 is relatively small. The second (and probably more important) cause of risk seeking in difficult situations is known as the *certainty effect*.

The certainty effect refers to the overweighting of outcomes that are certain, relative to outcomes that are merely probable (Tversky and Kahneman 1981: 455). Kahneman and Tversky illustrated this effect by the game of Russian roulette. Most people share the strong intuition that one should be willing to pay more to reduce the number of bullets from 1 to 0 than from 4 to 3 (1979: 265). The reduction of the probability of dying is the same in the two cases, but removing the single bullet achieves the certainty of a good outcome, while reducing the number of bullets from 4 to 3 does not eliminate the uncertainty. Utility Theory, in contrast, assumes that the rational response to probability is linear and does not distinguish between the two cases.

In the domain of gains, the certainty effect and the shape of the value function both favor risk aversion. For example, a large majority of people will prefer a sure gain of $850 over a 90 percent chance to win $1,000. The certainty effect contributes to this preference because the "decision weight" that is associated with a probability of 0.90 is significantly *less* than 90 percent of the decision weight of a sure thing (Kahneman and Tversky 1979: 280–281). The overweighting of the sure gain relative to a gain that is merely probable favors the risk-averse choice in this example. When an actor faces a choice between a sure loss and a possible loss, however, the certainty effect contributes to risk-seeking preferences by exactly the same logic. Certainty enhances the aversion to a sure loss just as it enhances the attractiveness of a sure gain.

In policy debates, arguments that draw on the certainty effect often appear more compelling and persuasive than they should be. Experimental evidence dovetails with the common-sense observation that the invocation of certainties has a rhetorical power that mere probabilities lack.

Evidence of the special aversiveness of sure losses and the attendant increase in risk acceptance can be found in a variety of domains. For instance, Fiegenbaum and Thomas argue that aversion to certain losses account for the negative correlation between risk and return in investment decisions. Their large-N analysis of companies' investment portfolios indicated that most firms are risk-acceptant when they are suffering losses or are below targeted "aspiration levels" and risk-avoidant when they are above those levels (1988: 97).

In another domain, Rachlinski examined choices in the context of a hypothetical litigation case. He showed that decisions concerning whether to pursue litigation or settle vary with the domain of the individual. He also showed that respondents who were in the weaker position (low stated probability of prevailing in court) *and* were in the domain of losses were far more likely than their counterparts (weak position but in the domain of gains) to pursue a costly and risky litigation with a small chance of success (Rachlinski 1996).

The prototypical risk-seeking behavior occurs in desperate situations: faced with a choice between a significant loss and the prospect of a bigger disaster – but with a chance to escape – actors are prone to accept gambles that appear unreasonable to an objective observer. This analysis applies to the losing side in a conflict. Faced with a choice between surrender or fighting on with a slim chance of escaping the worst, the leaders of the losing side will be tempted to persevere. If there is one thing that is worse than a sure loss it is a loss that is both sure and immediate.

The risk seeking behavior of losers is closely related to the phenomenon known as escalation of commitment, which is observed when a project that has consumed considerable resources appears to be failing. The rational prescription is to "ignore sunk costs" and evaluate the costs of new efforts against the value of their expected outcome, but decision makers often persevere even with poor odds of success (Brockner 1992; Bazerman 1998).

An agency problem often compounds the psychological difficulties of giving up a lost cause. The leaders of the losing entity will not personally do well by giving up now, and the threat they face may not be worse if they go on fighting. But the slim chance of victory is often enough even for followers to support a lost cause, although they are likely to suffer for it. Indeed, the tendency to escalate commitment seems to be exacerbated when decisions are considered by groups, and when the actor who made the original decision is still in charge, circumstances that are often observed in political decision-making (Staw 1976: 27; Whyte 1993: 430; Schaubroeck and Davis 1994: 59).

Pseudo-certainty

The pseudo-certainty effect refers to a decision-making bias in the response to multi-stage decisions. Specifically, it describes the tendency for individuals contemplating multiple-stage problems/scenarios to assign a high decision weight to an outcome that is certain if the second stage is reached, neglecting its contingent nature. Pseudo-certainty was illustrated by Tversky and Kahneman (1981: 453) using the following two problems:

Problem 2   Assume a two-stage game. In the first stage, there is a 75 percent chance to end the game with nothing and a 25 percent chance to move into the second stage. If you reach the second stage, your choice is between:

>   **A.** a sure win of $30
>   **B.** 80 percent chance to win $45
>   Your choice must be made before the game starts.

In this problem, a substantial majority (74 percent) chose **A**, which has the appeal of a seemingly certain gain. Now consider the next problem:

Problem 3   Which of the following options would you prefer?
>   **C.** 25 percent chance to win $30
>   **D.** 20 percent chance to win $45

A and **C**, and **B** and **D**, are respectively identical in terms of outcomes and probabilities. And yet, the single-stage version and the sequential version are treated differently (for further experimental support for this phenomenon, see Quattrone and Tversky 1988: 731; Kahneman and Tversky 1995: 52–53). In Problem 3, the majority (58 percent) prefers **D**, because the difference between the probabilities appears smaller than in Problem 2. When contemplating multiple-stage problems in which the first-stage is probabilistic and the second-stage contains a certain outcome, individuals tend to ignore the first-stage altogether. The preference for the option that yields a sure gain in the second stage is an example of the certainty effect that was discussed in the preceding section. In this case, however, the certainty that actors find attractive is only illusory: choice **A** is no more certain than **C**, it only seems to be so.

This effect has significant implications for international politics, in which decision-makers often encounter situations that involve multiple stages or interactions. In particular, pseudo-certainty is likely to exacerbate the reluctance to make strategically significant concessions. The dilemma that confronted Israel in the peace negotiations with Egypt in the 1970s illustrates the problem. At the conclusion the 1967 Six-Day War, Israel had gained control over the Sinai Peninsula, a strategically valuable region between the Mediterranean and Red Seas. If war broke out, the territory would be immensely valuable by providing strategic depth to prevent a large massing of Arab troops near Israel's borders (McPeak 1976: 429–430; Middletown 1991). Yigal Allon (1976), writing when he was Deputy Prime Minister and Minister of Foreign Affairs for Israel, declared the Sinai to be "critical to Israeli defense."

Though Israel eventually ceded control over the Sinai in the Camp David Accords of 1978, Israeli hawks fought stubbornly against such a concession, and came close to carrying the day. The intuitive appeal of their argument is easy to explain as an instance of pseudo-certainty. The decision whether to give up the Sinai involved a two-stage dilemma. In the first-stage, the question was whether another war would occur between Israel and Egypt. The second-stage was the outcome of a war if one broke out. There was apparent certainty in the second-stage: the Sinai was definitely an advantage if that stage was reached. In truth, however, the Sinai was only contingently valuable: holding it was important only *if* war broke out, but pseudo-certainty tends to mask such truths. The hypothesis of pseudo-certainty is that the probabilistic element in the first-stage of the problem – the possibility that war may not break out – will be ignored or neglected, while the certain element of the second-stage is over-emphasized. The actual probability that the war will be lost is the product of P (WarOccuring) × P (LosingWar), and is influenced by the possible effect of an agreement in reducing the probability of war, as well as by the increased risk in case of war. However, pseudo-certainty leads actors to frame the problem in their minds as P (Losing War | War Occurring) rather than the more accurate P (Losing War | War Occurring) × P (War Occurring).

By ignoring the first-stage of such games, actors under-emphasize the effect of their own actions. The focus of Israeli hawks on the strategic advantage conferred by the Sinai *if war occurs* caused a correspondent neglect of the effect that giving up the Sinai might have on diminishing the probability of war in the first place. Decades of peace between Israel and Egypt strongly suggest that the hawks were wrong.

As this case illustrates, focusing attention on considerations that will become relevant only if war occurs leads decision-makers to plan for the worst-case scenario – often a recipe for self-fulfilling prophecies. Dovish arguments, such as "we should not assume that war will surely occur" or "doing this now increases the chances of war later" sound feeble. The rhetorical force of a "sure thing" is a powerful advantage for hawks, even if the certainty they invoke is illusory.

Reactive devaluation

As already noted, the "bad behavior" of rivals is likely to be attributed to long-term hostile intentions, even when these inferences are not logically or factually supported. Similar distortions are observed in the context of negotiations, where actors must assess the offers presented by their adversaries. Here, the evidence suggests that individuals assign different values to proposals, ideas and plans of action based on their authorship. This bias, known as "reactive devaluation," is likely to be significant stumbling block in negotiations between adversaries.

In one recent experiment, Israeli Jews evaluated an actual Israeli-authored peace plan less favorably when it was attributed to the Palestinians than when it was attributed to their own government, and Pro-Israeli Americans saw a hypothetical peace proposal as biased in favor of Palestinians when authorship was attributed to Palestinians, but as "evenhanded" when they were told it was authored by Israelis. In fact, the phenomenon is visible even within groups. In the same experiment, Jewish "hawks" perceived a proposal attributed to the dovish Rabin government as bad for Israel, and good for the Palestinians, while Israeli Arabs believe the opposite (Maoz *et al*. 2002).

The effect of reactive devaluation in international politics is that leaders and their advisors are likely to significantly underestimate the value of proposals made by adversaries. We recognize, of course, that leaders have a duty to be wary of seemingly beneficial proposals or plans advanced by potentially untrustworthy sources. Our point is only that the evidence of reactive devaluation suggests that politicians are likely to be more wary and more suspicious than an unbiased observer would consider appropriate.

Conclusion

In our view, neither psychology nor decision science can provide a theory of interstate conflict (Kahneman and Tversky 2000: xi). It is simply unreasonable to expect a theory of choices between gambles with specified probabilities and monetary outcomes to predict or explain the decisions of national leaders as they wage war and negotiate peace (Kahneman and Tversky 2000: xi). It is similarly impossible to derive confident predictions about the future judgments and choices of national actors from notions such as the fundamental attribution error or loss aversion. There is too much else going on. By the same token, post hoc explanations of the judgments and decisions of national leaders in terms of the psychological mechanisms that we have illustrated are at best tentative and incomplete. A legitimate question can be asked – and often has been asked: if the psychology of judgment and decision-making supports neither confident predictions nor complete explanations of the actions of national leaders, how useful can it be?

A possible answer is that the concepts of psychology – including the seven biases that we discussed in this chapter – provide templates for patterns that can be recognized in complex situations. The training of histologists provides a useful analogy. Histologists are not born with an ability to differentiate different types of cancer cells, and cancer cells of a particular type do not look exactly alike and are hard to distinguish from other cells. The trained histologist has seen multiple examples of cells that share the same label, and has learned to identify them in microscope slides. The slides look different to the trained eye, they make more sense. We offer the observations discussed in this chapter as templates that may help make sense of past events and provide expectations about the future. Sense making and expectation are much weaker than explanations and predictions, but still potentially useful. The notion of the endowment effect, for example, prepares us to distinguish truly painful concessions that are treated as losses from other concessions in which bargaining chips are exchanged. And the FAE prepares us to find that participants in a conflict underestimate their role in provoking the opponent's hostility. We believe these intellectual tools may be useful, but repeat that "No warranty is implied … The scholars who use the tools to explain complex behaviors do so at their own risk" (Kahneman and Tversky 2000: xi).

The theme of this chapter was a chance observation, made while drawing a list of the biases of judgment and choice uncovered during the last few decades: it appeared that these biases were themselves biased in a hawkish direction. We started out by imagining a decision maker exposed to competing advisors, a hawk and a dove. If the decision maker is susceptible to the usual list of biases, she will tend to find the hawk's arguments more believable and the hawk's recommendations more attractive than they ought to be. We have found no deep reason for this observation, and we do not present it as a general and exceptionless claim. The most we can say for it is that it is intriguing.

Notes

* Space constraints limited the length of this chapter. A more complete version can be found on the authors' websites.

1 There is an important caveat to the findings described in this section, which is that there may well be cultural variation in unrealistic optimism. "Collectivist cultures," for example, seem less prone to self-enhancing biases (Heine and Lehman 1995).
2 While most social psychologists agree on the existence of the FAE, there is a still ongoing debate about why the attribution error occurs. For further information, the reader is referred to Heider (1958), Tversky and Kahneman (1974) and Quattrone (1982).
3 The exception to this is if the territory is taken and held as a bargaining chip (or "exchange good"), in which case one would not expect loss aversion to factor in the decision-making. Of course, part of the art of negotiation is to convince your opponent of your aversion to losing things that in fact you consider to be mere bargaining chips.

References

Allon, Y. (1976) "Israel: The case for defensible borders," *Foreign Affairs*, 55: 38–53.
Ariely, D., Huber, J. and Wertenbroch, K. (2005) "When do losses loom larger than gains?" *Journal of Marketing Research*, 42: 134–138.

Bazerman, M. H. (1998) *Judgment in Managerial Decision Making*, New York: John Wiley & Sons.

—— (2001) "Why negotiations go wrong," in I. G. Asherman and S. V. Asherman (eds) *The Negotiation Sourcebook*, MA, Human Resources Development Press.

Brockner, J. (1992) "The escalation of commitment to a failing course of action: Toward theoretical progress," *Academy of Management Review*, 17: 39–61.

Camerer, C. and Lovallo, D. (1999) "Overconfidence and excess entry: an experimental approach," *American Economic Review*, 89: 306–318.

Campbell, J. D. (1986) "Similarity and uniqueness: The effects of attribute type, relevance, and individual differences in self-esteem and depression," *Journal of Personality and Social Psychology*, 50: 281–294.

Carmon, Z. and Ariely, D. (2000) "Focusing on the forgone: How value can appear so different to buyers and sellers," *Journal of Consumer Research*, 27: 360–370.

Cooper, A., Woo, C. and Dunkelberg, W. (1988) "Entrepreneurs' perceived chances for success," *Journal of Business Venturing*, 3: 97–108.

Crary, W. G. (1966) "Reactions to incongruent self-experiences," *Journal of Consulting Psychology*, 30: 246–252.

Cross, K. P. (1977) "Not can, but will college teaching be improved?" *New Directions for Higher Education*, 17.

Darley, J. M. and Batson, D. (1973) "From Jerusalem to Jericho": A study of situational and dispositional variables in helping behavior," *Journal of Personality and Social Psychology*, 27: 100–108.

Fiegenbaum, A. and Thomas, H. (1988) "Attitudes toward risk and the risk-return paradox: Prospect theory explanations," *Academy of Management Journal*, 31: 85–106.

Friedland, N., Keinan, G. and Regev, Y. (1992) "Controlling the uncontrollable: Effects of stress on illusory perceptions of controllability," *Journal of Personality and Social Psychology*, 63: 923–931.

Gilovich, T. and Savitsky, K. (1999) "The spotlight effect and the illusion of transparency: Egocentric assessments of how we are seen by others," *Current Directions in Psychological Science*, 8: 165–168.

Gilovich, T., Savitsky, K. and Medvec, V. H. (1998) "The illusion of transparency: Biased assessments of others' ability to read one's emotional states," *Journal of Personality and Social Psychology*, 75: 332–346.

Glaser, M., Langer, T. and Weber, M. (2005) "Overconfidence of professionals and lay men: Individual differences within and between tasks?" Online. Available: <http://papers.ssrn.com/sol3/papers.cfm?abstract_id=712583> (Accessed September 30, 2006)

Heider, F. (1958) *The Psychology of Interpersonal Relations*, Lawrence Erlbaum Associates New York: John Wiley & Sons.

Heine, S. J. and Lehman, D. R. (1995) "Cultural variation in unrealistic optimism: Does the west feel more vulnerable than the east?" *Journal of Personality and Social Psychology*, 68: 595–607.

Heradstveit, D. (1981) *The Arab-Israeli Conflict: Psychological Obstacles to Peace*, New York: Oxford University Press.

Jervis, R. (1980) "The impact of the Korean War on the Cold War," *Journal of Conflict Resolution*, 24: 563–592.

Johnson, D. D. P. (2004) *Overconfidence and War: The Havoc and Glory of Positive Illusions*, Cambridge, MA: Harvard University Press.

Johnson, D. D. P., McDermott, R., Barrett, E. S., Cowden, J., Wrangham, R., McIntyre,

M. H. and Rosen, S. P. (2006) "Overconfidence in wargames: Experimental evidence on expectations, aggression, gender and testosterone," *Proceedings of the Royal Society of London*, 273: 2513–2520.

Jones, E. E. and Harris, V. A. (1967) "The attribution of attitudes," *Journal of Experimental Social Psychology*, 3: 1–24.

Kahneman, D., Knetsch, J. L. and Thaler, R. H. (1990) "Experimental tests of the endowment effect and the Coase theorem," *Journal of Political Economy*, 98: 1325–1348.

—— (1991) "Anomalies: The endowment effect, loss aversion, and status quo bias," *Journal of Economic Perspectives*, 5: 193–206.

Kahneman, D. and Renshon, J. (2007) "Why hawks win," *Foreign Policy*, 158: 34–38.

Kahneman, D. and Tversky, A. (1979) "Prospect theory: An analysis of decision under risk," *Econometrica*, 47: 263–292.

—— (1995) "Conflict resolution: A cognitive perspective," in Arrow, K., Mnookin, R. H., Ross, L., Tversky, A. and Wilson R. (eds) *Barriers to Conflict Resolution*, New York, W.W. Norton: 44–62.

—— (2000) *Choices, Values, and Frames*, New York: Cambridge University Press.

Kramer, R. M. (1994) "The sinister attribution error: Paranoid cognition and collective distrust in organizations," *Motivation and Emotion*, 18: 199–230.

Langer, E. J. (1975) "The illusion of control," *Journal of Personality and Social Psychology*, 32: 311–328.

Levy, J. S. (1997) "Prospect theory, rational choice, and international relations," *International Studies Quarterly* 41: 87–112.

List, J. A. (2003) "Does market experience eliminate market anomalies?" *Quarterly Journal of Economics*, 118: 41–71.

McPeak, M. A. (1976) 'Israel: Borders and security', *Foreign Affairs*, 54: 426–443.

Maoz, I., Ward, A., Katz, M. and Ross, L. (2002) "Reactive devaluation of an 'Israeli' vs. 'Palestinian' peace proposal," *Journal of Conflict Resolution*, 46: 515–546.

Marks, G. (1984) "Thinking one's abilities are unique and one's opinions are common," *Personality and Social Psychology Bulletin*, 10: 203.

Martin, D. J., Abramson, L. Y. and Alloy, L. B. (1984) "Illusion of control for self and others in depressed and nondepressed college students," *Journal of Personality and Social Psychology*, 46: 125–136.

Middletown, D. (1991) "Sinai pullout: Israel to lose in air power," *New York Times*, November, 8: 9.

Neale, M. A. and Bazerman, M. H. (1985) "The effects of framing and negotiator overconfidence on bargaining behaviors and outcomes," *Academy of Management Journal*, 28: 34–49.

Novemsky, N. and Kahneman, D. (2005) "How do intentions affect loss aversion?" *Journal of Marketing Research*, 42: 139–140.

Perloff, L. S. and Fetzer, B. K. (1986) "Self-other judgments and perceived vulnerability to victimization," *Journal of Personality and Social Psychology*, 50: 502–510.

Pietromonaco, P. R. and Nisbett, R. (1982) "Swimming upstream against the fundamental attribution error: Subjects' weak generalizations from the Darley and Batson Study," *Social Behavior and Personality*, 10: 1–4.

Quattrone, G. A. (1982) "Overattribution and unit formation: When behavior engulfs the field," *Journal of Personality and Social Psychology*, 42: 593–607.

Quattrone, G. A. and Tversky, A. (1988) "Contrasting rational and psychological analyses of political choice," *American Political Science Review*, 82: 719–736.

Rachlinski, J. (1996) "Gaines, losses and the psychology of litigation," *Southern California Law Review*, 70: 113–185.

Regan, D. T., Straus, E. and Fazio, R. (1974) "Liking and the attribution process," *Journal of Experimental Social Psychology*, 10: 385–397.

Robertson, L. S. (1977) "Car crashes: Perceived vulnerability and willingness to pay for crash protection," *Journal of Community Health*, 3: 136–141.

Ross, L. (1977) "The intuitive psychologist and his shortcomings: Distortions in the attribution process," in L. Berkowitz (ed.) *Advances in experimental social psychology*, New York, Academic Press. 10: 173–220.

Samuelson, W. and Zeckhauser, R. (1988) "Status quo bias in decision making," *Journal of Risk and Uncertainty*, 1: 7–59.

Schaubroeck, J. and Davis, E. (1994) "Prospect theory predictions when escalation is not the only chance to recover sunk costs," *Organizational Behavior and Human Decision Processes*, 57: 59–82.

Sen, S. and Johnson, E. J. (1997) "Mere-Possession effects without possession in consumer choice," *Journal of Consumer Research*, 24: 105–117.

Sherman, S. J. (1980) "On the self-erasing nature of errors of prediction," *Journal of Personality and Social Psychology*, 39: 211–221.

Silverman, I. (1964) "Self-esteem and differential responsiveness to success and failure," *Journal of Abnormal Psychology*, 69: 115–119.

Staw, B. M. (1976) "Knee-deep in the big muddy: A study of escalating commitment to a chosen course of action," *Organizational Behavior and Human Performance,* 16: 27–44.

Svenson, O. (1981) "Are we all less risky and more skillful than our fellow drivers?" *Acta Psychologica*, 47: 143–148.

Taylor, S. E. and Brown, J. D. (1988) "Illusion and Well-Being: A Social Psychological Perspective on Mental Health," *Psychological Bulletin* 103(2): 193–210.

Thaler, R. (1980) "Toward a positive theory of consumer choice," *Journal of Economic Behavior and Organization*, 1: 39–60.

Tversky, A. and Kahneman, D. (1974) "Judgment under uncertainty: Heuristics and biases," *Science*, 185: 1124–1131.

—— (1981) "The framing of decisions and the psychology of choice," *Science*, 211: 453–458.

Van Boven, L., Gilovich, T. and Medvec, V. H. (2003) "The illusion of transparency in negotiations," *Negotiation Journal*, 19: 117–131.

Van Evera, S. (1999) *Causes of War: Power and the Roots of Conflict*, New York: Cornell University Press.

Weinstein, N. D. (1980) "Unrealistic optimism about future life events," *Journal of Personality and Social Psychology*, 39: 806–820.

Whyte, G. (1993) "Escalating Commitment in Individual and Group Decision Making: A prospect theory Approach," *Organizational Behavior and Human Decision Processes*, 54: 430–455.

Wilson, T. D. and Kraft, D. (1993) "Why do I love thee?: Effects of repeated introspections about a dating relationship on attitudes toward the relationship," *Personality and Social Psychology Bulletin*, 19: 409.

6 Threat inflation and the failure of the marketplace of ideas

The selling of the Iraq War

Chaim Kaufmann

Mature democracies such as the United States are generally believed to be better at making foreign policy than other regime types. Especially, the strong civic institutions and robust marketplaces of ideas in mature democracies are thought to substantially protect them from severe threat inflation and "myths of empire" that could promote excessively risky foreign policy adventures and wars (Snyder 1991; Van Evera 1999; Russett 1993; Reiter and Stam 2002). The marketplace of ideas helps to weed out unfounded, mendacious, or self-serving foreign policy arguments because their proponents cannot avoid wide-ranging debate in which their reasoning and evidence are subject to public scrutiny.

The marketplace of ideas, however, failed to fulfill this function in the 2002–03 U.S. foreign policy debate over going to war with Iraq. By now there is broad agreement among U.S. foreign policy experts, as well as much of the American public and the international community, that the threat assessments that President George W. Bush and his administration used to justify the war against Iraq were greatly exaggerated, and on some dimensions wholly baseless.

Post-war revelations have made clear that President Bush and top officials of his administration were determined from early 2001 to bring about regime change in Iraq (Suskind 2004; Woodward 2004; Clarke 2004). It was not until the summer of 2002, however, that they began their public campaign to generate support for preventive war to achieve this objective. They made four main arguments to persuade the public of their case against Saddam Hussein:

1 he was an almost uniquely undeterrable aggressor who would seek any opportunity to kill Americans virtually regardless of risk to himself or his country;
2 he was cooperating with al Qa'ida and had even assisted in the September 11, 2001 terrorist attacks against the United States;
3 he was close to acquiring nuclear weapons; and
4 he possessed chemical and biological weapons that could be used to devastating effect against American civilians at home or U.S. troops in the Middle East.

Virtually none of the administration's claims held up, and the information needed to debunk nearly all of them was available both inside and outside the U.S. government before the war (Cirincione *et al.* 2004). Nevertheless, administration officials persistently repeated only the most extreme threat claims and suppressed contrary evidence.

Most important, the marketplace of ideas failed to correct the administration's misrepresentations or hinder its ability to persuade the American public. The administration succeeded, despite the weakness of the evidence for its claims, in convincing a majority of the public that Iraq posed a threat so extreme and imme-diate that it could be dealt with only by preventive war. Overall, this policy debate resembles what Stephen Van Evera (1988) calls "non-evaluation": that is, a debate in which little real evaluation takes place because those in power ignore or suppress assessments from internal sources that might contradict their preferred policy, and use their ability to influence political and media agendas to focus public attention on their own arguments at the expense of attention to external criticisms.

The question now is, why was this threat inflation so successful? The answer has both theoretical and policy implications. Although the Iraq debate is certainly not the first instance of threat inflation in the United States or other democracies, it mat-ters whether this episode should be considered an uncommon exception to the rule that democratic marketplaces of ideas can usually restrain policies based on dubi-ous claims and rationales, or whether there is a risk of repeated equally severe failures, perhaps with much higher costs for U.S. national security.

Understanding the limits of threat inflation has become especially important because of the Bush administration's adoption of a preventive war doctrine, which substantially expands the potential, compared with previous U.S. grand strategies, for involving the United States in multiple military adventures. This in turn greatly increases the possible consequences if democratic processes and the marketplace of ideas fail repeatedly to weed out exaggerated threat claims and policy proposals based on them. Although conquering Iraq could not do much to improve U.S. national security because the supposed Iraqi threat was mostly chimerical, the costs have been remarkably serious considering the weakness and unpopularity of the opponent and the short time that has elapsed. These include the direct costs of combating the ongo-ing resistance, damage to the United States' reputation among publics worldwide, and increased support for Islamist views similar to those of terrorist groups such as al Qa'ida (Pew 2004). Some observers argue that other major powers, including U.S. allies, are already seeking ways to balance against U.S. power and that further mili-tary adventures comparable to Iraq would accelerate this process (Pape 2003).

Assessing the risk of future failures of the marketplace of ideas requires an explan-ation of the causes of the failure in the Iraq case, which is the purpose of this article. Five factors appear critical in having determined the outcome.

First, democratic political systems may be inherently vulnerable to issue manip-ulation. The logic of the marketplace of ideas in foreign policy is based on the proposition that median voters have strong incentives to scrutinize expansionist arguments and reject those that seem to serve only narrow interests or risk weaken-ing, rather than strengthening, national security (Snyder 1991: 49–52; Downs 1957). There is reason to believe, however, that median voter logic can often be bypassed by elite manipulation of how issues are framed in debate (Arrow 1963; Riker 1988). In this case, the critical manipulation involved redefining the threat posed by Hussein from containing regional aggression to deterring direct terrorist attack on the United States. Second, the Bush administration benefited from its control over the government's intelligence apparatus, which it used to distort the public record by selectively publicizing favorable analyses while suppressing contrary information. Third, the White House enjoys great authority in foreign policy debate, which, in the Iraq case, gave it a credibility advantage over independent critical analyses regardless of the strength of the critics' information or analyses. The authority advantage of the presidency also enhanced the administration's ability to manipulate the framing of the issues. Fourth, the countervailing institutions on which the marketplace of ideas theory relies to check the ability of those in power to control foreign policy debate – especially the press, independent experts and opposition parties – failed to do so, and may generally lack the power to fulfill the functions that the theory expects of them. Finally, the shock of the September 11 atrocities created a crisis atmosphere that may have reduced public skepticism about both diagnoses of threats and proposed solutions.

We cannot predict the future based on a single case. Yet because the first four of these five critical factors are embedded in the structure of the American political system, the implication is that we should not be confident that similar failures will not be repeated in the future.

The remainder of this article is organized into four sections. The first section describes the Bush administration's efforts to inflate alleged threats posed by Iraq and evaluates the validity of their claims. The second section describes the success of the administration's threat inflation in swaying U.S. public opinion, while the third seeks to assess why the marketplace of ideas failed. The final section discusses potential implications for the likelihood and scale of possible future failures.

Threat inflation in the Iraq debate

Assessments of threat normally involve some ambiguity. Threat inflation, as opposed to ordinary conservatism, can be defined as

1   claims that go beyond the range of ambiguity that disinterested experts would credit as plausible (Snyder 2000: 55);
2   a consistent pattern of worst-case assertions over a range of factual issues that are logically unrelated or only weakly related – an unlikely output of disinterested analysis;
3   use of double standards in evaluating intelligence in a way that favors worst-case threat assessments; or
4   claims based on circular logic, such as Bush administration claims that Hussein's alleged hostile intentions were evidence of the existence of weapons of mass destruction (WMD) whose supposed existence was used as evidence of his intentions (Cramer 2004).

Administration exaggerations of the Iraqi threat during 2002–03 qualify on all four grounds. The errors did not result from mistakes by U.S. intelligence agencies.

Rather, top officials knew what policy they intended to pursue and selected intelligence assessments to promote that policy based on their political usefulness, not their credibility. Deputy Secretary of Defense Paul Wolfowitz came close to admitting as much in May 2003 when he stated, "We settled on the one issue that everyone could agree on, which was weapons of mass destruction, as the core reason." An unnamed administration official came still closer when he told an ABC News reporter, "We were not lying [about Iraqi weapons]. But it was just a matter of emphasis" ("Secretary Wolfowitz Interview with Sam Tannenhaus," *Vanity Fair*, 10 May 2003; John Cochran, "Reason for War? White House Officials Say Privately the Sept. 11 Attacks Changed Everything," ABCNews.com, 25 April 2003). As an intelligence official who supported the war described it, "You certainly could have made strong cases that regime change was a logical part of the war on terrorism, given Baghdad's historic terror ties, but that didn't have enough resonance. You needed something that inspired fear" (Vest 2004).

Deterring Hussein: Saddam the madman

Prior to 2002, the main challenge in U.S. policy toward Iraq was framed as containment of potential regional aggression, and a general consensus existed that containment did not require regime change. Few experts doubted that Iraq had been deterred since the 1991 Persian Gulf War, or that the vast military superiority of the United States could deter it, as would be expected for almost any other midsized state. Yet most agreed that Hussein could be contained. This consensus included some Bush administration officials. Condoleezza Rice, who would become Bush's national security adviser, wrote in 2000, "If they [the Iraqis] do acquire WMD, their weapons will be unusable because any attempt to use them will bring national obliteration" (Rice 2000). Similarly, in February 2001, Secretary of State Colin Powell expressed confidence that Iraq could be kept contained (Secretary of State Colin L. Powell, "Briefing for the Press Aboard Aircraft En Route Brussels," 2 February 2001). Arguments by Iraq hawks that containment would fail, leading to a "destabilizing effect on the entire Middle East," made almost no impact (Letter to President Clinton from Project for a New American Century, 26 January 1998).

As long as the debate was framed in this way, attempts to argue that Iraqi WMD programs required preventive war would have faced an uphill battle. Instead, during 2002–03 administration officials sought to redefine Hussein as not an ordinary regional despot careful to protect his power, but an evil madman bent on the destruction of the United States and willing to run virtually any risk to himself or his country to fulfill this goal.

In September 2002, President Bush declared, "The first time we may be completely certain he has nuclear weapons is when, God forbid, he uses one." In March 2003, he asserted, "The danger is clear: using chemical, biological, or, one day, nuclear weapons provided by Iraq, the terrorists could one day kill hundreds of thousands of people in our country or any other" (George W. Bush, "President's Remarks at the United Nations General Assembly," 12 September 2002). In making the administration's case for going to war, Secretary of State Powell asked the UN Security Council in a speech on February 5, 2003,

> Should we take the risk that he will not someday use [WMD] at a time and a place and in a manner of his choosing? . . . The United States will not and cannot run that risk for the American people. Leaving Saddam Hussein in possession of weapons of mass destruction for a few more months or years is not an option, not in a post-September 11th world.

The administration's claims about the supposed threat Hussein posed were not backed by evidence. An October 2002, Special National Intelligence Estimate concluded that Hussein was unlikely to initiate an unprovoked WMD attack against the United States (Director of Central Intelligence, "Key Judgments from the National Intelligence Estimate on Iraq's Continuing Programs for Weapons of Mass Destruction," October 2002). Officials did not present a serious rationale for the administration's position: they failed to address the question of why even a nuclear-armed Hussein would be unfazed by the United States' ability to defeat him conventionally or to retaliate for any Iraqi use of WMD (Vice President Richard B. Cheney, speech to VFW convention, 26 August 2002).

The administration benefited, however, from parallel claims made by friendly analysts, most important Kenneth Pollack, whose book persuaded numerous moderates and liberals who would not have otherwise trusted threat assessments emanating from the Bush administration (Pollack 2002). Pollack argued that Hussein was "one of the most reckless, aggressive, violence-prone, risk-tolerant, and damage-tolerant leaders of modern history," even "inadvertently suicidal." He also claimed that Hussein believed that "possession of nuclear weapons would deter [the United States] from taking action against him" over any regional aggression, regardless of U.S. military superiority (Pollack 2002: 270–276).

Contrary to claims by the Bush administration and other pro-war advocates, however, the record does not show that Saddam Hussein was especially difficult to deter. He was a vicious dictator and had international ambitions, but paid attention to limiting risk and took U.S. power very seriously (Mearsheimer and Walt 2002). Hussein's behavior since the first Gulf War showed him to have been successfully deterred at almost every turn. After the war, Hussein acquiesced in the loss of part of northern Iraq rather than fight the United States and Britain to retake it. He also acquiesced in the destruction of his nuclear weapons program by International Atomic Energy Agency (IAEA) inspectors in 1991–92, and apparently also eventually suspended his chemical and biological weapons programs for fear of the consequences of discovery. After the passage of United Nations Security Council resolution 1441, in November 2002, Iraq cooperated with intrusive inspections to a degree rarely seen in a country not militarily occupied. All of this suggests not a crazed aggressor prone to wild chances, but a ruler profoundly concerned with retaining power and aware that his greatest danger was that the United States might exert itself to remove him. In sum, Bush administration assertions that Hussein might be undeterrable had little foundation.

Inventing links to September 11 and to al Qa'ida: Saddam the terrorist

The second main component in the Bush administration's strategy for shifting the issue from containment to deterrence was to persuade Americans that Hussein was cooperating with terrorists who were already attacking American civilians.

Administration officials made two main claims in this regard, neither of which was supported by credible evidence. The first was that Hussein was personally responsible for assisting in the September 11 attacks. This assertion was based on an alleged meeting between Mohammed Atta, the pilot of the first plane to hit the Twin Towers, and an Iraqi intelligence officer in Prague in April 2001. The source for this was a single Czech informant whom Czech intelligence reported was not credible (John Tagliabue, "No Evidence Suspect Met Iraqi in Prague," *New York Times*, 20 October 2001; Isikoff 2002). The FBI and the CIA quickly also concluded that no such meeting had taken place. Evidence suggested that Atta had been in Virginia at the time in question (Patrick E. Tyler, "U.S. Drops Last Link of Iraq to 9/11," *New York Times*, 2 May 2002; Isikoff 2002; Cam Simpson, "Al Qaeda Allegation Is Weakest Link in Justifying War," *Chicago Tribune*, 20 March 2003).

Administration officials nevertheless continued to repeat the story despite the lack of evidence. Vice President Dick Cheney stated in September 2002, "We have reporting that places [Atta] in Prague with a senior Iraqi intelligence official a few months before September 11.... It is credible" (Vice President Richard V. Cheney, NBC Meet the Press, 8 September 2002). In one of the few Iraq threat claims that the administration has retracted, President Bush acknowledged in September 2003, "We've had no evidence that Saddam Hussein was involved with September the 11th" (President George W. Bush, media availability, Federal Document Clearing House, 17 September 2003).

The administration's second main claim linking Iraq to al Qa'ida concerned Abu Musab al-Zarqawi, the head of a mainly Jordanian and Palestinian terrorist group called al-Tawhid. In September 2002, Secretary of Defense Donald Rumsfeld said that he had "bulletproof evidence" of a link between Hussein and al Qa'ida (Eric Schmitt, "Rumsfeld Says U.S. Has 'Bulletproof' Evidence of Iraq's Links to Al Qaeda," *New York Times*, 28 September 2002). The fullest version of this claim came in Powell's famous speech to the UN Security Council, where he made three assertions:

1   Iraq was "harboring" Zarqawi, "a collaborator of Osama bin Laden," and had allowed him to "establish a base of operations [in Baghdad] for al Qaeda affiliates";
2   "the Zarqawi network helped establish another poison and explosive training center" in a camp belonging to a mainly Kurdish Islamist group called Ansar al-Islam; and
3   "Baghdad has an agent in the most senior levels" of Ansar (Colin L. Powell, "Remarks to the United Nations Security Council," 5 February 2003).

Zarqawi and Ansar al-Islam may indeed have been allied to al Qa'ida; since the U.S. invasion of Iraq, Zarqawi has sought al Qa'ida's help in organizing resistance to the occupation (Peter Finn and Susan Schmidt, "Al Qaeda Is Trying to Open Iraq Front; Plot Said to Be Hatched in Iran Last February," *Washington Post*, 7 September 2003). There was no evidence, however, that Ansar or Zarqawi was cooperating with Hussein. Ansar al-Islam was formed in 2001 for the purpose of overthrowing Hussein's regime and transforming Iraq into an Islamic state. It operated in an area of northern Iraq not under Baghdad's control (Walter Pincus, "Alleged Al Qaeda Ties Questioned; Experts Scrutinize Details of Accusations against Iraqi Government," *Washington Post*, 7 February 2003). Before Powell's speech, U.S. intelligence officials had complained both privately and publicly that the evidence did not support administration claims (Smith 2003). Afterward a senior U.S. government official admitted that it was not known whether the Iraqi "agent" in Ansar represented any form of influence or was simply an informer. Meanwhile CIA Director George Tenet told the Senate Intelligence Committee that he could not characterize Iraq's relationship with Zarqawi as "'control' in any way, shape or form" (Simpson 2003) Powell retracted the Zarqawi claims in January 2004.

Inflating Iraqi WMD threats: the nuclear weapons program that did not exist

In addition to introducing the new issue of the deterrability of Hussein, administration officials sought to persuade Americans that Iraq could not be contained from acquiring weapons of mass destruction, meaning that Hussein would be able to carry out the horrific intentions attributed to him. They claimed that he possessed large arsenals of chemical and biological weapons and was close to acquiring nuclear weapons.

The allegations about Iraq's nuclear potential were the most important to the administration's case for war because only the prospect of nuclear attack could frighten Americans to a degree qualitatively more terrible than September 11. The administration made four claims about the Iraqi nuclear threat. First, President Bush proclaimed in September 2002 that after the first Gulf War, IAEA inspectors had found that Iraq was just "six months away from developing a [nuclear] weapon" (Text of President Bush's News Conference, Associated Press, 7 September 2002). This claim was of no direct relevance to current threats in 2002–03, but was important because it largely became conventional wisdom and was used by administration officials to discredit IAEA and CIA assessments that Iraq was not close to building a nuclear weapon. According to Secretary of Defense Rumsfeld,

> Some have argued that the nuclear threat from Iraq is not imminent – that Saddam is at least 5–7 years away from having nuclear weapons. I would not be so certain. Before Operation Desert Storm in 1991, the best intelligence estimates were that Iraq was at least 5–7 years away. . . . The experts were flat wrong.
>
> ("Rumsfeld's Remarks before the House Armed Services Committee," Federal News Service, 18 September 2002)

Second, the administration declared that Iraq had continued a productive nuclear weapons program after 1991, despite the inspections designed to dismantle it and the ongoing sanctions. According to Vice President Cheney, "For 12 years [Hussein] has violated [his agreements], pursuing chemical, biological and nuclear weapons even while UN inspectors were in Iraq" ("Vice President's Remarks at 30th Political Action Conference," 30 January 2003). Third, President Bush and other officials argued in 2002 that only immediate war could prevent Iraq from completing a nuclear bomb. Cheney said that Iraq had "reconstituted its nuclear weapons program" and that "many of us are convinced that Saddam Hussein will acquire nuclear weapons fairly soon. Just how soon, we cannot really gauge" (Cheney, NBC Meet the Press, 8 September 2002). Fourth, Bush and other officials contended that because Iraq already possessed a design for a nuclear weapon, "with [imported] fissile material [it] could build [a bomb] within a year" ("Transcript of President's Remarks on Iraq Resolution," *New York Times*, 27 September 2002).

The first three claims were wholly inaccurate. Although Hussein may still have been interested in acquiring nuclear weapons, evidence available both inside and outside the U.S. government throughout the mid-1990s as well as the first two years of the Bush administration showed beyond reasonable doubt that by 2002 Iraq had not had an active nuclear weapons program for more than a decade. It also almost certainly could not have reconstituted an indigenous program as long as sanctions remained in place. The fourth claim, concerning nuclear smuggling, was not impossible, but unlikely. The only evidence that Iraq was seeking to acquire fissile material turned out to be fabricated. Moreover, by 2002 Iraq lacked the capability to enrich imported uranium or to manufacture a weapon even if it could have acquired weapons-grade material.

Contrary to later Bush administration claims, pre-1991 assessments of Iraq's nuclear weapons programs were basically accurate. IAEA inspections after the first Gulf War found that – based on optimistic assumptions for Iraq – it was at least 18 months and probably four to five years away from producing enough U-235 to build a nuclear weapon.

Bush administration success in swaying U.S. public opinion

The debate in the United States over the second Gulf War qualifies as a failure of the democratic marketplace of ideas. Numerous internal experts, independent experts, some media outlets and opposition politicians, and responsible international agencies all pointed out before the war that the Bush administration's claims concerning the Iraqi threat were not based on credible evidence. Nevertheless, the administration had succeeded in persuading most Americans, if not many foreigners, to accept its assessments.

The Bush administration's effort to shift the main issue in the Iraq debate from containment of potential regional aggression to deterrence of direct attacks on the United States was more or less completely successful, so much so that public debate in the months before the war includes few dissents from the proposition that Hussein was intensely motivated to attack Americans if he could. Polls in late 2002 showed that 70–90 percent of the American public believed that Hussein would sooner or later attack the United States with weapons of mass destruction (Gallup poll, 13–16 September and 10–12 December 2002). Between 45 percent and 66 percent also believed that he had assisted the September 11 attackers (Gallup poll, 19–21 August 2002). The administration's WMD claims were also widely accepted. Pre-war polls showed that 55–69 percent of Americans believed that Hussein already possessed WMD, and better than 95 percent believed that he was building them (Gallup poll, 7–9 February 2003). In one poll, 69 percent believed that Iraq already had nuclear weapons, and in another, 80 percent thought this likely (Fox News poll, 8–9 September 2002; Time/CNN poll, 15–16 January 2003).

These beliefs translated directly into American support for preventive war. There was a brief blip in support for invading Iraq immediately after September 11, 2001, with as high as 74 percent supporting this in November. Support for war then declined steadily, to about 50 percent in August 2002, when the administration began to ramp up its public campaign for removing Hussein by force. From this point onward, support for invasion rose gradually and more or less steadily to 66 percent in March 2003. The percentage favoring invasion even without UN sanction or allied cooperation rose from 20 percent in June 2002 to 45 percent in August 2002 and to 55 percent in March 2003, matching the evolution of the administration's public positions (Gallup polls, 17–19 June and 19–21 August 2002; *New York Times* poll, 11 March 2003).

The political class was also either persuaded or intimidated. Not one of the more than 30 senators and 100 representatives who attended hearings in July–October 2002 questioned administration claims concerning Hussein's intentions or the supposed Iraqi nuclear threat (see, for example, Senate Foreign Relations Committee, 31 July–1 August and 25–26 September 2002). Many of the 77 senators and 296 representatives who voted in October 2002 to authorize the president to use force against Iraq gave the nuclear threat as the main or one of the main reasons for their votes.

This failure of the marketplace of ideas was probably necessary to obtain political support for invading Iraq. If the public and opposition politicians had understood the weakness of the evidence of Hussein's determination to attack the United States, links to September 11 or al Qa'ida, or nuclear, chemical, or biological weapons programs, the administration probably could not have made a persuasive case for war.

The marketplace also has not operated to correct these misperceptions since the invasion. Although postwar searches failed to find evidence of Iraqi WMD or al Qa'ida connections, a year after the March 2003 invasion, public belief in the administration's pre-war threat claims had declined only slightly. According to polls taken between February and April 2004, 57 percent of Americans still believed that Iraq had possessed weapons of mass destruction, while 52 percent believed that Iraq still had WMD that have not yet been found (NBC News poll, 6–8 March 2004; CBS News poll, 24–27 February 2004). Forty-seven percent thought that "clear evidence that Iraq was supporting Al Qaeda has been found in Iraq," while 36 percent believed that Hussein was personally involved in the September

11 attacks (Harris poll, 9–16 February 2004; CBS News poll, 20 March–1 April 2004), and 55 percent that the U.S. invasion had been the right thing to do (PIPA poll, 16–22 March 2004). In one poll, 45 percent of Americans said that they would be as likely as before to accept such claims by President Bush, while 50 percent said they would be less likely (PIPA poll, 11–20 July 2004).

Public approval of President Bush's conduct of the Iraq War and of his overall job performance did decline between March 2003 and April 2004, from 71 percent to 41–46 percent and from 71 percent to 46–52 percent, respectively (CNN/Harris polls, 29–30 March 2003 and 8 April 2004). However, given the perseverance of public belief in the original rationales for the war, this probably represents dissatisfaction with the continuing armed resistance in Iraq and mounting U.S. casualties. If, however, rising costs in Iraq were to lead not only to reduced public support for the war itself, but also to reduced receptiveness to foreign military adventures for a substantial length of time, that would count in favor of the marketplace of ideas theory.

Why the marketplace failed

Five factors were crucial in determining the outcome of the debate prior to the second Gulf War:

1 the administration's ability to shift the framing of the issue from containment of potential Iraqi regional aggression to the question of whether Hussein could be deterred from direct attacks on Americans;
2 the ability of the White House to control the release of intelligence information;
3 the authority advantage of the presidency in national security policy debates;
4 the failure of countervailing institutions – mainly the press, independent experts, and opposition parties – on which the marketplace of ideas theory relies to combat threat inflation; and
5 the crisis atmosphere created by the shock of September 11.

Political manipulation in democracies

There is reason to doubt that the democratic marketplace of ideas can enforce policy accountability in the manner generally attributed to it. The argument for the relative superiority of democratic foreign policymaking is based on the logic of the median voter, developed by Anthony Downs (1957). The potential costs of war give median voters strong incentives to scrutinize expansionist arguments. This logic allows relatively little scope for elite manipulation, at least when the marketplace of ideas functions well. A robust marketplace of ideas ensures thorough policy debate, making it unlikely that median voters will be persuaded by arguments that cannot withstand independent evaluation (Snyder 1991: 49–52).

Median voter logic, however, applies primarily to situations in which voters are confronted with trade-offs between just two important values arrayed along a single value dimension. It also assumes that voters have fairly good understandings of the implications of different policy choices for their own interests, which in turn may require that the policy debate be framed in much the same way for a considerable time.

There is, however, another logic of public choice in democracies, based on Kenneth Arrow's Impossibility Theorem, which allows more scope for elite manipulation. Arrow showed that whenever there are three or more policy choices involving two or more value dimensions, no majoritarian system can reliably integrate preferences to produce something that can meaningfully be called the "will of the majority" (Arrow 1963: 26–33). Regardless of institutional arrangements, all democracies are vulnerable to manipulation of outcomes by means such as agenda control, strategic voting, or manipulation of issue dimensions (Arrow 1963: 30–31, 118–120). Of these, manipulation of issue dimensions best explains why the marketplace of ideas failed in the Iraq debate.

The motive for this type of manipulation arises when a policy question has become defined in terms of a single dominant issue dimension. Over time, median voters may develop settled preferences for one policy, so that the opposing political faction finds itself consistently in the minority. The minority may be able to reverse its fortunes, however, if it can introduce a second issue and make it the dominant issue in the debate. The newly introduced issue need not be literally new or invented, as long as its political salience was previously low compared with the first issue but can still increase. If the second issue dimension is cleverly chosen to crosscut preferences on the old main issue, many of those who opposed the minority faction on the old issue may now support it (Riker 1988: 197, 212). If enough do, the former minority can form a new majority around the new issue dimension and thereby gain power. This technique can work even when those who are being manipulated understand what is happening. Once persuaded that the second issue is at least as important as the first one, they have little choice but to vote their real preferences on it, regardless of the consequences for their interest in the first issue (Riker 1986: 150–151).

Arrovian issue manipulation usually has better prospects of success than direct attempts to shift views on a long-standing issue, which would have to overcome what may be deeply settled views of most people, not only elites. Although voters must be persuaded to treat the new issue as much more important than they did previously, this task is made easier by the previous low salience of the new issue, so that many people, especially nonexperts, may not have settled views on it.

This situation best describes what happened in the 2002–03 debate on U.S. policy toward Iraq. The Bush administration and like-minded advocates transformed the debate in a manner strikingly consistent with the dynamics of political manipulation identified by Arrow and Riker. To bypass the existing consensus that Iraqi regional aggression could be contained, they introduced the new issue of potential direct Iraqi attack on the United States.

This manipulation of the issue dimensions was relatively easy for the administration to carry out, for two reasons. First, the fact that Iraq was a foreign policy issue helped by concentrating debate on issues that were largely unfamiliar to most Americans, reducing the burden of arguing uphill against settled views. Had Iraq received as much public attention over several years before 2002 as, say, abortion, the administration could not so easily have persuaded so many people to adopt a changed formulation of the issue. One reason why median voter logic accounts better for domestic than for foreign policy outcomes is that it implicitly assumes that no one has any great authority advantage in political debate; without this assumption, voters' issue judgments would always be vulnerable to elite manipulation in Arrovian fashion.

Second, the new issue that administration officials introduced – Hussein's supposed terrorist intentions – was one on which it was politically difficult for opponents to challenge their claims. Although the administration failed to make a strong case that Hussein had particularly extreme intentions, it was still successful in persuading most Americans, in part because the ordinary human tendency toward patriotism makes it too hard to publicly defend the proposition that foreign opponents may not have hostile intentions or may be justified in some of their actions. Neither politicians, mainstream media, nor most public intellectuals can afford to be painted as soft on national security. This probably explains why, compared with the administration's other three major threat claims, there was so little debate on the hostility or deterrability of Hussein, and why there seem to be no polls directly on these issues.

The administration's introduction of this new issue dimension reduced barriers to making arguments for preventive war in three ways. First, reformulating the issue as the possibility of an Iraqi terrorist attack on the United States crosscut the previously dominant framing of the debate as regional containment versus regime change, in which the most serious possible consequence of containment failure was considered to be regional aggression by Iraq. This created a new rationale for war that split the previous consensus; many policy elites who had supported containment were persuaded to support preventive war once the issue was framed as direct defense of the United States. This in turn removed a major barrier to persuading the public. Second, it indirectly supported administration claims about Iraqi WMD, even if it did not logically imply them. Allegations that Hussein intended to attack American civilians were not evidence about the state of his WMD programs, but they did supply an additional reason why he might try. This likely lowered the standards of proof needed to persuade many Americans that Iraq's WMD programs were making dangerous progress. Finally, by accusing Hussein of having supported the September 11 terrorist attacks, the administration created a new rationale for war – retaliation for actual harm – unrelated to forestalling future threats.

This issue manipulation was probably a necessary condition for building public support for the second Gulf War. As long as the Iraq issue remained framed as regional containment versus regime change, the administration would face the uphill battle of overturning a settled consensus, at least among elites. The only obvious argument that it could have made would have been that, contrary to conventional wisdom, Iraqi WMD capabilities could be expected to grow enough to overturn the regional balance of power. The administration, however, lacked credible new evidence of such a change, and few experts doubted that Iraq could be deterred even then. An effort to persuade experts, political elites, and the public to change policy would likely have met considerable opposition.

Control of information

Only the White House has direct access to all national intelligence resources, giving it a unique ability to shape public perceptions through selective release – or suppression – of analyses and information. The Bush administration used this control to present to the public and the world a false picture of U.S. information about Iraqi threats. Analyses that supported the administration's inflated claims were publicized, while those that contradicted pro-war claims remained classified. Further, at least some of the favorable analyses were produced by coercion of intelligence agencies and analysts. This control was probably a necessary condition for the war because the administration built much of its case around release of intelligence documents.

The administration used its control of intelligence information in four ways. First, it consistently published or leaked intelligence analyses that favored its threat claims while suppressing contrary analyses. For instance, shortly before the congressional votes in October 2002, giving President Bush the authority to go to war against Iraq, the administration released part of a Special National Intelligence Estimate on Iraq to support its claims about nuclear, chemical, and biological programs, but kept secret 40 distinct caveats or official dissents.

Second, important intelligence information tending to undermine administration claims was suppressed or distorted. For instance, statements taken from the UN debriefing of Gen. Hussein Kamel, the head of Iraq's WMD programs until his defection in 1995, were used to support claims that after the 1991 Gulf War, Iraq had continued to lie to UN inspectors about pre-war programs. However, his additional statements that Iraq's biological weapons were destroyed after the war, and that Iraq had ended chemical weapons production before that war for fear of U.S. nuclear retaliation, were not released (Debriefing of Kamel, 22 August 1995; Vice President Cheney, speech to VFW convention, 26 August 2002; President Bush, speech at the Cincinnati Museum Center, 7 October 2002).

Third, administration officials publicized claims provided by Iraqi exiles linked to Ahmed Chalabi's Iraqi National Congress (INC), which stood to benefit from the overthrow of Hussein. In addition to other funding to the INC, at the beginning of the Bush administration, the U.S. government began funding an "Information Collection Program" to pay for intelligence from INC defectors. The practical effect was that the United States paid for intelligence that would promote a preventive war policy (Eli J. Lake, "Is Bush Getting the Whole Story on Iraq?" *Pittsburgh Post-Gazette*, 22 September 2002). At least two of the administration's major claims about the Iraqi threat – the aluminum tubes and the mobile bioweapons laboratories – were derived from defectors (see, for example: Judith Miller, "Iraqi Tells of Renovations at Sites for Chemical and Nuclear Arms," *New York Times*, 20 December 2001).

CIA and DIA analysts pointed out repeatedly that such sources could not be rated as reliable, prompting Secretary of Defense Rumsfeld to set up an *ad hoc* agency known as the Office of Special Plans (OSP) that would be willing to validate INC-based claims (Hersh 2003a; Pollack 2004: 88). OSP also collected raw, unverified intelligence data from the CIA and other agencies and passed it directly to top decisionmakers, bypassing the regular intelligence agencies (Bradley Graham and Dana Priest, "Pentagon Team Told to Seek Details of Iraq–Al Qaeda Ties; Effort Bypasses Regular Intelligence Channels," *Washington Post*, 25 October 2002).

Fourth, administration officials coerced intelligence agencies and analysts to provide politically useful conclusions. Numerous serving and retired analysts from the CIA, DIA, State Department, and FBI reported pressure from administration officials. The most succinct description came from Pollack, who said that Bush officials

> dismantle[d] the existing filtering process that for fifty years had been preventing the policymakers from getting bad information. They created 'stovepipes' to get the information they wanted directly to the top leadership. Their position is that the professional bureaucracy is deliberately and maliciously keeping information from them. . . . They were forcing the intelligence community to defend its good information so aggressively that the intelligence analysts didn't have the time or the energy to go after the bad information.
>
> (Quoted in Hersh 2003: 77)

The main counter that intelligence agencies have against such distortions is individual leaks, but serving analysts are inhibited by the danger of retaliation, while retired ones may not be listened to. For these reasons, we will probably never know the full extent of the information tending to discredit administration claims about Iraq.

Authority in foreign policy

Government agencies usually have a large authority advantage in debate with anyone else. This is especially so in realms where they have an information advantage and do not face competing authorities of comparable stature, which is the White House's normal situation in national security policy. The situation is unlike that of domestic policy, where authority is more widely spread among the executive, Congress, the courts, and in some circumstances non-governmental institutions such as political parties, unions, and churches.

The White House's authority advantage facilitated the administration's campaign for preventive war in five ways. First, it helped the administration control the agenda for debate, which in turn assisted the effort to redefine the Iraq policy problem from regional containment to homeland defense. Although Arrovian issue manipulation is routinely used in domestic politics – for instance, the competing efforts to define the 2000 presidential election as being about the economic performance of the Clinton administration versus about the moral character of Bill Clinton – in domestic settings, normally no side has a great advantage in controlling which issue formulation becomes dominant. In national security policy, the executive branch does have such an advantage, at least in the United States; once the administration decided to redefine the issue as one of deterrence rather than containment, there was no equally prestigious institution that could contest this shift.

Second, the White House's authority concentrated attention on the administration's claims, compelling critics to counterpunch point by point with limited if any opportunity to present a coherent opposing narrative. In addition, throughout the Iraq debate mainstream press and even opposition politicians often simply accepted administration claims uncritically, while even those criticisms most compelling on logic or facts were rarely reported without simultaneously granting administration claims at least equal respect. Internal critics, who were important because of the centrality of intelligence analyses in the debate, were at a special disadvantage. Internal opponents of government policy generally lack independent authority and can make their dissents public only by way of leaks, which are often delayed until after the critical decisions have been made. There have been far more anti-Iraq War leaks since the invasion than there were during the invasion debate. Further, leaks – except those by the White House itself – necessarily lack governmental authority and are treated as less credible by most of the public and the press.

Third, the administration's authority advantage allowed it to attack the credibility of independent experts. This was important in discrediting IAEA inspection findings that Iraq did not have an active nuclear weapons program. For instance, Vice President Cheney stated in March 2003,

> I think Mr. ElBaradei [director general of the IAEA] frankly is wrong. And I think if you look at the track record of the International Atomic Energy Agency and this kind of issue, especially where Iraq's concerned, they have consistently underestimated or missed what it was Saddam Hussein was doing.
>
> (Vice President Cheney, NBC Meet the Press, 16 March 2003)

In fact, the IAEA's track record on Iraq from the 1980s onward consistently demonstrated better accuracy than more alarmist critics, as U.S. intelligence agreed until the Bush administration took office. Such attacks on independent experts achieved some success; public confidence in the existence of Iraq's nuclear program did decline during the inspection period, but only marginally. Ordinary nationalist suspicion of foreign sources of authority probably helped: in a December 2002 poll, Americans said they would trust the administration over international inspectors by a margin of 52 percent to 36 percent (Gallup poll, 10–11 December 2002).

Fourth, careful phrasing of official rhetoric can allow even claims with especially weak evidentiary bases to be persuasive to the public, because often only experts are in a position to parse what certain official statements did and did not say. As noted above, Bush's 2003 State of the Union address attributed the Niger uranium story to British intelligence to avoid having to state in so many words something known to be false.

The most important use of this tactic was in encouraging public belief that Hussein had been involved in the September 11 atrocities. Without quite saying so, President Bush and other officials routinely used carefully juxtaposed formulations that placed the September 11 attacks and the alleged threat from Hussein within a few words of each other, giving the impression that there was a causal link without actually saying so. In his 2003 State of the Union address, Bush said: "Imagine those 19 hijackers with other weapons and other plans – this time armed by Saddam Hussein." In January 2003, Wolfowitz declared,

> As terrible as the attacks of September 11th were, however, we now know that the terrorists are plotting still more and greater catastrophes. . . . Iraq's weapons of mass terror and the terror networks to which the Iraqi regime are linked are not two separate themes – not two separate threats.
>
> (Deputy Secretary of State Wolfowitz, speech at Council on
> Foreign Relations, 23 January 2003)

Use of such rhetorical jujitsu undoubtedly accounts for why so many Americans believed that Hussein had supported the September 11 attacks.

Fifth, the authority of the White House allows even discredited claims to be repeated with some persuasive effect. Administration officials made use of this frequently during the pre-war debate, and some continued to do so after the invasion. For instance, the same week the Iraq Survey Group reported that evidence of Iraqi WMD had not been found, Vice President Cheney declared that there was "conclusive evidence [that Hussein did] have programs for weapons of mass destruction" as well as "overwhelming evidence that there was a connection between al-Qaeda and the Iraqi government" (Vice President Cheney, NPR Morning Edition, 22 January 2004).

The weakness of countervailing forces

One of the main institutions that the marketplace of ideas theory counts on to counter myths of empire – political opposition – was largely unavailable in the Iraq case and probably cannot be counted on reliably in foreign policy debates, more generally. The other two – the press and independent experts – did not and probably cannot do much independently to contain threat inflation.

Part of the reason that the Bush administration encountered minimal organized political opposition was that the Democrats faced the classic dilemma of a faction faced with a well-designed Arrovian issue manipulation – they were split. Many prominent Democrats were persuaded that the possibility of direct attack on the United States trumped any confidence they might have had in containment as well as their qualms about regime change, while those who were not persuaded had no options. Just as slavery split the Democrats of 1860, Democratic die-hards in 2002 could not oppose the administration's march to war and still carry the rest of their party with them.

Non-evaluation can also benefit from political opponents' fears of seeming weak in the face of an external threat, which makes it difficult to organize unified opposition to foreign policies with muscular symbolism. In the Iraq case, more prominent Democratic politicians, especially presidential candidates, preferred to criticize administration policy from the right rather than the left. Robust opposition is typically seen only after costly policy failures, and even then with considerable delay, as in the example of congressional opposition to Vietnam in 1973–75.

Throughout the pre-war debate on Iraq, the media were relatively supine, tending to report administration claims credulously, while devoting much lesser effort to investigating the validity of those claims or to reporting the views of experts who were doing so (Massing 2004). Administration and pro-war advocates also simply got disproportionate distribution. A study of network television news stories on Iraq over two weeks in January–February 2003 found that more than half of the 393 sources quoted were U.S. officials. Only 17 percent of sources quoted expressed skepticism about administration policy, most of whom were Iraqi or other foreign government officials. Only 4 percent were skeptical expressions by Americans, and only half of these had any affiliation to advocacy or expert organizations (FAIR 2003). In part, options for critical reporting were limited by the relative absence of organized political opposition, depriving the media of prominent figures around whom to center controversy.

Second, reporters may have feared loss of access to official sources if they published critical stories; during the war, numerous reporters signed agreements allowing the military to vet their stories. The impact of this on the content of reporting is uncertain.

Third, news organizations may judge that Americans do not want to be confronted with complex information or criticism of national policy. Such a judgment was reflected in CNN's decision to provide two separate versions of war coverage – a "cheerleading" version for U.S. audiences, and a more balanced and complex version for the rest of the world (Massing 2003: 17).

Fourth, a number of authors have proposed that conservative bias in the media favors Republican presidents and policies (Tomasky 2003; Chomsky 2002; Alterman 2003). During the 1990s most radio and television talk shows adopted conservative orientations, as has one mainstream news network, Fox. Polls show that viewers who got their news primarily from Fox were more likely than others to accept inaccurate pro-war statements (Kull *et al.* 2003/4: 581–585). Moderate and liberal outlets, however, are by no means excluded. The attitudes of Fox viewers could be more a self-selection effect than anything else.

Whether or not the mainstream news media are characterized by conservative bias on average, one effect of ideological fragmentation is that even the most egregious administration-promoted myths will receive support from friendly media. This in turn undermines the credibility of the media as an independent source of authority, reducing it from Walter Cronkite's "That's the way it is" to the staccato "I say, you say" exchanges of Crossfire.

Independent experts, mainly think tank analysts and university academics, also could not carry out the functions the marketplace of ideas assigns to them for many of the same reasons that the media could not. Academic experts are normally divided in their views and rarely present consensus opposition to administration claims. Relatively few presented comprehensive critiques, and fewer of those received wide media attention.

Further, as with the media, ideologically committed conservative think tanks such as the Heritage Foundation and the American Enterprise Institute made it possible to confuse debate by contradicting any expert criticism with experts of apparently equal authority. Since most of the public lacks the ability to evaluate experts' qualifications or disinterestedness, this undermined the possibility that any criticisms might be seen as authoritative or have much persuasive effect.

The impact of September 11

The World Trade Center and Pentagon terrorist attacks helped to support the Bush administration's case for war in two ways. First, it assisted the transformation of the Iraq issue from containment to deterrence of terrorism. The attack by one enemy on American civilians made it more plausible that others might also attack, and the authority advantage of the executive branch helped to focus that fear on Iraq, rather than on proposals to concentrate first on al Qa'ida. Second, as Robert Jervis has suggested, elevated fears of terrorism reduced Americans' skepticism about almost any promises to decrease their personal security fears (Jervis 2003: 317–318).

It is more difficult to assess, however, whether September 11 was a necessary condition for the second Gulf War. The uniqueness of the events of September 11 makes it impossible to specify all the categories of external shocks that could have been used to promote the administration's policy goals, if not necessarily in the same way. It is even more difficult to imagine all the possible stimuli that could be used to support other, future adventures. The successful use of September 11 to promote a preventive war against an opponent unrelated to the original provocation suggests that there may often be flexibility in the use of external events to promote preferred policies.

Prospects and risks for the future

Should we expect the marketplace of ideas to fail again, either in the United States or other democracies, possibly with worse consequences? Some dimensions of the failure in the Iraq case appear especially egregious, but a study of a single case cannot determine whether it is an outlier or part of a pattern of more or less normal market failures. It is not even clear which interpretation should be cause for more concern: if Iraq is an outlier, that could mean either that we should have relatively little concern for the future or that the robustness of the marketplace in the United States is deteriorating in a way not yet understood. If, however, the Iraq case is a relatively normal example, then we must fear equally severe failures, which could be especially dangerous if combined with a preventive war doctrine. What can be said is that most of the dynamics that appear to explain the Iraq outcome – the effectiveness of Arrovian issue manipulation, the information control and authority advantages of the executive in national security policy, and the fragmentation of countervailing institutions – are normally present in democracies, at least those with strong executives such as the United States.

How much danger this poses of further military adventures based on equally weak justifications is unclear, but there is some evidence that the Bush administration, at least, views preventive war as a foreign policy tool that could be used repeatedly. According to one senior official, "Iraq is not just about Iraq. [It was] a unique case," but in Mr Bush's mind, "it is of a type" (David E. Sanger, "Viewing the War as a Lesson to the World," *New York Times*, 6 April 2003). According to Bush's National Security Strategy, the United States "possesses unprecedented – and unequalled – strength and influence" and will seek "to dissuade potential adversaries from pursuing a military buildup in hopes of surpassing, or equaling, the power of the United States" (National Security Strategy of the United States, pp. 7, 33).

How common are threat inflation and failures of the marketplace?

No depth of investigation of the Iraq case alone can provide confident predictions about future risks. That will require systematic testing across cases that vary on the key factors suggested both by the marketplace of ideas theory and by my explanation of this case. Three categories of cases must be examined: previous instances of successful (or unsuccessful) threat inflation in the United States or other democracies with strong executives; instances in democracies with weaker executives, such as Britain in the Iraq case, and assessments such as that in 1955–56 of the threat posed by President Gamal Abdel Nasser of Egypt; and non-democratic cases. Across all cases, scholars should seek to evaluate the robustness of the institutions making up the marketplace of ideas, the power of the executive to manipulate issues and control information, the methods used to bypass or suppress the functioning of the marketplace, and the apparent reasons why the marketplace succeeded or failed as far as it did in each case.

References

Alterman, E. (2003) *What Liberal Media? The Truth about Bias in the News*, New York: Basic Books.

Arrow, K. J. (1963) *Social Choice and Individual Values*, 2nd edn, New York: Wiley.

Chomsky, N. (2002) *Media Control: The Spectacular Achievements of Propaganda*, 2nd edn, New York: Seven Stories.

Cirincione, J., Mathews, J. T. and Perkovich, G. with Orton, A. (2004) *WMD in Iraq: Evidence and Implications*, New York: Carnegie Endowment for International Peace.

Clarke, R. A. (2004) *Against All Enemies: Inside America's War on Terror*, New York: Free Press.

Cramer, J. K. (2004) "Sounding the tocsin redux: Persistent patterns of threat inflation," Paper presented to the 2004 meeting of the International Studies Association, Montreal, Canada.

Downs, A. (1957) *An Economic Theory of Democracy*, New York: Harper.

Fairness and Accuracy in Reporting. (2003) *In Iraq Crisis, Networks Are Megaphones for Official Views*. Online. Available: <http://www.fair.org/reports/iraq-sources.html> (Accessed March 18, 2003).

Hersh, S. (2003a) "Selective intelligence," *New Yorker*, May 12.

—— (2003b) "The stovepipe," *New Yorker*, August 8.

Isikoff, M. (2002) "The phantom link to Iraq: A spy story tying Saddam to 9–11 is looking very flimsy," Available: <http://www.newsweek.com> *(*Accessed April 30, 2002).

Jervis, R. L. (2003) "The confrontation between Iraq and the U.S.: Implications for the theory and practice of deterrence," *European Journal of International Relations*, 9: pp. 315–337.

Kull, S., Ramsay, C. and Lewis, E. (2003/4) "Misperceptions, media, and the Iraq war," *Political Science Quarterly*, 118: pp. 569–599.

Massing, M. (2003) "The unseen war," *New York Review of Books*, May 29, pp. 16–19.

—— (2004) "Now they tell us," *New York Review of Books*, February 26, pp. 43–49.

Mearsheimer, J. J. and Walt, S. M. (2002) *Can Saddam Be Contained? History Says Yes*, Cambridge, Mass.: Belfer Center for Science and International Affairs, John F. Kennedy School of Government, Harvard University.

Pape, R. A. (2003) "The world pushes back," *Boston Globe*, March 23.

Pew Global Attitudes Survey (2004) "Mistrust of America ever higher, Muslim anger persists," Washington, DC: Pew Foundation.

Pollack, K. M. (2002) *The Threatening Storm: The Case for Invading Iraq*, New York: Random House.

Pollack, Kenneth (2004) "Spies, Lies, and Weapons," *Atlantic*, January/February, pp. 78–92.

Reiter, D. and Stam, A. C. (2002) *Democracies at War*, Princeton, NJ: Princeton University Press.

Rice, C. (2000) "Campaign 2000 – promoting the national interest," *Foreign Affairs*, 79: pp. 45–62.

Riker, W. H. (1986) *The Art of Political Manipulation*, New Haven, CT: Yale University Press.

—— (1988) *Liberalism against Populism*, Prospect Heights, IL: Waveland.

Russett, B. (1993) *Grasping the Democratic Peace: Principles for a Post-Cold War World*, Princeton, NJ: Princeton University Press.

Smith, M. (2003) "Spies force retreat on 'al-Qa'eda link,'" *Telegraph* (London), February 4.

Snyder, J. (1991) *Myths of Empire: Domestic Politics and Political Ambition*, Ithaca, NY: Cornell University Press.

Snyder, J. (2000) *From Voting to Violence: Democratization and Nationalist Conflict*, New York: W.W. Norton.

Suskind, R. (2004) *The Price of Loyalty: George W. Bush, the White House, and the Education of Paul O'Neill*, New York: Simon and Schuster.

Tomasky, M. (2003) *Whispers and Screams: The Partisan Nature of Editorial Pages*, Cambridge, MA: John F. Kennedy School of Government, Harvard University, July 2003.

Van Evera, S. (1988) "Why States Believe Foolish Ideas: Non-Self-Evaluation by Government and Society," unpublished manuscript.

—— (1999) *The Causes of War,* Ithaca, NY: Cornell University Press.

—— (2003) "Why states believe foolish ideas: Non-Self-Evaluation by states and societies," in A. Hanami (ed.) *Perspectives on Structural Realism,* New York: Palgrave.

Vest, J. (2004) "Wrong target," *American Prospect*, Available <http://theamericanprospect.com>. (Accessed April 15, 2004).

Woodward, B. (2004) *Plan of Attack*, New York: Simon and Schuster.

7 The sound of silence

Rhetorical coercion, Democratic acquiescence, and the Iraq War

Ronald R. Krebs and Jennifer Lobasz

The Iraq War has been accused of, among other things, alienating young Muslims and revitalizing the Islamist threat, distracting the US government from the "war on terror" properly conceived, breaking the US Army and the military's reserve components, and estranging America's allies. The war has yet to be blamed for contributing to global warming. And yet it could, not just because the US military's inefficient vehicles in Iraq and Afghanistan produce many greenhouse gases, but because the debate over these wars, their conduct and their legacy has led to the destruction of innumerable trees. Eager to learn how the United States might avoid such needless and costly wars in the future, journalists (Gordon and Trainor 2006; Isikoff and Corn 2006; Ricks 2006), pundits (Fukuyama 2006; Rich 2006), and scholars (Dueck 2004; Flibbert 2006; Freedman 2004; Kaufmann 2004; Monten 2005; Mueller 2005; Western 2005a) have all sought to understand how the United States came to launch a misguided war against Iraq and how that war, once undertaken, could have been bungled so badly.

Many of the proposed answers revolve around asserted motives including the influence of a neoconservative cabal and its dreams of falling autocratic dominoes, Bush and Cheney's ties to the oil industry, "unfinished business" for those who had played leading roles in the 1991 Gulf War, and the impact of the September 11 attacks on decision-makers' tolerance for risk. Motives are important as driving forces of human behavior, but they are often unknown, even to the actors themselves, and are perhaps in principle unknowable. Even more importantly, these motives, whatever they were, are only the beginning of the story insofar as the Bush administration still had to effectively legitimate the war with Iraq – that is, to provide publicly acceptable reasons or justifications for the war.

The concept of "threat inflation" speaks directly to this point. President George W. Bush and his aides, it is claimed, exploited the "bully pulpit" to frame the national dialogue on Iraq and the looming prospect of military action, and manipulated intelligence to exaggerate the threat Iraq posed to the United States and US interests. Leading Democrats remained relatively quiet, silenced by their party's dovish reputation and their fear of seeming soft on security and perhaps also by an atmosphere of "militarized patriotism." We argue, however, that these explanations are either problematic or at least insufficient to account for the constrained nature of the pre-war debate and specifically for leading Democrats' accession to a large zone of consensus.

We maintain that the successful legitimation of the Iraq War was made possible by the effective fixing of the meaning of the September 11 attacks in terms of the "War on Terror." Elsewhere we have explained how and why this particular narrative became relatively "hegemonic" (Krebs and Lobasz 2007). Here we explain how this dominant narrative hindered the potential opposition in the debate over the looming Iraq War. Leading figures who might have been expected to resist the administration's program of aggressive democratization contested its claims only at the margins. We argue that they were the victims of successful "rhetorical coercion": a strategy that seeks to rhetorically constrain political opponents and maneuver them into public assent to one's preferred terms of debate and ideally to one's policy stance (Krebs 2006; Krebs and Jackson 2007). The administration's triumph was not inevitable, and thus its particular rhetorical strategies – implying an operational relationship between Al Qaeda and Hussein's Iraq, emphasizing the domestic brutality of Hussein's regime even in unrelated discussions about weapons of mass destruction, confusing warranted suspicions about Iraq's biological and chemical weapons programs and stocks with lingering concerns about continuing nuclear weapons research – were relevant to the outcome. Nevertheless, the consolidation of the War on Terror had already heavily stacked the deck in the administration's favor.

We should note at the outset that we are uncomfortable with the concept of "threat inflation" that organizes this volume. It implies that threats exist independent of the viability of their articulation, that they can be objectively measured, as can the degree to which they are exaggerated. It suggests that the legitimation of national projects is sometimes, even often, unproblematic, that the construction of a national consensus calls for explanation only when it departs from "reality." Proceeding from a more social ontology, we hold that threats are necessarily socially constructed and that the assertion of threat and of threat inflation are equally and inherently political interventions. We believe legitimation and the construction of (zones of) consensus to be always problematic, always worthy of explanation. In our view, the question should be framed differently. Rather than inquire why the Bush administration's "inflation" of the Iraq threat succeeded, we instead ask: how and why did the administration succeed in carrying the nation to war?

Our essay proceeds in four sections. First, we argue that the usual explanations of the successful "inflation" of the Iraq threat are insufficient. Second, we briefly present the familiar interpretation of the September 11 attacks – what we call the War-on-Terror narrative – that became dominant. Third, we show how it, in combination with existing representations of Iraq and its leadership, structured the subsequent contestation over the war. In the conclusion, we reflect on the relationship between structure and agency – that is, whether things might have turned out differently.

Existing arguments and their flaws

The war in Iraq and especially the subsequent revelation that its chief justification – the alleged existence of active Iraqi research programs to develop and acquire weapons of mass destruction and of sizable chemical and biological weapons stocks – was mistaken has led scholars to accuse the Bush Administration of having hyped, or "inflated," the threat Iraq posed. They claim that sufficient evidence was available prior to the onset of combat operations to have cast severe doubt on the administration's charges, and the war won popular assent only because the threat had been so exaggerated. While these accounts highlight factors of substantial import, they are ultimately not satisfying.

First, some correctly note that presidents in the United States enjoy particular authority with regard to foreign affairs. Thanks to the deference historically accorded the president, Congress' abdication of its responsibilities, and the executive's control over classified information, they argue that presidents' preferred frames dominate public debate, particularly in foreign policy (Kaufmann 2004: 37–43; Western 2005b: 108–109, 117–120). However, attributing Bush's success to his institutional position alone overstates presidents' power to set the terms of debate (frame) and to lead public opinion (persuade), even on matters about which they care deeply. The bully pulpit's influence is often overblown, and on a wide range of issues – including national security – presidents have served more as "facilitators" who reflect and perhaps intensify and channel widely held views than as "directors" who lead opinion or impose dominant frames (Edwards III 2003).[1] When presidents "go public," they *can* effectively shift policy and shape legislation, but only when their stance is popular (Canes-Wrone 2005; Kernell 2007). The recent rise of cable television and, arguably, of a generally more independent media has further undercut presidents' (already limited) capacity to control public debate. Presidents have many times faced substantial opposition and have been compelled to abandon pet projects abroad. The fact that leading Democrats typically did not vocally oppose the Iraq War is, therefore, the central puzzle.

Second, and closely related, John Mueller has observed that politicians (and by extension the media) accede to representations of threat because the political and reputational costs of underplaying risks exceed the costs of exaggerating them (Mueller 2005). This calculus can explain the long history of threat representations among democratic politicians, and it can account for the weakness of congressional opposition to war. The problem, however, is that this logic tends to overprediction: if Mueller were right, moves toward war would rarely meet with resistance, yet efforts to legitimate threats have hardly proved universally successful, even when the president leads the charge. The same problem bedevils Jane Cramer's argument, in this volume, that a post-World War II "militarized patriotism" accounts both for the lack of vocal opposition to Bush's drive for war and for the absence of an assertive media (Cramer 2009). In fact, the list of failed recent presidential efforts to build support for particular threats abroad is long – among others, Reagan on Lebanon, El Salvador, Grenada, and especially Nicaragua; G.H.W. Bush on Haiti; Clinton on Haiti, Bosnia, Iraq, and Kosovo.

Third, it is commonly argued that potential Democratic opponents went along with the Iraq War because they feared the accusation that they are soft on national security – a perception, and political vulnerability, that dates to Vietnam or even the "loss" of China. Republicans, the argument goes, have "owned" the security issue and have enjoyed an advantage when debate occurs on its terrain. While this logic seems intuitive, it overstates Democrats' reluctance to challenge Republicans on security questions. Recall, for example, the fits that congressional Democrats gave Reagan over Contra aid, despite his efforts to paint them as Soviet sympathizers or their unwitting dupes. Nor did Republican critiques of Clintonian engagement with China have much traction. Republicans have, according to polls, enjoyed greater trust on national-security matters, at least until recently, but that has not always silenced Democrats or ensured Republicans' triumph. Moreover, this presumes that Democrats could not themselves have deployed a powerful security argument to counter the drumbeat for war. However, they might have argued – and in fact some did and many more recently have – that war in Iraq would distract from the central mission of the War on Terror: the campaign against Al Qaeda. If this claim was unavailable to most Democrats, it was not because Republicans "owned" security, but because the dominant War-on-Terror narrative bound Iraq into that larger struggle.

Fourth, it is often suggested that the executive branch's control over intelligence, combined with limited congressional oversight, confers overwhelming informational advantages (Kaufmann 2004: 37–41; Western 2005a: Ch. 6). Mueller (2005: 228) has further argued that the public typically harbors "irrational fears about remote dangers," is uninformed, and is easily influenced.[2] That informational asymmetries exist, that they favor the chief executive, and that the manipulation of information occurred in the case of the Iraq War is beyond doubt, yet it is not clear that it was *causally* critical. If Kaufmann (2004) is right that there was enough information publicly available to demonstrate that Iraq was not an imminent threat, then the manipulation of intelligence cannot have had the effects he and others have ascribed to it. What becomes puzzling is why the administration's misrepresentations and misleading statements carried the day over the discrepant evidence.[3]

Fifth, many have pointed to the mainstream media's uncritical presentation of the administration's claims as contributing to the skewed public debate (Jamieson and Waldman 2003: Ch. 6; Kaufmann 2004: 44–45; Massing 2004; Western 2005b: 127–128). Yet if the press did in fact abdicate its professional obligation as government watchdog, the question is why it did so. In fact, existing studies suggest that the mainstream media is *generally* more dependent than independent, more mirror of official debates than participant in them. When the opposition is vibrant, the press can be feisty: criticism in official circles opens space for coverage of criticism outside Washington. When the opposition is itself relatively silent, voices not represented in the official debate are ignored. The media thus "indexes" high-profile debates, and these dynamics are only exacerbated in times of war (Bennett 1990, 2004; Cook 1998; Mermin 1999).[4] To the extent that journalists do criticize, they do so *within* the terms of the Washington consensus. The media's relatively uncritical presentation reflected Democrats' inability to advance a strong and united opposition. Again, the relative silence of leading Democrats calls for explanation.

Sixth, observers have invoked the psychology of risk to explain why threats may be inflated relatively easily and how the Iraq threat was made plausible. Human beings tend to overestimate risk, particularly with regard to rare events over which they feel they have no control. The September 11 attacks aggravated this, leading Americans to see still far-off concerns (Iraq's acquiring nuclear weapons) and low probability events (Iraq's sharing such weapons with Al Qaeda) as more imminent and more likely (Huddy *et al.* 2003; Sunstein 2003). With decisions made on the basis of possibility rather than probability, the Bush administration's case for invading Iraq seemed strong. However, this account is not supported by data. As late as February 2003, a majority of Americans said the United States should not attack Iraq without the United Nations' imprimatur, suggesting that they distinguished between possibility and probability (Kull *et al.* 2003–2004).

These claims about "threat inflation" and the Iraq War highlight important dynamics, but they are incomplete. They are rooted in arguments that tend toward overprediction, and many point back to a critical under-explained question: why did most leading Democrats either support the administration or at best offer a modest critique? Any adequate account of how the Iraq threat was successfully "sold" must be based upon a more general argument that can explain both the dogs that bark (when the assertion of a national-security threat successfully takes hold) and those that do not (when such assertions fail to hold sway). They must explain why and how actual or at least conceivable arguments to the contrary are marginalized (or not) and why and when a vibrant political opposition coalesces (or not). This is equally true of "inflated" and "uninflated" threats, at least in regimes that permit a modicum of political contestation.

The notion of threat inflation implies that how political actors represent circumstances is critical. Yet the causal mechanisms in these existing accounts focus seemingly on everything *but* the language and rhetorical strategies employed in the construction of consent. We argue that, to understand how the Iraq War was made possible, one should explore the legacy of the September 11 attacks on US political discourse, in conjunction with other genealogical elements. "September 11" was not just a political resource cynically deployed by administration figures to create the impression that the Iraqi regime was somehow responsible and thus to facilitate a war they had wanted all along (Freedman 2004: 18–20; Kaufmann 2004: 16–19, 46). Supporters of the Iraq War certainly did associate the Hussein regime with the attacks, but this was made possible by the way in which "September 11" was represented and its meaning fixed in place.

The meaning of 9/11

The conventional wisdom has been that 9/11 "changed everything." "History begins today," Deputy Secretary of State Richard Armitage recalled telling Pakistan's intelligence chief. Yet neither the Bush administration's militarized and unilateral policies of aggressive democracy promotion nor their legitimating discourse were radically new (Gaddis 2004; Leffler 2004). Faced with an event that demanded an interpretive response, US elites unsurprisingly fell back on older tropes. Multiple interpretations remained possible, however, and these strove to dominate the public sphere. But only one – that favored by the Bush administration – did.

The administration's narrative has been widely noted and need not be belabored. Within days, Bush and his advisers consistently portrayed the attacks as the latest stage in a terrorist "war" on "America" and its "values." Deploying a series of binaries, they contrasted the goodness and virtue of America with the "evil" of her terrorist adversaries, the freedom that Americans prized with the despotism that her enemies represented, the victims' commitment to civilization with the "evildoer" perpetrators' barbarism. "Evil" could not be negotiated or reasoned with, violence had to be met with violence, and a "war on terror" was proclaimed (Bostdorff 2003; Jackson 2005; Silberstein 2004).

The United States was thus cast as victim, blameless for the perpetrated outrage: the horrific attacks were not a response to its deeds and misdeeds abroad. This claim was central to several strands of argument, which variously saw the attacks as a backlash against globalization, as rooted in popular frustration with repressive government at home, and as part of an intra-Arab and Muslim civil war. At the core of these contending accounts lay a common narrative element: "we" were attacked because of "who we are," not because of "what we have done."

This narrative soon proved dominant. In reportage, national identity discourse – including the invocation of core American values and the demonization of the enemy – overshadowed all others in the ensuing weeks (Coe *et al.* 2004; Hutcheson *et al.* 2004). The administration's political opponents rallied behind not only the president's policies, but his rhetoric. "Save for a few criticisms of [Bush's] offhand remarks about a 'crusade' and wanting Osama bin Laden 'dead or alive,'" one scholar observes, "no significant domestic public criticism of [Bush's] discourse about evil was voiced" (Bostdorff 2003: 293). Public opinion surveys over the coming years questioned not whether the United States should engage in a War on Terror, but rather how that war might be most effectively waged. As Lustick concludes, "The War on Terror has thus achieved the status of a background narrative" (Lustick 2006: 17). Five years after the attacks, many self-identified progressives continued to criticize the administration's approach on this terrain, re-inscribing the War on Terror as the defining discourse of the age (Judt 2006).

There was a prominent alternative of course. In this narrative, "we" were attacked precisely because of "what we have done": financially and politically assisting repressive regimes, giving Israel unquestioned political support and implicitly sanctioning its occupation of Palestinian territory, spreading neoliberal economic policies and threatening traditional ways of life. In short, on September 11 the United States reaped what it had sowed. Overall, however, this narrative made little headway beyond those predisposed to it: opinion remained steady between 2001 and 2004 in denying that US wrongdoing abroad was primarily responsible for the September 11 attacks (Kohut *et al.* 2004). Explaining why this alternative failed to make much headway is itself an important question, and one we have taken up elsewhere (Krebs 2008; Krebs and Lobasz 2007). For our purposes here, it suffices to note that the War-on-Terror narrative swiftly came to dominate the national security imaginary.

The war on terror, rhetorical coercion, and the invasion of Iraq

As the Bush administration worked to frame Iraq as a "gathering storm," it maintained that Iraq either had acquired or would soon acquire weapons of mass destruction, particularly nuclear weapons, that this development would spark intolerable instability in a region of strategic significance, and that Iraq might share nuclear weaponry with non-state actors who could not be deterred. At least in principle, such justifications can be countered, and the administration might have faced substantial opposition. Yet leading Democrats passed up this opportunity to challenge its central claims. Why? We argue that the dominance of the War on Terror narrowed the space for debate over foreign policy and led many Democrats to hold their tongues. The established terms of debate after September 11 had repercussions that extended well beyond those first months after the World Trade Center towers fell. Moreover, challenging the war in Iraq required challenging a portrait of Saddam Hussein as evil and as a terrorist, terms in which he had long been cast. A large and critical group of Democrats, whose national profiles might have bolstered the opposition to war, shied away from criticizing the popular president leading the War on Terror: while a handful jumped enthusiastically on the Iraq bandwagon, many others quietly favored invasion or at most criticized unilateral action. Countering the president's clarion call was seen as unsustainable in the post-9/11 rhetorical environment.

Some conservatives began calling for the invasion of Iraq immediately after the September 11 attacks, but the president's own rhetoric was notably restrained until the 2002 State of the Union. Following that address, in which Bush famously (or perhaps notoriously) characterized Iraq, Iran, and North Korea as comprising an "axis of evil," the president's depiction of Saddam Hussein and the Iraqi regime remained consistent.[5] Hussein supported terrorism, sought and possessed weapons of mass destruction, killed and tortured "his own people," and could not be trusted. As Bush put it in the State of the Union:

> Iraq continues to flaunt its hostility toward America and to support terror. The Iraqi regime has plotted to develop anthrax, and nerve gas, and nuclear weapons for over a decade. This is a regime that has already used poison gas to murder thousands of its own citizens – leaving the bodies of mothers huddled over their dead children. This is a regime that agreed to international inspections – then kicked out the inspectors. This is a regime that has something to hide from the civilized world.
>
> (Bush 2002a)

In the months that followed, Bush and other leading administration figures repeated and reinforced this portrait of Iraq and its regime. In the late summer and early fall of 2002, as the administration launched an aggressive campaign to sway public opinion, three additional elements were grafted on to the basic narrative. First, previously acceptable risks with regard to Iraqi weapons programs were no longer tolerable in the wake of September 11 (see also Susskind 2006). Second, Iraq was a "grave and growing" danger. Third, Saddam Hussein hated (and was not merely hostile to) America and its values. Through the start of major combat operations, the administration did not waver from these core arguments (Bush 2002c, 2003 a,b).

Many have noted how administration figures regularly slyly mentioned Iraq in the same breath as the September 11 attacks, implying an operational link with Al Qaeda where there was none (Freedman 2004: 18–20; Kaufmann 2004: 16–19), but the administration's rhetoric, widely reflected in media coverage (Gershkoff and Kushner 2005), forged more durable bonds between the Iraqi regime, Saddam Hussein, and the War on Terror. By regularly referring to Iraq as a member of the "axis of evil," Bush and key administration spokespeople suggested that the Iraqi regime and its president were on the same moral plane as "the terrorists" and were probably terrorists themselves. By emphasizing that the Iraqi regime killed its own citizens, the administration elided any distinction between the state terror in which Iraq had engaged and the international terrorism to which the United States had been subjected. By maintaining that the Iraqi regime had "something to hide from the civilized world," Bush placed it in the realm of barbarism, where Al Qaeda prominently resided. By emphasizing Saddam Hussein's unyielding hatred of the United States and its values, Bush and others suggested a common agenda with Islamist terrorists. By continuously focusing on Saddam Hussein, rather than on Iraq or even its regime, Bush suggested a further parallel with Osama bin Laden; their organizations reflected their leaders' political programs and personal pathologies, in contrast to democracies in which law, not personal whim, ruled. The link between the Iraqi regime and Al Qaeda was established not just through blunt tactics of continual misrepresentation, but perhaps more through these subtle rhetorical deployments that capitalized on the relatively settled meaning of September 11, reflected in the dominant discourse of the War on Terror.

Part of the reason for the Bush administration's success in fashioning a link between Iraq and the War on Terror lies in the very nature of discourse on terrorism. Terrorism threatens the very logic of inside/outside that sustains the modern nation-state, and states consequently respond by asserting anew their territorial identity, reimposing a geopolitics of identity and difference, and emphasizing the primacy of territorial defense (Coleman 2004: 88–93; Keohane 2002). As Americans daily reproduced this statist counterterrorist discourse, it seemed natural to posit close links between Al Qaeda and a state sponsor, as the administration regularly insinuated. Not any state could have been reasonably inserted into that role, but Iraq was a prime candidate, largely because it had already been well established in US politics that Saddam Hussein and his regime were demonstrably evil and terroristic.[6]

The rhetorical treatment of Saddam Hussein and Iraq in the decade after the first Gulf War further helps explain why the essential terms of the administration's frame went largely uncontested. As early as October 1990, President George H. W. Bush depicted Saddam Hussein as "Hitler revisited," and he regularly suggested that Hussein was as great a threat as Hitler, that the invasion of Kuwait was akin to Hitler's invasion of Poland, and that the world's failure to respond forcefully to

Hussein's aggression would equal British and French appeasement at Munich in 1938 (Bush 1990 a,b,c,d). "In most of the West," Lance Morrow notes, "Hitler is the 20th century's term for [the] Great Satan," and to invoke Hitler is to evoke "evil's icon" (Morrow 1991, 2003: 137–138). This characterization of Saddam Hussein was echoed in the press, and thus in January 1991 nearly as many West Virginians identified Saddam Hussein as the most evil statesman of the twentieth century as named Hitler (West Virginia Poll, 23 January 1991, www.poll.orspub.com). Like Hitler, Saddam was not only brutal but evil: his appetite for fearsome weapons was insatiable, and he was an inveterate aggressor who could be neither permanently contained nor appeased.

Rhetoric equating Saddam Hussein with Hitler and Baathist Iraq with Nazi Germany did not taper off much during the 1990s. In 1998 Clinton's secretary of state, Madeleine Albright, called Saddam Hussein "the most evil man the world has seen since Hitler" (Bennet 1998), and this portrait of Iraq's president had become so well entrenched that, in "person on the street" interviews conducted that same year, citizens based their analysis of Iraq on the Hitler analogy (Wilgoren 1998). Hussein's credentials as a figure of imposing evil were thus well established by the time Bush included his regime in the "axis of evil." In issuing an ultimatum to Iraq in March 2003, Bush invoked past Western errors and alluded to Hitler: "in the 20th century, some chose to appease murderous dictators . . . In this century . . . a policy of appeasement could bring destruction of a kind never before seen on this Earth" (Bush 2003b). Representing Saddam Hussein as a pathetic petty tyrant, as one who aspired to be Hitler but lacked the competence or the resources, was theoretically available to anti-war forces, but it flew in the face of a decade-old discourse that had treated Iraq as a threat to national security on par with Nazi Germany.

The second rhetorical engine driving the case for war was that Saddam Hussein and his regime were terrorists, and this also found support in the rhetoric of the Clinton administration. Eschewing the Hitler analogy himself, Clinton argued from the beginning of his presidency that Saddam Hussein was responsible for acts of terrorism. After discovering an Iraqi plot to assassinate former President George H.W. Bush, Clinton authorized missile strikes against Iraqi intelligence assets, announcing that "Saddam Hussein has demonstrated repeatedly that he will resort to terrorism or aggression if left unchecked" (Clinton 1993). Whether this was an appropriate use of the terrorism label or not, it was widely repeated by administration figures and in the press throughout the Clinton years. American newspapers openly speculated that Iraq had a hand in the 1993 World Trade Center bombing, and Iraq was fingered for other potential and actual terrorist activity at home and abroad (Broad and Miller 1998; Erlanger 1998; Sennott 1995; Weiner 1993). The image of Saddam Hussein as terrorist had struck sufficiently deep roots that George W. Bush could credibly accuse him of "harboring terrorists and the instruments of terror, the instruments of mass death and destruction" (Bush 2002d). Like the barbaric terrorists, his regime had no place in the family of civilized nations.

This rhetorical history left Americans well disposed to see Saddam Hussein as capable of committing or at least supporting the most nefarious acts, and the administration's rhetorical efforts to link his regime to the horrific attacks of

September 11 tilled a fertile soil and swiftly brought forth fruit. Bush's representations of Hussein were by no means irrelevant – the seeds required active cultivation to pierce the surface – but linking Iraq to the War on Terror was hardly an imposing task (Althaus and Largio 2004: 795–799; Foyle 2004).[7] This articulation was essential in undercutting Democrats who might have otherwise opposed war with Iraq. As Bush put it, "you can't distinguish between Al Qaida and Saddam when you talk about the war on terror . . . because they're both equally as bad and equally as evil and equally as destructive" (Bush 2002b). One cannot negotiate with unquestionable evil, one can only wage war against it. Thus, the United States was compelled to invade Saddam Hussein's Iraq.[8] Given the dominance of the War-on-Terror narrative, opponents of war with Iraq had few rhetorical resources with which to challenge these "logical" steps leading down the path to war.

Opposition to the war among Democrats was muted. True, Democrats in the Senate only narrowly authorized military force against Iraq, voting 27–21 for Joint Resolution 114, and Democrats in the House of Representatives voted down the resolution, 81–126. But nearly all leading Democratic figures and particularly the front runners for the presidential nomination supported the war in its essence, even if some took issue with the details (Western 2005a). At the leadership level, there was by the summer of 2002 "broad bipartisan support for ousting" Saddam Hussein by "a military invasion if other options fail": in other words, by the summer before the war, the question of the Iraqi regime's removal was, even among Democrats, not if, but when and how (Dao 2002). Party leaders made it "very hard," according to Senator Dianne Feinstein, for lower-ranking Democrats to speak out against the war. A "rift" reportedly emerged between the party leadership and prospective presidential candidates, on the one hand, and rank-and-file Democrats on the other, and the rift was even greater between Beltway Democrats and the core Democratic constituency outside Washington. Opponents of the war, both inside and outside Congress, were placed "on the defensive" (Traub 2004; VandeHei 2002).

Part of the reason for this group's public acquiescence to the invasion of Iraq lies in the rhetorical obstacles erected after September 11. The establishment of the War on Terror as the organizing narrative in foreign policy, in combination with the existing portrait of Saddam Hussein as evil and as a terrorist, deprived leading Democrats of socially sustainable arguments with which to oppose the administration. In short, these Democrats were "rhetorically coerced": they had been left without access to the rhetorical materials needed to craft an acceptable rebuttal.[9] What they could do – and what they did – was raise questions about the timing and circumstances of an invasion. The boundaries of sustainable rhetoric had been narrowed after September 11, limiting the space for vocal opposition.

What arguments did Democrats offer, and why could they make at best limited headway in post-9/11 politics? First, a small number of Democrats, some quite prominent in the party, opposed an invasion of Iraq from the very beginning, arguing that the status quo was tolerable and sustainable.[10] Senator Ted Kennedy maintained that "there are realistic alternatives between doing nothing and declaring unilateral or immediate war. War should be a last resort, not the first response." He, along with Senator Robert Byrd, accused the administration of pushing for war so as to divert the nation's attention from the faltering economy and the rash of corporate corruption scandals with ties to the White House. These Democrats did not argue that Saddam Hussein was not a threat or that he could be turned aside with sweet reasonableness. Rather, they suggested that containment, combined with a continued inspections regime, remained an adequate response to an Iraq that had been weakened by a decade of economic sanctions ("Senate to Debate" 2002).[11] Former Clinton deputy William Galston similarly argued, "We should contain Hussein, deter him and bring him down the way we brought down the Evil Empire that threatened our existence for half a century – through economic, diplomatic, military and moral pressure, not force of arms" (Galston 2002). By invoking the Cold War, Galston suggested that evil need not be destroyed or conquered. Yet such a view of evil was difficult to sustain after September 11. The War-on-Terror narrative, to which Democrats had acceded and which they reproduced, implied that evil could not be tolerated. Nor could Democrats challenge the long-standing charge, made first by a fellow Democrat, that Saddam Hussein supported terrorism. If the evil of transnational terrorism could be eliminated only through the application of military force – that is, war – and if Saddam Hussein was in fact a fellow terrorist, then there was little reason not to apply those same means to Iraq in pursuit of the consensus goal of regime change.

Second, other Democrats suggested that the costs of a war would be prohibitive and that the United States had higher priorities on which to expend resources. Senator Mark Dayton claimed that "we know that the United States would defeat Iraq and depose Saddam Hussein. But we don't know the cost in bloodshed, destruction and subsequent occupation. And we don't know the consequences of violating our national principle of not starting wars." Former Vice President Al Gore likewise challenged the administration's priorities, arguing that an invasion of Iraq would jeopardize the campaign against the perpetrators of the September 11 attacks and undermine US global leadership; the United States needed to focus on ensuring the safety of nuclear materials in the former Soviet Union and on rooting out Al Qaeda. A minority of congressional Democrats challenged the administration's claim that Iraq was in fact a "grave and growing danger," maintaining instead that Iraq posed a *continuing*, not an immediate and imminent, threat.

Yet the administration's rebuttals were compelling in the post-9/11 public sphere, for reasons that should now be clear. While it sought to some extent to respond by adducing evidence that the Iraqi threat was in fact pressing, it also contended that the criterion of imminence that critics had applied was irrelevant and that the argument revealed how little its political opponents grasped the realities of the threats facing the United States. In its 2002 *National Security Strategy*, the administration had argued that imminence was, as a criterion for war, outmoded, for the September 11 attacks had proved that one could not wait until forces gathered at the border. While the administration did insist that the costs of invasion and reconstruction would be far lower than the critics forecast, the articulation of Iraq to the War on Terror put potential critics in the uncomfortable position of having to argue that they would sacrifice national security for the sake of a few dollars. Finally, attempts to insert space between Iraq and the War on Terror, along the lines

Gore had suggested, failed to comprehend how firmly the two were now linked in public discourse.

In the post-September 11 rhetorical space, Democratic politicians who might normally have helped lead a vigorous opposition to the invasion were relatively silent or at least very tempered in their criticism. This was less because they had been persuaded of the Bush administration's logic and factual claims than because the fixing of the War on Terror as the dominant discourse after September 11 had deprived them of winning arguments, of socially sustainable avenues of reply.[12] They were the victims of successful rhetorical coercion. Recognizing that their justifications for opposing the war were unlikely to gain rhetorical traction, many Democrats either jumped on the administration's bandwagon or offered a more modest critique. Democrats could, and did, argue that violating Iraq's national sovereignty, as opposed to the pursuit of non-state actors like Al Qaeda, required the imprimatur of the United Nations and the support of the international community. This argument carried much weight with the American public: just a month before the invasion began, a clear majority of Americans opposed going to war without UN sanction (Kull *et al.* 2003–04: 569–570). But this was necessarily a far weaker form of argument that already conceded the administration's most fundamental points. Nor was it particularly constraining to the Bush administration, which co-opted such selective multilateralist critiques by recasting the issue: would the United Nations uphold its own previously articulated commitment to shut down Iraqi WMD and ballistic missile programs (Western 2005a: 201–206)? The administration also correctly predicted that Americans' objections to a unilateral course of action would fall away once the war began. Over the long run, thought the administration, their view of the war would be shaped by the success and/or the cost of the operation, not the lack of UN approval.

Democratic politicians undoubtedly possessed varied reasons for withholding vigorous criticism of the administration's plans for war in Iraq. We do not have access to internal memos that might lay out the logic behind these politicians' policy choices, and even these documents might very well be strategically framed, undermining their value for revealing "true motives." Since we cannot here – and probably no research can definitively – establish what motives were in fact paramount, our purpose has been more modest: to establish the plausibility of an account centered on rhetorical coercion. Rhetorical coercion, we believe, is an essential piece of the story, even in "straightforward" accounts of anticipated political punishment for opposing the war. Had arguments against removing Saddam Hussein from power by military means been socially sustainable, opposition to the war would not have been politically costly. The combination of existing representations (Iraq as personified in Saddam, Saddam as Hitler revisited and as a terrorist) with the post-9/11 War on Terror narrowed the space for sustainable political debate. To have opposed the war in Iraq would have seemed to toss in the towel in the unquestioned War on Terror, and to have opposed the pursuit of the War on Terror because of a dispute over the (unilateral military) means seemed, given the all-too-concrete costs of the September 11 attacks, to misplace one's priorities.

Conclusion

As the war in Iraq festers, as the numbers of wounded and killed American and Iraqi soldiers and civilians climb ever upwards, as America's foreign policy elite searches desperately for a way to extricate the United States from the morass without sparking a region-wide conflagration, as the prospect of an Iraq Syndrome, paralleling that which followed the Vietnam War, looms, making sense of how this situation arose and was legitimated is necessarily of great import. For those who think they understand how the United States became embroiled in Iraq – through a combination of ideology, institutional prerogatives, deception, and psychological pathology – this essay seeks to demonstrate what a more rhetorical perspective may contribute to our comprehension of the implications of September 11 and the road to war in Iraq.

Dominant narratives deeply shape political contestation and policy outcomes. The administration's successful campaign to bring the United States into war with Iraq hinged on a post-9/11 rhetorical environment dominated by the War on Terror. In this context, and given the characterizations of Saddam Hussein and Iraq prominent in US political rhetoric since the first Gulf War, the link between Al Qaeda and Iraq that would buttress the invasion was eminently sustainable. The burden of proof fell on those who denied that Iraq was a central front in the War on Terror. Potential opponents were rhetorically hemmed in, unable to offer a powerful case against the administration's aggressive policy.

The foregoing argument conveys an air of inevitability regarding the outcome of the Bush administration's push for war with Iraq. Indeed, in the moment, during the debates of fall 2002 and winter/spring 2003, there was little Democrats could have done to have waylaid a Bush administration determined to launch a war. But, viewed through a longer time-frame, the outcome was far from inevitable. The Bush administration need not have cast the perpetrators and planners of September 11 as "evil-doers," and it need not have called for an expansive War on Terror – even if it had opted for a militarized response. The administration certainly had much discretion about how broad or narrow a War on Terror it would pursue. And Democrats might have given voice to an alternative to the War on Terror, accepting the short-run political costs that resistance would have entailed in favor of the long-run flexibility that it might have afforded. Once Democrats assented to the War on Terror, however, the rhetorical resources available to them in the run-up to war in Iraq were meager indeed. At that point, preventing the march to war may well have been impossible, but leading Democrats might nevertheless have taken a braver stance. When the war turned sour, a consistent Democratic opposition would have profited. Instead, during the 2004 presidential primaries, nearly all the Democratic candidates were compelled to explain why they now opposed a war that they had earlier authorized. Their arguments were often reasonable, but they came off as tortured. Had Sen. John Kerry voted initially against the war, he might have claimed the White House. Accepting such political gambles, however, would have required leading Democrats to have long time horizons and be risk acceptant, which politicians often do not and are not. We have argued that the political opposition faced an unenviable set of circumstances after September 11 that impeded, but certainly did not eliminate, its capacity to oppose either the War on Terror or the war in Iraq.

The War on Terror need not always be with us. Discourse is always subject to challenge and is always laced through with contradictions. Hegemonies may be disrupted, creating space for political change. As contradictions accumulate, the space for resistance grows as well. The stubborn lack of progress with regard to security or development in Iraq, the climbing casualties among civilians and soldiers alike, and the regular revelations regarding the manipulation of pre-war intelligence caused Bush's approval rating to plummet and led to a stunning Democratic victory in the 2006 midterm elections. Increasingly Americans endorsed the view that the war was not justified in the first place and that, even if it was, the United States was now doing more harm than good and should withdraw. While criticism of the war grew immensely, it remained too often divorced from any criticism of the War on Terror. The failures of Iraq opened a space for resistance to this dominant narrative, but Democrats, for the most part, remained trapped within the War on Terror.[13] Even the 2008 Democratic President elect of US Barack Obama (Obama 2008), reproduced that narrative, even while he downplayed its more Manichean elements. Challenging hegemonic understandings is never easy, but it is essential if alternative policies are to be not only envisioned but socially and politically sustained.

Notes

1 See also Jacobs and Shapiro 2000; Sobel 2001. But see Cohen 1997.
2 However, public opinion is *collectively* rational (Page and Shapiro 1992), and the operative mechanism appears to be elite cuing. The problem regarding Iraq was that elites spoke largely with a single voice – highlighting again the relative silence of the Democrats.
3 Of course Kaufmann may be wrong, and information contradicting the administration's claims may not have existed or may have lacked credibility. On the contemporaneous plausibility of the administration's assessments regarding Iraqi WMD programs, see Jervis 2006.
4 The reasons for indexing include, among others: the efficiency of relying on official sources; the predictability and credibility of official sources; the interests of major news corporations; and the journalistic norm of "balance." With regard to the use of force abroad, journalists' concerns about appearing unpatriotic also foster subservience to official narratives. For critical views of "indexing," see Edwards III 2003: 172–183; Wood and Peake 1998.
5 This conclusion is based on a careful reading of every presidential address related to Iraq between September 2001 and March 2003, located in Public Papers of the Presidents [hereafter PPP], http://www.presidency.ucsb.edu/ws/ (Accessed 15 August 2008).
6 Moreover, other conceivable candidates – such as Afghanistan and Sudan – were not sufficiently state-like to sustain allegations that they had facilitated the attacks' remarkable coordination. Thanks to Bud Duvall for this observation.
7 Thrall 2009, in this volume, focuses on the public's predispositions, and this argument seems to us complementary, rather than competing.
8 A final noteworthy element is that Congress had overwhelmingly approved the Iraq Liberation Act in October 1998, and Clinton himself had publicly endorsed regime

change as a US objective the following month. These moves narrowed the rhetorical space available to potential opponents in 2002–2003, since many Democrats had voted in 1998 in favor of regime change.

9 Space constraints prevent us from presenting the theoretical logic of rhetorical coercion in greater detail. For more on this mechanism, see Krebs 2006; Krebs and Jackson 2007.

10 The most prominent among these early opponents – Senators Robert Byrd, Carl Levin and Edward Kennedy – are the exceptions that prove the rule: old lions of the party, they could speak freely because they held secure seats and no longer harbored aspirations for national office.

11 This was apparently the view, before the war, among many military officers: see Ricks 2002. For an academic endorsement of containment, even of a nuclear-armed Iraq, see Mearsheimer and Walt 2003.

12 Western (2005: 197–198) similarly, if briefly, suggests that Bush's framing of the war "boxed in" opponents.

13 Questions about the War on Terror finally began to penetrate the mainstream in 2006: see Fallows 2006; Lustick 2006; Mueller 2006. For specific suggestions about what an opposition hegemonic project would look like, well beyond the War on Terror, see Lakoff 2004; Tomasky 2006.

References

Althaus, S. L. and Largio, D. M. (2004) "When Osama Became Saddam: Origins and consequences of the change in America's public enemy #1," *PS: Political Science and Politics*, 37: 795–799.

Bennet, J. (1998) "Clinton sets out to revive support for stand on Iraq," *New York Times*, 20 February.

Bennett, W. L. (1990) "Toward a theory of press-state relations in the United States," *Journal of Communication*, 40: 103–125.

—— (2004) "Gatekeeping and press-government relations: A multigated model of news construction." In L. L. Kaid (ed.) *Handbook of Political Communication Research*, Mahwah, NJ: Lawrence Erlbaum.

Bostdorff, D. M. (2003) "George W. Bush's post-September 11 rhetoric of covenant renewal: Upholding the faith of the greatest generation," *Quarterly Journal of Speech*, 89: 293–319.

Broad, W. J. and Miller, J. (1998) "Germ defense plan in peril as its flaws are revealed," *New York Times*, 7 August.

Bush, George H. W. (1990a) "Remarks, fundraising luncheon for gubernatorial candidate Clayton Williams," 15 October, PPP.

—— (1990b) "Remarks, republican fundraising breakfast," 23 October, PPP.

—— (1990c) "Remarks, republican party fundraising breakfast," 1 November, PPP.

—— (1990d) "Remarks, republican campaign rally," 3 November, PPP.

Bush, George W. (2002a) "Address before a joint session of the congress on the state of the union," 29 January, PPP.

—— (2002b) "Remarks prior to discussions with President Alvaro Uribe of Colombia and an exchange with reporters," 25 September, PPP.

—— (2002c) "Iraqi regime danger to America is 'grave and growing,'" 5 October, PPP.

—— (2002d) "The Iraqi threat," 7 October, PPP.

—— (2003a) "Address before a joint session of the congress on the state of the union," 28 January, PPP.

—— (2003b) "Address to the nation on Iraq," 17 March, PPP.

Canes-Wrone, B. (2005) *Who Leads Whom? Presidents, Policy, and the Public*, Chicago: University of Chicago Press.

Clinton, William J. (1993) "Address to the nation on the strike on Iraqi intelligence headquarters," 26 June, PPP.

Coe, K., Domke, D., Graham, E. S., John, S. L., Pickard, V. W. (2004) "No shades of gray: The binary discourse of George W. Bush and an echoing Press," *Journal of Communication*, 54: 234–252.

Cohen, J. E. (1997) *Presidential Responsiveness and Public Policy-Making: The Public and the Policies That Presidents Choose*, Ann Arbor: University of Michigan Press.

Coleman, M. (2004) "The naming of 'terrorism' and 'evil outlaws': Geopolitical place-making after 11 September," in S. D. Brunn (ed.) *11 September and Its Aftermath: The Geopolitics of Terror*, London: Frank Cass.

Cook, T. (1998) *Governing with the News: The News Media as a Political Institution*, Chicago: University of Chicago Press.

Cramer, J. K. (2009) "Militarized patriotism and the success of threat inflation," in A. T. Thrall and J. K. Cramer (eds) *American Foreign Policy and the Politics of Fear: Threat Inflation Since 9/11*, London: Routledge.

Dao, J. (2002) "Call in congress for full airing of Iraq policy," *New York Times*, 18 July.

Dueck, C. (2004) "Ideas and alternatives in American grand strategy, 2000–2004," *Review of International Studies*, 30: 511–535.

Edwards III, G. C. (2003) *On Deaf Ears: The Limits of the Bully Pulpit*, New Haven, CT: Yale University Press.

Erlanger, S. (1998) "Republicans back Clinton on the use of force on Iraqis," *New York Times*, 27 January.

Fallows, J. (2006) "Declaring victory," *Atlantic Monthly*, September: 60–73.

Flibbert, A. (2006) "The road to Baghdad: Ideas and intellectuals in explanations of the Iraq war," *Security Studies*, 15: 310–352.

Foyle, D. C. (2004) "Leading the public to war? The influence of American public opinion on the Bush administration's decision to go to war in Iraq," *International Journal of Public Opinion Research*, 16: 269–294.

Freedman, L. (2004) "War in Iraq: Selling the threat," *Survival*, 46: 7–50.

Fukuyama, F. (2006) "After neoconservatism," *New York Times Magazine*, 19 February.

Gaddis, J. L. (2004) *Surprise, Security, and the American Experience*, Cambridge, MA: Harvard University Press.

Galston, W. A. (2002) "Why a first strike will surely backfire," *Washington Post*, 16 June.

Gershkoff, A. and Kushner, S. (2005) "Shaping public opinion: The 9/11–Iraq connection in the Bush administration's rhetoric," *Perspectives on Politics*, 3: 525–537.

Gordon, M. R. and Trainor, B. E. (2006) *Cobra II: The Inside Story of the Invasion and Occupation of Iraq*, New York: Vintage.

Hess, G. R. (2006) "Presidents and the congressional war resolutions of 1991 and 2002," *Political Science Quarterly*, 121: 93–118.

Huddy, L., Feldman, S., Taber, C. and Lahav, G. (2003) "Fear and terrorism: Psychological reactions to 9/11." In P. Norris, *et al.* (eds) *Framing Terrorism: The News Media, the Government, and the Public*, New York: Routledge.

Hutcheson, J., Domke, D., Billeaudeaux, A. and Garland, P. (2004) "U.S. national identity, political elites, and a patriotic press following September 11," *Political Communication*, 21: 27–50.

Isikoff, M. and Corn, D. (2006) *Hubris: The Inside Story of Spin, Scandal, and the Selling of the Iraq War*, New York: Crown.

Jackson, R. (2005) *Writing the War on Terrorism: Language, Politics, and Counter-Terrorism*, Manchester: Manchester University Press.

Jacobs, L. R. and Shapiro, R. Y. (2000) *Politicians Don't Pander: Political Manipulation and the Loss of Democratic Responsiveness*, Chicago: University of Chicago Press.

Jamieson, K. H. and Waldman, P. (2003) *The Press Effect: Politicians, Journalists, and the Stories that Shape the Political World*, Oxford: Oxford University Press.

Jervis, R. (2006) "Reports, politics, and intelligence failures: The case of Iraq," *Journal of Strategic Studies*, 29: 3–52.

Judt, T. (2006) "Bush's useful idiots," *London Review of Books*, 28.

Kaufmann, C. (2004) "Threat inflation and the failure of the marketplace of ideas: The selling of the Iraq War," *International Security*, 29: 5–48.

Keohane, R. (2002) "The Globalization of informal violence, theories of world politics, and 'the liberalism of fear,'" in C. Calhoun *et al.* (eds) *Understanding September 11*, New York: Social Science Research Council/New Press.

Kernell, S. (2007) *Going Public: New Strategies of Presidential Leadership*, 4th edn., Washington, DC: CQ Press.

Kohut, A., *et al.* (2004) *News Audiences Increasingly Politicized*, Washington, DC: Pew Research Center for the People and the Press.

Krebs, R. R. (2006) *Fighting for Rights: Military Service and the Politics of Citizenship*, Ithaca, NY: Cornell University Press.

—— (2008) *Rhetoric and the Making of U.S. National Security*, unpublished manuscript, University of Minnesota.

Krebs, R. R. and Jackson, P. T. (2007) "Twisting tongues and twisting arms: The power of political rhetoric," *European Journal of International Relations*, 13: 35–66.

Krebs, R. R. and Lobasz, J. K. (2007) "Fixing the meaning of 9/11: Hegemony, coercion, and the road to war in Iraq," *Security Studies*, 16: 409–451.

Kull, S., Ramsay, C. and Lewis, E. (2003–04) "Misperceptions, the media and the Iraq war," *Political Science Quarterly*, 118: 569–598.

Lakoff, G. (2004) *Don't Think of an Elephant! Know Your Values and Frame the Debate: The Essential Guide for Progressives*, New York: Chelsea Green.

Leffler, M. P. (2004) "Think again: Bush's foreign policy," *Foreign Policy*, September: 22–28.

Lustick, I. S. (2006) *Trapped in the War on Terror*, Philadelphia: University of Pennsylvania Press.

Massing, M. (2004) *Now They Tell Us: The American Press and Iraq*, New York: New York Review of Books.

Mearsheimer, J. J. and Walt, S. M. (2003) "An unnecessary war," *Foreign Policy*, January–February: 50–59.

Mermin, J. (1999) *Debating War and Peace: Media Coverage of U.S. Intervention in the Post-Vietnam Era*, Princeton, NJ: Princeton University Press.

Monten, J. (2005) "The roots of the Bush doctrine: Power, nationalism, and democracy in U.S. strategy," *International Security*, 29: 112–156.

Morrow, L. (1991) "Evil," *Time*, 10 June: 48–53.

—— (2003) *Evil: An Investigation*, New York: Basic Books.

Mueller, J. (2005) "Simplicity and spook: Terrorism and the dynamics of threat exaggeration," *International Studies Perspectives*, 6: 208–234.

—— (2006) *Overblown: How Politicians, the Terrorism Industry and Others Stoke National Security Fears*, New York: Free Press.

Obama, B. (2008) "A New Strategy for a New World," 15 July, Online available: <http://www.barackobama.com/2008/07/15/remarks_of_senator_barack_obam_96.php. (Accessed August 15, 2008)

Page, B. I. and Shapiro, R. Y. (1992) *The Rational Public: Fifty Years of Trends in Americans' Policy Preferences*, Chicago: University of Chicago Press.

Rich, F. (2006) *The Greatest Story Ever Sold: The Decline and Fall of Truth in Bush's America*, New York: Penguin.

Ricks, T. E. (2002) "Some Top Military Brass Favor Status Quo in Iraq," *Washington Post*, 28 July.

—— (2006) *Fiasco: The American Military Adventure in Iraq, 2003 to 2005*, New York: Penguin.

"Senate to debate Iraq resolution; Key democrats have doubts, but measure on track for passage" (2002) *Washington Post*, 4 October.

Sennott, C. M. (1995) "Blast probers say trail leading to Iraq," *Boston Globe*, 10 February.

Silberstein, S. (2004) *War of Words: Language, Politics and 9/11*, London: Routledge.

Sobel, R. (2001) *The Impact of Public Opinion on U.S. Foreign Policy since Vietnam*, New York: Oxford University Press.

Sunstein, C. R. (2003) "Terrorism and probability neglect," *Journal of Risk and Uncertainty*, 26: 121–136.

Susskind, R. (2006) *The One Percent Doctrine: Deep Inside America's Pursuit of its Enemies Since 9/11*, New York: Simon & Schuster.

Thrall, A. T. (2009) "Framing Iraq: Threat Inflation in the Marketplace of Values," in J. K. Cramer and A. T. Thrall (eds) *American Foreign Policy and the Politics of Fear: Threat Inflation Since 9/11*, Oxford: Routledge.

Tomasky, M. (2006) "Party in search of a notion," *American Prospect*, May.

Traub, J. (2004) "The things they carry," *New York Times Magazine*, 4 January.

VandeHei, J. (2002) "Louder war talk, and muffled dissent: Party leaders make opposition difficult, wary democrats say," *Washington Post*, 25 September.

Weiner, T. (1993) "Attack is aimed at the heart of Iraq's spy network," *New York Times*, 27 June.

Western, J. (2005a) *Selling Intervention and War: The Presidency, the Media, and the American Public*, Baltimore, MD: The Johns Hopkins University Press.

—— (2005b) "The war over Iraq: Selling war to the American public," *Security Studies*, 14: 106–139.

Wilgoren, J. (1998) "Around the U.S., cynicism and a showing of support," *New York Times*, 17 December.

Wood, B. D. and Peake, J. S. (1998) "The dynamics of foreign policy agenda setting," *American Political Science Review*, 92: 173–184.

8 Militarized patriotism and the success of threat inflation

Jane K. Cramer

> Simply stated, there is no doubt that Saddam Hussein now has weapons of mass destruction. There is no doubt he is amassing them to use against our friends, against our allies, and against us.
>
> (Vice President Cheney, August 26, 2002)

In the fall of 2002 dire warnings by the Bush Administration about Iraq's weapons of mass destruction (WMD) were consistently combined with suggestions that a substantial link existed between Iraq and al-Qaeda, and even between Iraq and the 9/11 attacks. It is now well known that the Bush Administration intentionally inflated the Iraqi threat as it worked to mobilize public and congressional support for an invasion of Iraq (Danner 2006; Cirincione Matthews and Perkovich with Orton 2004). Debate continues over why the administration's obvious threat inflation efforts were so successful. In this chapter I argue that the key political fight that determined the success of the Bush Administration's push for an invasion of Iraq was the debate in Congress over the Iraq War Resolution which passed in the House and Senate on October 10–11, 2002, and was signed into law by President Bush on October 16, 2002. After this legislative victory, where the Administration succeeded in pushing through a "blank check" resolution that authorized the president to use the armed forces of the United States "as he determines to be necessary and appropriate," all supporters of this resolution had to then fall into line and either justify why they supported this extreme resolution or be silent. Leaders who supported the resolution could no longer stand in opposition and question the president or the intelligence, and those who had opposed generally went silent as well since they knew they had lost and they could gain little to nothing by standing in opposition to an increasingly popular war. Thus, after this resolution passed, the debate in the "marketplace of ideas" was for all intents and purposes over – the leaders of the political opposition had signed on to allowing the President to wage war in Iraq at his discretion, leaving only outsiders with no real political clout or leverage to criticize.

This chapter analyzes what happened in the marketplace of ideas by first detailing the political struggle of this period that reveals two important facts:

1   the executive branch did not have important information advantages that enabled it to mislead or persuade the Congress and the public (compare to Kaufmann, Western, this volume), and

2   the 9/11 attacks did not pre-determine the outcome of this political struggle – the Congress did not feel cornered or silenced by the 9/11 attacks or the administration's rhetoric after these attacks (compare to Krebs and Lobasz, this volume; in support, see Holsti 2004: 279).

Instead, the bipartisan opposition, led by leading Democrats and Republicans in the Senate, thought the connection between Iraq and 9/11 was so weak that the President's urgent push for war could be crucially restrained if not derailed. A sudden political maneuver, a "match point" game changer as Senator Joe Biden termed it, happened on October 2, 2002 and after this time the strong opposition in the Congress fell apart. When it was clear that the opposition would fail, then there appeared to be no political benefit to opposing the President, and possibly high political costs, so a strong majority switched from opposing the President's Resolution to supporting it.

Recognizing how close the opposition was to victory at this critical moment, and investigating the actual reasons why the strong opposition to the executive branch suddenly lost this crucial political fight leads me to propose to explain this case through a hypothesis I term "militarized patriotism." This hypothesis points out that the main reason the opposition was silenced in the end was the immediate political need of congress members with presidential aspirations – leaders who I term "politicians of national stature" – to not appear "weak" on defense and to patriotically defer to the president on issues of war powers. I argue that these were considered the politically safe positions to take in order to remain a viable national political contender in the future. I point out that these "safe" political positions became "norms" of behavior for leading politicians during the Cold War.

In 2002, politicians questioned and resisted the need to act in accordance with these norms (Byrd 2004), but ultimately fell back on these norms in this uncertain political situation even though they clearly wanted to oppose the executive branch. This analysis focuses on the political pressures of this period that drove leading congress members to behave "patriotically" in a traditional Cold War style rather than to do what they actually believed was the right thing to do for their country. Ultimately, I argue that this perversion of patriotism, where patriotism silences dissent and insists on deference to the executive branch, became firmly established during the Cold War along with the rise of militarism. Thus, to begin to repair the democratic marketplace of ideas in the United States, the problem of militarism needs to be addressed.

The fight over the Iraq War Resolution and the end of debate in the marketplace of ideas

On most issues, Democrats had been unified in 2001 and 2002 in their opposition to the Bush administration. National security issues were a different story right after 9/11 when the whole country came together to back the President and almost all leaders backed the U.S. invasion of Afghanistan. Some analysts have argued the Iraq War issue was similar in that Democrats needed to back the President in the "War on Terror." I argue that, most Democrats did not perceive the situation this way. Although Democrats were tentative and uncertain, almost all resisted supporting the Bush administration on Iraq the way they had supported the invasion of Afghanistan, and many believed they had the political space to organize an opposition to the executive branch's plans for Iraq. Other analysts argue Democrats were divided because many had been convinced that attacking Iraq was the best policy. I show below that there is strong evidence that almost all Democrats were not actually convinced, even though Democrats did end up divided. Democrats ended up almost perfectly divided along lines of political necessity: those who had national political aspirations along with those in tight congressional races ended up supporting the administration once chances for a unified opposition collapsed, and Democrats who had no national aspirations or were not facing immediate electoral challenges were opposed to the Iraq War Resolution. Ultimately, it is likely most Democrats were actually opposed to the Iraq War Resolution (as their speeches – "signing statements" – often revealed) but it was thought to be politically safer by many to vote in support of the administration, especially after it was clear the administration was going to prevail anyhow.

In this section, I present extensive evidence strongly indicating that most Democrats, as well as many Republicans, were *not* convinced by the administration. Instead, a large majority of the Senate (if not the House) believed the administration's case concerning a WMD threat from Iraq was weak and unproven, they did not agree that the United States should attack Iraq unilaterally, they strongly preferred disarming Iraq through weapons inspections, they opposed regime change without real proof there was a "grave" threat, and they feared the costs and consequences of invading Iraq. In fact, because so few in Congress were actually convinced regime change in Iraq was a good idea, in late August 2002, many administration leaders and Democrats thought the Bush administration would not get support from Congress to attack Iraq unilaterally. Even in late September, after the Iraq War Resolution had been presented by the administration and discussed extensively, congressional support was still a very open question.

However, in a political maneuver at the beginning of October, with no significant new intelligence discussed, the executive branch prevailed. There, as will be explained, is strong evidence that most Democrats and many Republicans deferred to the executive branch not on the merits of the case, but because they did not want to appear weak on defense or unpatriotic. In the end, this evidence suggests that the marketplace of ideas failed in 2002 because of the dual norms of militarized patriotism discussed below – congressional leaders, especially those who were presidential hopefuls and needed to be of "national stature," understood they needed to be "strong" on national defense and they felt it was politically safer to defer to the executive branch on major issues of national security because it was deemed to be perceived as more patriotic by the public.

That there was virtually no debate at all about invading Iraq in the first seven months of 2002 appears to provide strong evidence Democrats feared being labeled unpatriotic in the wake of 9/11. In January, President Bush had labeled Iraq as part of the "axis of evil" in his State of the Union speech, and presented his arguments against Saddam Hussein. In the succeeding months he repeatedly asserted his intention of removing Saddam Hussein from power and his administration began visibly to prepare extensively for a "possible" invasion of Iraq (O'Hanlon and Gordon 2002). Over this period, many U.S. allies overseas stood up in opposition to a possible invasion, yet most Democrats did not even ask questions. One commentator asked, in March 2002, "Where is the debate?" and argued:

> It isn't treason for a party out of power in wartime to talk about these matters. If anything, it's the Democrats' patriotic responsibility not just to hold up their end of the national dialogue over the war's means and ends, but to say where they want to take the country in peace. . .
>
> (Rich 2002)

Another commentator observed: "Democrats [have] been tiptoeing around [the Iraq war issue] like teen-agers sneaking in after curfew. . . ." and argued "The Democrats' silence coupled with the Republicans' enthusiasm put the nation in the difficult position of being taken into a questionable war without any questions being asked" (Goldsborough 2002). Likewise, an editorial remarked that the beating of war drums in Washington, DC, had "been met by a cowed silence from most Democrats" (Atlanta Journal-Constitution 2002). Even though there was no strong Democratic opposition to the Bush administration over Iraq, there was also no agreement either.

Leading Democrats all stated they agreed that it would be better if Saddam Hussein was out of power, but most strongly hedged about whether it was necessary or advisable to use force against Iraq. Sen. Joseph Lieberman (D-Conn.) notably came out in full support of using force, but he was virtually alone. If others agreed, it likely would have been to their political advantage to speak up. House Minority Leader Dick Gephardt (D-Mo.) also tentatively favored military action in early summer, but with the strong caveat that only *if all other efforts failed.* By mid-July, Gephardt was a firm believer there should be a national dialogue with evidence presented to Congress before any large-scale invasion (Dao 2002).

Other leading Democrats, such as former Vice President Al Gore, Senate Majority Leader Tom Daschle (D-S.D.), and Senators John Edwards (D-N.C.), John Kerry (D-Mass.), and Hillary Clinton (D-N.Y.), repeatedly tried to sidestep the issue altogether. One report said: "Democrats fear being labeled unpatriotic. They don't want to force a debate now that would divert attention from domestic issues that they think boost their chances in November's elections." This report also noted that Senator Edwards said: "It is overly simplistic to say are we in favor of a war or against a war. Saddam is dangerous, and he needs to be gone. But there are many things that need to be done before any decision is made or action taken" (Thomma and Hutchinson 2002). It was widely perceived that Democrats were cautious because they believed they could only lose politically if they tried to debate the Iraq issue. One typical report stated in August: "Iraq is emerging as the wild-card issue in the 2002 election, with Democrats nervously watching a growing debate . . . fearful that it could shift attention away from economic issues that now dominate the agenda" (Balz 2002). According to Rep. Dennis Kucinich (D-Ohio), who came out in strong opposition to invading Iraq: "There's a certain amount of fear [among Democrats], let's face it. The nature of politics is caution. People are just watching and wondering what's going on here" (Thomma and Hutchinson 2002). Since Democrats had openly favored the invasion of Afghanistan, their silence in the first half of 2002 indicated they were not convinced an invasion of Iraq was necessary, and further they did not feel they necessarily had to support the executive branch in the wake of 9/11.

Further confirming these observations about early 2002, in mid-April, prominent outside observers recognized the striking congressional reticence to debate a possible war in Iraq. An ongoing Brookings/Harvard Forum convened a panel of eminent "Congress-watchers" to discuss: Where was Congress? Was it perhaps premature for a serious congressional debate [on Iraq]? Was Congress intimidated by the White House? All four panelists agreed that in the wake of 9/11, Congress had been in essential agreement with the White House about the invasion of Afghanistan based on the merits of the case, but each predicted there would soon be much more debate over Iraq. One stated: "[Earlier] Congress did support the president on the merits of these things and as issues become less black and white and more complicated, I think you'll certainly see more congressional involvement." Likewise, another remarked:

> I think in times of war there is a natural tendency for everybody to rally together and to support the chief executive and that inhibits this kind of questioning that you want to erupt. I think you will have a debate over Iraq. I'm a little surprised that there hasn't been more of it up to now, but I think it's going to happen.
>
> (Hess and Kalb 2003: 249)

These observers believed in the spring of 2002 the time of rallying behind the president after 9/11 was fading (as was indicated in public opinion polls), they did not think Congress simply agreed about Iraq, and they had expected more debate already.

Democratic silence continued through most of the summer of 2002 even as public support for invading Iraq – despite scarce voiced opposition – fell to just over 50 percent. Additionally, there was over 60 percent support among the public for multilateralism, giving the Democrats clear public support for opposing unilateralism. The silence about Iraq was finally broken by congressional leaders with strong questioning by Sen. Joseph Biden (D-Del.) and Sen. Richard Lugar (R-Ind.), the leaders of the Senate Foreign Relations Committee, who decided in early August to begin hearings about U.S. policy toward Iraq. The questions posed by the senators emphatically implied they were not convinced invading Iraq was urgent or even necessary:

First, what threat does Iraq pose to our security? How immediate is the danger?
... Second, what are the possible responses to the Iraqi threat? ... Third, when
Saddam Hussein is gone, what would be our responsibilities?

(Biden Jr. and Lugar 2002)

These hearings were quite substantial in that many felt they revealed how weak the
administration's case actually was. For example, testimony from the CIA chief
George Tenet admitted that there was no "technically collected" evidence – no
physical proof – on Iraq's WMD programs. Thus, the intelligence services were
basing every claim of current programs on defector statements. This clearly took
many senators and staffers by surprise because they knew human intelligence alone
was a shaky proposition. Moreover, the main piece of evidence the administration
had presented at this point for an Iraqi nuclear program was intercepted aluminum
tubes that were allegedly for nuclear centrifuges. However, the senators heard during these hearings from the State Department and the Energy Department (which
had the strongest technical expertise to judge the aluminum tubes) that the tubes
were not likely meant for a nuclear program. Thus, the senators knew the administration's case was not strong. One Senate science advisor recalled that after watching the administration's presentation of its evidence, he said in private, "They're
going to war and there's not a damn piece of evidence to substantiate it" (Isikoff and
Corn 2006: 117–19).

At the same time, in August 2002, prominent Republicans and former military
officers began launching a credible challenge to the executive branch. Brent
Scowcroft, retired Air Force general and former national security adviser to
Presidents Ford and George H.W. Bush, led the opposition arguing there was
"scant evidence" to tie Saddam Hussein to terrorism. Scowcroft also reasoned that
Saddam Hussein, whom he believed then devoted enormous efforts to equipping
his forces with WMDs, would not make common cause with terrorists because he
was a "power-hungry survivor" who would know that this would open him to a devastating response from the U.S. (Scowcroft 2002). Scowcroft was joined in his
charge to stop the administration from unilaterally invading Iraq by two secretaries
of state from the George H.W. Bush administration, James W. Baker III
and Lawrence S. Eagleburger. Others joining in opposition included Richard C.
Holbrooke and numerous Republican politicians, including House Majority
Leader Dick Armey (R-Tex.) and Sen. Chuck Hagel (R-Neb.), a likely Republican
presidential hopeful. It was widely reported that State Department officials, including Secretary of State Colin Powell and his assistant Richard Armitage were
opposed to the invasion and were working behind the scenes to rally the opposition.

Other respected military professionals also openly opposed an invasion of Iraq
and made their voices heard during this critical period of debate. They included
Gen. Wesley Clarke, the head of the U.S. NATO force in the Kosovo War, Gen.
Norman Schwarzkopf, head of U.S. forces in the 1991 Gulf War, and Gen. Anthony
Zinni, who had then just recently served as Bush's top envoy to the Middle East. All
warned strongly against a war with Iraq. Other military professionals were also
calling for more debate, such as Retired Army Lt. Col. Ralf Zimmerman, who

wrote in the *Army Times* that it was time for the U.S. public to think through this issue and "have an open public debate over war vs. containment as the proper option when dealing with Iraq" (Ricks 2006: 48). Even with all of these credible allies, and public support for an invasion dropping, no leading Democrats from Congress decided to take a strong stand in opposition.

By the end of August 2002, after many Republican and military voices came out in opposition some Democrats were arguing that the president needed Congress's approval before invading Iraq. A number of Democrats made it clear that they were not convinced an attack was necessary and were not ready to give the president authority under the War Powers Act. "Based on what the administration has shared with Congress, I'd say the administration is far short of being able to count on Congress's support for any action," said Rep. Rick Larsen (D-Wash.) (Postman 2002). It was at that time reported that White House lawyers were arguing the president did not need a vote in Congress because the 1991 congressional resolution for the first Gulf War was still in effect. Other administration officials were arguing authorization under the War Powers Resolution was not necessary at all anyhow. These arguments were being made because administration leaders feared a resolution would likely include restrictions on military action.

In response to the strong challenge from Republicans and some Democrats that the President should not go to war without the clear support of the Congress, the Bush Administration ultimately decided to change tactics. Instead of insisting it could go ahead unilaterally, it decided to take the issue to the United Nations. The administration then framed the issue so that Congress was asked to rally behind the president to help pressure the United Nations to act but should not tie the president's hands if the United Nations failed to act.

Beginning in full force on September 11, 2002, the administration launched a campaign to press its case to the United Nations, Congress, and the public. It held special briefings and emphasized evidence that, they argued, made a strong case against Iraq, including the evidence of aluminum tubes for centrifuges, unmanned aerial vehicles that could possibly carry WMD and new evidence of "associations" and "relationships" between Saddam and al-Qaeda. Many leaders were unconvinced. Dick Armey said later: "It wasn't very convincing. If I'd gotten the same briefing from President Clinton or Al Gore, I probably would have said, 'Ah, bullshit.' But you don't do that with your own people" (Isikoff and Corn 2006: 124).

Also in September, Democratic Party leaders held their own briefings for congressional Democrats. These briefings were led by men and women who shaped national security strategy for Bill Clinton, including Kenneth Pollack, Dennis Ross, and Madeleine Albright. They all argued Saddam Hussein was dangerous and military force was the only permanent solution, although they included strong caveats about the need for a broad international coalition and sufficient post-war planning. Many Democrats would later argue it was these briefings that changed their minds, but there is evidence to suggest this information and advice did not actually convince the majority (at least in the Senate) that there was a grave threat – or to support a unilateral invasion. Clear opposition persisted after these briefings so it appears that only after Democrats ended up voting for the "blank check" resolution did they rationalize that these briefings convinced them.

The administration introduced its preferred language for the Iraq War Resolution on September 19, and was still negotiating the language of the resolution at the end of September. Even at the *end of the month* – after all the briefings – the president's war resolution was no sure thing. Democratic Senator Joe Biden and two Republican Senators, Richard Lugar and Chuck Hagel, were gaining overwhelming support for an alternative proposal that would drastically narrow the president's authority. These Senators all served on the Senate Foreign Relations Committee and they had heard extensive testimony from the intelligence services on the alleged Iraqi threat. They were not convinced the administration had sufficient evidence and they wanted to draw the resolution about Iraq very narrowly. The Biden–Lugar–Hagel Resolution was crafted to allow Bush to attack Iraq only for the purpose of destroying Iraq's WMD (not regime change), and only after seeking UN approval. If the United Nations said no, their proposal required the president to come back to Congress and demonstrate that the Iraqi threat was so "grave" that only military action could eliminate it.

The resolution reportedly had the backing of at least 60 to 70 senators, including as many as 25 Republicans. According to Biden, the resolution was being encouraged by Powell and Armitage at the State Department. The widespread support for this resolution demonstrates that there were substantial bipartisan doubts about a "grave" threat requiring unilateral military action.

The White House was worried about the Biden proposal. Bush was reportedly furious and told Sen. Trent Lott (R-Miss.), "I don't want a resolution such as this to tie my hands," and he ordered Lott: "Derail the Biden legislation and make sure its language never sees the light of day" (Isikoff and Corn 2006: 127). In the end, Lott did not need to derail the resolution. The White House had been negotiating the language of its preferred resolution with leaders from both the House and Senate. The Democrats were a minority in the House, and although Democratic Minority Leader Dick Gephardt had been pushing for small changes to the resolution, he could not get much. The White House had Republican support in the House and decided to call deliberations to a close and introduce the legislation in the House – most likely to preempt the Biden Resolution in the Senate. According to Gephardt,

> At some point, the White House said, "This is as good as it gets," and I became convinced we couldn't get more. You had to make a decision whether you were for giving the president the authority or not. Everything else was window dressing.
>
> (Isikoff and Corn 2006: 127)

On October 2, the White House held a Rose Garden press conference announcing that it had finalized the draft Iraq War Resolution to be introduced in the House. The press conference was highly notable because Dick Gephardt agreed to appear with the president in support of the resolution. Democratic Majority Leader Senator Tom Daschle had also taken part in the negotiations with the White House but had refused to appear in the Rose Garden and endorse the broad language of the proposed resolution. Gephardt's appearance in the Rose Garden caught both Senators Daschle and Biden off guard (Newshour with Jim Lehrer, "Kwame Holman reports on the House resolution authorizing military action against Iraq," October 2, 2002). Daschle abruptly canceled his morning press briefing. A stunned Biden remarked to reporters,

> I believe from my discussions with the Republicans who support this [the Biden resolution] that there are up to twenty-four, twenty-five Republican members who would much prefer to see this [resolution] narrowed along the lines that we have suggested. I believe there are as many as a dozen who, prior to this sort of being potentially, you know, match point already occurred here [referring to Gephardt's Rose Garden appearance], who were prepared to vote for this.

> (PBS Holman Report 2002)

Gephardt's support of the president's resolution effectively killed Biden's proposal. Thereafter, the Republicans responded to Biden's requests for support by stating that they could not afford to "be to the left of Dick Gephardt" (Isikoff and Corn 2006).

Why would many Republican senators and almost all Democratic senators, who believed they should support a narrow resolution precluding a unilateral invasion without more proof of a "grave" threat, change their minds just because one congressman decided to support the "blank check" resolution? Republicans felt they could not be seen as "weaker" on national security than a leading Democrat. Moreover, they could not be seen as less loyal to the commander-in-chief. With the collapse of Republican support, all Democrats who faced tight races in the 2002 midterm elections (except Sen. Paul Wellstone [D-Minn.]) – and presidential hopefuls from both parties (including Senators Hagel and Biden) – decided they also needed to be "strong" on national security and support the commander-in-chief.

Why did Dick Gephardt decide to support Bush and even appear in the Rose Garden before any debate of the resolution had taken place in Congress? Most observers were as surprised as Daschle and Biden, and considered his appearance in the Rose Garden out of character and even a betrayal of sorts to his party. According to Gephardt, his thinking was shaped by the former Clinton national security aides who argued that Iraq would have to be confronted. Indeed, Gephardt made an impassioned speech about how Iraq posed a serious threat. However, there is also significant evidence he was not actually convinced a unilateral invasion was a good idea and was instead conforming to the norm to be "strong" on national defense. First, he repeatedly revealed that he had deep reservations and regrets at the time and felt he was in a difficult political position. He later recalled saying: "I'm sorry he's the president. I didn't vote for him. But we're in a tight spot" (Isikoff and Corn 2006: 128). Second, he contended that Democrats had no choice but to go along with Bush on Iraq and they had to try to keep Iraq from becoming the defining issue in the upcoming elections. However, it should be noted that

Democrats really did have a choice here because bipartisan opposition to the administration's resolution was widely known. All leaders of Congress knew there was possible political cover for Democrats if bipartisan support could be arranged and no one could tag one party or a few leaders as unpatriotic, especially because opposition included many prudent hawks and military professionals. Even leading political science realists advertised their opposition to an invasion of Iraq at this time in a full page ad in *The New York Times* (September 26, 2002). Thus, the Biden–Lugar–Hagel proposal was a missed opportunity that would have given the Democrats the ability to neutralize the war issue during the election season by being full participants rather than rubber-stampers.

Gephardt's claim, therefore, that there was no real option for Democrats appears self-serving; it appears he jumped at the chance to look extra tough on national security in the Rose Garden, rather than working for the benefit of the Democratic party and the country. Others also noted that Gephardt perceived himself to be in a particularly tight spot because he was determined to run for the presidency in 2004, and, like other leading Democrats, he had voted against the 1991 Gulf War. Other members of Congress reasoned Gephardt felt that if he cast a similar vote against a possibly popular war, he could expect the Republicans to tag him as soft and too hesitant to use military force. Instead, if he came out strong on national security, this could be to his definite advantage and set him apart from other Democratic contenders for the presidency. His political advisers urged him to appear on the Rose Garden lawn.

Gephardt was not alone on the lawn with the president. Bush had support at that point from many known hawks on this issue, such as Senators Joseph Lieberman, John McCain (R-Ariz.), and John Warner (R-Va.), and Republican Speaker of the House Dennis Hastert (R-Ill.), all of whom were in the Rose Garden. However, it was notable that Republican House Majority Leader Dick Armey was not there. The absence of both Armey and Daschle was known to be because both of these leaders hoped to leave open the possibility of real debate over the resolution. Thus, the presence of Gephardt was striking to all. Daschle, like Gephardt, was also a presidential hopeful and would likely have benefited politically by being seen as "standing tough" on national security. Daschle's colleagues recognized it took political courage to not appear on the lawn standing "strong" on national security and praised him for his courage and leadership on the Senate floor during the debate of the resolution (Byrd 2002: S10242).

Even though senate members clearly preferred not to unilaterally attack Iraq, after the collapse of the bipartisan support for the Biden Resolution, everyone on Capitol Hill began predicting the president's resolution would pass easily so the subsequent debate was anticlimactic. The media hardly covered the House debate with only one reporter in the press gallery when it began. At the most intense points in both the House and the Senate debates fewer than 10 percent of each body's members attended. One seasoned observer remarked: "Usually, when there are few people around, it means they don't like what's happening but don't feel they can do anything about it" (Ricks 2006: 61). Overall the Senate decided to go to war in Iraq after only six days of debate. This brief debate stands in stark contrast to the 21 days spent debating the Elementary and Secondary Education Act, the 23 days on the energy bill, the 19 days on the trade bill, and 18 days on the farm bill (Byrd 2004: 175).

It is even more remarkable how perfunctory the debate was given that senators received the crucial National Intelligence Estimate (NIE) on Iraq on October 1, 2002, a mere three days before the debate. Gephardt, in fact, made up his mind without consulting the new NIE on Iraq, further indicating that he made up his mind based on political pressures rather than reasonably considering the full merits of the case. Congress had requested in September that the CIA produce an NIE on Iraq. The fact that members of Congress needed to request an NIE should have set off alarm bells: such requests were normally unnecessary because the CIA routinely produces NIEs about possible major threats. When the intelligence estimate on Iraq's WMD capabilities finally arrived in Congress on October 1, 2002, some congressional aides were anxious to review it, but no more than a half dozen members of Congress ever went to the secure room to examine the document. Senate aide Peter Zimmerman, the scientific adviser to the Senate Foreign Relations Committee, later explained why:

> We had an election coming up. The Democrats were afraid of being seen as soft on Saddam or on terrorism. The whole notion was, "Let's get the war out of the way as fast as possible and turn back to the domestic agenda".
>
> (Isikoff and Corn 2006: 133–38)

I argue here, that while congress members ultimately wanted to avoid appearing "soft" and unpatriotic, normal electoral pressures of wanting to merely change the issue are not the full story. Congress, despite electoral pressures, came very close to standing together in opposition to the executive branch. It was the acute pressures on Gephardt – that were also perceived to be acute for all politicians of national stature so no Democrat took an early lead in opposition – that led to the wholesale change of many votes that nearly were cast in opposition despite the election season.

Finally, most Democrats and even many Republicans made speeches that further reveal that they understood the weakness of the intelligence and that they thought attacking unilaterally was unwise. For example, Senator Clinton warned strongly against a unilateral invasion multiple times, and ultimately said: "I take the President at his word that he will try hard to pass a United Nations resolution and seek to avoid war, if possible [through weapons inspections]" (Clinton 2002: S10289). Likewise Daschle made it clear to all there were major controversies over the intelligence that were being reported in the media as they debated on October 10, 2002: "A report in yesterday's *Washington Post* suggests 'an increasing number of intelligence officials, including former and current intelligence agency employees, are concerned the agency is tailoring its public stance to fit the administration's views'" (Daschle 2002: S10241). Additionally, Senator Biden stated: ". . . Iraq's illegal weapons of mass destruction program do not – do not – pose an imminent threat to our national security . . ." (Biden 2002: S10290). Strong reservations abounded.

Senator Daschle, among others, also pointed out that there was no debate about the real costs and consequences of the possible war they were authorizing, nor was there any discussion of the new, and in his view, dangerous policy of preemption they were adopting if they went forward with attacking Iraq. Daschle made these points by asking tough questions of the resolution – questions so tough, it sounded like he really would not support the resolution. In the end, he defended his right to ask tough questions in these words:

> Some people think it is wrong to ask questions or raise concerns when the President says our national security is at risk. They believe it is an act of disloyalty. I disagree. In America, asking questions is an act of patriotism. For those of us who have been entrusted by our fellow citizens to serve in this Senate, asking questions is more than a privilege, it is a constitutional responsibility.
>
> (Daschle 2002: S10242)

Daschle expressed strong reservations about the Iraq War Resolution while he also expressed in this statement strong awareness of the pressure to conform with the norms of militarized patriotism. The next day, on October 11, 2002, Daschle voted with 77 other senators for the Iraq War Resolution.

Militarized patriotism explains success of threat inflation

A major debate has developed concerning why the U.S. "marketplace of ideas" failed so profoundly in this period. I hypothesize that the failure of the marketplace of ideas can best be understood by recognizing the powerful silencing effect of norms of behavior that delineate what is considered "patriotic" behavior in the U.S. Two important norms emerged for politicians during the Cold War as the political culture within the U.S. became increasingly militarized – first to support "strong" national security policies, and second, to defer to the executive branch on war powers in times of perceived crisis. These norms have often precluded genuine democratic deliberation of foreign policy alternatives in the marketplace of ideas in the United States since World War II. Ultimate adherence to these norms, although questioned by many, created the market failure in the run-up to the Iraq War. This argument, focused on norms, stands in sharp contrast with other leading explanations that point to the institutional power of the executive branch or public fear combined with powerful rhetoric after the terrorist attacks of September 11, 2001 as the critical factors leading to the success of threat inflation.

Scholars, politicians and pundits noticed that patriotism played a role in silencing political opposition and sharply prejudiced the media during the run-up to the Iraq War (McGovern 2005; Krugman 2006). Others have argued that the silencing effect of patriotism was simply the unavoidable effect of "ordinary patriotism" and that it may have silenced some opposition but was not the central obstacle to the efficient functioning of the marketplace of ideas (Kaufmann 2004: 36). I contend that the norms enforced by patriotism – i.e., what behavior is considered "patriotic" – were not "ordinary" norms of patriotism for a democracy, but were relatively recent anti-democratic norms generated by the militarized political culture that emerged during the Cold War (Duffield 1999; Berger 1996; Jepperson *et al.* 1996). These norms largely account for the lack of debate in early 2002, the lack of strong opposition leadership and ultimately for the total collapse of the nearly successful opposition to the "blank check" Iraq War Resolution.

Patriotism is simply "love and devotion to one's country" and therefore in a democracy, where free and open debate are necessarily respected and valued as essential to the health of the democracy, "love and devotion to one's country" should not brand any particular political opinions "unpatriotic." Indeed, dissent should be considered patriotic. Dissenters, and especially mild, responsible and logical dissenters, should not fear being labeled as unpatriotic. However, militarism exists in a state when there is a general political orientation of the people or the government to maintain a strong military force and to be prepared to use it aggressively to defend or promote national interests. Thus, I argue that the rise of militarism during the Cold War, caused by perceived large external threats and the growth of a very large military industrial complex, led to the distorting of "ordinary patriotism" into "militarized patriotism" where citizens or leaders who questioned or opposed maintaining strong military forces or questioned or opposed reflexively using military force to defend or promote national interests were labeled as "unpatriotic." Hence, "militarized patriotism" is the causal mechanism through which a militarized political culture is manifested and affects behavior in the marketplace of ideas (Yee 1996).

Unlike most constructivists who discuss political culture, I do not argue that the militarized political culture in the United States created a shared world view where the public and politicians prefer, or can only "imagine," highly militarized security policies (in contrast with Duffield 1999). On the contrary, a majority of the public and the politicians recognized and preferred a multi-lateral solution to the Iraq threat, with a strong preference for disarming Iraq through weapons inspections rather than a military invasion (see Thrall, this volume). However, individual political actors, especially prominent politicians of national stature, were constrained in their individual behavior by cultural norms of behavior. It was imperative for them in particular to avoid being labeled "unpatriotic," thus they could not espouse policies that could be construed as "weak" on national security or as unsupportive of the executive branch in a time of crisis. A cultural domestic environment established in an earlier period in response to a different international environment embodied a set of norms that later constrained the behavior of rational political actors (Schimmelfennig 2003: 283–286).

During, and especially after World War II, the U.S. political culture was transformed from relatively isolationist and anti-militarist to wholly internationalist and militarist (Hogan 1998; Sherry 1995). Rapid militarization of the United States happened early in the Cold War with the creation of a large, permanent standing army, a vast network of overseas bases, and the blossoming of what has been called the "national security state;" the defense budget jumped sharply from $13.7 billion in 1950 to $52.8 billion in 1953 and remained at higher levels. This militarization happened because the United States came to fear a large threat from the Soviet Union and communism, and this collective fear led to what has been called the "Cold War consensus" and a transformation to a militarized political culture during the Cold War (Fordham 1998).

For almost two decades at the beginning of the Cold War, the period of the "Cold War consensus," the U.S. public was highly unified in its embrace of very "strong" national security policies; this was the time when a unified political culture is easiest to discern. When the United States fought in Vietnam, the Cold War consensus significantly eroded. Many Americans began to question the size and necessity of the massive military, and they began to question many other U.S. foreign policies. During the 1970s there was even widespread agreement that the United States had perhaps gone too far in its militarization and that "overkill" existed, and therefore the United States could safely and securely pursue arms control (Rosenberg 1983). However, while there were disagreements about national security policy in terms of whether the United States needed to keep building its forces up or if it could limit its forces to some degree, there remained intact a widespread consensus in favor of "strong" national security policies.

No politicians of national stature ever advocated significant reductions in military spending or any other major lessening of militarization throughout the Cold War or after. Advocates of isolationism or any position supporting merely national defense rather than a strong global military presence were not to be found in the mainstream. This was a profound change in U.S. political culture from the more than 150 years of U.S. history before World War II when many citizens and leaders openly and forcefully advocated for un-militarized, even isolationist, foreign policies. While there was nearly a decade of post-Vietnam questioning, widespread popular support for "strong" national security policies returned in full force in 1979 at a time of perceived increased threat. Militarization returned with a vengeance in the 1980s, when the United States – with its highest peacetime military budgets of the Cold War – spent over $2.2 trillion in eight years on the military. Military spending continued at Cold War levels even after the end of the Cold War and the disappearance of the Soviet threat.

The Cold War embrace of "strong" national security policies was matched by public and apparent congressional willingness to support increased presidential war powers. The Cold War was an era of nuclear threats, and many believed national security interests could no longer allow for a slow, deliberative, and open debate of U.S. military interests and decisions for war. With the possibility that devastating weapons could attack the United States quickly, it was apparently assumed that a president needed the prerogative to act quickly and make independent credible threats to preserve national security.

U.S. presidents have used force abroad over 300 different times throughout U.S. history, whereas Congress has officially declared war only five times (Hendrickson 2002: 1). Thus, one could argue that the War Powers Clause of the Constitution granting Congress full powers and responsibility to declare war has never held sway. However, historians maintain that from the founding of the Republic through the nineteenth century and until the Cold War, presidents generally sought congressional authorization or approval prior to using force (Sofaer 1976; Fisher 1995).

This political practice was essentially overturned with the Korean War, when President Truman sought no formal declaration of war or prior approval before committing troops. Instead the Truman administration noted: "That the President's power to send the Armed Forces outside the country is not dependent on congressional authority has been repeatedly emphasized by numerous writers" (Hendrickson 2002: 3) Moreover, Truman maintained he had the constitutional authority as commander-in-chief to use the military forces for a "police action." These arguments were accepted and even defended by some members of Congress. Ryan Hendrickson writes: "With such a precedent in place and repeatedly reaffirmed by presidential leadership in military affairs during the cold war, it seems that a norm of presidential leadership is now an accepted part of the U.S. foreign policy process" (Hendrickson 2002).

After the Vietnam War, Congress attempted to re-assert its power over war powers by passing the War Powers Resolution over President Nixon's veto in 1973. However, the War Powers Resolution has been widely criticized for actually ceding war powers to the president that the Constitution does not allow: It permits the president to commit troops for up to 90 days without congressional authorization, whereas under the Constitution the president can only use force to "repel sudden attacks." Other critics of the War Powers Resolution argue it was an unnecessary effort to establish powers that Congress already had. In the end, most observers argue that the War Powers Resolution has generally failed because Congress has been unwilling to meaningfully exercise its power and subsequent presidents have been unwilling to truly abide by it.

No politicians of national stature significantly questioned the United States' "strong" national security policies at the end of the Cold War even though the massive size and scope of the United States' military establishment in the absence of a peer-competitor was historically without precedent. In 2002, U.S. defense spending was 25 times greater than "the *combined* defense budgets of the seven 'rogue states' then comprising the roster of U.S. enemies" (emphasis added) (Bacevich 2005: 17). It is clear the United States remained highly militarized after the Cold War, and the "norm of behavior" that no politician of national stature could afford to be viewed as "weak" on national security remained intact.

Moreover, no significant congressional challenge of executive authority in war powers was ever mounted after the Cold War, despite the dramatically changed threat environment. In fact, after the Cold War there has been a significantly increased U.S. willingness to use force, but no marked increase of congressional participation in decision making. During the forty-year Cold War, although the United States liberally used clandestine force, it only engaged in six separate large-scale military actions. Since the end of the Cold War, beginning with Operation Just Cause in Panama in 1989, the United States has engaged in nine large-scale military operations, along with many other smaller actions such as cruise missile attacks and frequent bombings in Iraq throughout the 1990s, and each use of force included vast congressional deference and little meaningful congressional participation in decision making (Bacevich 2005: 19).

Thus, I argue it is these two norms of behavior that account for congressional silence and the executive branch victory in the run-up to the Iraq War. A majority of Congress members clearly wanted to oppose the Bush Administration's push for a possible unilateral invasion of Iraq to oust Saddam Hussein. Congress members understood the evidence and almost succeeded in joining together in opposition despite the 9/11 attacks and despite the normal electoral pressures. However, the opposition coalition ultimately fell apart because it was deemed too politically risky by some members of Congress to be viewed as not being "strong" on national security and it was perceived as much safer politically to avoid being labeled "unpatriotic" by deferring to the executive branch on issues of war powers in a time of alleged crisis. In short, skeptics were silenced and Congress could not conduct a genuine debate on the most important national security question – whether or not to go to war – because of the pressures of militarized patriotism. If Congress is para-lyzed and cannot democratically deliberate, then the entire marketplace of ideas fails, and the executive branch wins, no matter the merits of its case.

Militarized norms and the marketplace of ideas

The theory of the democratic marketplace of ideas is based on the notion that open debate and discussion can ultimately influence policy outcomes in a democracy. I have argued that the militarized political culture created in the United States during the Cold War forged two norms of behavior that drastically curtailed open debate in the marketplace of ideas during the Cold War and after, and especially again dur-ing the run-up to the Iraq War. These militarized norms of patriotism pressured politicians of national stature to appear "strong" on national security and to unify behind the executive branch during this uncertain period that could be perceived as a period of crisis (although they recognized the crisis did not emanate from Iraq). Although it is impossible to prove the existence or power of norms definitively and it is further impossible to know why politicians voted as they did, there is strong evidence that a vast majority in the Senate preferred to vote to curtail the executive branch's plans for unilateral regime change, but many Republican and Democratic votes suddenly changed their position apparently based on political calculations when the bipartisan effort to drastically narrow the Iraq War Resolution collapsed on October 2, 2002.

The evidence that many in Congress strongly opposed the executive branch's plans for unilateral regime change is extensive and even overwhelming. Further, many observers readily concur that pressures to be patriotic silenced debate and likely changed many votes in the electoral season of 2002. I have attempted here to make the additional argument that the problem with the marketplace of ideas was not simply the problem of ordinary patriotism or the electoral season. I have argued that to fix the problems of patriotism – to protect dissent and to get Congress to assert its responsibilities in war powers – underlying militarism needs to be recog-nized and guarded against. Leaders and the public need to recognize that using force should truly be a last resort and not a first option, so those opposing force should have the benefit of the doubt while those advocating force should be viewed skeptically (and certainly not viewed as more patriotic). Further, the root causes of militarism need to be studied and better understood, rather than accusing those who study militarism as being unpatriotic.

The fact that the United States shares a militarized political culture is widely recognized by the rest of the world, but sharply denied within the United States. Evidence of the U.S. militarized world view in sharp contrast with the rest of the world was perhaps most clear and striking during the run up to the Iraq War, when Colin Powell went before the United Nations to argue the case for invading Iraq. The United States generally loudly lauded Powell's performance and declared the evidence he presented for using military force against Iraq as overwhelming, while the rest of the world remained unconvinced, thought the evidence for using force was stunningly lacking and collectively shook their heads at the United States in disbelief.

References

Atlanta Journal-Constitution (2002) "Bush can't circumvent Congress to initiate war," 23 August: 19A.

Bacevich, A. (2005) *The New American Militarism: How Americans are Seduced by War*, New York: Oxford University Press.

Balz, D. (2002) "Democrats worry about Iraq as issue; Debate on war seen as diversion from economy," *Washington Post*, 19 August: A01.

Berger, T. U. (1996) "Norms, identity and national security in Germany and Japan," in Katzenstein, P. J. (ed.) *The Culture of National Security: Norms and Identity in World Politics*, New York: Columbia University Press.

Biden Jr., J. R. and Lugar, R. G. (2002) "Debating Iraq," *New York Times*, 31 July: A19.

Biden Jr., J. R. (2002) Congressional Record–Senate, 10 October.

Byrd, R. C. (2002) Congressional Record–Senate, 10 October.

—— (2004) *Losing America: Confronting a Reckless and Arrogant Presidency*, New York: W.W. Norton.

Cirincione, J., Matthews J. T. and Perkovich, G. with Orton, A. (2004) *WMD in Iraq: Evidence and Implications*, New York: Carnegie Endowment for International Peace.

Clinton, H. (2002) Congressional Record–Senate, 10 October.

Dao, J. (2002) "Call in Congress for full airing of Iraq policy," *New York Times*, July 18: A1.

Danner, M. (2006) *The Secret Way to War: The Downing Street Memo and the Iraq War's Buried History*, New York: New York Review of Books.

Daschle, T. (2002) Congressional Record–Senate, 10 October.

Duffield, J. (1999) "Political culture and state behavior: Why Germany confounds neorealism," *International Organization*, 53: 765–803.

Fisher, L. (1995) *Presidential War Power*, Lawrence: University Press of Kansas.

Fordham, B. O. (1998) *Building the Cold War Consensus: The Political Economy of U.S. National Security Policy, 1949–51*, Ann Arbor: University of Michigan Press.

Goldsborough, J. O. (2002) "Democrats finally awaken over Iraq," *San Diego Union-Tribune*, 30 September: B7.

Hendrickson, R. C. (2002) *The Clinton Wars: The Constitution, Congress, and War Powers*, Nashville, Tenn.: Vanderbilt University Press.

Hess, S. and Kalb, M. (2003) "Transcript of forum on Congress," in S. Hess and M. Kalb, (eds), *The Media and the War on Terrorism*, Washington, D.C.: Brookings Institution Press.

Hogan, M. (1998) *A Cross of Iron: Harry S. Truman and the Origins of the National Security State, 1945–1954*, Cambridge: Cambridge University Press.

Holsti, O. R. (2004) *Public Opinion and American Foreign Policy*, (2nd edn), Ann Arbor: MI: University of Michigan Press.

Isikoff, M. and Corn, D. (2006) *Hubris: The Inside Story of Spin, Scandal, and the Selling of the Iraq War*, New York: Crown.

Jepperson, R. L., Wendt, A. and Katzenstein, P. J. (1996) "Norms, identity, and culture in national security," in P. J. Katzenstein (ed.) *The Culture of National Security: Norms and Identity in World Politics*, New York: Columbia University Press.

Kaufmann, C. (2004) "Threat inflation and the failure of the marketplace of ideas: The selling of the Iraq war," *International Security*, 29: 5–48.

Krugman, P. (2006) "The treason card," *New York Times*, 7 July.

McGovern, G. (2005) "Patriotism is nonpartisan: Challenging a mistaken war can take more courage than fighting one," *Nation*, 24 March: 30–31.

O'Hanlon, M. E. and Gordon, P. H. (2002) "Is fighting Iraq worth the risks?" *New York Times*, 25 July: A17.

PBS news video and transcript, (2002) *A Newshour with Jim Lehrer*, "Kwame Holman reports on the House resolution authorizing military action against Iraq," Online. Available: <http://www.pbs.org/newshour/bb/middle_east/july-dec02/bkgdiraq_10–2. html> (Accessed October 30, 2002).

Postman, D. (2002) "Washington congressional Democrats say they're wary of attack on Iraq," *Seattle Times*, 28 August: A12.

Rich, F. (2002) "The wimps of war," *The New York Times*, 30 March: A15.

Ricks, T. E. (2006) *Fiasco: The American Military Adventure in Iraq, 2003 to 2005*, New York: Penguin.

Rosenberg, D. A. (1983) "Origins of overkill: Nuclear weapons and American strategy, 1945–1960," *International Security*, 7: 3–71.

Scowcroft, B. (2002) "Don't attack Saddam," *Wall Street Journal*, 15 August, A12.

Schimmelfennig, F. (2003) *The EU, NATO, and the Integration of Europe: Rules and Rhetoric*, Cambridge: Cambridge University Press.

Sherry, M. (1995) *In the Shadow of War: The United States Since the 1930's*, New Haven, Conn.: Yale University Press.

Sofaer, A. (1976) *War, Foreign Affairs, and Constitutional Power*, Cambridge, Mass.: Ballinger.

Thomma, S. and Hutchinson, R. (2002) "Democrats cautious on attack on Iraq," *Pittsburgh Post-Gazette*, 22 August: A8.

Yee, A. S. (1996) "The causal effects of ideas on policies," *International Organization*, 50: 69–108.

Yergin, D. (1977) *Shattered Peace: The Origins of the Cold War and the National Security State*, Boston, Mass.: Houghton Mifflin Company.

9 The war over Iraq

Selling war to the American public

Jon Western

This chapter examines how, in the absence of any link between Iraq and the events of September 11, President George W. Bush was able to lead the United States into a preventive war against Iraq with such widespread public and political support. How was he able to build and sustain broad public and political support for military action against Saddam Hussein as part of the war on terror despite no factual link between Iraq and the September 11 attacks and despite the existence of counter-arguments on the anticipated consequences of postwar occupation?

As each of the chapters in this volume shows, it is clear that President Bush and his advisors manipulated and inflated the threat emanating from Saddam Hussein's regime in Iraq. The question is how, and under what circumstances, does threat inflation work to influence public opinion and to open the political space for launching such an aggressive and ambitious strategy as preventive war? I begin with a brief discussion of the theoretical literature on the role of public opinion and the use of force. Next I present a case study of the Bush administration's domestic mobilization strategy that explores the mechanisms by which threat inflation influenced public opinion. Specifically, I examine the influence of four variables:

1 latent public opinion and the public's broad views on the nature and history of the Iraqi regime and behavior, and ultimately, the plausibility of the administration's arguments in support of war,
2 executive-branch information and propaganda resources and agenda-setting advantages;
3 executive cohesion and oppositional fragmentation; and
4 crisis duration.

The presence of all four of these factors enabled President Bush to launch his war against Saddam Hussein.

Public opinion and the use of force: predispositions and information

One of the basic features of democratic politics is that military force is not used without some consideration of the will of the public. Although elites do not make decisions on the use of force by referendum, the literature on public opinion and foreign policy has long recognized that elites are somewhat sensitive to public opinion on matters related to the use of force. Scholars also have found several consistent trends in public predispositions toward the use of force (Klarevas 2002). First, when Americans believe their security is threatened – real or perceived – they will back the use of force. Second, in a run-up to war, Americans consistently prefer diplomacy and multilateral efforts – including through the United Nations – over unilateral action (Kull and Destler 1999). Third, Americans are sensitive to costs and casualties, but they often remain committed to the use of force once it is engaged as long as they believe there is a clear theory of victory and that the costs are necessary to achieve the stated objectives (Feaver and Gelpi 2004). Fourth, although the public frequently supports the use of force to restrain threatening foreign-policy behavior by an adversary, it is less likely, on balance, to support the use of force to engineer internal political change (Jentleson 1992; Jentleson and Britton 1998). Finally, especially in the past decade, Americans have been willing to contemplate the use of force to respond to terrorism and threats posed by the illicit proliferation of weapons of mass destruction (Jentleson and Britton 1998).

Despite these broad predispositions, however, public support for or opposition to going to war is not simply a reflection of underlying predispositions. Public opinion is also highly dependent on the information the public receives. Even in a thriving democracy, information can be shaped to frame the public's understanding and interpretation of events. Because most citizens rarely have the time, inclination, or expertise to form independent opinions on national security matters, their perceptions of the costs and stakes involved in a particular crisis are routinely influenced principally by the information presented to them. Elites such as the president, senior administration officials, congressional leaders, and representatives of the national media organizations play a significant role in the transmission of information about foreign events to the public.

Of these conveyors of information, however, presidents are particularly important and influential. More than two decades ago, Richard Brody found that, especially early in crises, presidents often hold information monopolies that give them an edge in establishing the initial framing of a crisis (Brody 1983–84).Others have since demonstrated that presidents often have advantages in early analysis, evaluation, and interpretation of regional and civil conflicts. The vast resources of official overseas missions, intelligence-collection assets, and privileged stature in international diplomatic channels allow the president to write the first draft of what a conflict means for the United States. Because much of this information is processed through a closed national-security apparatus that does not allow for open public debate, opportunities for mobilized opposition against a governing group's position may be significantly disadvantaged without some independent ability to confirm or refute the veracity of executive information. Furthermore, presidents, especially popular ones, frequently are given wide latitude and deference on national-security issues.

These information advantages are most notable when there is strong consensus among elites – especially within the executive branch. Several scholars have found in independent studies that elite consensus within the executive branch significantly influences public support (Zaller 1992; Larson 1996; Klarevas 1999). Conversely, when elites are divided, the "dissensus" exposes the public to alternative arguments and analytical narratives and often leads to polarization of public views.

Information advantages are also significant when a crisis is relatively short in duration or when the crisis is framed in such a way to compress the decision-making time frame. Under such circumstances, oppositional elites and the media often are unable to challenge or carefully scrutinize information – including intelligence reports – and arguments concerning the magnitude of the threat and the potential costs of military actions. Longer crises often allow oppositional elites time to access new and existing information, to scrutinize embedded assumptions, and to challenge initial framing narratives of a crisis.

In short, public support for or against the use of force is a function of both the public's general predispositions and the information it receives. The public will not accept arguments for war willy-nilly; there must be some plausible connection to long-standing beliefs and experiences. Nonetheless, a cohesive administration intent on framing and selling the need for war can frequently influence and mobilize public support by controlling, managing, and even distorting information (Lowi 1989). The administration's information advantages and its ability to sell its arguments are especially strong when the decision-making time frame within a given crisis is compressed. When information is controlled and manipulated, and when counterarguments are suppressed, co-opted, or delegitimized, even rational publics may end up endorsing policies that later seem irrational (Page and Shapiro 1992).

Latent public opinion on terrorism and Iraq

In the 10 years prior to the terrorist attacks of 9/11, extensive polling data revealed that Americans had shifted their concerns from traditional cold war threats to a new set of dangers. By overwhelming and increasing numbers throughout the 1990s, Americans believed that two issues posed the most critical threats to U.S. security: the illicit proliferation of weapons of mass destruction – particularly nuclear weapons – and terrorism (see Table 9.1) (Chicago Council on Foreign Relations 2002). In addition, during this same time period, Gallup polling data revealed that a majority of Americans consistently favored taking military action against Iraq to remove Saddam Hussein from power (see Table 9.2) (Moore 2001).

Table 9.1 American's perceptions of critical security threats

	Percentage of Americans who believe threat to be critical	
Year	*Terrorism*	*Possibility of unfriendly countries' becoming nuclear powers*
1994	69	72
1998	84	75
2002	91	85

Source: U.S. General Population Topline Report, World Views 2002, Chicago Council on Foreign Relations and the German Marshall Fund of the United States, October 2002.

Table 9.2 Public opinion on going to war with Iraq

Date	Do you favor sending American troops back to the Persian Gulf to remove Saddam Hussein from power? (Percent responding)		
	Yes	No	No opinion
March/April 1992	55	0	5
June 1993	70	27	3
February 2001	52	42	6

Source: David W. Moore, "Americans Believe U.S. Participation in Gulf War a Decade Ago Worthwhile," Gallup News Service, February 21, 2001.

Note: In 1998, during the crisis over inspections, Gallup found, in a slightly differently worded question, that 76 percent of Americans supported "using military power to remove Saddam Hussein," while 19 percent were opposed.

In the immediate aftermath of the events of September 11, most Americans already had strong concerns about terrorism and weapons of mass destruction. These perceptions, coupled with their longstanding views that Saddam Hussein was intent on harming the United States, meant that most Americans were willing to assume Iraq's complicity – directly or indirectly – in those attacks even absent compelling evidence. As Bush and his advisers began their initial efforts to mobilize the public for war in Iraq in late 2001, they found that the American public already was largely predisposed to a focus on Iraq as the logical second phase in the war on terror.

Nonetheless, the administration was well aware of the limitations of those opinions. Despite the consistent majorities in favor of removing Saddam Hussein from power, that support was tempered by a number of conditions. First, the decade of polling data also revealed a strong preference for giving diplomacy time to run its course before military action (Moore 2002). Second, Americans were willing to countenance regime change but generally only within the context of multilateral action and with explicit UN support. Finally, the attitudes on Iraq were expressed in response to hypothetical questions on the use of force, not in the context of an actual troop mobilization and deployment.

Within the Bush administration at the time, concern was expressed that although the public was eager to lash out in response to the events of September 11, no one knew how long that anger would be sustained or if that support for war would transfer from a hypothetical question to a real military deployment. Launching a preventive war in Iraq would involve months of planning, extensive logistical preparations, and major deployments of combat troops. Given such a time frame, the Bush administration worried that residual support would likely evaporate and alternatives to war would be presented by liberal Democrats and others most likely to balk at military action. In short, Bush and his advisers had support for war in Iraq in the initial months after September 11 and the fall of the Taliban in Afghanistan. The question was, could they keep it? The public might have been predisposed to consider war in Iraq, but it was not a certainty that the public would support war without concerted effort by the administration.

The global war on terror: enhancing executive-branch information and propaganda advantages

One of the most significant contributing factors to the success of the administration's efforts in selling the war in Iraq was its ability to control and manage much of the flow of information regarding the magnitude and "imminence" of the threat posed by Saddam Hussein. A key factor was not simply linking the war in Iraq to the events of September 11, but more broadly to define and develop the Iraq war mobilization strategy within the context of the global war on terror. In the immediate days following September 11 attacks, the administration consolidated the national-security apparatus and enhanced the executive branch's information advantages.

The strategy was to define the American response to the attacks as broadly as possible and to set-up a war-time posture with expanded presidential powers. In his nationally televised address on the evening of September 11, 2001 President Bush announced that the United States was a nation at war – a global war on terror. The administration immediately solicited full Congressional support for going to war against those responsible for the terrorist attacks. On 14 September, both the House and Senate passed broad language authorizing the president to use "all necessary and appropriate force" against those who planned or helped the terrorist attacks of September 11. Despite the broad language, the administration still wanted more expansive language – including the ability to "wage war against suspected terrorists not just abroad but also inside the United States" (Mayer 2008, p. 44). When Congress refused to support the more expansive language, the White House solicited secret Justice Department guidance that vastly expanded interpretation of the president's war-time powers. The Justice Department memoranda argued that as commander-in-chief, the president had the inherent authority to conduct a whole range of activities including the use of military force inside the United States to prevent or deter terrorist activity and warrantless eavesdropping. In sum, the president could act to defend the country and to "override existing laws that Congress specifically designed to curb him" (Mayer 2008, p. 47).

In addition to carving out a legal justification for expanding executive authority, key administration officials began discussions about the manner in which the administration could gain information control over the events and manage the U.S. message and response. Secretary of Defense, Donald Rumsfeld had expressed concern about the role of public opinion and the use of force after September 11, and he asserted that sustaining public support for the war on terror would require new and creative ways of controlling information and selling the administration's strategies. He advocated that the administration consider "waging the war on terror . . . like a political campaign with daily talking points" (Woodward 2004).

Furthermore, Bush and his senior advisers were well aware of history of the domestic context of American war fighting efforts. They were especially aware of the domestic fate that befell President Lyndon Johnson and the nation during the war in Vietnam. The constraining influence of the Vietnam experience is not only well established in the academic literature but remains a highly salient concern among policy-makers in Washington (Mueller 1972; Sobel 2001). In explaining his concern for the relationship between public relations and war, Bush later told journalist Bob Woodward, "I am a product of the Vietnam era. I remember presidents trying to wage wars that were very unpopular, and the nation split" (Woodward 2004, p. 95). During the military actions in Afghanistan, Bush repeatedly told his staff that it was imperative that he control how issues related to the war on terror were framed (Woodward 2004, p. 227).

This initial response – to consolidate executive authority – set both the tone and the procedures by which the administration would subsequently approach the global war on terror and all of its broad components. Despite, and perhaps because of the expressed concerns from key members of Congress, the Justice Department rulings on expanding executive authority were deliberately kept secret – kept from the public, from Congress, and even from many within the administration who might object (Mayer 2008, pp. 45–46). The overall importance of this effort was to ensure that the president and his team maintained their absolute control over the global war on terror. Furthermore, as the issue of Iraq emerged within the internal and then the national discourse in the spring and summer of 2002 – the issue was defined in terms of its relationship to the global war on terror. Correspondingly, as the initial considerations of Iraq progressed, the senior advocates for war – Cheney and Rumsfeld – applied the extraordinary procedures and information strategies developed in the days after September 11 to the planning, decision-making, and public mobilization campaign on Iraq.

Selling the war in Iraq: consolidating information and framing advantages

In mid-November, the Taliban forces fell at Mazar-e-Sharif in northern Afghanistan, precipitating the rapid collapse of the Taliban regime throughout Afghanistan. Within days, Secretary Rumsfeld sent his first "snowflake" on Iraq to U.S. Central Command (CENTCOM) war planners in Tampa, Florida. Rumsfeld asked the planners to consider how many troops the United States would need to overthrow Saddam Hussein from power.

The quick shift to Iraq reflected a deep seeded view held by many senior administration hardliners that Saddam Hussein's regime posed a potential threat to the United States and a persistent threat to the Middle East, to Israel, and to the free-flow of oil (Western 2005). The question was how to link Iraq to the global war on terror.

The war in Afghanistan provided valuable insights into the domestic response the administration might expect as it turned its attention to Iraq. The country was solidly supportive of military action and the post-September 11, 24-hour cable news media culture was by-and-large editorially supportive of expanding the war on terror. And, Bush's approval ratings soared and then hovered around 90 percent. Bush's team understood and appreciated the advantages that came from their position (Moore and Slater 2003, pp. 288–291).

While the Pentagon and CENTCOM began their secret planning for an invasion of Iraq, White House officials began to develop the initial mobilization campaign to introduce the concept of regime change in Iraq. The first order of business was to attack the two principal arguments against regime change: first, 10 years of containment strategies had effectively boxed in Saddam Hussein; and second, the public would not sustain its support for war in Iraq because there was no direct link between Saddam Hussein and Al Qaeda.

To counter these arguments, Bush's advisers began to construct a link between Iraq and Al Qaeda and demonstrate that containment would not work (Frum 2003, p. 233). Bush's speechwriters invented a term, "axis of evil," that was consciously intended to convey that Al Qaeda and Iraq were linked. If not directly connected regarding September 11, they were most certainly linked (and hence allied) in their desire to harm the United States. In addition, "evil" was designed to convey that Iraq and groups like Al Qaeda were irrational. This was meant to suggest that containment could not work against either of them (DeYoung and Millbank 2002). Finally, the term alluded to the Second World War – that is, total war – and the need for massive commitment.

Bush introduced the phrase in his State of the Union address. He proclaimed, "The Iraqi regime has plotted to develop anthrax, and nerve gas, and nuclear weapons for over a decade." He added that Iraq, along with North Korea and Iran – all of whom, he said, were intent on acquiring nuclear weapons – and their "terrorist allies, constitute an *axis of evil*, arming to threaten the peace of the world" (Bush 2002a). The speech triggered immediate reactions. Critical editorial boards chastised the "belligerent" tone of the speech while others wondered if this signaled that the administration was preparing to fight simultaneous wars in Iraq, Iran, and North Korea. Despite criticism, the speech did trigger a flurry of news media coverage on Saddam Hussein's historical efforts to develop weapons of mass destruction. The *Washington Post*, for example, warned that "Iraq, busy rebuilding its weapons of mass destruction in the absence of UN inspectors, represents the most immediate threat, and the ... tool of forcible regime change – of military action – must also be considered" (*Washington Post* 2002a). Meanwhile, leading members of Congress endorsed Bush's position. Senators John McCain and Joseph Lieberman, among others, warned that the threat from Saddam was growing each day and that "time is not on our side" (Rubin 2002).

Throughout the spring of 2002, Bush's popular approval continued to hover between 70 percent and 80 percent, giving him widespread credibility and legitimacy to set the agenda on Iraq. On 1 June 2002, Bush used his commencement speech at the U.S. Military Academy at West Point to argue against containment and deterrence. He argued they no longer made sense in a world in which rogue regimes could acquire and use weapons of mass destruction or hand them off to terrorist organizations. Bush proclaimed, "Our security will require all Americans to be forward-looking and resolute, to be ready for pre-emptive action, when necessary, to defend our liberty and to defend our lives" (Bush 2002b). His message was clear: new threats required new thinking.

Amid this effort, however, and as anticipated, the public and political discourse on Iraq began to shift from a largely theoretical discussion of a future attack on Iraq to a more realistic assessment of the likely costs and benefits of actually doing so.

As this occurred, public support for invading Iraq began to drop: from the peak of 74 percent in November 2001 to 61 percent in June 2002 (Gallup Poll 2002).

Despite this slippage, the administration was effective in setting the agenda and framing the debate. By June 2002, the troika of threats – the proliferation of weapons of mass destruction; terrorism, and Iraq – far outpaced all other threats in the international system as the most critical to Americans. Eighty-six percent of Americans polled believed that the threat of Iraq's developing weapons of mass destruction was a "critical" threat to the vital interests of the United States. In addition, the president's framing of the debate had put political opponents in an awkward position. Saddam Hussein's record demonstrated a willingness to use chemical weapons against civilian populations; he had invaded Iran in 1980 and Kuwait in 1990; and he had a record of seeking nuclear capabilities. Those potentially opposed to regime change were left to argue why, in the face of extensive evidence of brutality and potential danger; they supported the continuation of Saddam's rule. As a result, by mid-summer 2002, potential opponents ultimately accepted the concept of regime change. Senate majority leader Tom Daschle, for example, acknowledged: "There is broad support for a regime change in Iraq. The question is, how do we do it and when do we do it?" (Kondrake 2002).

Confronting elite dissensus

By early August, nonetheless, several prominent Democrats and Republicans sensed that the hard-liners within the administration, and the president himself, were increasingly intent on unilateral military action against Iraq. Senate Foreign Relations Committee chairman Joseph Biden argued for the need for allies, and he warned of the dangers, the long-term implications, and the costs of unilateral action. Republican senators Richard Lugar and Chuck Hegel both warned the administration not to press ahead on Iraq without international support and a carefully crafted plan for "winning the peace." Furthermore, in what was almost certainly an organized campaign, Powell and two of former president George H.W. Bush's chief advisers, former national security adviser Brent Scowcroft and former secretary of state James A. Baker III, weighed in to slow the move toward war. On 5 August, Powell, in a private dinner with President Bush, warned that acting without broader international support "Bush would look like a bully, like he didn't care, like the administration was only interested in getting its own way, was not interested in what the rest of the world had to say" (PBS 2003). After the meeting, a series of op-ed commentaries from Scowcroft and Baker appeared, warning that the hard-liners were dismissing the costs of war. On 15 August, Scowcroft wrote in the *Wall Street Journal* that Saddam Hussein did not pose an imminent threat and that war in Iraq would divert resources and international goodwill from the war on terrorism (Scowcroft 2002). Former secretary of state Lawrence Eagleburger was even more alarmist in expressing his concern. Speaking on Fox News about the influence of Wolfowitz, Defense Policy Board chairman Richard Perle, and other neoconservatives, he said, "I must tell you, I think they're devious. . . . I am scared to death that they are going to convince the president that they can do this overthrow of Saddam on the cheap, and we'll find ourselves in the middle of a swamp because we didn't plan to do it in the right way" (Eagleburger 2002). Four days later, Baker wrote in the *New York Times* that regime change "cannot be done on the cheap. . . . If we are to change the regime in Iraq, we will have to occupy the country militarily. The costs of doing so, politically, economically and in terms of casualties, could be great" (Baker 2002a). He concluded that it was imperative to develop a broad international coalition for the action.

Stung by the criticism, Vice President Cheney used his speech before the annual convention of the Veterans of Foreign Wars (VFW) to respond. He warned that the costs of inaction would be much higher than the costs of action: "Simply stated, there is no doubt that Saddam Hussein now has weapons of mass destruction. There is no doubt that he is amassing them to use against our friends, against our allies, and against us." He also stressed that Iraq was intent on acquiring nuclear weapons and would likely use those weapons against the United States: "Just how soon, we cannot really gauge. Intelligence is an uncertain business. . . . Let me give you just one example of what I mean. Prior to the Gulf War, America's top intelligence analysts would come to my office in the Defense Department and tell me that Saddam Hussein was at least five or perhaps even 10 years away from having a nuclear weapon. After the war we learned that he had been much closer than that, perhaps within a year of acquiring such a weapon" (Cheney 2002). He then postulated that Saddam was likely to acquire nuclear weapons "fairly soon."

The overall effect of this open feuding within the Republican Party led to a noticeable shift in public opinion. By late August, Gallup polling data revealed that those supporting invading Iraq with ground troops had dropped to 53 percent while those opposed rose to 41 percent. In addition, even though a majority still backed invading Iraq, additional polling data revealed that by significant margins most Americans felt that Bush had not done enough to "explain why the U.S. might take action in Iraq" (CNN/USA Today/Gallup Poll 2002b). Furthermore, significant majorities also expressed their view that the United States should wait and give the United Nations more time to get weapons inspectors back into Iraq (CBS/New York Times Poll 2002).

Amid the disarray, Bush returned to Washington in early September intending to tighten and refocus his campaign. He had three priorities: first, to restore consensus within his administration; second, to develop a comprehensive strategy to sell the administration's case for war; and third, to develop a strategy that would effectively accommodate and ultimately co-opt opposition to American action in Iraq.

Restoring consensus

The first order of business was to get his advisers unified in support of the effort to remove Saddam Hussein. Throughout August, Powell had advocated that the president use his speech before the UN General Assembly slated for 12 September to focus on Iraq and to develop broader international support. Cheney and Rumsfeld remained not only skeptical of the UN but convinced that deference to an international coalition, and to the UN in particular, would ultimately harm American interests (Calibrisi 2002). Bush resolved the dispute by agreeing to go to the UN – but he announced that he would shift the focus of the debate to the UN Security Council and its failure to enforce its own resolutions on Iraq.

In addition, on 7 and 8 September, Bush assured British Prime Minister, Tony Blair that he would go to the UN. In exchange, Bush obtained a private assurance from Blair that regardless of what happened at the UN, the United Kingdom would join in the military action with the United States – Bush would have a partner (PBS 2004). The British position seemed to seal the deal. Bush would accept the Security Council process – as long as any resolution was backed with firm teeth. Cheney and Rumsfeld reluctantly acquiesced to the UN process for the time being.

Co-opting opposition

Second, Bush and his advisers were intent on reclaiming the agenda and reframing the discourse on Iraq. The administration quickly decided to press Congress for a formal vote authorizing the president to use force. According to Woodward's account, Cheney in particular was eager for a vote before the November midterm elections, so that "voters would know before the election where every congressman and senator stood on Saddam Hussein and his dangerous regime" (Woodward 2004, p. 168).

Furthermore, by pledging to go to the UN, Bush not only tempered congressional opponents but also argued that his efforts at the UN would be strengthened if he could demonstrate firm American support for action. In short, he framed the need for a congressional resolution as the last, best hope for building international consensus and ultimately, peace, rather than as a blank check for war.

Marketing strategy and message discipline

Finally, President Bush also tasked his key communications staff with developing a comprehensive strategy to sell the administration's case for war. Chief of Staff, Card said in a candid comment that later would be widely criticized, "From a marketing point of view you don't introduce new products in August" (Buhmiller 2002). Despite the criticism, Card's strategy and timing were effective. He and his staff created the White House Iraq Group to coordinate the "daily message on Iraq" (Woodward 2004, p. 172). The team produced a website titled "Iraq: A Decade of Deception and Defiance" that was unveiled during Bush's UN speech. The team also monitored much of the public comments of senior administration officials and worked to keep them in line with the daily message. For example, they pressed Rumsfeld to withdraw a 2,300 word article he had submitted to the *Washington Post*'s Outlook section. The piece made a pointed case for the right of the United States to conduct a unilateral, pre-emptive strike against an adversary intent on developing weapons of mass destruction – a line that deviated from the focused message in the run-up to the president's speech to the UN General Assembly (DeYoung and Allen 2002; Sanger 2002).

Card's team also coordinated public appearances by the president's senior advisers. On Sunday, 8 September, Cheney, Rice, Powell, and Rumsfeld were all dispatched to the Sunday morning talk shows. Their message was clear and disciplined: Saddam Hussein's regime was aggressively pursuing weapons of mass destruction, including nuclear weapons; it had links to international terrorism, and to Al Qaeda in particular; and Iraq, along with Al Qaeda, was intent on inflicting harm on the United States (*New York Times* 2002). To add greater urgency to the case, Rumsfeld warned, "Imagine a Sept. 11 with weapons of mass destruction. It's not 3,000; it's tens of thousands of innocent men, women and children" (Purdam 2002).

The mobilization campaign was carefully timed to coincide with the first anniversary of the terrorist attacks. On 12 September 2002, the president delivered his speech to the UN General Assembly. He warned that Saddam Hussein was defying the Security Council and that Iraq was intent on developing nuclear weapons. To mollify critics among liberals and selective engagers in Congress, Bush added, "We will work with the UN Security Council for the necessary resolutions." He issued a warning, however: "We want the United Nations to be effective. We want the resolutions of the world's most important multilateral body to be enforced. And right now those resolutions are being unilaterally subverted by the Iraqi regime" (Bush 2002c). He concluded by threatening that if the United Nations did not protect international security, the United States would.

The speech produced its intended effect. Many of those previously skeptical of the administration's position concluded that the pressure was on the UN to enforce its existing resolutions. For example, Baker wrote in the *Washington Post* that the speech had made the case against Iraq: "The question is no longer why the United States believes force is necessary to implement resolutions involving Iraq, but why the United Nations, after years of inaction, does not now agree. . . . The administration's challenge now is to persuade the United Nations to act on its principles" (Baker 2002b).

The combined effect of the efforts of the first two weeks in September was to slow and reverse the downward trend in support for invading Iraq. Gallup poll results, which had revealed that public support for war had fallen to 53 percent in late August, rebounded five percentage points to 58 percent. A CBS News poll revealed even stronger support, with 68 percent saying they would approve taking military action against Iraq to remove Saddam Hussein from power (CBS News 2002).

In addition, the residual effect of Cheney's emphatic declaration about Saddam Hussein's military capabilities at the VFW convention in August had triggered extensive news commentary and analysis during the last week in August and the first week in September and precipitated a shift in the number of Americans who believed Saddam Hussein actually possessed weapons of mass destruction. In mid-August, before Cheney's speech, a CNN/USA Today/Gallup poll found that 55 percent of those polled believed Iraq "currently possessed" weapons of mass destruction, while 39 percent thought Saddam was trying to develop them (CNN/USA Today/Gallup Poll 2002a). By early September, a CBS/New York

Times poll reported that 79 percent of Americans believed Iraq "currently possessed" such weapons (CBS/New York Times Poll 2002a). Perhaps most notable, in a survey of registered voters, Fox News reported that 69 percent of those surveyed believed Saddam Hussein already possessed nuclear weapons (Fox New/Opinion Dynamics Poll 2002).

Al Qaeda and Iraq: constructing the link

Still, the polling data continued to reflect two concerns on the part of the public. On the one hand, the public expressed significant concern over the threat posed by Iraq: 62 percent thought that Iraq was planning to use weapons of mass destruction against the United States (CBS/New York Times Poll 2002). On the other hand, the polling data continued to reflect that the public wanted the administration not only to secure a congressional resolution authorizing the use of force, but also to gain support from its allies and the United Nations.

Over the next week, the hard-liners sought to add a sense of urgency to American and international action. On 18 September, Rumsfeld told the House Armed Services Committee, "No terrorist state poses a greater and more immediate threat to the security of our people and the stability of the world than the regime of Saddam Hussein" (Vandehei and DeYoung 2002). That was followed the next day by a draft war resolution sent by the president to Congress. It stated specifically that the events of September 11 underscored the "threat that Iraq will transfer weapons of mass destruction to international terrorist organizations," and it cited the "high risk that the current Iraqi regime will either employ those weapons to launch a surprise attack against the United States or its armed forces or provide them to international terrorists who would do so" (*Washington Post* 2002b).

Perhaps even more significant was the fact that Powell was now fully on board with the overall effort. Although Powell was widely reported to be waging a constant battle with the hard-liners at the Pentagon, after Bush's pledge at the United Nations to secure a Security Council resolution and after Prime Minister Blair announced his firm backing of Bush's position, Powell consistently participated in the effort to sell the administration's policy on Iraq (except for an occasional critical extemporaneous remark). On 20 September, Powell appeared before the House International Relations Committee and urged lawmakers to pass the resolution by arguing that it was imperative that the United States present a unified face to the world in order to enlist the support of other countries in a showdown with Iraq. Powell was still the most respected figure in the Bush administration: his own popular approval rating (88 percent in September 2002) routinely exceeded that of Bush (78 percent) (Moore 2002). Powell used this stature to counteract the concerns of some of the moderate Republicans and Democrats who believed that the president was rushing too quickly into a confrontation with Iraq. Powell reassured the lawmakers that he had long been "known as a reluctant warrior" and he believed that in order for diplomacy to have a chance, "the threat of war has to be there" (Woodward 2004, p. 187).

Opposition dissensus

Meanwhile, as Congress began debate on a resolution authorizing the president to use force to remove Saddam Hussein, the pressure of election-year politics put many liberals on the defensive. Democrats were well aware that Republicans had a significant advantage over them in the eyes of Americans on national security matters. Following September 11, polling data also revealed that most Americans believed Republicans were more able to protect national security than Democrats (Pew Research Center 2002b). Within this politicized context, according to a *Washington Post* report, more than a dozen Democrats who opposed the resolution nonetheless concluded that it was better to support the resolution than face a "backlash from voters" (Vandehei 2002). Senior Democratic strategists also pointed out that every Democrat facing a tough race in the House of Representative had lined up in support of the resolution.

Over the course of the next several weeks, administration officials continued their full-court press with inflated threat assessments. Condoleezza Rice speaking on PBS proclaimed forcefully "there clearly are contacts between al-Qaida and Iraq that can be documented" (Warner 2002). Rumsfeld, speaking to reporters that evening, said that he had "very reliable" and "credible" reporting that Iraq and Al Qaeda had "discussed safe haven opportunities in Iraq, reciprocal nonaggression discussions, . . . and that al Qaeda leaders have sought contacts in Iraq who could help them acquire weapons of mass destruction capabilities" (Schmitt 2002). The evidence, he declared, was "bullet-proof."

The campaign that had begun in earnest in early September ultimately paid off. Public opinion polls continued to reveal overwhelming support for the president. By early October, the Pew Research Center for the People and the Press reported that two-thirds of the American public believed that Saddam Hussein was involved in the September 11 attacks. Seventy-nine percent of Americans believed that Iraq either possessed or was on the verge of acquiring nuclear weapon (Pew Research Center 2002a).

On 10 and 11 October, the House of Representatives and then the Senate passed resolutions authorizing the president to use force if necessary. In just over 10 months, the administration had effectively employed executive-branch information, framing, and mobilization advantages to weigh in on the debate and shift and shape the political discourse.

Deciding on a military plan and mollifying the critics

Following passage of the congressional resolutions, Bush tentatively decided in mid-October on a military plan prepared by General Tommy Franks (Sanger, Schmitt and Shanker 2002b). Because of the logistical requirements of the plan, it would be early February, at the earliest, before an invasion could begin.

Meanwhile, the administration had committed itself to seeking a new Security Council resolution. Over the course of the next three weeks, Powell pressed the international community for such a resolution (Woodward 2004, pp. 220–227). On

8 November, the Security Council unanimously passed Resolution 1441, which proclaimed that Iraq was in material breach of its disarmament obligations under a series of previous resolutions, called for the immediate and unrestricted access by UN inspectors to facilities in Iraq, and warned the Iraqi government that it would "face serious consequences" if it obstructed inspectors or in any way violated its obligations. The resolution also set up a 60 day time period for preparation of an initial inspections report to the Security Council and set 27 January 2003 as the due date for that report.

Bush immediately declared that the international community was in complete agreement that Saddam Hussein's "cooperation must be prompt and unconditional or he will face the severest consequences" (Lynch 2002). In an op-ed piece in the *Washington Post* two days later, Powell likewise asserted that the UN resolution revealed that most of the world was unified in its demands on Iraq (Powell 2002). The effort seemed to resonate with the public: support for invading Iraq with ground troops rose from 54 percent to 59 percent.

Despite the rhetoric, however, Resolution 1441 did not reflect or produce an international consensus. For example, Hans Blix, the United Nations Monitoring, Verification, and Inspection Commission's chief weapons inspector, sent his advance team to Iraq on 18 November, but he believed he was to submit only an interim report by 27 January and that then he would conduct further inspections under the auspices of UN Security Council Resolution 1284 before submitting a report on 27 March that would identify the "key remaining disarmament tasks" (DeYoung and Pincus 2003). In addition, France, Germany, and Russia demanded that no action be taken in Iraq until the inspectors issued their report and the Security Council passed a second resolution.

Wavering public opinion?

The inspections process and the conflicting positions among Security Council members triggered their own dynamic with respect to American public opinion. On the one hand, most Americans wanted the inspections process to proceed because they hoped it would avert war. They also desired that the administration continue to work through the UN. On the other hand, a majority of Americans highly approved of Bush's handling of the situation and expressed confidence in his leadership. Several polls also suggested that, while a majority of Americans wanted the Bush administration to pursue a second UN resolution before undertaking military action, they also would support Bush if he chose to go to war without a second resolution.

For his part, by early January, Bush had become increasingly frustrated with the inspections process and concerned about the sustainability of his public and political support. American troops were now shipping out in large numbers to wait at the ready in the middle of the Kuwaiti desert or on offshore naval vessels. Their morale and that of their families and neighbors certainly required that they not be stationed there merely to contain Saddam. In a meeting with Rice in mid-January, Bush observed, "Time is not on our side here. Probably going to have to, we're going to have to go to war" (Woodward 2004, p. 254).

As the military finalized its war plans and neared completion of the deployment of the forces needed for a military offensive, the administration launched a final campaign to rally the country. On 23 January, Rice wrote an op-ed in the *New York Times* titled "Why We Know Iraq Is Lying," which argued that it was "clear and resounding" that Iraq was not voluntarily disarming and that it was treating the UN weapons inspections process as a "game" (Rice 2003). On 25 January, three days before Bush was scheduled to deliver the State of the Union speech, several senior deputies assembled to go through the CIA information and package it to sell it to the public (Woodward 2004, pp. 288–292). The advisors scoured the intelligence and disproportionately compiled the data that supported their positions and ignored countervailing evidence.

They assembled the evidence for Bush's State of the Union address, in which he again repeated the long list of dangers that he and the hard-liners saw in Iraq. Bush stressed that secret intelligence evidence revealed that Saddam Hussein was aiding and protecting terrorists, including members of Al Qaeda, and that he could provide weapons of mass destruction to terrorists without detection. Bush concluded, "If this threat is permitted to fully and suddenly emerge, all actions, all words, and all recriminations would come too late" (Bush 2003).

Bush's speech was followed by Powell's presentation to the United Nations on 5 February. Bush's senior political advisers had suggested that Powell be the one to take the evidence to the UN and sell the case to anyone still sitting on the fence. (Woodward 2004, p. 291). Powell presented what he claimed was conclusive evidence of Iraqi intransigence and violations regarding compliance with the UN resolutions. He presented satellite imagery and communications intercepts of what he reported were secret mobile biological laboratories and Iraqi efforts to relocate banned chemical and biological munitions – none of which proved to be valid intelligence.

Bush's State of the Union speech and Powell's presentation had their intended effect. The *Washington Post* titled its editorial the day after Powell's' presentation "Irrefutable"; and pronounced, "It is hard to imagine how anyone could doubt that Iraq possesses weapons of mass destruction"; and further added that Powell's efforts would "stand as a worthy last effort to engage the United Nations" (*Washington Post* 2003). The *New York Times*, long a skeptic of military action in Iraq, concluded that Powell "may not have produced a 'smoking gun,' but he left little question that Mr. Hussein had tried hard to conceal one" (*New York Times* 2003). Polls showed that more than two-thirds of Americans believed that Bush had made a "convincing case" (CNN/USA Today/Gallup Poll 2003b). A CNN/USA Today/Gallup poll conducted in early February revealed that 87 percent of Americans were convinced or thought it likely that Iraq had direct ties to Al Qaeda (CNN/USA Today/Gallup Poll 2003b). The numbers also confirmed that there would likely be no major political backlash for war. Polling data, which had shown a softening of public support for war in December and January during the inspections process, increased 11 points, from 52 percent to 63 percent, in the two-week period that included Bush's State of the Union address and Powell's presentation.

As the administration made the case for war, however, neither Bush nor Powell discussed the potential costs of war or the risks that could follow the defeat of Saddam Hussein's regime. In January, the National Intelligence Council (NIC) prepared two analyses for Bush that predicted that toppling Saddam Hussein's regime would trigger broader Iraqi and Arab support for Islamic fundamentalism and that there was a real possibility of the development of a coordinated insurgency and guerilla warfare aimed at American troops (Jehl and Sanger 2004). Because of the highly classified nature of the documents, however, their circulation within the administration was tightly controlled and war opponents and skeptics in Congress and the media were unaware of the NIC's conclusions.

Further bolstering the administration's case was the fact that the media remained largely hamstrung by its inability independently to confirm or refute much of what the administration reported. Journalists in Iraq were under strict control by the Iraqi government and unable to collect information independently. Meanwhile, those reporting from Washington and New York continued to rely extensively on U.S. government sources. Furthermore, as the *New York Times*'s ombudsman reported 15 months after the war began (and following a scathing criticism of the media's role by Michael Massing in the *New York Review of Books*), much of the *Times* reporting during the pre-war period – especially in January 2003 – was flawed because it was premised on unsubstantiated claims by parties with "vested interests" and because reporters were frequently writing with an eye toward "coddling sources" and maintaining access (Okrent 2004). Even the *New York Times* editors themselves conceded that several articles published between fall 2001 and 2003 had been based on information that was "controversial" and "insufficiently qualified or allowed to stand unchallenged" (*New York Times* 2004).

The Bush administration had so effectively controlled information and sold its agenda that when the antiwar movement did gain momentum in the United States and around the globe, and even after an unprecedented global demonstration in hundreds of cities in dozens of countries on 16 February, there was no significant shift in American public or political support for military action.

In early March, General Franks reported that his military preparations were complete and that he was ready to launch his plan. On 17 March, Bush issued a final ultimatum to Saddam Hussein to leave the country or face military attack. Two days later, Bush gave the order for American forces to begin the war with Americans now rallying around the flag.

The implications of selling war in Iraq

In the immediate aftermath of the September 11 tragedy, large numbers of Americans already believed that Iraq was a probable threat to the United States. Republicans and Democrats routinely had identified Saddam Hussein over the past decade as a menace and a threat to regional and international security. In addition, Iraq had increasingly become intertwined in the national discourse of the two other major threats – terrorism and the proliferation of weapons of mass destruction – that had emerged within the consciousness of the American public in the past decade.

The Bush administration nonetheless concluded that transforming general predispositions into overt support for war would require a carefully constructed campaign to control and manipulate the flow of information – both to convince the public of the necessity of military action and to delegitimize any political opposition. The administration relied on executive privileges in information collection, analysis, and dissemination to emphasize the threat posed by Iraq and to discount the potential costs. It also took full advantage of the fact that after September 11, President Bush's popular approval had skyrocketed to levels well above 80 percent. The public, the media, and even political opponents gave him wide latitude to respond to the terrorist attacks. He relied on that public trust and political capital to sell the case for war in Iraq.

The evidence presented here suggests, however, that not only did Bush rely on that public trust – he also abused it. The post-invasion evidence now reveals that much of the information and many of the assessments of threat used by the Bush administration in its pre-war public relations campaign were inflated, distorted, or selectively disclosed to the public. The administration did not simply rely on rhetorical devices – such as invoking rhetorical images of mushroom clouds and the like – it deliberately and selectively used its executive advantages on intelligence collection and analysis to frame a particular version of the threat in order to influence public opinion. When the intelligence reports supported their positions, the hard-liners routinely proclaimed them to be "highly credible" or, in the case of Rumsfeld's portrayal of interview data provided by detainees at Guantánamo Bay, as "bullet-proof." When intelligence reports contradicted or weakened the president's case for war, however, the administration waged a systematic campaign to discount the integrity of intelligence analysis and evidence. This was evident in the administration's portrayal of intelligence analyses that concluded that Iraq was several years away from developing its own nuclear capacity; in response to those assessments, first Cheney and then Bush, Rice, and Rumsfeld all stressed the inherent limitations and "uncertainty" of intelligence analysis.

Bush and his advisers also released intelligence when it suited them to bolster their case for war. Powell's presentation to the UN Security Council in February 2003 included audiotape of highly classified electronic intercepts – an unprecedented disclosure by the United States of its signal intelligence sources and methods. Yet the NIC's predictions on the likely postwar violence and insurgency or other internal analysis of the potential costs were tightly restricted and unknown to the public and to most of Congress.

Throughout the run-up to the war in Iraq, the Bush administration inflated the threat on Iraq and then effectively sold it to the American public. Ultimately, the evidence presented here demonstrates the extent of power held by the presidency in controlling and manipulating public opinion when it comes to matters of war and peace.

References

Baker III, J. A. (2002a) "The right way to change a regime," *New York Times*, 25 August: A9.
—— (2002b) "The UN route," *Washington Post*, 15 September: B7.

Brody, R. (1983–84) "International crises: A rallying point for the president?" *Public Opinion*, 6: 41.

Buhmiller, E. (2002) "Bush aides set strategy to sell policy on Iraq," *New York Times*, 7 September: A1.

Bush, G. W. (2002a) "State of the union address," Online. Available: <http://www.whitehouse.gov/news/releases/2002/01/iraq/20020129-11.html> (Accessed 1 June 2008).

—— (2002b) "Remarks by the president at 2002 graduation exercise of the United States Military Academy, West Point, New York," Online. Available: <http://www.whitehouse.gov/news/releases/2002/06/20020601-3.html> (Accessed 1 June, 2008).

—— (2002c) "President's remarks at the United Nations General Assembly,' Online. Available: <http://www.whitehouse.gov/news/releases/2002/09/20020912-1.html> (Accessed 31 May 2008).

—— (2002d) "President Bush outlines Iraqi threat," "Remarks by the President on Iraq," Online. Available: <http://www.whitehouse.gov/news/releases/2002/10/iraq/20021007-8.html> (Accessed 1 June 2008).

—— (2003) "State of the union address," Online. Available: <http://www.whitehouse.gov/news/releases/2003/01/iraq/20030128-19.html> (Accessed 1 June 2008).

CBS/New York Times Poll. (2002a), 7 September 2002, *Polling the Nations Database*, Online. Available: <http://poll.orspub.com/poll/lpext.dll?f=templates&fn=main-h.htm> (Accessed 2 October 2004).

—— (2002b) *Polling the Nations Database*, 24 September, Online. Available: <http://poll.orspub.com/poll/lpext.dll?f=templates&fn=main-h.htm> (Accessed 2 October 2004).

CNN/USA Today/Gallup. (2002a) 23 August, Online. Available: <http://poll.orspub.com/poll/lpext.dll?f=templates&fn=main-h.htm> (Accessed 2 October 2004).

—— (2002b) *Polling the Nations Database*, 5 September, Online. Available: <http://poll.orspub.com/poll/lpext.dll?f=templates&fn=main-h.htm> (Accessed 2 October 2004).

—— (2003a) *Polling the Nations Database*, 1 January, Online. Available: <http://poll.orspub.com/poll/lpext.dll?f=templates&fn=main-h.htm> (Accessed 2 October 2004).

—— (2003b) *Polling the Nations Database*, 5 February, Online. Available: <http://poll.orspub.com/poll/lpext.dll?f=templates&fn=main-h.htm> (Accessed 2 October 2004).

Calibrisi, M. (2002) "Colin Powell: Planning for an exit," *Time*, 9 September: 14.

Carroll, J. (2004) "American public opinion about the situation in Iraq," Online. Available: <http://www.gallup.com/poll/focus/sr030610.asp> (Accessed 30 June 2008).

Cheney, R. (2002) 'Vice president speaks at 103rd national convention," Online. Available: <http://www.whitehouse.gov/news/releases/2002/08/iraq/20020826.html> (Accessed 1 June 2008).

Chicago Council on Foreign Relations and the German Marshall Fund of the United States (2002) "U.S. general population topline report," *WorldViews,* October.

DeYoung, K., and Allen, M. (2002) "Disarm Iraq quickly, Bush to urge UN; Failure to move may lead to U.S. action," *Washington Post*, 7 September: A1.

DeYoung K., and Millbank, D. (2002) "U.S. repeats warnings on terrorism; Bush urges other nations to 'get their house in order'", *Washington Post*, 1 February: A1.

DeYoung, K., and Pincus, W. (2003) "Iraq hunt to extend to March, Blix says; Arms search timetable complicates U.S. plans," *Washington Post*, 14 January: A1.

Eagleburger, L. (2002) interview on Fox News, Online. Available: <http://www.foxnews. com/story/0,2933,60704,00.html> (Accessed 1 June 2004).

Feaver, P. and Gelpi, C. (2004) *Choosing Your Battles: American Civil-Military Relations and the Use of Force*, Princeton: Princeton University Press.

Fox News/Opinion Dynamics Poll. (2002) *Polling the Nations Database*, 12 September, Online. Available: <http://poll.orspub.com/poll/lpext.dll?f=templates&fn=main-h.htm (Accessed 2 October 2004).

Frum, D. (2003) *The Right Man*, New York: Random House.

Jentleson, B. (1992) "The pretty prudent public: Post post-Vietnam American opinion on the use of force," *International Studies Quarterly*, 36 (March).

Jentleson, B. and Britton, R. (1998) "Still pretty prudent: Post-Cold War American public opinion on the use of military force," *Journal of Conflict Resolution*, 42, August: 395–417.

Gallup Poll. (2002) "Iraq," Tuesday Briefing, Online. Available: <http://www.gallup.com/ content/default.aspx?ci=1633&pg=3> (Accessed 14 April 2004).

Hart, G. (2002) "Note to democrats: Get a defense policy," *New York Times*, 3 October: A27.

Jehl, D. and Sanger, D. E. (2004) "Prewar assessment on Iraq saw chance of strong divisions," *New York Times*, 28 September: A1.

Kaufmann, C. (2004) "Threat inflation and the failure of the marketplace of ideas: The selling of the Iraq war," *International Security*, 29: pp. 5–48.

Klarevas, L. (1999) *American Public Opinion on Peace Operations: The Cases of Somalia, Rwanda, and Haiti*, Ph.D. diss., American University, 1999.

—— (2002) "The 'essential domino' of military operations: American public opinion and the use of force," *International Studies Perspectives*, 3: pp. 417–37.

Kondrake, M. (2002) "Congress should hold great debate over policy on Iraq," *Roll Call*, 27 June.

Kull, S. and Destler, I. M. (1999) *Misreading the Public: The Myth of a New Isolationism*, Washington: Brookings Institution Press.

Larson, E. (1996) *Casualties and Consensus: The Historical Role of Casualties in Domestic Support for U.S. Military Operations*, Santa Monica: Rand, 1996.

Lowi, T. (1989) "Making democracy safe for the world: On fighting the next war," in G. John Ikenberry (ed.) *American Foreign Policy: Theoretical Essays*, Glenview, IL: Scott, Foresman.

Lynch, C. (2002) "Security council resolution tells Iraq it must disarm; Baghdad ordered to admit inspectors or face consequences," *Washington Post*, 10 November: A26.

Massing, M. (2004) "Now they tell us," *New York Review of Books*, 26 February: pp. 43–49.

Mayer, J. (2008) *The Dark Side: The Inside Story of How the War on Terror Turned Into a War on American Ideals*, New York: Doubleday.

Moore, D. W. (1998a) "Support increasing for military action with Iraq: Men in favor, women opposed," 5 February, Online. Available: <http://www.gallup.com/content/ default.aspx?ci=4252&pg=1> (Accessed 1 June 2004).

—— (1998b) "Public ready for war with Iraq, support wavers if substantial U.S. military casualties," 18 February, Online. Available: <http://www.gallup.com/content/default. aspx?ci=4252&pg=1> (Accessed 1 June 2004).

—— (2001) "Americans believe U.S. participation in gulf war a decade ago worthwhile: Small majority favor new war to remove Saddam Hussein from power," 26 February, Online. Available: <http://www.gallup.com/content/default.aspx?ci=1963&pg=1> (Accessed 1 June 2004).

—— (2002) "Powell remains most popular political figure in America," *Gallup News Service*, 30 September, Online. Available: <http://www.gallup.com/poll/content/?ci= 6886> (Accessed 1 June 2004).

Moore, J. and Slater, W. (2003) *Bush's Brain: How Karl Rove Made George W. Bush Presidential*, New York: Wiley.

Mueller, J. (1972) *War, Presidents, and Public Opinion*, New York: Wiley.

New York Times. (2002) "With few variations, top Bush advisers present their case against Iraq," 9 September: A8.

New York Times. (2003) "The case against Iraq," 6 February 2003: A38.

New York Times. (2004) "The times and Iraq," 26 May: 6.

Okrent, D. (2004) "Weapons of mass destruction? Or Mass Distraction?" *New York Times*, 30 May, 4: 2.

PBS. (2003) "The long road," *Frontline*, transcript. Online. Available: <http://www.pbs.org/ wgbh/pages/frontline/shows/longroad/etc/script.html>, (Accessed 1 June 2004).

PBS. (2004) "Blair's war," *Frontline*, Online. Available: <http://www.pbs.org/wgbh/pages/ frontline/shows/blair/etc/script.html, (Accessed 1 June 2004).

Page, B. I. and Shapiro, R. (1992) *The Rational Public: Fifty Years of Trends in Americans' Policy Preferences*, Chicago: University of Chicago Press.

Pew Research Center for the People and the Press. (2002a) "Americans thinking about Iraq, but focused on the economy," Midterm Election Preview, Pew Research Center for the People and the Press, 10 October, Online. Available: <http://people-press.org/reports/ display.php3?ReportID=162> (Accessed 1 June 2004).

Pew Research Center for the People and the Press. (2002b) "Support for potential military action slips to 55%: Party images unchanged with a week to go," 30 October, Online. Available: <http://people-press.org/reports/display.php3?ReportID=163> (Accessed 12 July 2004).

Powell, C. (2002) "Baghdad's moment of truth," *Washington Post*, 10 November: B7.

Purdam, T. S. (2002) "Bush officials say time has come for action on Iraq," *New York Times*, 9 September: A1.

Rice, C. (2003) "Why we know Iraq is lying," New *York Times*, 23 January: A25.

Rubin, D. (2002) "U.S. warns NATO on Iraq; Allies urged to join new war on terrorism, or America will go it alone," *Pittsburgh Post Gazette*, 3 February, A1.

Sanger, D. (2002) "Blair, meeting with Bush, fully endorses U.S. plans for ending Iraqi threat," *New York Times*, 8 September: A23.

Sanger, D., Schmitt, E., and Shanker, T. (2002b) "War plan for Iraq calls for big force and quick strike," *New York Times*, 10 November: A1.

Sanger, D. E., and Shanker, T. (2002a) "Exploring Baghdad strike as Iraq option," *New York Times,* 29 July: A1.

Schmitt, E. (2002) "Rumsfeld says U.S. has 'bulletproof' evidence of Iraq's links to Al Qaeda," *New York Times,* 27 September: A9.

Scowcroft, B. (2002) "Don't attack Saddam," *Wall Street Journal*, 15 August: A12.

Sobel, R. (2001) *The Impact of Public Opinion on Foreign Policy since Vietnam: Constraining the Colossus*, New York: Oxford University Press.

Vandehei, J. (2002) "Daschle Angered by Bush Statement; President 'Politicizing' Security Issue, He Says," *Washington Post*, 26 September: A1.

Vandehei, J., and DeYoung, K. (2002) "Bush to seek broad power on Iraq," *Washington Post*, 19 September: A1.

Warner, M. (2002) interview with Condoleezza Rice, *The NewsHour with Jim Lehrer*, transcript no. 7463, 25 September.

Washington Post. (2002a) "Yes they are evil," 3 February 2002: B7.
—— (2002b) "Text of proposed resolution," 20 September: A20.
—— (2003) "Irrefutable," 6 February: A36.
Woodward, B. (2004) *Plan of Attack*, New York: Simon and Schuster.
Western, J. (2005) *Selling Intervention and War: The Presidency, the Media, and the American Public*, Baltimore, MD: Johns Hopkins University Press.
Zaller, J. R. (1992) *The Nature and Origins of Mass Opinion*, Cambridge: Cambridge University Press.

10 Framing Iraq

Threat inflation in the marketplace of values

A. Trevor Thrall

> There is a bear in the woods. For some people the bear is easy to see. Others don't see it at all. Some people say the bear is tame. Other people say it's vicious and dangerous. Since no one can really be sure who's right, isn't it smart to be as strong as the bear, if there is a bear?
>
> (1984 Reagan television ad)

After the invasion of Iraq, in the wake of the failure to uncover weapons of mass destruction or any link between Iraq and Al Qaeda or the events of 9/11, accusations of "threat inflation" became commonplace, with scholars arguing that the Bush administration pumped up the Iraq threat beyond the facts available and made arguments based on far-fetched worst case scenarios (Kaufmann 2004; Cirincione 2005; Prados 2004; Hersh 2003). Worse, many observers believe the administration was extremely successful in its efforts to build public support for war on false grounds.

Five years into the effort to explain exactly how and why the Bush administration succeeded in inflating the threat, the most popular line of argument is that Bush was able to induce a failure in the marketplace of ideas. A healthy and functional American marketplace of ideas would have produced a more robust debate over the administration's assessment of the Iraq threat and its justifications for war. The implication is that the administration would have lost such a debate and that America would have been unlikely to go to war. Some, like Krebs and Lobasz (Chapter 7), argue that Bush adopted powerful rhetorical arguments that put opponents on the defensive and made them risk looking unpatriotic for criticizing the president. Cramer (Chapter 8) takes a similar argument further back into the Cold War, identifying the birth of a norm she calls "militarized patriotism," which made Americans more likely to support military solutions and made it more difficult for opponents to gain traction in public debate. Kaufmann and Western argue that the president's information advantage over Congress and his ability to dominate news coverage, thanks to news routines and a lapdog media, made it difficult for elite debate to spark opposition to the invasion (Kaufmann, Chapter 6; Western, Chapter 9). The consequences of such marketplace failures, according to this line of thinking, are dire. As Cramer summarizes the invasion of Iraq: "This case of successful threat inflation calls into question the widely accepted notion that mature democracies have well-developed 'marketplaces of ideas' that can reliably steer democracies toward smarter, well-considered foreign policies" (2005).

In this chapter, I take a contrary track and argue that these arguments rely on an improperly specified model of the marketplace of ideas. Hence, they mischaracterize the true nature and impact of threat inflation. Although threat inflation is an important and potentially costly political process, the American marketplace of ideas is quite robust and Iraq, in fact, does not represent a failure of the marketplace. Contrary to most of the other contributions in this volume, I argue that successful threat inflation is much more difficult than recent work suggests, has been fairly rare in recent years, and is not likely to lead to unwarranted support for aggressive foreign policy proposals concerning Iran, North Korea, or other trouble spots in the near to medium term.

The reasons for the health of the American marketplace of ideas, however, are not those usually considered by scholars of threat inflation, liberal theory or political communication. Since the work of John Stuart Mill, scholars have assumed that the genius of a democratic marketplace of ideas lies in the fact that weak ideas and falsehoods get exposed through competition as better and more accurate ideas gain acceptance from the public. I argue, to the contrary, that the strength of the marketplace lies not in its ability to move the nation toward truth, but in its tendency to divide the public into countervailing factions, each seeking its own "truth" based on competing sets of values. Historically, for several reasons I describe in this chapter, the American system has been quite (some might say increasingly) effective at maintaining a state of polarization on important issues. This polarization is not a perfect constant, of course, but under most circumstances in such a marketplace, no single idea gains enough currency to achieve consensus. Bold policy initiatives falter, radical ideologies find few customers, and threats fail to inflate.

To develop this argument I first elaborate on this alternate conception of the marketplace of ideas. I then redefine threat inflation as a process of competitive efforts by elites to frame national security issues for the public. I use the new model to explain the Bush administration's successes and failures in building and maintaining public support for the war in Iraq. I conclude with a discussion of the implications of this argument for American foreign policy.

Reconceptualizing the marketplace of ideas

Recent claims of threat inflation rely on a time-honored model of the marketplace of ideas. This model rests on two related assumptions about the nature and operation of the marketplace. The first assumption concerns the opinion formation process at the individual level and the incentives it provides for elites to advance truthful arguments. The second concerns the role of the news media and the ways in which its performance helps lead to truth under normal circumstances or to threat inflation in cases of "market failure." In this section I outline and challenge these assumptions, offering a fresh perspective from which to assess both the marketplace and threat inflation.

In the conventional view of the marketplace of ideas, political elites have strong incentives to tell the truth because public has strong preferences for truth over falsehood and because the media provide a free marketplace that allows the public to test claims against one another. The result is that over time the public identifies and supports truth and good ideas over falsehoods and bad ideas. As Mill wrote: "Wrong opinions and practices gradually yield to fact and argument. . . ." (Gray and Smith 1991: 40). In this view, the invisible hand of the market guides the public toward truth and honest public debate about the conditions of the day, with sound policy resulting from the interplay of ideas and argument.

Mill's formulation in turn has long provided one of the cornerstones of democratic theory generally and liberal theory regarding foreign policy in particular. Citizens who are going to bear the costs of war will pay close attention to the justification for war along with its costs and benefits. Insofar as it helps citizens gain an accurate understanding of the facts surrounding a possible conflict, open debate in the marketplace of ideas helps prevent elites from conducting wars when they are not justified by the situation (Bentham 1999; Kant 1983; Mill 1913; Owen 1994; Fishkin 1995; Elster 1998).

Recent work on threat inflation and nationalist mythmaking echoes Mill's preoccupation with facts and truth. Kaufmann's (2004: 5) understanding of the marketplace dynamic sums up the standard model well: "The marketplace of ideas helps to weed out unfounded, mendacious, or self-serving foreign policy arguments because their proponents cannot avoid wide-ranging debate in which their reasoning and evidence are subject to public scrutiny." Van Evera (1990: 27) argues that nationalist myths "should be dampened by norms of free speech, which permit the development of evaluative institutions that can challenge errant ideas." Snyder and Ballantine (1996: 6) worry that states in the early stages of democratization may be unable to "create common public forums where diverse ideas engage each other under conditions in which erroneous arguments will be challenged."

As a result of the first assumption about the importance of information to public deliberation, the second assumption about the marketplace of ideas is that a robust and unfettered news media system is required to make it work (Kaufmann 2004; Van Evera 1990; Snyder and Ballantine 1996). Freedom of speech, press, and the ability of competing groups to gain access to the news are central. Scholars have placed great emphasis on the professional norms, ethics, and objectivity of journalists, as well as the independence and willingness to challenge government elites of their news organizations. In the standard view, adversarial-minded news media watchdogs are critical safeguards and promoters of free and full debate. Media performance to these standards has thus been viewed as central to gaining the benefits of a marketplace of ideas.

Modern work on the marketplace of ideas has acknowledged that markets do not always work as Mill described. Imperfect competition can stem from many sources including government control of the media, immature media systems lacking norms of objective journalism, or manipulative political elites who exaggerate and lie. Critical to all their work, however, is that, like economists, these authors view such imperfections as departures from the normal operation of a healthy marketplace of ideas in the modern Western democratic setting. As Snyder and Ballantine (1996: 12) put it, "The better institutionalized the market, the better it scrutinizes arguments and forces ideas to confront each other in common forums, and therefore the better the information the market provides." Thus, though many have pointed at poorly developed marketplaces causing trouble and conflict around the world, a great number of scholars have concluded that mature Western democracies generally enjoy the benefits of healthy marketplaces in the creation of foreign policy (Becker 1983; Bennett 2005; Van Evera 1990).

Despite the beauty and parsimony of this formulation of a rational, pluralist, economic exchange between buyers and sellers, the traditional model of the marketplace of ideas does not describe the social, emotional, and political nature of a healthy and mature marketplace much better than it describes an unhealthy one. The most important reason for this is that the driving force behind public acceptance of what political elites have to sell is not truth, but values. Certainly people prefer truth to lies, but for most important matters in politics and society, truth is beside the point. People hold opinions and support political elites not because they are more accurate or make truer claims than others, but because those opinions and claims resonate more deeply with their value systems, beliefs, and cherished identities (Lakoff 1996; Kinder 1994; Sears 1993).

Further, contrary to the conception that all citizens share a passion for good arguments and universal truth, the real marketplace is characterized by wildly varying attitudes and beliefs about the most fundamental questions of politics including how society should look and how the government should behave. Crucially, these differences are not merely the result of inadequate deliberation or information but rather the result of conflicting values, worldviews, and emotional connections to various ideas, groups, symbols, and (at times) myths. As a result, the greatest rewards for elites lie in seeking resonance with strongly held values, not in telling "the truth" (Edelman 1971; Sears 1993; Kaufman 2001). Clearly, the natural equilibrium of such a marketplace of ideas is not policy consensus but conflict, not a singular public truth but contending value judgments about the world and how it should look.

Skeptics of this value-based perspective will complain that facts are often central to policy debates – does Iraq have WMD, will tax cuts lead to higher rates of economic growth, will stricter gun control policies lead to reduced gun violence? I contend, however, that even these straightforward factual questions are the product of a worldview that gives those questions meaning. Many factual questions would never be asked in the first place were it not for the motivating force of a value system that helps identify this or that fact as a critical one. Not even the most bland or objective facts can be interpreted without relying on a set of values to make them salient and to give them context.

Even when people can agree about a fact and its relevance to the matter at hand they may disagree about its meaning. Examples of this type of disjuncture abound in politics. Liberals and conservatives may agree that Bush's tax cuts will spur economic growth but disagree about whether they are a good idea for the nation. Liberals and conservatives may agree that Saddam Hussein is seeking weapons of mass destruction, but disagree about whether this is something that justifies imme-diate military action. Moreover, because elites understand this process, political communication becomes an iterative process of interpretation by elites and public (Kuklinski and Hurley 1996; Edelman 1998).

In this alternate view of the marketplace of ideas, the news media must also play a very different role from that imagined by traditional theories. Previous work has typically argued that even if elites have incentives to play to specific audiences with biased arguments or false comforts, the news media will provide the necessary counterbalance. In the conventional vision of the ideal marketplace, the news media are by bound by norms of objectivity, motivated by a desire to publish the truth in the public interest, and thus ensure that elite arguments must contend with each other in the public sphere (Van Belle 1997). In this 'strong media' model, mature democracies can punish elites who tend too often toward vague promises or false claims. Market failures, from this perspective, occur whenever the news media fail to be critical enough of elite claims or fail to provide enough information to the public to make informed opinions about events (Page and Shapiro 1992; Bennett *et al.* 2007).

Viewed from the perspective of a "marketplace of values," however, the ability of the modern American news media to guide elites toward truth telling is sharply constrained by the fact that elites primarily seek support not by appeal to truth but through appeals to values couched in statements that gain their strength from unfal-sifiable visions of the "good society." Examples of this would include such com-mon appeals as spending more money on national defense to enhance security, upholding the death penalty in the name of public safety, or ending late-term abor-tions to preserve the sanctity of life. In none of these cases, so common in American politics, can one predetermine the most relevant facts of the case or observe a sin-gle Truth about an issue. One can disagree with these appeals but one cannot some-how prove them wrong through public debate. What we see is debate about *which* facts and *which* truth should take priority in policy making with the dividing lines in the debate typically revolving around competing value systems (Kaufman 2001; Van Evera 1994; Snyder 1991; Lakoff 1996). In each case political leaders may bolster their arguments with an array of facts that support their case, but in the end the success of their appeals rests more heavily on how well the underlying world-view of their communication resonates with the public than on the accuracy of the particular facts of the case.

The result is that the media's role in the *healthy* marketplace of values is not to lead public debate toward the higher ground of consensus and truth but in fact to help elites polarize society into opposing camps. Modern debates over abortion, the death penalty, affirmative action, gun control, gay marriage, and US foreign policy illustrate an iron law of the American marketplace of values: when elites sell com-peting policy preferences, their success is primarily determined by the distribution of the underlying values among the public, not by the quality of factual reporting by the news media. The eventual level of public polarization will depend both on the initial distribution of values as well as on the level of elite conflict over particular issues. When elites are in lock step, the public will gravitate toward higher levels of agreement; when elites clash, the public will tend toward greater polarization (Zaller 1992; Larson 1996).

Ironically, perhaps, the mainstream news media's role stems in large part from the commitment to the ideals of modern journalism. The very processes and norms that traditional theories of the marketplace identify as powerful agents for seeking truth in fact help keep the media on the sidelines during the real game. Objective news media systems are not supposed to espouse partisan values, or to judge events or people on the basis of partisan values. As a result the traditional news media have little choice but dutifully to report the facts of a situation while remaining mute about the contending worldviews producing the claims made by elites. Recent comments from Judith Miller, a *New York Times* reporter, provide insight into this dynamic. Responding to sharp questions about *Times* coverage of Iraqi WMD before the invasion, Miller defended her work saying, "My job isn't to assess the government's information and be an independent intelligence analyst myself. My job is to tell readers what the government thought of Iraq's arsenal" (Massing 2004).

This reduced role for the press suggests a different standard of performance from that applied by traditional theories. If people do not rely very heavily on facts to form opinions, then the media should not be blamed for failing to provide them. And since information is not the critical driver of opinion and policy preference, we should not look to information as the proximate source of "market failures." Instead, the metric to be used becomes the extent to which the media encompass the full range of elite cues about a threat. In other words, do the news media make it obvious to the audience that Republicans feel this way but Democrats another? If so, the media have played their essential role in the marketplace of values by helping citizens align their opinions with their values, regardless of how far from ideal we might consider the information they have provided.

Redefining threat inflation

Following the marketplace of ideas tradition, most work on threat inflation defines the process in terms of elite manipulation of facts and the subsequent distortion of debate upon which the public must form its opinions. Kaufmann, for example, offers this definition of threat inflation:

> Threat inflation, as opposed to ordinary conservatism, can be defined as
>
> 1   claims that go beyond the range of ambiguity that disinterested experts would credit as plausible;
> 2   a consistent pattern of worst-case assertions over a range of factual issues that are logically unrelated or only weakly related – an unlikely output of disinterested analysis;
> 3   use of double standards in evaluating intelligence in a way that favors worse-case threat assessments; or
> 4   claims based on circular logic, such as Bush administration claims that Hussein's alleged hostile intentions were evidence of the existence of

weapons of mass destruction whose supposed existence was used as evidence of his intentions.

(Kaufmann 2004: 8–9)

Cramer (2005: 3) likewise notes that "Threat inflators are not simply 'prudent' or 'conservative' threat estimators, but are actually guilty of portraying threats that exceed the bounds of uncertainty or ambiguity which are associated with the assessment of a threat." Both definitions echo Snyder and Ballantine's (1996: 10) definition of nationalist myths: "assertions that would lose their credibility if their claim to a basis in fact or logic were exposed to rigorous, disinterested public evaluation." These definitions of threat inflation are close cousins to the discussion of elite manipulation in the broader public opinion literature. Zaller (1992: 313), for example, defines elite domination as a "situation in which elites induce citizens to hold opinions that they would not hold if aware of the best available information and analysis."

More simply put, these definitions contend that threat inflation is a form of exaggeration or lying that degrades the quality of public deliberation. Though these definitions strike one as commonsensical, even obvious, they lose much of their usefulness when we acknowledge that the motive force underlying the marketplace is not truth but values.

The marketplace of values perspective challenges the conventional definition on several fronts. First, as noted above, a worldview is required before one can even determine which facts about a potential threat are the relevant facts. Taking the case of Iraq, for example, many have come to take for granted the primacy of the WMD debate, both in terms of judging the Bush administration and with respect to supporting the war. In fact, however, the "truth" about Iraqi WMD development only became important once the President had evoked it in service to constructing a larger argument about the threat posed by Iraq. What made WMD salient for the Bush team were the values and the worldview that Bush and his foreign policy team shared. The secondary importance of Iraqi WMD became clearer as the facts became clear-cut. Asked in late 2005 by Fox News if he would have invaded Iraq even if he had known that Iraq did not have WMD, Bush answered, "absolutely" (Stevenson 2005).

Second, life in the marketplace of values means that even when people agree on the relevant facts, there will be disagreement on the interpretation of those facts as they apply their values and worldviews to the facts in order to give them meaning. The Reagan "Bear in the Woods" campaign advertisement quoted at the start of this Chapter illustrates this point. In 1984, the USSR had thousands of nuclear warheads targeting the US and a massive conventional army in Eastern Europe. These facts were not in dispute – the threat was obvious. Or was it? In fact, the meaning of these obvious facts was the subject of continuous and contentious debate. Should the US have concluded from these facts that the Soviets were bent on world domination and thus responded aggressively and confrontationally? Or should the US have assumed instead that the Soviets were as afraid of US military might as we were of theirs and sought instead to cooperate? A "disinterested" analyst could not answer the key questions: how scared should we be and how should we respond to a powerful adversary when we don't know what they will do? The Reagan team, however, with a worldview that defined communism as an immoral and dangerous political system, was readily able to answer the question. The ad explicitly admitted that in fact the truth *could not be known*. Instead, it promoted a position on national defense based on Reagan's view of the world and appealed for support from those who shared it.

Finally, this alternate conception of the marketplace also suggests that the very definition of national security, and thus of a security threat, might be very different depending on one's worldview. Scholarship over the past 20 years has shown that some people hold a very narrow notion of national security that defines threats only as direct military threats against the US homeland. Others, however, carry around a very broad notion of national security that includes quality of life elements such as unemployment levels and environmental protection, or "the American way of life" (Wittkopf 1990; Nye 2002).

In sum, threat perception at the individual level requires first a system for understanding and evaluating the world, then second requires 'facts' (information) that trigger and support concerns based on that system. Policy guidance also requires a value system to allow officials to establish priorities, make decisions, and justify their own actions. Disagreements over which facts matter and how they matter thus spring eternally from the competing values and perspectives held by the American public and their leaders. Debates over facts do matter, but it is clear that defining threat inflation as simply a matter of exaggerating, lying or imperfect debate obscures the bigger picture.

Framing the threat

In light of the discussion earlier I propose that we view threat inflation as a subset of a broader and more common phenomenon: the effort to *frame* the world and thus persuade a mass audience to adopt a cause. Framing, to borrow Robert Entman's (2004: 5) definition, is "selecting and highlighting some facets of events or issues, and making connections among them so as to promote a particular interpretation, evaluation, and/or solution."

Consider again the "Bear in the Woods." The Reagan campaign referred to the Soviet Union as a bear in order to increase the salience of Soviet military strength and potentially violent nature and intentions, thereby encouraging people to support a more aggressive response to the possibility of bear trouble. Implied in the ad as well is the notion that not to respond would be irresponsible. Clearly the ad is an effort to frame the Soviet threat by promoting a particular problem definition (the USSR is a strong and potentially dangerous bear), a moral evaluation (anyone who doesn't think there is a bear is incompetent and people who see the bear but don't respond are irresponsible), and a treatment recommendation (increase US military power to defend against the bear).

With due credit to Entman, then, I define threat framing as "the process of selecting and highlighting some facets of national security-related events or issues and making connections among them so as to promote a particular threat definition, causal interpretation, moral evaluation, and/or policy recommendation through the activation of values, attitudes, and beliefs held by the public." Threat inflation (or deflation), in turn, is simply an instance of threat framing in which the goal is to increase (or decrease) public concern with a threat.

These definitions of threat framing and threat inflation offer an improvement over an exaggeration-based definition of threat inflation. Framing allows for a more complete explanation for how elites communicate about threats and how the public reasons about threats than exaggeration-based arguments. Framing theory also acknowledges what is missing from previous discussions of the marketplace of ideas and threat inflation: the centrality of values, the fact that we cannot interpret reality in a purely objective way but instead must choose a perspective from which to view it, and the fact that our opinions flow from the frames we use to interpret the world. In so doing, it locates the dynamic in a rich theoretical literature. A growing body of work across several fields has established the importance of framing to strategic political communication (Riker 1983; Edelman 1998; Kaufman 2001; Entman 2004), to news coverage of the world (Gans 1980; Gitlin 1980; Hallin 1994; Norris *et al.* 2003), and to how individuals interpret the world and the formation of mass public opinion (Tversky and Kahneman 1981; Goffman 1974; Sniderman and Theriault 2004; Druckman and Chong 2007). These research agendas have much to tell us about how threat framing and threat inflation work.

Iraq: a failure of the marketplace of ideas?

Chaim Kaufmann's 2004 article in *International Security* offers the most complete and compelling argument that the Bush administration exaggerated the threat from Iraq and did so successfully, persuading a majority of the public to support the invasion on false grounds. Kaufmann argues that Bush was able to mobilize support for war by misusing intelligence, dominating news coverage thanks to a compliant press and cowed opposition, thereby stoking unfounded fears about Iraqi WMD. In his view and from the perspective of the standard marketplace of ideas theory, elite manipulation led the public to hold opinions they would not have held under conditions of full information.

I argue that although Kaufmann's critique may be devastating to the factual basis for Bush's march to war, it pays too little attention to the true engines of opinion formation. To illustrate this I use threat framing theory to assess the impact the Bush administration's efforts had on public support for the war. I argue later that the Iraq case both supports threat framing theory's focus on frames over facts and also, contrary to Kaufmann and others, that it represents not a failure of the marketplace of ideas but standard operating procedure for a healthy marketplace of values. Far fewer people supported the war for the "wrong" reasons than Kaufmann and others believe. I conclude that Iraq suggests that the American public sphere is quite robust for all its deficits, real and imagined.

Critical information? Iraqi WMD and support for war

If Kaufmann and the standard marketplace of ideas model are correct, the Iraq case should reveal three pieces of evidence: first, that factual information about WMD shaped public opinion about Iraq; second, that support for the decision to go war dropped as misperceptions about WMD faded; and third, a convergence of opinion about the decision to go to war as the marketplace guided citizens toward a more objective and truthful assessment of the situation.

The alternative hypothesis of threat framing theory is that competing frames about the war dueled for acceptance from the public throughout the crisis, with the balance of opinion resulting not from the facts of the situation but instead from the marriage of elite cues and individual predispositions. If threat framing theory is correct, then we should instead see first, that threat perceptions and support for an invasion followed from the frames held by citizens rather than from facts, both in the pre-war and post-war phases; second, that threat perceptions were less responsive to changes in facts than changes in elite framing; and third, increasing opinion polarization over time rather than convergence as people gained the necessary information to align their opinions more closely with their values.

The average support for an invasion of Iraq between August 2002 (when Kaufmann argues the Bush threat inflation campaign began in earnest) and March 15th on the eve of the invasion was 57 percent (see Figure 10.1). Though certainly a majority, it sounds less impressive when we note that public support was already at 53 percent in August 2002, having dropped from almost 70 percent at the

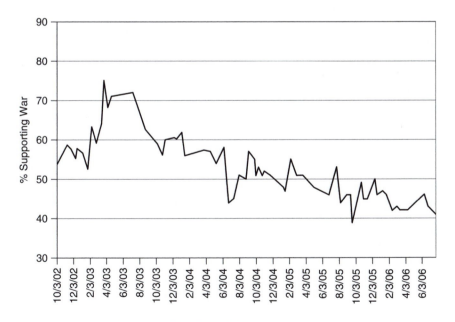

Figure 10.1 Support for the Iraq War, 2002–2006

Source: Gallup Poll.

beginning of 2002. Bush thus made very little head way between August 2002 and January 2003 despite a joint resolution from Congress authorizing him to use force against Iraq, despite committing US credibility by sending American forces to forward positions in the Persian Gulf, and despite the fact that Saddam Hussein continued to behave as the evil dictator Bush argued that he was. The fact that support for the invasion only began to rise from its Fall 2002 levels once troops were positioned in the Gulf and the media were discussing the war as a foregone conclusion suggests that the rally effect of crisis, rather than President Bush's threat inflation rhetoric, was responsible for the appearance of last minute support for the policy. Support for the invasion then peaked in late April with the fall of Baghdad and began a long slide that would eventually stabilize below 50 percent within two years.

If Kaufmann is correct, pre-war opinion about Iraq should be the result of mistaken beliefs that Iraq had or was actively developing weapons of mass destruction. And indeed, by early February 2003, 56 percent of the public was "certain" that Iraq had the facilities to develop weapons of mass destruction (Gallup Poll, 7 February 2003). Further, support for the war did correlate with certainty about Iraq's WMD efforts. Those who were certain that Iraq had WMD facilities were far more likely to support the war than those less certain. In early February 2003, 77 percent of those who were certain supported an invasion compared to 51.5 percent of those who believed it was likely but not certain that Iraq had WMD facilities, and just 17 percent of those who felt it was certain Iraq did not have WMD facilities.

What is missing from these figures, however, is the *cause* of people's certainty about Iraqi WMD. Kaufmann argues that this is where the marketplace failed by reporting Bush's exaggerations uncritically and giving little room to his critics to challenge his assertions. A study by Jason Barabas (2005) provides support for Kaufmann's thesis, illustrating that the overall level of certainty expressed by journalists and political actors about the presence of Iraqi WMD in media reports was high before the war and then waned over time. The result of the changing information environment, Barabas argues, is that at first many people but later fewer people were certain that Iraq was developing WMD and in turn, support for the war dropped over time.

The real answer, however, lies beneath the impressive correlations between certainty and overall support for the war. At each step of the way the public was sharply divided about whether or not Iraq was developing weapons of mass destruction. In February 2003, for example, at the supposed height of Bush's threat inflation efforts, Gallup found that 62 percent of republicans were "certain" Iraq was doing so compared to only 40 percent of independents and 39 percent of democrats. The traditional model cannot explain this response to supposedly brute facts. What made some people certain that Iraq had weapons of mass destruction while others were certain Iraq had none?

Threat framing theory suggests that people's preexisting frames for viewing security issues predisposed them to come to conclusions – often unwarranted in both directions – about the state of the Iraq WMD program. In the absence of sure knowledge, Republicans (and some independent and Democrats) who shared

Bush's worldview concerning national security were more responsive to the overall assessment of Iraq as a critical threat. As a result, they were also more trusting of Bush's use of US intelligence regarding WMD to support the argument for war. Thus, where Kaufmann and Barabas argue that misperceptions about WMD led people to support the war, I argue instead that people's reliance on differing frames led to differences of opinion about WMD and the war from the outset. By January 2004, 42 percent of Republicans were still certain Iraq had been developing WMD, compared to just 17 percent of Democrats (Gallup Poll, 29 January 2004).

Standard marketplace of ideas logic also assumes that over time support for the war should have faded as people learned the truth about WMD. The public did develop more accurate assessments of Iraq WMD over time, but as Figure 10.2 reveals, the predicted drop in support for the war only occurred among Democrats and independents. Republican support for the decision to go to war never dropped below 80 percent despite the failure to find any WMD in Iraq. Moreover, when asked about the justification for war, 83 percent of Republicans polled in January 2004 responded that the war would be justified even if WMD *were never found* (Gallup Poll, 29 January 2004). The suggestion that the fact of Iraqi WMD was the central driver of support for war thus begins to look like an argument that the tail wagged the dog.

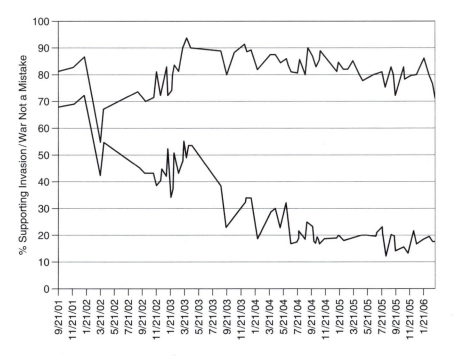

Figure 10.2 Partisan Polarization over Iraq, 2002–2006

Source: Gallup Poll.

Further, the traditional conception of the marketplace of ideas holds that as Bush's dominance over debate faded in the wake of the invasion (as the market "corrected" itself, in other words), the more free and fair debate should have helped guide the public toward enlightened consensus about the facts and policy preferences. However, though we see an imperfect trend toward a more accurate grasp of certain facts about Iraq, Iraq itself remained a Rorschach test. Two years after the invasion the public was more polarized than ever about the war, despite more information. Republicans did not waver in their support for Bush's decision to go to war, nor did they waver in the face of a stronger than predicted insurgency, waves of suicide bombers, the tragedy of Abu Ghraib, or sustained attacks by democratic candidates for president. Republicans continued to argue that the war was going well, that it was justified, and that it had produced important benefits. Democrats, meanwhile, solidified into firm opposition, arguing that the war was going poorly, was not justified, and had eroded US security rather than strengthened it.

Threat framing theory again offers an explanation. Contrary to the assumption that people supported the war because they misperceived the situation, threat framing theory suggests that republicans correctly perceived the alignment of their values with the thrust of Bush's arguments and thus supported the war both before and after the invasion. An important implication is that value-based frames are sturdier constructs than facts and that frames generate support, often times in spite of the facts. Threat framing theory suggests that republicans used WMD as a rallying point in the beginning to justify the conclusion, based on their framing of the situation, that the US must deal with Iraq sooner rather than later. When the initial factual justification proved weak, Bush and others moved on to other justifications such as the need to rescue the Iraqi people from a brutal dictator and the need to spread democracy in the Middle East as part of the war on terror (Gershkoff and Kushner 2005; Western 2005). Republicans, because their support was never truly dependent on the facts about Iraqi WMD but instead was secured by Bush's framing of the invasion, never missed a beat and continued to support the president's policies.

Democrats, meanwhile, provide mirror image support for threat framing theory. Beginning with a very different conception of security and the best way to ensure it, Democrats never fully bought into Bush's arguments about the need to invade Iraq and were never as convinced about Iraqi WMD either. Although Democrats would later make political use of the fact that WMD had not been found in Iraq, it was just one of many reasons that Democrats would cite for their opposition to the war including casualties (both American and civilian Iraqi), the rise of terrorism and insurgency within Iraq, and the impact of the war on America's relationship with the rest of the world. Thus, the facts of the case are convenient shorthand for identifying the divisions in society over key issues, but they should not be confused with the more fundamental *reasons* that people disagree.

If we accept Kaufmann's argument that pre-war debate was relatively one-sided, with Bush holding all of the information and doing the lion's share of the talking, then we can explain his success in mobilizing Republicans and lack of success in mobilizing Democrats as the result of differential responses to his framing of the situation. When Bush argued for war his underlying frame was that after 9/11 the world was a different place, one in which gathering threats must be dealt with and in which Iraq had become a critical front in the war on terror. In response, republicans overwhelmingly agreed, democrats mostly disagreed, and independents were somewhere in the middle. Later, the facts had changed, but the underlying frame from which republicans were viewing the situation had not, and thus their support remained steady.

Democrats and independents, however, eventually turned in greater numbers against the war as they picked up enough information from both Bush and opposing elites to understand the competing frames at stake and identify the one that resonated best with their own values. Again, assuming Kaufmann is correct in his assessment of the pre-war debate, this took more time for Democrats and independents than for Republicans because they were exposed to less frame-relevant information to help them identify their side of the fence. Over time, as the news provided more information about the war and opposing elites spoke up in greater numbers, the polarization process picked up steam as the marketplace divided the public into warring factions.

Thus to summarize, Kaufmann identifies the president's unchecked exaggeration as the linchpin of his effort to sell the war in Iraq. The failure of the marketplace lay in the inability or unwillingness of the media to confront the factual inaccuracies and flawed arguments about US intelligence and the Iraqi threat. Threat framing theory, on the other hand, argues that the president's success was much more modest than Kaufmann suggests and that it stemmed primarily from the president's ability to communicate his general framework for interpreting the Iraq threat, not from his ability to trick people into holding misperceptions about Iraq. In short, threat framing theory suggests that Iraq was not a failure of the marketplace of ideas but a case study of the healthy marketplace of values in action. Bush's argument about the threat from Iraq before the invasion simply appealed to more people than the oppositional frame at the time. To argue that this support required a foundation of misperception is to underestimate the power of values and to overestimate the importance of facts and our ability to use them to come to consensus about important policy matters.

A robust marketplace

I have argued that the marketplace of ideas operates more like a marketplace of values and that threat framing provides a more useful explanatory tool than elite manipulation of information in understanding threat perceptions. The most important conclusion from this analysis is that the American marketplace is more robust than many have suggested recently and that the pessimists have looked for both crisis and comfort in the wrong place. The ability of a political system to resist threat inflation lies not in its ability to come to rational consensus through debate and deliberation but in the degree to which it encourages competition among elites and the public over the appropriate frame with which to view threats.

The United States enjoys a robust marketplace for at least three major reasons. First, as noted, the public does not typically agree on the nature of threats, even in the face of substantial elite rhetorical pressure. The United States is simply fortunate that its public is polarized enough to make wars of choice an unpopular course of action most of the time. Second, the highly competitive U.S. electoral system provides a brake on threat inflation by ensuring that candidates design moderate foreign policies. This does not ensure wise foreign policy directly, but it does discourage threat inflation in pursuit of extreme agendas. Finally, the U.S. news media provide an important check on threat inflation. Where the standard marketplace of ideas model requires full and free debate of current events, the marketplace of values requires only that the news media provide more basic information about how elites view the situation more generally and cues about where each party stands on key policies. Despite their many flaws, American news organizations manage to meet this lower bar on most occasions.

Still, even a robust marketplace may fail. Threat framing theory suggests that the critical failure mode of the marketplace of values is not when one group dominates debate but when there is simply no competition among elites at all. In such cases a large majority of the public will be predisposed to view a potential threat in the same way. This prediction echoes the literature on nationalism and ethnic conflict, where authors argue that elites stoke fears by appealing to widely shared cultural myths and mobilizing public emotions. In such cases elites have an easy time getting the public riled up about threats to the extent that they share the myths, symbols, and preexisting frameworks for thinking about the world. Most literature on nationalism imagines that the free press in democratic societies is the regulator on such strategies. However, a careful read of American history suggests that democratic publics have no special ability to find truth and that there is no magic in a free press by itself.

Despite this polarization on most issues Americans do share certain core cultural values related to security including the need to defend the American homeland proper and the desire to maintain the American way of life in the face of competition with other "isms." In the cases where a large majority of Americans have been in broad agreement on something, leaders have been able to motivate the public in ways quite similar to those used by nationalist leaders in Serbia, Rwanda, and elsewhere. Many have argued that the Cold War provides a long running example of this dynamic as American anticommunism provoked needless military spending and military intervention (Mueller 2006; Hermann and Chomsky 2002).

Some might complain that this view of the democratic marketplace of ideas is too cynical. I argue, on the contrary, that the marketplace is built upon a solid foundation. The standard conception of the marketplace of ideas demands that politicians, journalists, and citizens discover, discuss, and agree on the Truth without perjury or prejudice. This, I submit, is an unrealistic hope, and one that the founders explicitly rejected when crafting the Constitution (Madison 1787). The founders, working from assumptions similar to those I have made about the marketplace of values, created a republican government that would embrace competition and make dominance difficult. Though they may have opposed the war as a foreign entanglement, they would nonetheless approve of a marketplace of values that assumes disagreement, occasional dishonesty, and an ignorant public, and yet manages to provide some protection against these imperfections.

References

Barabas, J. (2005) "Certitude: uncertain knowledge and message clarity in mediated deliberation," Paper presented at the American Political Science Association Conference for International Communication and Conflict, Georgetown University, Washington, DC.

Becker, G. (1983) "A theory of competition among pressure groups for political influence," *Quarterly Journal of Economics*, 98: 371–400.

Bennett, W. L. (2005) *News: The Politics of Illusion*, 6th edn, New York: Longman.

Bennett, W. L., Lawrence, R. G. and Livingston, S. (2007) *When the Press Fails: Political Power and the News Media from Iraq to Katrina*, Chicago, IL: Chicago University Press.

Bentham, J. (1999) *Works of Jeremy Bentham*, Oxford: Oxford University Press.

Cirincione, J. (2005) "Not one claim was true," *Bulletin of the Atomic Scientists*, January/February.

Cramer, J. K. (2005) "Sounding the tocsin redux: Persistent patterns of threat inflation in the marketplace of ideas," Paper delivered at the 2005 meeting of the International Studies Association.

Druckman, J. N. and Chong, D. (2007) "Framing public opinion in competitive democracies," *American Political Science Review*, 101: 637–655.

Edelman, M. (1971) *Politics as Symbolic Action: Mass Arousal and Quiescence*, New York: Academic Press.

—— (1998) *Constructing the Political Spectacle*, Chicago, IL: University of Chicago Press.

Entman, R. M. (2004) *Projections of Power: Framing News, Public Opinion, and U.S. Foreign Policy*, Chicago, IL: University of Chicago Press.

Elster, J. (1998) *Deliberative Democracy*, Cambridge: Cambridge University Press.

Fishkin, J. S. (1995) *The Voice of the People*, New Haven, CT: Yale University Press.

Gallup/CNN/USA Today (2003) *Gallup/CNN/USA Today Poll*. 7 February. Online. Available HTTP: www.ropercenter.uconn.edu/data_access/ipoll/ipoll.html (Accessed August 31, 2008).

Gallup/CNN/USA Today (2004) *Gallup/CNN/USA Today Poll*. 29 January. Online. Available HTTP: www.ropercenter.uconn.edu/data_access/ipoll/ipoll.html (Accessed August 31, 2008).

Gans, H. J. (1980) *Deciding What's News*, New York: Vintage Press.

Gershkoff, A. and Kushner, S. (2005) "Shaping public opinion: The 9/11-Iraq connection in the Bush administration's rhetoric," *Perspectives on Politics*, 3: 525–37.

Gitlin, T. (1980) *The Whole World Is Watching: The Making and Unmaking of the New Left*, Berkeley: University of California Press.

Goffman, E. (1974) *Frame Analysis: An Essay on the Organization of Experience*, New York: Harper & Row.

Gray, J. and Smith, G. W. (eds) (1991) *John Stuart Mill On Liberty: In Focus*, London: Routledge.

Hallin, D. C. (1994) *We Keep America On Top: Television Journalism and the Public Sphere*, Oxford: Oxford University Press.

Hermann, E. and Chomsky, N. (2002) *Manufacturing Consent: The Political Economy of the Mass Media*, Updated edn, New York: Pantheon Books.

Hersh, S. (2003) "The stovepipe," *The New Yorker*, 27 October.

Holsti, O. (2004) *Public Opinion and American Foreign Policy*, rev. edn, Ann Arbor, MI: University of Michigan.

Kant, I. (1983) *Perpetual Peace, and Other Essays on Politics, History, and Morals*, trans. T. Humphrey, Indianapolis, IN: Hackett.

Kaufman, S. J. (2001) *The Symbolic Politics of Ethnic War*, Ithaca, NY: Cornell University Press.

Kaufmann, C. (2004) "Threat inflation and the failure of the marketplace of ideas: The selling of the Iraq war," *International Security*, 29: 5–48.

Kinder, D. (1994) "Reason and emotion in American political life," in R. C. Schank and E. Langer (eds) *Beliefs, Reasoning, and Decision Making: Psycho-Logic in Honor of Bob Abelson*, Mahwah, NJ: Lawrence Erlbaum Associates.

Kuklinski and Hurley (1996) "A matter of interpretation," in D. C. Mutz, P. M. Sniderman and R. A. Brody (eds) *Political Persuasion and Attitude Change*, Ann Arbor, MI: University of Michigan Press.

Lakoff, G. (1996) *Moral Politics: How Liberals and Conservatives Think*, Chicago, IL: University of Chicago Press.

Larson, E. (1996) *Casualties and Consensus: The Historical Role of Casualties in Domestic Support for U.S. Military Operations*, Santa Monica, CA: Rand.

Massing, M. (2004) "Now they tell us: The American press and Iraq," *New York Review of Books*, February 26.

Madison, J., Hamilton, A., Jay, J. and Kramnick, I. (1987) *The Federalist Papers*, New York: Penguin Classics.

Mill, J. (1913) *On Liberty of the Press for Advocating Resistance to Government: Being Part of an Essay Written for the Encyclopedia Britannica*, 6th edn, New York: Free Speech League.

Mueller, J. (2006) *Overblown: How Politicians and the Terrorism Industry Inflate National Security Threats, and Why We Believe Them*, New York: Free Press.

Norris, P., Kern, M. and Just, M. (2003) *Framing Terrorism: The News Media, the Government, and the Public*, New York: Routledge.

Nye, J. (2002) *The Paradox of American Power: Why the World's Only Superpower Can't Go It Alone*, Oxford and New York: Oxford University Press.

Owen, J. (1994) "How Liberalism Produces Democratic Peace," *International Security*, 19.

Page, B. I. and Shapiro, R. Y. (1992) *The Rational Public*, Chicago, IL: University of Chicago Press.

Prados, J. (2004) *Hookwinked: The Documents That Reveal How Bush Sold the War*, New York: The New Press.

Riker, W. H. (1983) "Political theory and the art of heresthetics," in A. Finifter (ed.) *Political Science: The State of the Discipline*, Washington, DC: American Political Science Association.

Sears, D. O. (1993) "Symbolic politics: A socio-psychological theory," in S. Iyengar and W. J. McGuire (eds), *Explorations in Political Psychology*, Durham, NC: Duke University.

Sniderman, P. M. and Theriault, S. M. (2004) "The structure of political argument and the logic of issue framing," in W. E. Saris and P. M. Sniderman (eds) *Studies in Public Opinion*, Princeton, NJ: Princeton University Press.

Snyder, J. (1991) *Myths of Empire: Domestic Politics and International Ambition*, Ithaca, NY: Cornell University Press.

Snyder, J. and Ballantine, K. (1996) "Nationalism and the marketplace of ideas," *International Security*, 21: 5–40.

Stevenson, R. W. (2005) "Bush says U.S. needs patience on Iraq war; Admits errors," *New York Times*, 15 December.

Tversky, A. and Kahneman, D. (1981) "The framing of decisions and the psychology of choice," *Science*, 211: 453–458.

Van Belle, D. (1997) "Press freedom and the democratic peace," *Journal of Peace Research*, 34: 405–414.

Van Evera, S. (1990) "Primed for peace: Europe after the Cold War," *International Security*, 15: 7–57.

—— (1994) "Hypotheses on nationalism and war," *International Security*, 18: 5–39.

Western, J. (2005) *Selling Intervention and War: The Presidency, the Media, and the American Public*, Baltimore, MD: Johns Hopkins University Press.

Wittkopf, E. (1990) *Faces of Internationalism: Public Opinion and American Foreign Policy*, Durham, NC: Duke University Press.

Zaller, J. (1992) *The Nature and Origins of Mass Opinion*, New York: Cambridge University Press.

11   Inflating terrorism

John Mueller

Homeland Security czar Michael Chertoff has proclaimed the "struggle" against terrorism to be a "significant existential" one – carefully differentiating it, apparently, from all those insignificant existential struggles we have waged in the past (Harris and Taylor 2008). Meanwhile, the *New York Times* editorial board assured us on April 23, 2008, that "the fight against al-Qaeda is the central battle for this generation," and Senator John McCain more expansively, and repeatedly, labels it the "transcendental challenge of the twenty-first century." Meanwhile Democrats routinely insist that the terrorist menace has been energized and much heightened by the Republicans' misguided war in Iraq.

"At the summit of foreign policy," political scientist Warner Schilling once observed, "one always finds simplicity and spook" (1965: 389). As part of this process it strongly appears that, with the benefit of hindsight, there has been a tendency to inflate national security threats in the past and then, partly in consequence, to overreact to them. These include anxieties over domestic and foreign Communism, fears about the imminence of thermonuclear war, apprehensions over challenges posed by various "rogue states" or devils du jour most of whom eventually faded into insignificance (remember Nasser, Sukarno, Qaddafi, Castro?), insecurities engendered by the Iran hostage crisis and the Japanese economic challenge of the 1980s, and worries about the "ethnic warfare" that was supposedly going to engulf the world in the 1990s (see Mueller 2006: Chapters 3–6; Johnson 1994).

Not all concerns that could potentially have been seized upon have evoked anxiety and overreaction. For example, the American public and its leaders have remained remarkably calm about the potential damage that could be inflicted by the planet's intersection with large meteors or comets, and (perhaps more pertinently) they do not seem to be exercised all that much by much-advertised dangers stemming from global warming or genetically modified food. But it does appear that every foreign policy threat in the last several decades that has come to be accepted as significant has then eventually been greatly exaggerated.

It does not automatically and necessarily follow, of course, that because foreign policy threats have been inflated in the past, we are doing so now. However, there has been a significant pattern of over-extrapolation and overreaction, not to mention simplicity and spook, that has often led to policies that were unwise, costly, unnecessary, and sometimes massively counterproductive. And we do seem now to be at it again (see also Chapman and Harris 2002; Seitz 2004; Lustick 2006; Furedi 2007). On examination, any threat presented by international terrorism hardly seems existential or transcendental. Nonetheless, it has been embraced by the American public, inflated by what might be called the "terrorism industry," and seems to have been internalized to the point where efforts to deal with it, no matter how expensive or unproductive, will be around for a long time.

The scope of the threat

In evaluating the threat, a good place to start is with analyses provided by Marc Sageman in lectures and in his book, *Leaderless Jihad* (2007). Now a professor at the University of Pennsylvania, Sageman is a former intelligence officer with experience in Afghanistan. Carefully and systematically combing through both open and classified data on jihadists and would-be jihadists around the world, Sageman sorts the al-Qaeda enemy – just about the only terrorists who seem to want to target the United States itself – into three groups.

First, there is a cluster left over from the struggles in Afghanistan against the Soviets in the 1980s. Currently they are huddled around, and hiding out with, Osama bin Laden somewhere in Afghanistan and/or Pakistan. This band, concludes Sageman, probably consists of a few dozen individuals. Second, joining them in the area are perhaps a hundred fighters left over from al-Qaeda's golden days in Afghanistan in the 1990s.

These key portions of the enemy forces would total, then, less than 150 actual people. They may operate something resembling "training camps," but these appear to be quite minor affairs. They also assist with the Taliban's far larger and very troublesome insurgency in Afghanistan.

Beyond this tiny band, concludes Sageman, the third group consists of thousands of sympathizers and would-be jihadists spread around the globe who mainly connect in internet chat rooms, engage in radicalizing conversations, and variously dare each other actually to do something.

All of these rather hapless – perhaps even pathetic – people, should of course be considered to be potentially dangerous. From time to time they may be able to coalesce enough to carry out acts of terrorist violence, and policing efforts to stop them before they can do so are certainly justified. But the notion that they present an existential threat to just about anybody seems at least as fanciful as some of their schemes.

The threat presented by these individuals is likely, concludes Sageman, simply to fade away in time. Unless, of course, the United States overreacts and does something to enhance their numbers, prestige, and determination – something that is, needless to say, entirely possible.

I've checked this remarkable and decidedly unconventional evaluation of the threat with three prominent experts who have spent years studying the issue. They generally agree with Sageman.

One of them is Fawaz Gerges, whose brilliant book, *The Far Enemy*, based on hundreds of interviews in the Middle East, parses the jihadist enterprise (Gerges

2005; see also Ignatius 2008). As an additional concern, he suggests that Sageman's third group may also include a small, but possibly growing, underclass of disaffected and hopeless young men in the Middle East, many of them scarcely literate, who, outraged at Israel and at America's war in Iraq, may provide cannon fodder for the jihad. However, these people would mainly present problems in the Middle East (including in Iraq), not elsewhere.

Although there are some who worry that al-Qaeda has been able to reconstitute itself and is now on the march (see Bergen 2007; Hoffman 2008; Mazzetti and Rohde 2008),[2] estimates of the size of al-Qaeda central generally come in with numbers in the same order of magnitude as those suggested by Sageman. Egyptian intelligence, for example, puts the number at less than 200, while American intelligence estimates run from 300 to upwards of 500 (Wright 2008). One retired U.S. intelligence officer suggests it could be "as many as 2000" (Mazzetti and Rohde 2008), but that number should obviously be taken essentially to define the upper range of contemporary estimates.

Another way to evaluate the threat is to focus on the actual amount of violence perpetrated around the world by Muslim extremists since 9/11 outside of war zones. Included in the count would be terrorism of the much-publicized and fear-inducing sort that occurred in Bali in 2002, in Saudi Arabia, Morocco, and Turkey in 2003, in the Philippines, Madrid, and Egypt in 2004, and in London and Jordan in 2005.

Three think-tank publications have independently provided lists of such incidents. Although these tallies make for grim reading, the total number of people killed comes to some 200 or 300 per year. That, of course, is 200 or 300 per year too many, but it hardly suggests that the perpetrators present a major threat, much less an existential one. For comparison: over the same period far more people have drowned in bathtubs in the United States alone. Another comparison comes from the consequences of policies instituted by the Transportation Security Administration. Increased delays and added costs at airports due to new security procedures provide incentive for many short-haul passengers to drive to their destination rather than flying. Since driving is far riskier than air travel, the extra automobile traffic generated by increased airport security screening measures has been estimated to result in 400 or more fatalities per year (Ellig *et al.* 2006: 35).

Another assessment comes from astronomer Alan Harris. Using State Department figures, he estimates a worldwide death rate from international terrorism outside of war zones of 1,000 per year – that is, he assumes in his estimate that there would be another 9/11 somewhere in the world every several years. Over an 80 year period under those conditions some 80,000 deaths would occur which would mean that the probability that a resident of the globe will die at the hands of international terrorists is about one in 75,000 (6 billion divided by 80,000). In comparison, an American's chance of dying in an auto accident over the same time interval is about one in 80. If there are no repeats of 9/11, the probability of being killed by an international terrorist becomes more like one in 120,000.

An important reason for these low numbers, note Sageman and Gerges, is that policing agencies around the world, often working cooperatively, have rolled up, or rolled over, thousands of potential jihadist terrorists since 9/11. These include not only the police in Europe, but also in Egypt, Jordan, Syria, Iran, Indonesia, Morocco, Saudi Arabia, and Pakistan. They have been energized not out of any love for the United States, much less for its foreign policy, but because the terrorists threaten them as well. In addition, terrorist acts mostly tend to be counterproductive. Before some Jordanian hotels were bombed by terrorists, some 25 percent of Jordanians viewed bin Laden favorably. After the attacks, this fell to less than one percent (see also Mack 2008; Abrahms 2006).

If this weren't enough, al-Qaeda has continually expanded its enemies list in its declarations to the point where, as one analyst notes, it has come to include "all Middle Eastern regimes; Muslims who don't share their views; most Western countries; Jews and Christians; the governments of India, Pakistan, Afghanistan, and Russia; most news organizations; the United Nations; and international NGOs" (Bergen 2007: 19). In sum, bin Laden and gang seem mainly to have succeeded in uniting the world, including its huge Muslim portion, against their violent global jihad.

Meanwhile, after years of well-funded sleuthing, the FBI and other investigative agencies have been unable to uncover a single true al-Qaeda sleeper cell in the United States (Isikoff and Hosenball 2007). (In interesting synergy, that would be exactly the number of weapons of mass destruction uncovered by the U.S. military in Iraq over the same period.)

Any "threat" appears, then, principally to derive from Sageman's leaderless jihadists: self-selected people, often isolated from each other, who fantasize about performing dire deeds. From time to time some of these characters may actually manage to do some harm, though in most cases their capacities and schemes – or alleged schemes – seem to be far less dangerous than initial press reports vividly, even hysterically, suggest. There is, for example, the diabolical would-be bomber of shopping malls in Rockford, Illinois, who exchanged two used stereo speakers (he couldn't afford the opening price of $100) for a bogus handgun and four equally bogus hand grenades supplied by an FBI informant (Lawson 2008). Had the weapons been real, he might actually have managed to do some harm, but he clearly posed no threat that was existential (significant or otherwise) to the United States, to Illinois, to Rockford, or, indeed, to the shopping mall.

For the number of terrorist casualties to change radically, terrorists would have to become *vastly* more capable of inflicting damage. In fact, they would pretty much need to acquire an atomic arsenal and the capacity to deploy and detonate it.

Nuclear weapons, can inflict massive destruction of course, and an atomic bomb in the hands of a terrorist group could kill tens of thousands of people or even, in exceptional circumstances, more. And warnings about the possibility that small groups could fabricate nuclear weapons have been repeatedly uttered at least since 1946 when A-bomb maker J. Robert Oppenheimer agreed that "three or four men" could smuggle atomic bomb units into New York and "blow up the whole city" (Allison 2004: 104). Such assertions proliferated after the 1950s when the "suitcase bomb" appeared to become a practical possibility, and dire warnings about nuclear terrorism have escalated with the stimulus of 9/11 – even though the terrorists used weapons no more sophisticated than box-cutters on that terrible day.

However, these cries of alarm have obviously so far proven to be much off the mark. It is also essential to note that making a nuclear weapon is an extraordinarily difficult task. As the Gilmore Commission, a special advisory panel to the President and Congress, stresses, building a nuclear device capable of producing mass destruction presents "Herculean challenges." The process requires obtaining enough fissile material, designing a weapon "that will bring that mass together in a tiny fraction of a second, before the heat from early fission blows the material apart," and figuring out some way to deliver the thing. And it emphasizes that these merely constitute "the *minimum* requirements." If each is not fully met, the result is not simply a less powerful weapon, but one that can't produce any significant nuclear yield at all or can't be delivered (Gilmore Commission 1999: 31, emphasis in the original). And after assessing this issue in detail, physicists Christoph Wirz and Emmanuel Egger conclude that fabricating a nuclear weapon "could hardly be accomplished by a subnational group" because of "the difficulty of acquiring the necessary expertise, the technical requirements (which in several fields verge on the unfeasible), the lack of available materials and the lack of experience in working with these" (2005: 501). If Sageman has it even roughly correct, any notion that al-Qaeda jihadists could come up with such weapons seems farfetched in the extreme.

A common concern envisions a newly nuclear country palming off a bomb or two to friendly terrorists for delivery abroad. However, this is exceedingly improbable because there would be too much risk, even for a country led by extremists, that the ultimate source of the weapon would be discovered. As Matthew Bunn puts it

> A dictator or oligarch bent of maintaining power is highly unlikely to take the immense risk of transferring such a devastating capability to terrorists they cannot control, given the ever-present possibility that the material would be traced back to its origin.
>
> (2007: vi)

Important in this last consideration are deterrent safeguards afforded by "nuclear forensics," the rapidly-developing science (and art) of connecting nuclear materials to their sources even after a bomb has been exploded (Levi 2007: 127–33). Moreover, there is a considerable danger the bomb and its donor would be discovered even before delivery or that it would explod in a manner and on a target the donor would not approve – including on the donor itself.

Nor is it likely that a working nuclear device could be stolen. "A theft," note Wirz and Egger, "would involve many risks and great efforts in terms of personnel, finances, and organization" while safety and security systems on the weapons "ensure that the successful use of a stolen weapons would be very unlikely" (2005: 502). Of particular concern in this are Russia's supposedly missing suitcase bombs. However, a careful assessment by the Center for Nonproliferation Studies has concluded that it is unlikely that any of these devices have indeed been lost and that, regardless, their effectiveness would be very low or even non-existent because they require continual maintenance (2002: 4, 12). By 2006, even some of the top alarmists on the issue were concluding that "It is probably true that there are no 'loose nukes', transportable nuclear weapons missing from their proper storage locations and available for purchase in some way" (Pluta and Zimmerman 2006: 56).

Moreover, no terrorist group, including al-Qaeda, has shown anything resembling the technical expertise necessary to fabricate or deal with a bomb. And contacts – "academic," it is claimed – between Pakistani scientists and al-Qaeda were abruptly broken off after 9/11 (Albright and Higgins 2003: 54–55; Suskind 2006: 69–70, 122). In testimony before the Senate Select Committee on Intelligence on January 11, 2007, FBI Director Robert Mueller, who had been highly alarmist about the terrorist potential in previous testimony, was stressing that his chief concern within the United States had become homegrown groups, and that, while remaining concerned that things could change in the future, "few if any terrorist groups" were likely to possess the required expertise to produce nuclear weapons – or, for that matter, biological or chemical ones.

If dealing with enemies like that is our generation's (or century's) "central battle," it would seem we are likely to come out quite well.

Embracing the threat

There are, then, several key facts for the American public to consider in evaluating how to respond to the terrorism challenge:

1   There have been no al-Qaeda attacks whatever in the United States since 2001,
2   No true al-Qaeda cell (nor scarcely anybody who might even be deemed to have a "connection" to the diabolical group) has been unearthed in the country,
3   The homegrown "plotters" who have been apprehended, while perhaps potentially somewhat dangerous at least in a few cases, have mostly been flaky or almost absurdly incompetent,
4   The total number of people killed worldwide by al-Qaeda types, maybes, and wannabes outside of war zones since 9/11 stands at some 300 or so a year, and
5   Unless the terrorists are able somehow massively to increase their capacities – something that appears highly unlikely – the likelihood a person living in the United States will perish at the hands of an international terrorist over an 80-year period is about one in 75,000.

However, the public apparently continues to remain unimpressed by this set of inconvenient observations. Polls suggest that people – or at any rate Americans – remain concerned about becoming the victims of terrorism, and the degree of worry doesn't seem to have changed much in the years since the 2001 attacks even though no terrorism whatever has taken place in the country since that year. Only somewhat less than a third profess that they do not worry at all about the chance that they will personally become a victim of terrorism – the correct response, one might imagine, to a one-in-75,000 lifetime threat. Another third worry "not too much," and fully a third worry "somewhat" or "a great deal" about this microscopic possibility.[3]

In some respects, fear of terror may be something like playing the lottery except in reverse. The chances of winning the lottery or of dying from terrorism may be microscopic, but for monumental events which are, or seem, random, one can irrelevantly conclude that one's chances are just as good, or bad, as those of anyone else. Cass Sunstein labels the phenomenon "probability neglect." He argues that "when their emotions are intensely engaged, people's attention is focussed on the bad outcome itself, and they are inattentive to the fact that it is unlikely to occur" (2003: 122).

The public appears to have chosen, then, to wallow in a false sense of insecurity (to apply a phrase suggested by Leif Wenar), and it apparently plans to continue to do so. Accordingly it will likely also presumably continue to demand that its leaders pay due deference to its insecurities and will uncritically approve as huge amounts of money are shelled out in a quixotic and mostly symbolic effort to assuage those insecurities.

Inflating the threat: the terrorism industry

In response to this apparent demand, something that might be called "the terrorism industry" has sprung up. This group consists of politicians, bureaucrats, journalists, and risk entrepreneurs who benefit in one way or another from exacerbating anxieties about terrorism.

There is no reason to suspect that George W. Bush's concern about terrorism is anything but genuine. However, his presidential approval rating did receive the greatest boost for any president in history in September 2001, and it would be politically unnatural for him not to notice. One study documents a consistent positive relationship between government-issued terror warnings and presidential approval (Willer 2004), while another observes Bush's approval ratings to rise when thoughts of death or terrorism become especially salient (Landau *et al.* 2004). The Bush administration also had a terrific political incentive to stoke fear by portentously pointing to bad people out there and citing evidence of terrorist intrigues.

Meanwhile, the Democrats, who have been at a decided political disadvantage on the terrorism issue, do not want to seem to underplay the terrorist threat, and so, like the Republicans, they find it – or believe it – politically expedient to exaggerate and to inflate, desperate not to be thought soft on terrorism. Opportunities for politicians of all stripes are opened up by the popular, sudden, and massive increases in expenditures designed to enhance security against terrorism. Not surprisingly, much of this hasty spending has been rendered inefficient as pork barrel and politics-as-usual formulas have been liberally applied.

Bureaucrats, too, are in on the act, and the interactive, if somewhat paradoxical, process between government and public is crisply described by Ian Lustick: the government "can never make enough progress toward 'protecting America' to reassure Americans against the fears it is helping to stoke" (2006: 97). Threat exaggeration is additionally encouraged, even impelled, because politicians and terrorism bureaucrats also have an incentive to pass along vague and unconfirmed threats to protect themselves from later criticism should another attack take place. There is a technical term for this behavior: CYA. And the result, as Bart Kosko points out, is a situation in which "government plays safe by overestimating the terrorist threat, while the terrorists oblige by overestimating their power" (2004; see also Rosen 2004: 79).

The media also play an important role. Politicians and bureaucrats may feel that, given the public concern on the issue, they will lose support if they appear insensitively to be downplaying the dangers of terrorism. But the media like to tout that they are devoted to presenting fair and balanced coverage of important public issues. As has often been noted, however, the media appear to have a congenital incapacity for dealing with issues of risk and comparative probabilities – except, of course, in the sports and financial sections. I may have missed it, but I have never heard anyone in the media stress that in every year except 2001 only a few hundred people in the entire world outside of war zones have died as a result of international terrorism.

Actually, there are quite a few elemental aspects of the terrorism issue that have been almost entirely ignored in the media. For example, the suggestion that an American's chance of being killed by a terrorist is very, very small. Or that another hijacking attack like the ones on 9/11 is impossible because passengers and crew would forcefully interfere – as was shown on the fourth plane. Or that chemical weapons can't wreak mass destruction. Notions like that may be controversial, but shouldn't they at least be *discussed* in the media? Whether one ends up agreeing or disagreeing, aren't they at least relevant to the public policy debate? A cynical aphorism in the newspaper business holds that "if it bleeds, it leads." There is a obvious, if less pungent, corollary: if it doesn't bleed, it certainly shouldn't lead and, indeed, may well not be fit to print at all.

Risk entrepreneurs form the final layer of the terrorism industry. The monied response to 9/11 has swelled their ranks, and its members would be out of business if terrorism were to be back-burnered. Accordingly, they have every competitive incentive (and they are nothing if not competitive) to conclude it to be their civic duty to keep the pot boiling. As "a rising tide lifts all boats," suggests Lustick, "an intractable fear nourishes all schemes" (2006: 98; see also Furedi 2007). As it turns out, many of your agile risk entrepreneurs just happen to have stuff to sell, such as data-mining software, anti-radiation drugs, detention-center bed space, and cargo inspection systems. There have also been creative efforts by people with political agendas to fold them into the all-consuming war on terror. The gun control lobby has proclaimed that "We have a responsibility to deny weapons to terrorists" while the National Rifle Association explains that people would rather face the terrorist threat "with a firearm than without one" (Lustick 2006: 83–84).

Moreover, notes Jeffry Rosen, dependent as they are on public acceptance for status and recognition, terrorism experts have an "incentive to exaggerate risks and pander to public fears" (2004: 222). Accordingly, like other members of the terrorism industry, they are truly virtuosic at pouring out, and poring over, worst case scenarios – or "worst case fantasies," as Bernard Brodie once labeled them in a different context (Brodie 1978: 68).

What we mostly get from the terrorism industry, then, is fear-mongering, and much of it borders on hysteria. James Carafano and Paul Rosenzweig assert that "because of the terrorists' skillful use of low-tech capabilities, their capacity for harm is essentially limitless," suggesting, apparently, that the bad guys would be *less* dangerous if they could only obtain high-tech weapons (2005: 93). Others, like Indiana senator Richard Lugar, are given to proclaiming that terrorists armed with weapons of mass destruction present an "existential" threat to the United States (Fox News Sunday, June 15, 2003), or even, in columnist Charles Krauthammer's view, to "civilization itself" (2004). Graham Allison, too, thinks that nuclear terrorists could "destroy civilization as we know it" (2004: 191). Not to be outdone, Michael Ignatieff warns that "a group of only a few individuals equipped with lethal technologies" threaten "the ascendancy of the modern state" (2004: 147). A best-selling book of 2004 by Michael Scheuer, formerly of the CIA, repeatedly assures us that our "survival" is at stake and that we are engaged in a "war to the death" (2004: 160, 177, 226, 241, 242, 250, 252, 263). Two years later, although there had been only a few sizeable terrorist attacks outside of war zones around the world and none whatever within the United States, Scheuer remained comfortable in his alarm: "America faces an existential threat," he proclaimed and, moreover, "time is short" (2006). It has become fashionable in some alarmist circles extravagantly to denote the contest against Osama bin Laden and his sympathizers as (depending on how the Cold War is classified) World War III or World War IV.

As the subtext (or sometimes the text) of these hysterical warnings suggests, the "existential" threat comes not from what terrorists would do to us, but what we would do to ourselves in response. It seems, then, that it is not only the most-feared terrorists who are suicidal. However, all societies are "vulnerable" to tiny bands of suicidal fanatics in the sense that it is impossible to prevent every terrorist act. But the United States is hardly "vulnerable" in the sense that it can be toppled by dramatic acts of terrorist destruction, even extreme ones. In fact, as military analyst William Arkin points out forcefully, although terrorists cannot destroy America,

> every time we pretend we are fighting for our survival we not only confer greater power and importance to terrorists than they deserve but we also at the same time act as their main recruiting agent by suggesting that they have the slightest potential for success
>
> (2006; see also Chapman and Harris 2002; Lustick 2006; Furedi 2007)

Ultimately, then, the enemy, in fact, is us. Thus far at least, terrorism is a rather rare and, appropriately considered, not generally a terribly destructive phenomenon. But there is a danger that the terrorism industry's congenital (if self-serving and profitable) hysteria could become at least somewhat self-fulfilling should extensive further terrorism be visited upon the Home of the Brave.

A key element in a policy toward terrorism, therefore, should be to control, to deal with, or at least productively to worry about the fear and overreaction that terrorism so routinely inspires and that generally constitutes its most damaging effect.

The communication of risk, however, is no easy task. In summarizing some of the literature on this issue, risk analyst Paul Slovic points out a number of regularities. People tend greatly to overestimate the chances of dramatic or sensational causes of death. Realistically informing people about risks sometimes only makes them more frightened. Strong beliefs in this area are very difficult to modify. A new sort of calamity tends to be taken as harbinger of future mishaps. A disaster tends to increase fears not only about that kind of danger but of all kinds. People, even professionals, are susceptible to the way risks are expressed – far less likely, for example, to choose radiation therapy if told the chances of death are 32 percent rather than that the chances of survival are 68 percent (1986: 403–415).

In fact, suggests Sunstein, the best response in emotion-laden situations like terrorism may be to "alter the public's focus." That is, "perhaps the most effective way of reducing fear of a low-probability risk is simply to discuss something else and to let time do the rest" (2003: 131). However, for all the gloomy difficulties, risk assessment and communication should at least be part of the policy discussion over terrorism, something that may well prove to be a far smaller danger than is popularly portrayed. By contrast, the constant unnuanced stoking of fear by politicians, bureaucrats, experts, and the media, however well received by the public, is on balance costly, enervating, potentially counterproductive, and unjustified by the facts.

Ultimately, however, the fundamental source of the alarm arises not from the terrorism industry as much as from the public. Edward R. Murrow's comment about McCarthy applies more broadly: "he didn't create this situation of fear, he merely exploited it." Hysteria and alarmism often sell. That is, although there may be truth in the "If it bleeds, it leads" newspaper adage, this comes about not so much (or at any rate not entirely) because journalists are fascinated by blood, but because they suspect, quite possibly correctly, that their readers are. Politicians, bureaucrats, and people with things to sell to the fearful react similarly. Thus, although the terrorism industry may exacerbate the fears, it does not create them, and its activities and cries of alarm are essentially lagging indicators of their existence.

Internalizing the threat

None of this should be taken to suggest that people spend a great deal of time obsessing over terrorism, spooking over it, or even paying all that much attention to it: terrorism has for years now scored rather poorly on polls asking about the country's most important problem. However, people don't constantly think about motherhood either. Nonetheless, they will not look kindly upon a politician or bureaucrat or journalist who is insufficiently sentimental about that venerable institution.

An apt comparison would be with the public's concern about the threat once presented by domestic Communism. Impelled by several spectacular espionage cases and by an apparently risky international environment, fears about the dangers presented by "the enemy within" became fully internalized in the years after World War II. In a famous public opinion study conducted at the height of the McCarthy period in the mid-1950s, sociologist Samuel Stouffer (1955) found that some 43 percent professed to believe that domestic Communists presented a great or very great danger to the United States. At the same time, however, when Stouffer asked more broadly about what their primary worries were, people mainly voiced concerns about personal matters. Unprompted, apprehensions about domestic Communism (or about restrictions on civil liberties) scarcely came up in the survey. There was, Stouffer concluded, no "national anxiety neurosis" over the issue.

That conclusion probably holds for present concerns about domestic terrorism as well. There was a lot of evasive behavior after the 9/11 attacks – indeed, several studies conclude that more than 1000 Americans died between September 11, 2001, and the end of that year because out of fear they avoided airplanes in favor of much more dangerous automobiles (Sivak and Flannagan 2004). However, behavior eventually settled down and people pretty much seem now to carry out their lives without spending a lot of time thinking about the dangers presented by domestic terrorism. There has been no great exodus from Washington or New York, and few people seem even to have gone to the trouble of stocking up on emergency supplies despite the persistent nanny-like urgings of the Department of Homeland Security.

Problems arise, however, not from a national anxiety neurosis, but more from other results of the terrorism concern. One is that when a consensus about a threat becomes really internalized, it becomes politically unwise, even disastrous, to oppose it – or even to seem to oppose it. Another is that the internalized consensus creates a political atmosphere in which government and assorted pork barrelers can expend, or fritter away, considerable public funds and efforts on questionable enterprises as long as they appear somehow to be focused on dealing with the threat. In the present context, the magic phrase, "We don't want to have another 9/11," tends to end the discussion. And the "war" on terror accordingly becomes, in a vivid Washington phrase, "a self-licking ice cream cone."

Once again, the parallel with domestic Communism is instructive. In that atmosphere politicians scurried to support billions upon billions to surveil, to screen, and to spy on an ever expanding array of individuals who had come to seem suspicious for one reason or another. Organizations were infiltrated, phones were tapped (each tap can require the full time services of a dozen agents and support personnel), letters were intercepted, people were followed, loyalty oaths were required, endless leads (almost all to nowhere) were pursued, defense plants were hardened, concentration camps for prospective emergency use were established, and garbage was meticulously sifted in hopes of unearthing scraps of incriminating information.

At the time, critics of this process focused almost entirely on the potential for civil liberties violations. This is a worthy concern, but it is not the only one. As far as I can see, at no point during the Cold War did anyone say in public "many domestic Communists adhere to a foreign ideology that ultimately has as its goal the destruction of capitalism and democracy by violence if necessary; however, they do not present much of a danger, are actually quite a pathetic bunch, and couldn't subvert their way out of a wet paper bag. Why are we expending so much time, effort, and treasure over this issue?" It is astounding to me, however, that plausible, if arguable, point of view seems never to have been publicly expressed by anyone – politician, pundit, professor, editorialist – during the Cold War, although some people may have believed it privately. On Stouffer's survey, only a lonely, and obviously politically insignificant share of the population – two percent – professed to believe that domestic Communists presented no danger at all.

Something similar is now happening in pursuit of the terrible, if vaporous, terrorist enemy within. Redirecting much of their effort from such unglamorous enterprises as dealing with organized crime and white collar embezzlement (which, unlike domestic terrorism, have actually happened since 2001), agencies like the FBI have kept their primary focus on the terrorist threat (Eggen and Solomon 2007). Like their predecessors during the quest to quash domestic Communism, they have dutifully and laboriously assembled masses of intelligence data and have pursued an endless array of leads – by August 2008, the agency was celebrating the receipt of its two millionth terrorism tip from the public. Almost all of this activity has led nowhere, but it will continue because, of course, no one wants to be the one whose neglect somehow led to "another 9/11" – or, as the assistant chief for the FBI's National Threat Center puts it, it's the lead "you don't take seriously that becomes the 9/11" (Leinwand 2008).

Criticisms of the Patriot Act and of the Bush administration's efforts to apprehend prospective terrorists focus almost entirely on civil liberties concerns, worrying that rights for innocent Americans might be trampled in the rush to pursue terrorists. A perfectly valid concern, but from time to time someone might wonder in public a bit about how much money the quest to ferret out terrorists and to protect ourselves is costing, as well as about how limited the results have been.

We can also expect continued efforts to reduce, or to seem to reduce, the country's "vulnerability" despite at least three confounding realities: there exist an essentially infinite number of potential terrorist targets, the probability any one of those targets will be hit by a terrorist is essentially zero, and inventive terrorists, should they ever actually show up, are free to redirect their attention from a target that might enjoy a degree of protection toward one of the many that don't. Nonetheless, hundreds of billions of dollars have been so far spent on this quest and the process seems destined to continue or even accelerate even though, as a senior economist at DHS has put it, "we really don't know a whole lot about the overall costs and benefits of homeland security" (Anderson 2006).

And there is more. The experience with domestic Communism suggests that once a threat becomes really internalized, the concern can linger for decades even if there is no evidence to support such a continued preoccupation. It becomes self-perpetuating.

In the two decades following the Stouffer survey, news about domestic Communism declined until it essentially vanished all together. In the mid-1950s, there were hundreds of articles in the *Readers' Guide to Periodical Literature* listed under the categories, "Communism-US" and "Communist Party-US". In the mid-1970s, in stark contrast, there were scarcely any. This of course reflected the fact that domestic Communism really wasn't doing very much of anything to garner attention. The Cold War continued elsewhere, but there were no dramatic court cases like the one concerning the State Department's felonious document-transmitter, Alger Hiss, and his accuser, Whittaker Chambers, or atomic spy cases like the ones involving Klaus Fuchs and Julius and Ethel Rosenberg, cases that had so mesmerized the public in the late 1940s and early 1950s.

In fact, despite huge anxieties about it at the time, there seem to have been no instances in which domestic Communists engaged in anything that could be considered espionage after the World War II. Moreover, at no time did any domestic Communist ever commit anything that could be considered violence in support of the cause – this, despite deep apprehensions at the time about that form of terrorism then dubbed "sabotage." (All notable terrorist violence within the United States since 2001 has taken place on television – most persistently on Fox's "24" – and the same was true about domestic Communist violence during the Cold War. FBI informant Herbert Philbrick's confessional book of 1952, *I Led Three Lives*, at no point documents a single instance of Communist violence or planned violence, but violence became a central focus when his story was transmuted into a popular television series.)

However, even though the domestic Communist "menace" had pretty much settled into well deserved oblivion by the mid-1970s, surveys repeating the Stouffer questions at the time found that fully 30 percent of the public *still* considered internal Communists to present a great or very great danger to the country, while those who found them to be of no danger had inched up only to around 10 percent (Mueller 1998).

Some have argued that unjustified fears (or "hysteria") about the Communist enemy within was created by the media, and some now say the same thing about apprehensions about the terrorist enemy within. But the fear of domestic Communism persisted long after the press had become thoroughly bored with the issue. That is, fears often have an independent source, and then take on a life of their own.

Something similar may have happened with the "war" on drugs. Over the last few decades the drug evil has so impressed itself on the American public psyche that the issue can scarcely be brought up for public discussion. At one time drugs were a big concern with the public – Ronald Reagan latched on to it, and then George H. W. Bush pushed it further, particularly after it soared into public anxiety in the first year of his presidency. Somewhere along the line it became a politically untouchable issue, and, certainly, neither Bill Clinton nor Bush the younger were tempted to tinker with, much less reexamine, the policy. In the meantime, it has picked up its own political constituency – in California the powerful prison guard lobby takes the lead.

One could, of course, suggest that the long and costly drug "war" has pretty much been a failure, particularly because drug use has scarcely plummeted and because strenuous efforts to interdict supplies have not been able notably to inflate the street price. But that discussion, considered by many to be political poison, never really happens, and the drug war and its attendant expenditures continue to ramble inexorably and consensually onward. This, despite the fact that it is severely hampering efforts to rebuild war torn Afghanistan by seeking to cut off that struggling country's only significant source of earned revenue.

Perspectives on terror, now thoroughly internalized, seem likely to take on a similarly unexamined, self-perpetuating trajectory. Moreover, since terrorism will always be with us – like drugs, but unlike threats which were capable of dying out entirely such as Communism and the threat supposedly presented by domestic Japanese during World War II – we could be in for a long siege.

This is suggested as well by the fact that routine fears and knee-jerk concerns continue to hold at impressive levels despite a perceptible decline in the ferocity of official warnings. Interested public officials have sometimes attempted to jigger things with various alarms and excursions, raising terror alerts from time to time, warning against "complacency," assuring all and sundry that the "war" must needs continue (and their budgets increase) because . . . well, because we have to do everything possible to prevent another 9/11.

However, we have been subjected to only a few such warnings lately. On April 29, 2007, former CIA Director George Tenet did reveal on CBS' "60 Minutes" that his "operational intuition" was telling him that al-Qaeda had infiltrated a second or third wave into the United States, though he added with uncharacteristic modesty, "Can I prove it to you? No." And DHS Secretary Michael Chertoff informed us a few months later that his gut was telling him there'd be an attack during the summer. (If it is illegal to cry "fire" in a crowded theater, one might be set to wondering where it should also be illegal for responsible public officials to stoke fear, with inevitable damaging consequences to health and policy, when their statements, by the officials' own admission, are based on nothing.)

But spooky misgivings inspired by guts and intuitions are nothing compared to the colorful and unqualified fire and brimstone warnings issued by public officials in the past. On December 21, 2003, Chertoff's predecessor at DHS, Tom Ridge, divined that "extremists abroad are anticipating near-term attacks that they believe will either rival, or exceed" those of 2001. And on May 25, 2004, Attorney General John Ashcroft, with FBI Director Robert Mueller at his side, announced that "credible intelligence from multiple sources indicates that al-Qaeda plans to attempt an attack on the United States in the next few months," that its "specific intention" was to hit us "hard," and that the "arrangements" for that attack were already 90 percent complete. (Oddly enough, Ashcroft fails to mention this memorable headline-grabbing episode in *Never Again*, his 2006 memoir of the period.)

Director Mueller himself has mellowed quite a bit over time. On February 11, 2003, he assured a Senate committee that, although his agency had yet actually to identify an al-Qaeda cell in the US, such unidentified (or imagined) entities nonetheless presented "the greatest threat," had "developed a support infrastructure" in the country, and had achieved "the ability and the intent to inflict significant casualties in the US with little warning." At the time, intelligence reports were asserting – that is, guessing – that the number of trained al-Qaeda operatives in the

United States was between 2,000 and 5,000 (Gertz 2002). On February 16, 2005, at a time when the FBI admitted it *still* had been unable to unearth a single true al-Qaeda cell, Mueller continued his dire I-think-therefore-they-are projections: "I remain very concerned about what we are not seeing," he ominously ruminated. However in testimony on January 11, 2007, Mueller had become notably reticent, and his chief rallying cry had been reduced to a comparatively bland "We believe al-Qaeda is still seeking to infiltrate operatives into the U.S. from overseas" (Mueller, R. S., 2007).

Impressively, even a specific (and, it appears, unique) effort on the part of an official to dampen terrorism fears has had no noticeable impact. In 2007, New York Mayor Michael Bloomberg actually went so far as to urge people to "get a life," pointing out that "you have a much greater danger of being hit by lightning than being struck by a terrorist."

It is possible, however, that Bloomberg's glancing brush with reality (which, most interestingly, does not seem to have hurt him politically) was undercut by the fact that his city expends huge resources chasing after terrorists while routinely engaging in some of the most pointless security theater on the planet. For example, New York often extracts police officers from their duties to have them idle around at a sampling of the city's thousands of subway entrances watching vacantly as millions of people wearing backpacks or carrying parcels descend into the system throughout the city. It is also fond of trumpeting the fact that thousands of people each year call the city's police counterterrorism hot line – 8,999 in 2006, it turns out, and more than 13,473 in 2007 – while managing to neglect to mention that not one of these calls has yet led to a terrorism arrest (Neuman 2008).

H. L. Mencken once declared "the whole aim of practical politics" to be "to keep the populace alarmed (and hence clamorous to be led to safety) by menacing it with an endless series of hobgoblins, all of them imaginary" (1949: 29). There is nothing imaginary about al-Qaeda, of course, though some of the proclaimed sightings of the group in the United States by officials do have an Elvis-like quality to them. However, the public seems to have internalized the terrorism concern and, accordingly, has been able to retain much of its sense of alarm about internal attacks even when the al-Qaeda hobgoblin doesn't actually carry any out and even when politicians, public officials, and other members of the terrorism industry, however belatedly, temper their scary – and at times irresponsible – bellowings.

Notes

1 This chapter updates and expands on themes discussed in John E. Mueller (2006).
2 This notion has been around for a long time. As early as 2002, CIA Director George Tenet was assuring a joint Congressional committee without even a wisp of equivocation that al-Qaeda was "reconstituted," planning in "multiple theaters of operation," and "coming after us" (New York Times, October 18, 2000, A12)
3 Online. Available: <http://www.pollingreport.com/terror.htm> (Accessed August 31, 2008). These and other poll data come from the information arrayed under "terrorism" at.pollingreport.com.

References

Abrahms, M. (2006) "Why terrorism does not work," *International Security*, 31: 42–78.
Albright, D. and Higgins, H. (2003) "A bomb for the Ummah," *Bulletin of the Atomic Scientists*, April: 49–55.
Allison, G. (2004) *Nuclear Terrorism: The Ultimate Preventable Catastrophe*, New York: Times Books.
Anderson, T. (2006) "Terror may be at bay at port; Shipping hubs too vulnerable," *The Daily News of Los Angeles,* 18 May: N1.
Arkin, W. M. (2006) *Goodbye War on Terrorism, Hello Long War*. Online. Available: <http://blogs.washingtonpost.com/earlywarning> (Accessed April 26, 2006).
Bergen, P. (2007) "Where you Bin? The return of Al Qaeda," *New Republic,* 29 January: 16–19.
Brodie, B. (1978) "The Development of Nuclear Strategy," *International Security*, 2: 65–83.
Bunn, M. (2007) *Securing the Bomb 2007*, Cambridge, MA: Project on Managing the Atom, Belfer Center for Science and International Affairs, John F. Kennedy School of Government, Harvard University.
Carafano, J. and Rosenzweig, P. (2005) *Winning the Long War: Lessons from the Cold War for Defeating Terrorism and Preserving Freedom*, Washington, DC: Heritage Books.
Center for Nonproliferation Studies. (2002) *"Suitcase Nukes": A Reassessment.* Monterey, CA: Monterey Institute of International Studies. Online. Available: <http://cns.miis.edu/pubs/week/020923.htm> (Accessed 22 September 2002).
Chapman, C. R. and Harris, A. W. (2002) "A skeptical look at September 11th: How we can defeat terrorism by reacting to it more rationally," *Skeptical Inquirer*, September/October: 29–34.
Eggen, D. and Solomon, J. (2007) "Justice dept.'s focus has shifted: Terror, immigration are current priorities," *Washington Post*, 17 October: A1.
Ellig, J., Guiora, A. and McKenzie, K. (2006) *A Framework for Evaluating Counterterrorism Regulations,* Washington, DC: Mercatus Center, George Mason University.
Fox News Sunday (2003) "Interview with Richard Lugar," Sunday, June 15. Online. Available: <http://www.lexis-nexis.com> Accessed August 31, 2008.
Furedi, F. (2007) *Invitation to Terror: The Expanding Empire of the Unknown,* London: Continuum.
Gerges, F. A. (2005) *The Far Enemy: Why Jihad Went Global*, New York: Cambridge University Press.
Gertz, B. (2002) "5,000 in U.S. suspected of ties to al Qaeda; Groups nationwide under surveillance," *Washington Times*, 11 July: A1.
Gilmore Commission (Advisory Panel to Assess Domestic Response Capabilities for Terrorism Involving Weapons of Mass Destruction). (1999) *First Annual Report: Assessing the Threat.* Online. Available: <http://www.rand.org/nsrd/terrpanel> (Accessed 15 December 1999).
Harris, S. and Taylor, S., Jr. (2008) "Homeland security chief looks back, and forward," Online. Available: <http://www.govexec.com/story_page_pf.cfm?articleid=39539> (Accessed 17 March 2008).
Hoffman, B. (2008) "The myth of grass-roots terrorism: Why Osama bin Laden still matters," *Foreign Affairs,* May/June.
Ignatieff, M. (2004) *The Lesser Evil: Political Ethics in an Age of Terror*, Princeton, NJ: Princeton University Press.

Ignatius, D. (2008) "The fading jihadists," *Washington Post*, 28 February: A17.

Isikoff, M. and Hosenball, M. (2007) "The flip side of the NIE," Online. Available: <http://www.newsweek.com/id/32962> (Accessed 15 August 2007)

Johnson, R. H. (1994) *Improbable Dangers: U.S. Conceptions of Threat in the Cold War and After*, New York: St. Martin's.

Kosko, B. (2004) "Terror threat may be mostly a big bluff," *Los Angeles Times*, 13 September: B11.

Krauthammer, C. (2004) "Blixful amnesia," *Washington Post*, 9 July: A19.

Landau, M. J., Solomon, S., Greenberg, J., Cohen, F., Pyszczynski, T., Arndt, J., Miller, C. H., Ogilvie, D. M. and Cook, A. (2004) "Deliver us from evil: The effects of mortality salience and reminders of 9/11 on support for president George W. Bush," *Personality and Social Psychology Bulletin*, 30: 1136–1150.

Lawson, G. (2008) "The fear factory," *Rolling Stone*, February.

Leinwand, D. (2008) "Psst – leads from public to FBI rise," *USA Today*, 15 February: 4A.

Levi, M. (2007) *On Nuclear Terrorism*, Cambridge, MA: Harvard University Press.

Lustick, I. S. (2006) *Trapped in the War on Terror*, Philadelphia, PA: University of Pennsylvania Press.

Mack, A. (2008) *Human Security Brief 2007*, Vancouver, BC: Human Security Report Project, Simon Fraser University.

Mazzetti, M. and Rohde, D. (2008) "Amid U.S. policy disputes, Qaeda grows in Pakistan," *New York Times*, 30 June: A1.

Mencken, H. L. (1949) *A Mencken Chrestomathy*, New York: Knopf.

Mueller, J. (1988, Spring) "Trends in political tolerance," *Public Opinion Quarterly*, 52: 1–25.

—— (2006) *Overblown: How Politicians and the Terrorism Industry Inflate National Security Threats, and Why We Believe Them*, New York: Free Press.

Mueller, R. S. (2007) "Statement before the Senate Select Committee on Intelligence," January 11. Online. Available: <http://www.fbi.gov/congress/congress07/mueller011107.htm> Accessed 31 August 2008.

Neuman, W. (2007) "In Response to M.T.A.'s 'Say Something' Ads, a Glimpse of Modern Fears," *New York Times*, B1.

Pluta, A. M. and Zimmerman, P. D. (2006) "Nuclear terrorism: A disheartening dissent," *Survival*, 48: 55–70.

Rosen, J. (2004) *The Naked Crowd*, New York: Random House.

Sageman, M. (2007) *Leaderless Jihad*, Philadelphia: University of Pennsylvania Press.

Scheuer, M. (2004) *Imperial Hubris: Why the West Is Losing the War on Terror*, Dulles, VA: Brassey's.

—— (2006) "Courting catastrophe: America five years after 9/11," *National Interest*, September/October: 20–23.

Schilling, W. R. (1965) "Surprise attack, death, and war," *Journal of Conflict Resolution*, 9: 385–390.

Seitz, R. (2004) "Weaker than we think," *American Conservative*, 6 December.

Sivak, M. and Flannagan, M. J. (2004) "Consequences for road traffic fatalities of the reduction in flying following September 11, 2001," *Transportation Research Part F*, 301–305.

Slovic, P. (1986) "Informing and educating the public about risk," *Risk Analysis*, 6: 403–415.

Stouffer, S. A. (1955) *Communism, Conformity, and Civil Liberties*, Garden City, NY: Doubleday.

Sunstein, C. R. (2003) "Terrorism and probability neglect," *Journal of Risk and Uncertainty*, 26: 121–136.

Suskind, R. (2006) *The One Percent Doctrine: Deep Inside America's Pursuit of Its Enemies Since 9/11*, New York: Simon and Schuster.

Willer, R. (2004) "The effects of government-issued terror warnings on presidential approval," *Current Research in Social Psychology*, 30 September: 10.

Wirz, C. and Egger, E. (2005) "Use of nuclear and radiological weapons by terrorists?" *International Review of the Red Cross*, 87: 497–510. Online. Available: <http://www.icrc.org/Web/eng/siteeng0.nsf/htmlall/review-859-p497/$File/irrc_859_Egger_Wirz.pdf> (Accessed 30 September 2005).

Wright, L. (2008) "The rebellion within," *New Yorker*, 2 June.

12 Perception and power in counterterrorism

Assessing the American response to Al Qaeda before September 11

Benjamin H. Friedman

This chapter explains the United States reaction to the Al Qaeda threat from the beginning of the Clinton administration until the September 11 attacks. It argues that Americans, especially the intelligence community and top officials in the Clinton administration, perceived the threat accurately – or even overestimated it. While the policies employed to combat Al Qaeda before September 11 appear lacking in hindsight, the failure cannot be attributed to misperception. This conclusion flies in the face of much political rhetoric and, more importantly for our purposes, much political science, which sees perception of danger as the chief cause of government responses to it.

This chapter argues instead that the U.S. government's failure in countering Al Qaeda, even during the Bush administration, resulted not from misperception but from the combination of political circumstance, the challenge of destroying a terrorist organization located in foreign country, and the difficulty of re-orienting national security institutions to meet new threats. Defense organizations develop interests in responding to threats like those that they were created to combat. The distribution of power in American government makes it hard for Presidents or anyone else to reorganize these institutions either by changing the purpose of one or shifting the balance of power among them. Absent a sense of crisis that excites the public, security policies continue much as they have, even when the circumstances that justified them in the first place end.

The main purpose of the chapter is to explain the case. The other purpose is to evaluate theories concerning what causes states to react to threats. The chapter first discusses these theories. Second, it gives an overview of the U.S. perception and response to the rise of the Al Qaeda threat in the 1990s, finding that perception was accurate but the policy response failed. Third, the chapter explains this outcome.

Theories of threat perception

This study is part of a larger study on what makes the United States react to security dangers. Although many theories offer explanations for what causes reaction, scholars agree that explanation is necessary – states do not calculate the odds of danger well. Even structural realists agree that states regularly do not respond to incentives the international system provides, often failing to balance the power of rising powers or overreacting and causing needless alarm. Scholars who study risk say that states are inconsistent in their approach to regulating harms. States guard zealously against certain risks and accept others that are far more dangerous.[1] Americans are less precautionary than Europeans about global warming and genetically modified foods, but are more cautious about secondhand smoke and nuclear proliferation (Sunstein 2002). The explanation for this variation is elusive, but it is evidently not the magnitude of harms themselves.

Theories about the origins of these national preferences for defenses fit in two categories. They can be explanations for what we fear and therefore what we seek protection from. Or they can explain policy outcomes without an intermediate perceptual step. These latter theories see defense policy as a product of elites' interests and values. Perception is secondary. These theories can incorporate public threat perception as an influence on elites however – a source of political energy that must be heeded or manipulated.

By demonstrating the accuracy of leaders' perception, this study dismisses the relevance of theories arguing that misperception causes policy failure. Perceptual theories sometimes predict accurate perception, however. So the finding of no misperception simply shows that the perceptual theories are not the explanation for policy failure, not that the theories are wrong.

An overview of some perceptual explanations for why states react to danger is useful so that the reader knows what is being dismissed. Psychological literature argues that risks' characteristics drive our estimation of them. Terrorism has many attributes that cause humans to fear it more than threats that cause more death (Friedman 2006). It creates ready mental images, employs technology, is uncontrollable, and was largely new to Americans in the late 1990s and early 2000s. (Slovic 1987; Sunstein 2003). Although risk perception in this analysis is sensitive to events and their portrayal in the media, this approach suggests that American leaders should always have overestimated the terrorist threat.

Ideology offers another set of explanations for what dangers states perceive. Ideological theories of risk perception say that social or cultural groups guide members' threat perception. They teach their members to fear what threatens the values that the group is organized around. Risks are social glue (Douglas and Wildavsky 1992). Threat perception in this view varies as social groups change, not as threats change. Members of groups adopt collective views about what to fear because they are motivated by social values and have limited time to evaluate threats themselves. Ideologies are cost effective risk selectors for members, including politicians.

Ideological theories of threat perception say that people's preference for protection against such risks is not a result of estimates of danger but of values. They misperceive the odds of threats because they care about them, not the reverse. Political fights about policy concerning risk, whether a health hazard or a state's military capability, are like theater (Thrall 2007). The disagreement is motivated by values, by disagreement about what government ought to do, but conducted in the language of science, the likely magnitude of harm.

The trouble with these theories is the complexity of social life. The United States has lots of groups. How do their various risk portfolios conglomerate? One way to deal with this problem is to look just at the two most powerful groups in the country: parties and the state itself. Each has an ideology that should lead to a focus on certain dangers.

Parties are conglomerations of groups with unique agendas concerning risk. They change agendas when dominant entities in the party change. Republicans tend to fear threats to American power, social order and market exchange. Thus, they highlight national security dangers, crime and economic decline. Democrats value the environment and economic equality and highlight threats to them. In this view, terrorism, as a national security threat, tends to be a Republican concern. However, because the party generally celebrates American military power, it may be less focused on terrorism than state threats and care about terrorism only as an offshoot of states.

The unifying ideology of the United States is liberalism. As Louis Hart observes, the purity of this ideology in the United States creates a paradoxical illiberal tendency to fear both internal groups who subscribe to other ideologies and illiberal states abroad (Hart 1955). Leaders, like the public, use ideology as shorthand for danger (Desch 2007). Thus, they fear terrorism insofar as it is seen as linked to threats to liberal values.

Organizational theory offers another explanation for misperception. Here, national views of security threats are skewed because countries see threats through the lens of the public organizations with an interest in exaggerating dangers that they were created to fight (Friedman and Sapolsky 2006). Organizations, or sub-organizations within them, are designed for a particular purpose. They develop methods of fulfilling their purpose that provide consistent outside support from funders in Congress and the executive branch and a clear guide to employees (Selznick 1957; Wilson 1989). That purpose gives them a preference for responding to dangers that create demand for their services.

Large organizations often combine various functions, creating a division of labor and hierarchy, with those that execute the organization's main task on top. (The dominance of fighter pilots in the Air Force is an example). Changes in purpose – innovation – would elevate new parts of the organization, changing its power structure (Wilson 1971). Therefore, the leaders often avoid innovation and responding to danger that requires organizational change. Organizations do not promote all threats, but those that fit their purpose; those that do not require innovation.

Powerful organizations like the military services use funded studies performed by nominally independent analysts, press leaks, strategy documents and other means to educate the public and supporters about preferred threats. Their views gain support from entities that share their interest – like military contractors and lawmakers whose districts have military facilities or a concentration of jobs that the organizations ultimately fund. This, the famous military-industrial complex, is not a conspiracy but a set of allied interests.

Truth about danger falls victim to a collective action problem. We all have a slight interest in the truth, but debate is dominated by entities with a concentrated interest in misrepresentation (Synder 1991; Van Evera 2003). The nature of national security information heightens the effect of this imbalance of interests. The information is difficult to collect, so it tends to be centralized and controlled by those inclined to hype it. It is often complex, requiring interpretation by experts with incentives to give worst case accounts. White House officials do have more time to consider threat reporting should they choose to, and they are more likely to understand the biases of the agencies providing information. But they too have limited time and rely on military organizations and intelligence organizations for their threat information.

Partially independent intelligence organizations like the Central Intelligence Organization should provide more accurate information than the military services and their intelligence organizations. The CIA's organizational interest lies less in promoting any particular threat than in a reputation for prescience (Kent 1994). But because the political punishment for underestimating danger is worse than the punishment for overstating, intelligence agencies tend towards worst case accounts.

This theoretical approach says that states will struggle to see new threats. Because states look through eyes fixed on past threats, they miss new ones. State fears are path dependent; circumstances at critical past junctures where organizations emerged produce lingering visions of danger (Pierson 2000). However, at times, military organizations may be in entrepreneurial mode, searching for justifications for their budgets. They may then tie emerging threats to their purposes to gain support, allowing these dangers to be perceived or overestimated.

Terrorism is arguably a threat that security organizations lack incentive to inflate. This theory predicts that the country should ignore it. But if it can be linked to threats that organizations looking for justification combat, they might exaggerate its danger.

Perceptual explanations for what dangers people react to can be reconceptualized as explanations only for the public's perception of danger and demand for defense. Here, these demands constrain leaders' options in making defense policy, but do not determine their perceptions of danger. Elites with more time to consider dangers might avoid psychological biases that skew judgment. They may echo the fears of their party members because that gets them elected, not because they share them. Liberalism likewise can be seen as motivating public fears, where other factors drive elite concern. Geopolitics may drive policy preferences that leaders sell with talk about liberalism (Mearsheimer 2001).

Likewise, a second cut on organizational theory says that organizational interests constrain leaders but do not guide their view of danger. This is the theory that explains U.S. policy failure in this case. Even in U.S. defense policy, where the president is dominant, power is distributed among the military services, congressional committees and White House and Pentagon officials. Because they share objectives in providing security and because they repeatedly bargain, these players seek compromise. The easiest way to achieve compromise on policy, the path of least resistance, is to recreate the prior bargain. The best guide for this year's budget is last year's (Schilling 1962). This need for compromise heightens the status quo bias created by organizational interests.

This does not mean that states cannot respond to threats that do not fit established interests. New organizations can be built. Old ones slowly change their stripes. But without a clear failure – rare without war – states are slow to respond.

One way to overcome this status quo bias is alarming the public with a crisis or the perception of it (Schilling 1962). The public is a source of potential energy that can disturb the incentive structures of the actors, changing hierarchies within organizations and the balance of power among them – changing foreign policy fast. Governing this way is what Theodore Lowi called oversell, the exaggeration of danger to overcome the stasis of the political system produced by its decentralization (Lowi 1979). E. E. Schattsneider compares politics to a street fight observed by a crowd, where a loser is well served to try to involve the audience, knowing it will change the dynamics of the fight (1960). Oversell broadens the audience or the relevant players in a political competition. It is a strategy of policy innovation.

According to this theory, the president may or may not perceive the terrorist threat, but short of a sense of public alarm, he will struggle to change policies to respond to it. He might employ terrorist attacks or their potential to excite the public to push policy changes impossible under normal conditions. But other factors – the impact of the event itself, the way the threat impacts human psychology, whether it impacts on the parties' ideologies or seems to threaten liberalism – contribute to his success.

U.S. perceptions of threat in the 1990s

Claims that the U.S. government underestimated the terrorist threat prior to September 11 are common in today's politics. But scholarly sources have not considered the claim, so far as I know, except to show that officials tended to overstate terrorist capability to kill Americans with chemical, biological and nuclear weapons in this period (Leitenberg 2005; Mueller 2006). Clinton administration counterterrorism officials have authored accounts casting themselves as Churchillian voices of alarm unheeded by the rest of the country (Benjamin and Simon 2003; Clark 2004). The leading example of the claim that September 11 attacks resulted from a government failure to perceive the threat is the *9/11 Commission Report*. It said that a "failure of imagination" allowed the attack to occur and writes that the "road to 9–11 again illustrates how the large, unwieldy U.S. government tended to underestimate a threat that grew ever greater" (National Commission 2004: 348).

This section disputes this view. It argues that the American government perceived the Al Qaeda threat accurately in the 1990s, although officials overstated its ability to use unconventional weapons. It argues that the government responded to the danger but still failed to destroy it. The reaction was maybe slow and insufficient, but the country was hardly asleep.

A few facts at the outset demonstrate that the U.S. government was aware and responsive to Al Qaeda in the 1990s. Al Qaeda declared war on Americans starting in the mid-1990s but had killed fewer than 50 Americans prior to September 11 (National Commission 2004: 340). Al Qaeda itself did not directly attack

Americans until 1998. President Clinton grew concerned about terrorism early in his presidency and proposed a variety of reforms to deal with it starting in the mid-1990s. He mentioned terrorism in every State of the Union Address starting in 1994, and nearly all his foreign policy addresses starting in 1995. He frequently warned of the danger of terrorists using weapons of mass destruction (Rovner 2005: 1, Benjamin and Simon 2003: 364). After his reelection, Clinton listed terrorism first among several security challenges facing the country (National Commission 2004: 101).

U.S. homeland security spending grew from around $9 billion in fiscal year 1995 to about $17 billion in FY 2001 (de Rugy 2005: 12). Counterterrorism spending rose from $5.7 billion in FY 1996 (the first year the Office of Management and Budget cared enough to count relevant activities across the government) to $11.3 billion in FY 2001 (Benjamin and Simon 2003: 248). This is pocket change compared to defense spending, – well over $300 billion at the time – but as a percentage, the growth outpaced that of the overall defense budget, which began to rise in FY 1998 after its post-Cold War decline.

American intelligence and FBI officials helped arrest Al Qaeda associates around the world in the decade prior to September 11 – disrupting various plots. The State Department and immigration officials used terrorist watch-lists by the mid-1990s (National Commission 2004: 76, 80). U.S. pressure on Sudan to stop hosting Osama Bin Laden contributed to its decision to push him out in 1996. The CIA employed Afghan proxies to try to capture or kill Bin Laden in Afghanistan starting in 1996, the year he moved there. The U.S. responded to the embassy bombings of 1998 with cruise missile assaults on Al Qaeda's Afghan terrorist camps and kept submarines off the coast of Pakistan between 1998 and 2000 to do so again. After 1998, the CIA funded teams of Uzbeks and Pakistanis meant to pursue Al Qaeda leaders in Afghanistan. It gave some aid to and shared intelligence with the Northern Alliance fighting the Taliban starting in 1997 in the hope that it could locate or kill Bin Laden. U.S. diplomats told the Taliban repeatedly to expel Al Qaeda and warned the Taliban that they were responsible for what their guests did. Warnings that terrorist attacks were coming were plentiful in the spring and summer of 2001. Just before September 11, the Bush administration approved a set of more aggressive policies to pursue Al Qaeda in Afghanistan.

Before the embassy bombings

Al Qaeda was never the global conspiratorial network of popular lore (Burke 2003). It began at the end of the Soviet war in Afghanistan in the late 1980s as a group of fighters that coalesced around the cleric Abdul Azzam and Bin Laden, a wealthy Saudi who had become a supporter of violent Sunni extremists – referred to here as jihadists (National Commission 2004: 55–56). The core group, several hundred at most, probably far less, were just a faction among the Islamic radicals who had come to Afghanistan from Arab states. Bin Laden returned to Saudi Arabia in 1990 but was known to fund radicals in Afghanistan from afar (Coll 2004: 221–230). After a conflict with Saudi rulers over the Gulf War, Bin Laden moved to Sudan in 1992, bringing much of his cohort there. He set up a council that aimed, with limited success, to coordinate with other jihadist groups. But these groups remained separate from Al Qaeda (National Commission 2004: 59–60). By 1994, the CIA's Sudan station noted in cables that Bin Laden had assembled a small private army of radicals from various Middle-Eastern states in Sudanese camps (Coll 2004: 271–272).

State Department cables and CIA reports in late 1980s and early 1990s raised concerns about the Arab fighters in Afghanistan, noting their potential to make trouble in their home countries (Coll 2004: 201, 227–228, 231, 239). These concerns began to get more attention from CIA analytical bureaucracy by 1992, although there was little policy response. Bin Laden's name emerged in this time in U.S. intelligence reports and briefings as a terrorist financier, which at the time was only a slight understatement, and his network was targeted for intelligence collection in 1993 (Coll 2004: 255–56).

Two attacks in the United States in the early 1990s were linked to the emerging Al Qaeda network. El Sayyid Nosair, who assassinated Meir Kahane in 1990 in New York City, had contact with several future Al Qaeda members and with an Al Qaeda associate, the Blind Sheikh, Omar Ahmad Abdel Rahman, and some of his followers in Brooklyn. The FBI found Al Qaeda promotional videotapes and documents in Nosair's home (Benjamin and Simon 2003: 4–6, 235–236). It took the agency two years to translate the documents and several more to share them with the CIA. The FBI also learned that Bin Laden had contributed to the cost of Nosair's legal defense (Coll 2004: 255).

The World Trade Center bombing in February 1993 was organized by Ramzi Yousef, the nephew of Khalid Sheikh Mohammed, who would later join Al Qaeda and organize the September 11 attacks. After fleeing the United States, Yousef lived in a Bin Laden-funded guest house in Pakistan (Coll 2004: 274). A man who was stopped entering the country with Yousef, carried a bomb-making manual with Arabic for "Al Qaeda" on the cover (Benjamin and Simon 2003: 235). Other plotters frequented the Al Qaeda-funded Al Kifah Center in Brooklyn (Clarke 2004: 79). The investigations led to a circle of radicals around the Blink Sheikh planning to bomb New York City landmarks (National Commission 2004: 72). The plotters had personal connections to several Al Qaeda members (Benjamin and Simon 2003: 234–236).

In the wake of heightened concern about terrorism in the mid-1990s, the Clinton administration submitted counterterrorism legislation to Congress. The legislation, which President Clinton promoted in his 1995 State of the Union speech, established a special deportation mechanism for suspected terrorists, expanded federal jurisdiction to prosecute terrorism and further criminalized fundraising for terrorist organizations. After the Oklahoma City bombing, the administration added to the bill. They attempted to enhance wiretap surveillance authority for the FBI, allow law enforcement agencies to gather business records in terrorism cases using national security letters, force chemical makers to put traceable materials in products used for explosives, and give a spending boost to the CIA and FBI's counterterrorism efforts. Congressional Republicans blocked parts of the legislation –

wiretapping, national security letters and explosive tracing – on civil liberties grounds, but much of it passed in compromise form in 1996 (Doyle 1996; National Commission 2004: 100; Clarke 2004: 99).

In the spring of 1995, the administration reorganized counterterrorism policy. The reform, accomplished by an executive order – Presidential Decision Directive 39 (PDD 39) – created a new annual counterterrorism budget review. It gave the FBI lead responsibility among U.S. government agencies in investigating terror attacks where Americans were victims, ordered the Health and Human Services and Defense departments to prepare for large-scale terrorist attacks, instructed the CIA to undertake covert action and intelligence action against foreign terrorists, and said the government had no higher priority than preventing terrorists from getting "weapons of mass destruction" (Benjamin and Simon 2003: 229–231; Clarke 2004: 90–92).

The Directive marked the beginning of a trend in increased spending on counterterrorism and WMD attack preparedness (Clarke 2004: 158; National Commission 2004: 97). In January 1996, after White House prodding, the CIA established a virtual station (meaning that unlike most CIA stations it would be located in the United States) to gather intelligence about Bin Laden. By mid-year, following instructions from Richard Clarke, the lead counter-terror official in the NSC, the station was looking at ways to attack Bin Laden's financial support and facilities (Benjamin and Simon 2003: 243; Coll 2004: 320, 376).

In mid-1996, Bin Laden relocated to eastern Afghanistan. Later that year, Bin Laden issued his first fatwa against the United States, a 19 page list of examples of the supposed American assault on Islam centering on the presence of U.S. troops in Saudi Arabia. The fatwa calls vaguely for attacks on Americans (Benjamin and Simon 2003: 140–143). Al Qaeda meanwhile continued to provide money and paramilitary training to various people who sought support for plots, even as its core group remained in the low hundreds (Burke 2003: 13). In late 1996, a former Al Qaeda member, who had fled over a money dispute, told the CIA that Bin Laden was planning attacks on the United States (Coll 2004: 336). He claimed involvement in an Al Qaeda effort to obtain uranium for a nuclear weapon (Benjamin and Simon 2003: 128–129). In early 1997, Bin Laden told interviewers from CNN and ABC that he was making jihad against the United States. (Benjamin and Simon 2003: 147) In February 1998, Bin Laden issued another fatwa reciting America's sins against Islam. It said that attacking Americans was a religious duty for Muslims. Signing on were various jihadist leaders, including Ayman al-Zawihiri – leader of the terrorist faction Egyptian Islamic Jihad, whose remaining members had been driven out of Egypt (Benjamin and Simon 2003: 148–150).

This fatwa generated a CIA memo noting the threat, a worldwide State Department travel warning and heightened Americans pressure on the Taliban and Pakistan to do something about Bin Laden. Bin Laden's sanctuary became a talking point in the routine demarches the department issued to the Taliban (Coll 2004: 328–330). The U.S. Ambassador to the United Nations, Bill Richardson, discussed Bin Laden for 45 minutes with the Taliban on a visit to Afghanistan in early 1998

(Coll 2004: 384–387). State pressed the Pakistanis and Saudis, who had good relations with the Taliban, for help. Prince Turki, the Saudi intelligence chief, visited Afghanistan to press for Bin Laden's expulsion in June. The Taliban leader, Mullah Omar, expressed willingness to help, proposing a religious council to justify Bin Laden's expulsion. (National Commission 2004: 115, Coll 2004: 400–402). A U.S. Attorney in New York indicted Bin Laden in June to make it easier for U.S. authorities to capture him (Clarke 2004: 154).

By spring 1997, the CIA had a deal with Ahmed Shah Massoud, the leader of Northern Alliance, to provide cash and communications gear that would allow the Alliance to send intelligence about Bin Laden's movement's to Langley (Coll 2004: 460). In late 1997, the CIA began developing a plan for the Afghan team to attacks Tarnak Farms, a compound where Bin Laden often stayed, and capture him there. The plan was cancelled due to concerns at the White House and top levels of CIA about its feasibility, risk of collateral damage, and whether it was an assassination plan (National Commission 2004: 113–114; Coll 2004: 394–396). After the cancellation, White House counterterrorism director Clarke pressed the Pentagon, via the Chairman of the Joint Chiefs of Staff, Hugh Shelton, to produce contingency plans for striking Al Qaeda's infrastructure. Central Command, which had responsibility for the region, produced a plan to strike eight camps in Afghanistan with cruise missiles fired by attack submarines (National Commission 2004: 116).

In June 1998, the White House issued three more counterterrorism related policy directives – PDD 62, 63 and 67. PDD 67 was a government continuity plan for an incapacitating attack. PDD 63 set out a plan to heighten protection of computer systems used for critical infrastructure. PDD 62 established lead agencies for 10 counterterrorism activities and four interagency committees to oversee them, with Clarke managing the committees. It allowed him to sit on the Cabinet-level Principles Committee, and gave him a limited role in counterterrorism budget creation (Clarke 2004: 168–171). Clinton announced the reorganization in a speech discussing the danger of terrorism at the Naval Academy in June 1998. In January 1999, he gave another speech focused on biological weapons threats to promote a counterterrorism and WMD preparedness budget increase (Clarke 2004: 171–175).

Advocates of the misperception hypothesis argue that Al Qaeda was a centrally organized efficient organization beginning in the early 1990s and that intelligence reporting failed to see this, contributing a national underestimation of the danger (Benjamin and Simon 2003: 235–237, 276; Clarke 2004: 78; National Commission 2004: 72–73, 118). But it appears what the U.S. government learned at the time was essentially accurate: there was loose-knit network of Sunni extremist terrorists, many of whom remained abroad, interested in attacking U.S. targets, and Bin Laden was an important part of this network; an organizer and fundraiser who should be stopped. The agencies were somewhat slow in warning that Al Qaeda would attack Americans, but there was little evidence that this would occur prior to Al Qaeda's arrival in Afghanistan, when Americans officials and analysts quickly came to view it as a threat.

After the embassy bombings

Truck bombs hit the U.S. embassies in Dar es Salaam, Tanzania and Nairobi, Kenya on August 7, 1998, nine minutes apart. The Nairobi blast killed 212 people, twelve American. The Dar es Salaam attack killed 11 Tanzanians and wounded 85. The investigation pointed to Al Qaeda. It was the first time the group directly attacked Americans.

The Clinton administration considered military options immediately (Coll 2004: 408). A week after the attacks, Clinton ordered a cruise missile strike on a camp near Khost, Afghanistan, where a meeting of Al Qaeda leader was supposed to take place and on a facility suspected of producing chemical weapons for Al Qaeda in Sudan. The first strike missed the Al Qaeda leadership but was reported to have killed several dozen people, mostly terrorists.

Shortly after the Embassy Attacks, Clinton instructed the NSC to create a plan to "get rid of" Al Qaeda (Clarke 2004: 185). One result was a political-military plan called Delenda. The plan said that the U.S. would use diplomacy to push other countries to deny Al Qaeda sanctuary, use covert action to disrupt its operations, freeze its assets where possible, harden overseas U.S. facilities against attack, and prepare for military action (Clarke 2004: 197–199).

After the embassy attacks, the CIA increased its reporting efforts on Al Qaeda. It began to develop more sources in Afghanistan (the Defense Intelligence Agency also had some), a process aided by growing Pashtun dissatisfaction with the Taliban. This effort produced the information on Bin Laden's movement that led to consideration of missile strikes and to increased threat reporting (Coll 2004: 495–497). A variety of reports in late 1998 drew attention to the threat to aviation, several involving supposed plots to crash explosives-laden airplanes into targets. Several other reports warned that Al Qaeda was attempting to set up cells in the United States and attack targets there (Coll 2004: 420–421). A bevy of more analytical reports appeared discussing Al Qaeda's danger (National Commission 2004: 342).

The agency's covert efforts increased. U.S. intelligence services worked with foreign agencies in the year after the attack to break up Al Qaeda-linked groups in Albania, Azerbaijan, Italy, Britain and Uganda. A high level Al Qaeda operative was arrested in Germany (National Commission 2004: 127). The CIA began participating in more renditions, where terrorist suspects were removed from one location to their home country without going through normal legal channels (Benjamin and Simon 2003: 251–252).

The Clinton administration pressed the Taliban to turn over Bin Laden and warned through various channels that otherwise it would be held responsible for Al Qaeda' actions. Along with senior officials in the CIA, Pentagon and State, Clinton pressed Pakistan to force the Taliban to act, pushing first Prime Minister Nawaz Sharif and, after the coup, the new Prime Minister, Pervez Musharaf (Coll 2004: 487). In July 1999, Clinton declared the Taliban a terrorist-supporting organization and froze some of their assets, overruling objections of some in State who saw this as counterproductive. The U.S. also succeeded in getting the UN Security Council to sanction the Taliban in October of that year (National Commission 2004: 125). The White House pushed the Saudi's to cut off several terrorist financing sources in their country, to little avail (Clarke 2004: 191–194). State Department officials made minor efforts to organize talks linking the Northern Alliance with Pashtuns who could gather support in the southern Afghanistan. But these talks produced little (National Commission 2004: 124–125).

Anxiety in the counterterrorism bureaucracy increased in 1999. The NSC held meetings three times a week where U.S. intelligence agency reported on possible terrorist plots (Benjamin and Simon 2003: 265). Concern about unconventional weapons attacks mounted with reports of chemical weapons production efforts at an Al Qaeda camp and Bin Laden's statement in a *Time Magazine* interview in January that acquiring nuclear weapons was a religious duty (Benjamin and Simon 2003: 161; Coll 2004: 491). In December, Jordanian police broke up a large Al Qaeda-linked bombing plot, and Ahmed Ressam, who had trained in Afghanistan, was caught trying to enter the United States with explosives and found to be planning attacks on airports in Los Angeles. Ressam's apprehension led to further arrests in Montreal, Boston and New York – most on visa violations (Benjamin and Simon 2003: 312; National Commission 2004: 174–177).

By early 1999, we now know, Bin Laden had approved Khalid Sheikh Mohammed's hijacking plan that would become the September 11 plot. In January 2000, CIA agents, working from an NSA wiretap, observed an Al Qaeda meeting in Kuala Lumpur. Several of attendees would become 9–11 hijackers. The CIA learned two of their names but did not place them on U.S. watchlists or inform the FBI, even after learning that they had traveled to the United States (Coll 2004: 487–488; National Commission 2004: 181–182).

In March 2000, the Principals Committee agreed to a three-part counterterrorism effort: increased funding for CIA counterterrorism, a crackdown on foreign terrorist organizations and fundraising in the United States and improved border patrol. In early 2000, after the NSC prodded them to improve technical intelligence, the Joint Staff at the Pentagon proposed using an unmanned aerial vehicle, the Predator, to gather intelligence in Afghanistan and enable strikes (Benjamin and Simon 2003: 321). After funding was negotiated, a successful trial was undertaken in June. In August, the principals approved Predator flights, for now unarmed (Coll 2004: 527–536).

The Bush administration

The Bush administration's attention to terrorism was limited before September 11, but they did not dismiss the threat. The new national security leaders came to office without strong ideas about terrorism. They did know that they did not like their predecessors' approach. Yet in the 8 months they were in office, they slowly adopted a slightly more aggressive version of that approach.

In transition briefings, the outgoing Clinton NSC repeatedly warned Bush administration officials about the Al Qaeda threat. National Security Advisor Sandy Berger told Condoleezza Rice, who was taking over as National Security

Advisor, that she would spend more time on that than anything else. Clinton says he told Bush that Al Qaeda was the biggest threat he would face. George Tenet, who stayed on as CIA Director, issued similar warnings (National Commission 2004: 199; Coll 2004: 556).

The White House slowly reviewed but ultimately enhanced the counterterrorism policies they inherited. The President himself did not make terrorism a priority, focusing on defense issues like China and missile defense. Still, the White House sent a letter to Musharraf in early 2001, saying better relations depended on a number of things, including resolution of the Al Qaeda problem (Coll 2004: 552). The administration's first defense budget included a 27 percent increase for the CIA's counterterrorism operations. Vice President Cheney undertook a review that spring of responses to WMD attacks (National Commission 2004: 204).

Rice had written a *Foreign Affairs* article during the campaign that mentioned terrorism only as a tactic of states (Rice 2000). Yet she described Clinton's counterterrorism policy as feckless, indicating a desire to do more. Like the new President, who said he wanted to avoid swatting at flies, she was dismissive of tit-for-tat retaliation (Benjamin and Simon 2003: 335; National Commission 2004: 202) She decided to keep the NSC counterterrorism staff and asked Clarke to lead an interagency review on counterterrorism. But she forced Clarke to report through the Deputies Committee, the second ranking officials in each national security agency, rather to the principals, as before.

Secretary of Defense Donald Rumsfeld focused on military transformation. Terrorism was a second tier issue in his view, especially for the Pentagon (Benjamin and Simon 2003: 336; National Commission 2004: 208). His top Deputy, Paul Wolfowitz, argued that terrorists associated with states, like Iraq, were a larger problem, but eventually went along with White House policy against Al Qaeda (Clarke 2004: 231). The new Attorney General, John Ashcroft, did not support an FBI request to fund 400 new counterterrorism agents (Benjamin and Simon 2003: 346). Secretary of State Colin Powell took a hawkish line against the Taliban and Al Qaeda (Coll 2004: 564–565).

In January 2001, Clarke pressed for a principals meeting to discuss arming the Predator and heightening collaboration with the Uzbeks and the Northern Alliance (Benjamin and Simon 2003: 336–338). These proposals were instead discussed at a deputies meeting in late April. The participants agreed that the destruction of Al Qaeda should be the top U.S. objective in the region and to aid the Uzbeks and test the armed predator. The deputies tabled a decision on aiding the Northern Alliance while they worked to develop regional policy (Coll 2004: 564–565). The CIA resisted flying lethal Predator flights, concerned about cost and the military nature of the mission (Coll 2004: 527). Meanwhile Clarke was asked to draft a new Presidential Decision Directive on counterterrorism – now called a National Security Directive. In June, he submitted a draft, updating his 1998 political-military plan. It called for more diplomatic, financial, and covert pressure on Al Qaeda, more aid to anti-Taliban groups and more military options (National Commission 2004: 202–206).

That summer, U.S. officials reported unprecedented amounts of intelligence about upcoming attacks. The FBI issued 216 threat reports in six months, six mentioning aviation-related attacks. The Federal Aviation Administration issued 15 warnings. Receiving these reports, President Bush expressed a desire to "bring down" Al Qaeda (Coll 2004: 566–567). CIA stations helped local police and intelligence agencies disrupt terrorist cells in Yemen and Jordan and chased other leads (Coll 204: 568).

On September 4, the principals met and approved Clarke's new National Security Directive but did not decide what agency should fly armed Predators when they were ready. The principles agreed to increase aid to the Northern Alliance and Uzbeks but not on where the money should come from (Benjamin and Simon 2003: 345).

Policy failure, not misperception

There is no scientific way to say what perception of danger is correct. We can only form impressions. By that standard, the executive branch perceived Al Qaeda accurately prior to September 11. U.S. intelligence agencies were somewhat slow in recognizing in the mid-1990s that the Al Qaeda network was becoming more organized and preparing attacks against Americans. But Al Qaeda never became traditional organization. And the agencies expressed considerable concern that Al Qaeda was dangerous before it began targeting Americans. Clinton concerned himself with Al Qaeda starting in the mid-1990s and spoke about the danger of terrorism regularly. His National Security Advisors and his longest serving CIA Director, George Tenet, shared these concerns. The most damaging claims of misperception can be leveled against the FBI and military, which were not eager to combat terrorism. But as demonstrated below, this was a result of organizational imperatives, not misperception. For the most part, the relevant officials saw the danger.

The Bush administration's top security officials came into office relatively less concerned about terrorism. One reason for this is that they had less exposure to information about Al Qaeda while out of office. Their limited attention to the threat and tendency (as demonstrated by Wolfowitz and Rice in her writing) to focus on its link to states may indicate ideological bias. During the 1990s, many conservatives discussed terrorism almost only as an offshoot of rogue states, which they saw as the major security danger to Americans. This gives some credence to the ideological party view of threat perception, but it is unclear how much impact this tendency had prior to September 11. The idea that Iraq sponsored anti-American terrorism mattered latter but seemed to wash out in policy reviews in this period. The evidence is limited, but overall the Bush administration, while slow to develop policy and less alarmed than the Clinton administration, did not differ a great deal in its overall analysis and seemed to comprehend the threat.

There is little indication that either administration misperceived terrorism because it was a threat to liberal values. Talk about terrorists gathering the Middle-East into a caliphate that would threaten the United States and its values as the Soviet bloc once did came later. This could indicate that this language is mostly used for sales purposes.

Nor is there much evidence that either president was prevented from getting good intelligence about terrorism by security agencies drawn to conventional threats. Organizational theories of threat perception may then be a one way street; a source of overestimation but not underestimation. Where military interests ignore dangers like terrorism, leaders might estimate them accurately. Of course, that might not have held were the terrorist threat larger.

If you believe that the terrorist danger is an existential danger to the United States, as officials from both administrations now claim, you are led to the conclusion that both administrations underrated the danger. But the threat was never that. It was a network of individuals somewhere in the low thousands, many of whom had a burning desire but limited means to kill Americans, with a somewhat organized core of about a hundred or so. The group lacked the division of labor and knowledge storing capacity that large hierarchical organizations like armies use to kill in larger numbers. They could kill in the hundreds with a large truck bomb, and on their best day in 2001, the thousands. There is, in fact, a good case that Clinton administration overestimated the threat, especially its ability to use unconventional weapons (Coll 2004: 434). Even in relatively unmolested sanctuaries in Sudan and Afghanistan, Al Qaeda never approached success in producing weapons of mass destruction (Leitenberg 2005; Mueller 2006).

In reviewing the case, in fact, it is not even obvious that U.S. counterterrorism policy was insufficient. The counterterrorism polices can be described as a rational response to the danger. Having seen the danger, the state reacted with a variety of policies across various agencies. It acted to defend itself at home and abroad. The policies largely survived a change in administration, after a time consuming review. Note also that success in this case is less evident than failure. Success means terrorists go to jail, are killed or simply fail to act. And lots of terrorist were apprehended and a few killed because of U.S. counterterrorism policy. We do not know Al Qaeda's ratio of successful to failed plots, but there appear to be more of the latter. Is there a policy failure to explain?

Al Qaeda kept its sanctuary during this period while planning attacks on Americans, including the September 11 attacks, with limited molestation. That is a failure because U.S. set out to change these conditions but did not. Moreover, the U.S. government did not carry out the plans it developed. Between 1996 and 1998 the United States knew Al Qaeda's intent and often its leader's location but did little to kill or capture him. After that, fleeting reports of Bin Laden's whereabouts were received but attacks were passed up. U.S. leadership was reluctant to use force. Why was the policy not more aggressive?

Explaining the failure of U.S. counterterrorism policy

This section explains the failure to disrupt Al Qaeda prior to September 11 with three arguments. First the problem itself was extremely difficult. Second, war and scandal limited the Clinton administration's options. Third, as discussed earlier, security policy tends to resist change, whatever the wishes of its nominal masters.

First, the problem that the United States confronted, a terrorist organization protected by a hostile government, is hard to solve, particularly where that government (Sudan or Afghanistan) is far off and culturally different and thus a difficult place to collect intelligence. The idea that we would destroy Al Qaeda (that is what Clarke's "Delenda" plan means) short of war was a recipe for failure. Most counterterrorism policy does nothing to confront the sanctuary problem. Policing only goes so far. Protecting the homeland does less. Adding counterterrorism funds or drawing up military options are what you do when there is little else to do. The covert actions undertaken – aiding Pakistani spies and Uzbeks, giving listening gear to the Northern Alliance, were long-shots; low cost, unlikely benefit.

U.S. diplomacy succeeded in pushing Bin Laden out of his sanctuary in Sudan (although it is possible that they simply tired of their guest). But his relocation to Afghanistan compounded the problem. The Taliban was less persuadable.

Another tactic to disrupt terrorist havens is to change the nature of the host regime. If that is possible without war, it is a long-term process. The United States was initially banking on this in Afghanistan, but it did not appear to be bearing fruit, and meanwhile, attacks occurred.

The final option is military attacks against the terrorists or their hosts. But even cruise missile strikes are acts of war, which are costly in every sense – they may produce backlash among voters, anger among allies, and hostility in the region attacked, aiding terrorists. This was certainly a concern and probably what happened in Afghanistan. The question becomes what level of provocation is worth a war? The expected costs of the terrorism you go to war to prevent have to be high. Up until September 11, they did not appear high enough to justify a full scale war. Still, by 2000, the U.S. government was moving toward joining in Afghanistan's civil war due to terrorism. Had things gone slightly differently, that might have occurred and become a course that the United States regretted.

Second, the Clinton administration was politically constrained from a larger commitment in Afghanistan, even if it had judged one worthwhile. Presidents these days go to war without Congress' vote, but they need some support – otherwise they jeopardize their agenda and their party's power. Divided government made leadership in foreign affairs difficult in the late 1990s. The Lewinsky scandal made it worse. The Republicans charged that Clinton attacked the Afghanistan to distract the public from his sex scandal. But the opposite seems more likely: scandals upset Presidential appetite for wars because they destroy political capital.

Military actions elsewhere also limited the Clinton administration ability to use force in Afghanistan. It sent troops to Haiti in 1994. The memory of Somalia was not a happy one. The Army had a peacekeeping force in the Bosnia starting in 1996, which was unpopular with Republicans. The Administration bombed Iraq in Operation Desert Fox in December 1998 and maintained sanctions on it. Through NATO, it bombed Kosovo in the spring of 1999. One could argue that this promiscuous use of military force should mean that another war would be no big deal. But there are limits to what the political traffic will bear. The Clinton administration probably could have sold another war with a campaign about the danger Al Qaeda posed, but its other commitments drove up the price. Prior to September 11, the

Bush administration did not have enough time in office to much consider war. After that the political constraints were gone.

The third reason that counterterrorism failed prior to September 11 is the theory of organizational politics and change discussed earlier. Presidential power is limited. The President and his staff have the biggest say making defense budgets and policy, but the agencies that execute policy and Congress, mostly through committees, also have a say. Agencies are protected from presidential control of personnel at the working level by civil service laws and at top levels by the fact that Presidents can only fire agency leaders so often. Because the agencies are tied to past purposes, and Congress usually goes along, the President typically struggles to make change.

Examples of such limits on presidential power are evident where the President or his appointees advocate a policy or budget change and fails to enact it. But the limits operate where the executive simply does not suggest a policy change because it would radically depart from the status quo and be rejected by interests serving it. A President that wanted to take $100 billion dollars out of the defense budget and spend it on counterterrorism activities, which by their nature would be conducted by different sorts of agencies than those on top of the Pentagon, would not fly. The President would have to proceed in small increments, building up a new entity to combat terrorism.

It is not clear how much Clinton would have shifted budgets and policies if he could fully control them, but one reason that is so is because he could not. While the budget shifted to counterterrorism seem substantial when measured against prior years – the amounts were tiny in the context of the federal budget; slivers of percentages. The change was marginal. Likewise, if he did not need to cooperation of the Pentagon, Congress and the public, Clinton might have endorsed Clarke's most hawkish plans.

The 1990s are an interesting time to consider the bureaucratic politics of national security because the agencies were suited to a conflict, the Cold War, which ended unequivocally early in the decade. The agencies were in entrepreneurial mode, looking for ways to justify their existence, but not ways that would reshape their identity. For some of these agencies counterterrorism was a godsend. For others, it was anathema.

The counterterrorism group in the NSC was, as the theory predicts, the biggest booster of the terrorist threat and vigorous reactions to it. The arrival of the Al Qaeda threat enhanced not only its budget and prestige but its power over executive branch agencies, via Presidential Decision Directives.

The State Department's first priority was diplomacy. In its view, diplomacy was the output of embassies. It was not eager to have its new counterterrorism coordinator make policy from Washington. So it is not surprising that it was unwilling to do Michael Sheehan's bidding and subordinate other interests to punish Pakistan for failing to confront terrorism (Coll 2004: 265).

For the CIA, the new danger was a mixed bag. Its intelligence arm is tied to past threats by professional habits and expertise – if you are expert on Soviet tanks, studying terrorism lacks appeal – but had no further reason to harp on past dangers.

As long as there are reports to be written for presidents, it will study new dangers. The CIA's dominant group, however, are its operations officers. They needed a mission in the 1990s. Without Cold War spying, its budget was decimated, its purpose in doubt. Recruiting informants in Pakistan to provide intelligence on terrorists is similar to recruiting Communists in Belgrade. Counterterrorism was fine with the operations side if it meant running agents. This is why the CIA wanted terrorism-related budget increases to go to its general operations budget (National Commission 2004: 184–185). Tenet declared war on Al Qaeda after the embassy bombing, but the only new money that the CIA put into pure counterterrorism activities came from supplemental appropriations. The operations budget would not be sacrificed for the "war" (National Commission 2004: 184–185, 357, Clarke 210). Even in 1999, the Bin Laden station was slashing budget because the CIA would not sacrifice other ends to pay for it (Coll 2004: 456–458). In the late 1990s, counterterrorism helped the CIA get the administration to fund a long-range rebuilding program for its clandestine service (National Commission 2004: 90).

While the CIA was eager to collect information about terrorists, it was wary of running risky operations against them. Past scandals caused by covert operations made the agency avoid risky operations, especially the paramilitary sort, despite the units it maintained for these purposes. Tenet deemphasized these missions (Coll 2004: 361). Although many operators were game, CIA leaders resisted going to battle with the Northern Alliance and flying armed drones (Coll 2004: 581).

The FBI had little desire to fight terrorism prior to September 11. Where it did, its structure inhibited success. The Bureau is a crime-fighting agency, one run in recent decades out of its 56 field offices. Agents get promoted by making cases. Experience with domestic intelligence gathering had ended amid public recriminations and the Church hearings in the early 1970s. Tracking terrorists is an intelligence job that runs against the FBI's grain (National Commission 2004: 76).

After becoming FBI Director in 1993, Louis Freeh created a counterterrorism center in headquarters but did not move major funds from other areas to run it. The center was part of the National Security division, where the priority remained counterintelligence. The field offices, where the action was, did not much increase their manpower and budget devoted to counterterrorism (National Commission 2004: 74–76). The result was that, while the FBI was the lead agency for tracking domestic terrorists, it struggled to conduct open-ended collection efforts or pull together intelligence its agents gathered in their investigations, let alone share it with other agencies. Confusion over what criminal material could be used for intelligence heightened this problem (Benjamin and Simon 2003: 297–304). This problem persisted despite a tripling of its counterterrorism funding in the mid-1990s and a doubling of the number of agents on counterterrorism missions from 1996 to 2001 (National Commission 2004: 77).

The military services had limited interest in counterterrorism in the 1990s. Their missions were to fight state militaries, not terrorists. There are various sub-organizations in the Pentagon, however, with incentive structures adverse to those of organizations containing them. Most relevant are the special operations forces, organized as a sort of fifth service in special operations command (SOCOM). There are divisions within SOCOM, but as a generalization, special operations forces were open to a variety of mission types because their existence is threatened by the services. Prior to September 11, this insecurity made them eager to take on new tasks, including counterterrorism (Jackson and Long, forthcoming). After September 11, SOCOM enthusiastically became the designated lead entity in the "global war on terrorism."

The problem in the 1990s was that to enlist SOCOM, the president had to go through the Joint Chiefs. The Chiefs represented the services' views. This perspective, along with operational difficulty, limited their willingness to endorse raids on Al Qaeda camps. Military planners tend to rely on large force packages, and mistrust special operations forces, viewing them as rivals who should be used only in support of regular troops. The Chiefs were not necessarily adverse to using military hardware for counterterrorism missions, but resistant to using such forces regularly for that purpose. Like the Navy, the Chiefs were thus unhappy leaving expensive attack submarines off the coast of Pakistan to fire cruise missiles at terrorists, which is why they got the submarines returned to normal duties in late 2000.

The power of organizational purpose was mixed bag for counterterrorism. Some entities in the bureaucracy took to the task, aiding policy, but more did not. This limited the president's power to shift budget to counterterrorism, enact counterterrorism policy, and make it work. Changes he might have made were not possible; changes he did make were constrained. These constraints may not have caused the policy failure, but an FBI more willing to hunt terrorists or a military service eager to man Clarke's proposed raids might have changed things.

As noted, a sense of alarm can excite the public and cause Congress to ally with the president and alter the incentives that these organizations face. That was missing. Congress showed only sporadic interest in terrorism. After attacks, it tended to push through legislation or hold hearings on issues like preparedness and then move to other topics (National Commission 2004: 104–107). Congress tended to outsource its duties in making counterterrorism policies to bipartisan commissions but to ignore their recommendations (Benjamin and Simon 2003: 367).

Although there was nothing like the alarm that occurred after September 11, much of change that did occur in this period came when terrorist attacks produced windows of fear. This is consistent with the idea that alarm allows policy innovation. The attacks in 1995 produced counterterrorism legislation that would likely not have passed Congress otherwise. The embassy bombing produced numerous policy initiatives and structural reforms in security agencies. Clarke and Berger intentionally hyped the danger of unconventional weapons to frighten their own cabinet officials into adopting expensive preparedness measures (Clarke 2004: 163). Clinton talked up the biological weapons threat to sell his policies, with some success. The Clinton administration, however, did not promote fear of terrorism as much as might have to accomplish its goals. Certainly, it did not oversell of the terrorist danger with the focus the Bush administration later used to sell the war in Iraq. Had he desired a war in Afghanistan, or even more airstrikes or aid to the Northern Alliance, Clinton might have found oversell a useful tool.

The conclusion is perverse. Responsive defense policy might require fear-mongering. Concentrated interests provide sufficient defense against old threats by hyping them. The military-industrial is something of blessing, a self-perpetuating method of overcoming collective action problems (Lee 1990). Because so much of the defense establishment is served by it, the United States is today unlikely to miss a Chinese threat. It is also likely to overestimate it. But to respond adequately to threats that do not benefit concentrated interests, the president may need to frighten the public and their representatives. That tact, however, will likely require exaggerating danger and creating excessive demand for protection. The choice may be between failing too much or too little.

Notes

1 The words danger and threat are used here interchangeably to refer to things that kill or harm. Risk is the probability of a danger arriving and therefore is generally used where the probability of occurrence can be calculated. Risk is different than uncertainty. Uncertainty generally refers to a situation where the probability of an event occurring cannot be stated. The threat of war or terrorism is usually seen as uncertainty. Because they result from social not physical phenomena, national security dangers are more uncertain than other dangers. But all events and dangers have some uncertainty, especially when viewed personally. Uncertainty is a matter of degree. This means that the risk-uncertainty distinction is not precise. We can talk about the risk of terrorism.

References

Benjamin, D. and Simon S. (2003) *The Age of Sacred Terror: Radical Islam's War against America*, New York: Random House.
Burke, J. (2003) *Al-Qaeda: Casting a Shadow of Terror*, New York: I.B. Tauris.
Clarke, R. (2004) *Against All Enemies: Inside America's War on Terror*, New York: Free Press.
Coll, S. (2004) *Ghost Wars: The Secret History of the CIA, Afghanistan, and Bin Laden: from the Soviet Invasion until September 10, 2001*, New York: Penguin.
de Rugy, V. (2005) "What does homeland security spending buy?" American Enterprise Institute, Working Paper.
Desch, M. (2007) "American's illiberal illusion: The ideological origins of overreaction in U.S. foreign policy," *International Security*, 32: 7–43.
Douglas, M. and Wildavsky, A. (1992) *Risk and Culture: An Essay on the Selection of Technical and Environmental Dangers*, Berkeley: University of California Press.
Doyle, C. (1996) "Antiterrorism and effective death penalty act of 1996: A summary," Congressional Research Service Report.
Friedman, B. (2006) "Why we overreact to terrorism," Paper prepared for the Annual Meeting of the American Political Science Association, Philadelphia, August.
Friedman, B. and Sapolsky H. (2006) "You never know(ism)," *Breakthroughs*, 15: 3–11.
Hart, L. (1955) *The Liberal Tradition in American Politics*, New York: Harcourt Brace and Company.
Jackson, C. and Long, A. (Forthcoming) "The fifth service: The rise of special operations command," in H. Sapolsky, B. Friedman and B. Green (eds) *U.S. Military Innovation after the Cold War: Creation without Destruction*, London: Routledge.

Kent, S. (1994) "Estimates and influence," in D.P. Steury (ed.) *Sherman Kent and the Board of National Estimates: Collected Essays*, Central Intelligence Agency, Center for the Study of Intelligence.

Lee, D. (1990) "Public goods, politics, and two cheers for the military-industrial complex," R. Higgs (ed.) *Arms, Politics, and the Economy: Historical and Contemporary Perspectives*, New York: Holmes and Meier.

Leitenberg, M. (2005) *Assessing the Biological Weapons and Bioterrorism Threat*, Carlisle, PA: Strategic Studies Institute of the U.S. Army War College.

Lowi, T. (1979) *The End of Liberalism: The Second Republic of the United States*, New York, W.W. Norton & Company.

Mearsheimer, J. J. (2001) *The Tragedy of Great Power Politics*, New York: Norton.

Mearsheimer, J. (2004) "Lying in international politics," paper presented at the Annual Meeting of the American Political Science Association, Chicago, IL.

Mueller, J. (2006) *Overblown: How Politicians and the Terrorism Industry Inflate National Security Threats, and Why We Believe Them*, New York: Free Press.

National Commission on Terrorist Attacks upon the United States (2004) *The 9-11 Commission Report: Final Report of the National Commission on Terrorist Attacks upon the United States*, New York: W.W. Norton & Company.

Pierson, P. (2000) "Increasing returns, path dependence and the study of politics," *American Political Science Review*, 94: 251–267.

Rice, C. (2000) "Campaign 2000: Promoting the national interest," *Foreign Affairs*, 79: 45–62.

Rovner, J. (2005) "Why intelligence isn't to blame for 9-11," MIT Center for International Studies Audit of Conventional Wisdom, Cambridge, MA.

Schilling, W. R. (1962) *Strategy, Politics, and Defense Budgets*, New York: Columbia University.

Selznick, P. (1957) *Leadership in Administration: A Sociological Interpretation*, New York: Harper & Row.

Schattsneider, E. E. (1960) *The Semi-Sovereign People: A Realist's View of Democracy in America*, New York: Holt, Rinehart and Winston.

Slovic, P. (1987) "Perception of risk," *Science*, 236: 280–285.

Snyder, J. (1991) *Myths of Empire: Domestic Politics and International Ambition*, Ithaca, NY: Cornell University Press.

Sunstein, C. (2002) *Risk and Reason: Safety Law and the Environment*, New York: Cambridge University Press.

Sunstein, C. (2003) "Terrorism and probability neglect," *Journal of Risk and Uncertainty*, 26: 121–136.

Thrall, A. T. (2007) "A bear in the woods? Threat framing and the marketplace of values," *Security Studies*, 16: 452–488.

Van Evera. S. (2003) "Why states believe foolish ideas: Non-Self-Evaluation by states and societies," in A Hanami (ed.) *Perspectives on Structural Realism*, New York: Palgrave.

Wilson, J. Q. (1971) "Innovation in organization: Notes toward a theory," in J.O. Thompson (ed.) *Approaches to Organizational Design*, Pittsburgh: University of Pittsburgh Press.

—— (1989) *Bureaucracy: What Government Agencies Do and Why They Do It*, New York: Basic Books.

Index